PETER DRYSDALE Editor

Direct Foreign Investment in Asia and the Pacific

UNIVERSITY OF TORONTO PRESS
1972

First published in Australia by the Australian National University Press

Published in Canada and the United States by University of Toronto Press 1972

Printed and manufactured in Australia

ISBN 0-8020-1933-1

Microfiche ISBN 0-8020-0273-0

Preface

Consideration of the effects of direct foreign investment, as of other aspects of international commerce, is often confused by superficial inquiry and analysis encouraged by nationalistic sentiment. It is often possible to separate the economics from the politics. Their separate analysis allows more rational formulation of policy in pursuit of varied national objectives. This book is primarily about the economic effects of direct foreign investment. But important political interactions are not neglected.

Economic development in an open economy can undoubtedly be greatly accelerated by foreign investment. But there are problems that have to be solved. Foreign investment commonly improves economic efficiency but, in some countries, it might also be associated with economic and political imbalances. In many ways, we are only beginning to understand the solutions to some of these problems and the ways in which foreign investment can be most efficiently used. The contributions in this volume represent a significant clarification of the issues and a substantial advance in our knowledge.

It emerges from the argument that direct foreign investment is an important object of political decision both within and between countries, giving rise to very different problems in different parts of the world. In the chapters that follow, it is interesting to observe different emphases from commentators from the American continent on one hand, and from Asia-Australasia on the other. The former's views contain the elements of what might be characterised as a 'conspiracy theory' approach to foreign investment. The latter argue more from an 'ignorance theory' approach. Both elements are important.

In the Asian-Pacific region there is more competition between North American and European investment and that from Japan. The prospective growth of Japanese investment, as well as the opening up of Japan to western investment, pose some of the most challenging policy problems in the area, and they have a prominent place in the argument of the book. The incentives offered to foreign investors by host countries come under scrutiny, as do host countries' own tariff and commercial policies which frequently reduce the gains from foreign investment.

Direct foreign investment has recently achieved new status in international economic policy and the ramifications of its massive growth are profound. There is every indication that it will continue to grow rapidly in the next few years. Most of the contributors to this volume would see this as a welcome development but it is clear that few are sanguine about the economic and political problems that will be generated in the process.

The volume collects together the papers and proceedings of the Third Pacific Trade and Development Conference held in Sydney in late August 1970 to discuss the general issues raised by direct foreign investment in Asia and the Pacific. The conference was attended by scholars and government officials from Canada, the United States, Australia, New Zealand, Japan, Mexico, Indonesia, Korea, the Philippines, and Thailand, as well as officials from the International Bank for Reconstruction and Development and the Asian Development Bank.

The book covers four broad subjects: general issues raised by direct foreign investment (Chapters 1-4); foreign investment among advanced countries in the Pacific (Chapters 5-7); case studies in foreign investment in developing countries (Chapters 8-12); and balance of payments and policy issues in the region (Chapters 13 and 14). There is a summary of the proceedings in Chapter 15.

There was intensive discussion of each contribution at the conference, and an attempt has been made to report its substance at the end of each chapter. In two cases papers were discussed together, so that the general discussion of Chapters 8, 9 and 10 is reported at the end of Chapter 10, and that of Chapters 11 and 12 at the end of Chapter 12. The reports do not pretend to be complete but they preserve some of the tone and spirit of the controversies.

It would have been impossible to compile the book without the assistance of a large number of people and organisations. It is impossible to mention them all here. To some I owe a very great deal. Professor Kiyoshi Kojima of Hitotsubashi University (who is the inspiration of the Pacific Trade and Development Conference series), Professor Sir John Crawford of the Australian National University, and Professor John Nevile of the University of New South Wales directed the organisation of the conference from which these papers derive, and to them I am especially indebted. Thanks are due to the University of New South Wales, the Australian National University, and the various governments, organisations and institutions which provided financial support. I am also grateful to Christopher Manning, Ben Smith, Thomas Parry, Edna Liu, and Barbara Payne for their help with the proceedings of the conference. Mrs Beryl Palmer assisted throughout the conference and with interpreting the record of discussion. To her and to Mrs Isobel Everitt I record my special thanks for cheerfully producing a fine manuscript under considerable pressure. My debt to the contributors is obvious.

Canberra, January 1972   Peter Drysdale

Participants

Editor

Peter Drysdale, Economics Faculty, Australian National University

Contributors

Donald Brash, International Bank for Reconstruction and Development
Koichi Hamada, Economics Faculty, University of Tokyo
Helen Hughes, International Bank for Reconstruction and Development
Stephen Hymer, Economics Department, Yale University
Harry G. Johnson, Economics Department, Universities of Chicago and London
Charles P. Kindleberger, Economics Department, Massachusetts Institute of Technology
Ryutaro Komiya, Economics Faculty, University of Tokyo
James O. N. Perkins, Economics Faculty, University of Melbourne
Mohammad Sadli, Investment Board, Indonesia
A. E. Safarian, Department of Political Economy, University of Toronto
Cesar Virata, Finance Secretary, Philippines
Amnuay Viravan, Board of Investment, Thailand
Miguel Wionczek, Centro de Estudios Monetarios Latinoamericanos
Yoonsae Yang, Economic Planning Board, Korea

Other Participants

H. W. Arndt, Economics Department, School of Pacific Studies, Australian National University
Donald Badger, Reserve Bank of Australia
Sir John Crawford, Australian National University
Ronald S. Deane, Reserve Bank of New Zealand
H. Edward English, School of International Affairs, Carleton University
Warren Hogan, Economics Department, University of Sydney
Hisao Kanamori, Japanese Economic Planning Agency

Kiyoshi Kojima, Economics Department, Hitotsubashi University
Gregory McColl, Economics Department, University of New South
    Wales
Fritz Machlup, Economics Department, Princeton University
John Nevile, Economics Department, University of New South Wales
Hugh T. Patrick, Economics Department, Yale University
Arthur Paul, Asia Foundation
George Rosen, Asian Development Bank
Richard Snape, Economics Department, Monash University

Contents

Tables

1 Survey of the Issues

HARRY G. JOHNSON

Technically speaking, direct foreign investment entails majority ownership or control of a domestic enterprise by foreigners, and such foreigners
may be merely individuals and not necessarily a foreign-domiciled
enterprise. However, foreign direct investment in the contemporary
world is almost exclusively the preserve of foreign enterprises, and it is
this type of direct investment that has recently been exciting political
concern in such heavy recipients of it as Canada, Australia, and Western
Europe, including the United Kingdom. Hence this chapter will be
confined to surveying the issues raised by direct investment by the
corporations of one country into the economies of others.

As has already been mentioned, there has been mounting concern in
the advanced-country recipients of direct foreign investment (primarily
from the United States) about its implications for their economies and
national independence—in Canada since the mid-1950s, in Western
Europe since the early 1960s, in Australia still more recently. This concern has frequently been based on ignorance or on faulty analysis of
partial evidence. It has moreover in all probability concentrated far too
heavily on the United States international corporation and on United
States direct investment abroad, to the neglect of a more general trend
towards world-wide operations by corporations of all countries.[1] On the
other hand, the developing countries, which have traditionally been highly
suspicious of the international corporation (especially the United States-
based corporation), are being pressed by both the attenuation of the flow
of official aid for economic development and the remarkable contributions
of foreign enterprises to the promotion of economic development in

[1] Stephen Hymer and Robert Rowthorn present an empirical refutation of the
Servan-Schreiber thesis, and argue that the European corporations will in their
turn become multinational and competitive with the American international corporations, in 'Multinational Corporations and International Oligopoly: The Non-
American Challenge', in Charles P. Kindleberger (ed.), *The International Corporation: A Symposium* (Cambridge: The M.I.T. Press, 1970), pp. 57-91.

1

various countries to a reconsideration of, and a more favourable attitude towards, the role of the corporation as an agency of economic change and growth. Meanwhile, economic theorists have begun to take an interest in the positive and normative analysis of the phenomenon of corporate direct foreign investment.

The growth of corporate direct foreign investment in the period since World War II raises issues at a variety of levels, both in economic science and in policy formation. For the purposes of this survey, these issues are most conveniently arranged for discussion under the following headings: issues in economic theory, home country issues, host country issues, issues special to developing countries, and international policy issues.

Issues in Economic Theory

It is evident at the outset that understanding of the economics of direct foreign investment requires a different orientation on the part of the economist than that of traditional trade theory (the so-called Heckscher-Ohlin-Samuelson model of international trade), with its assumption of international immobility of factors of production and complete mobility of technical knowledge, for the essence of direct foreign investment is the transmission to the 'host' country of a 'package' of capital, managerial skill, and technical knowledge. The major issues posed for theory are the reasons why the transmission of such a 'package' of capital and knowledge is more profitable than the alternative of transmitting either the capital or the knowledge or both separately, and what the welfare implications are for the 'home' and the 'host' countries respectively. Along with the first issue goes the important empirical question of which industries are likely to be characterised by direct foreign investment and which are not. Economic theory offers two approaches to these questions, that of the theory of industrial organisation and that of traditional trade theory. These approaches must be used as complements, since the former is microeconomic in character whereas the latter stresses the requirements of general macroeconomic equilibrium.

The industrial organisation approach to the problem was pioneered by Stephen Hymer,[2] who emphasised the competition for market shares among oligopolists. The same sort of approach, but with an emphasis on the economics of new product development, characterises the work of Raymond Vernon's group at Harvard.[3] This approach has been elaborated in a paper by R. E. Caves[4] which also surveys the empirical evidence and synthesises the industrial organisation and trade theory approaches.

---

[2] S. H. Hymer, The International Operations of National Firms: A Study of Direct Investment (M.I.T. doctoral dissertation, Cambridge, Mass., 1960).

[3] See especially Raymond Vernon, 'International Investment and International Trade in the Product Cycle', *Quarterly Journal of Economics*, Vol. 80, No. 2, May 1966, pp. 190-207.

[4] R. E. Caves, 'International Corporations: The Industrial Economics of Foreign Investment', *Economica*, Vol. 48, No. 149, February 1971, pp. 1-27.

Caves's central theme is the parallelism between direct international investment and horizontal and vertical integration of firms in a geographically segregated market. In order to be able to invest successfully in production in a foreign market, the firm must possess some asset in the form of knowledge of a public-goods character (production technology, managerial or marketing skills) which can be transferred to a new location at little cost. This is necessary for it to be able to surmount the excess costs of production in an alien location. For it to be induced to produce abroad rather than license its know-how, moreover, the rent it can obtain from its knowledge must be tied to the actual process of production and distribution, and the firm must be large enough to undertake the required investment. Thus Caves argues that direct foreign investment is associated with product-differentiated oligopoly, a hypothesis which is broadly consistent with Vernon's emphasis on new product development. In similar fashion, direct foreign investment of the 'vertical' variety, that is, investment in the extraction of raw materials, is associated with oligopoly, differentiated or not, and the corresponding incentives to reduce uncertainty and to forestall potential competition. An important theoretical consequence of 'horizontal' direct foreign investment is the tendency towards the equalisation of profit rates in the same industry across nations, but not across industries within the national economy. Other implications are 'cross-hauling' in investments by national corporations in each others' markets, and a tendency towards overcrowding of the smaller markets by an excessive number of relatively inefficient firms.[5]

Trade theory, as developed by Vernon, myself,[6] Caves, and others, contributes to this general picture the notion of national comparative advantages and disadvantages in the generation of new differentiated products, and in the attraction of direct foreign investment. It also raises the general equilibrium question of the effects of such investment on the distribution of income within the home and the host country and on their respective economic welfare. A case can be constructed in which inward direct investment benefits domestic capital at the expense of labour;[7] and R. W. Jones has developed an interesting model of international but not inter-industrial mobility of capital, in which the attraction of foreign investment by a tariff benefits domestic labour.[8]

[5] An alternative theory of direct foreign investment in terms of exchange risk, according to which investors in the strongest-currency country have an advantage over investors elsewhere because their investment converts local into internationally desirable assets, has been offered by R. Z. Aliber ('A Theory of Direct Foreign Investment', in Kindleberger, op. cit., pp. 17-34).

[6] Harry G. Johnson, *Comparative Cost and Commercial Policy Theory for a Developing World Economy* (The Wicksell Lectures, Stockholm: Almqvist & Wicksell, 1968). See also 'The Efficiency and Welfare Implications of the International Corporation', in Kindleberger, op. cit., pp. 35-56.

[7] Ibid., pp. 45-7.

[8] R. W. Jones, 'A Three-Factor Model in Theory, Trade and History', cited in Caves, loc. cit.

As regards welfare effects, it has been generally and rather uncritically assumed that the impact of a package of capital, technology and managerial skill must be beneficial to the host country. Closer investigation of this issue, however, shows that the gains are not so obviously inevitable or significant.[9] To illustrate, if the foreign firm simply replaced imports by domestic output, charging the same price and paying the going wages for domestic labour, and remitting the interest on its capital and the rent on its superior knowledge as profits, the host country would gain nothing. In fact, if the foreign investment were attracted by a tariff or by fiscal subsidies, the host country might well lose.

However, under existing double-taxation agreements, the host country more or less pre-empts the right to tax the profits of the foreign enterprise, and thus captures a share of both the earnings of the foreign capital and the rents of the foreign knowledge. This is one source of gain from inward foreign investment, which may be particularly important for developing countries both because the foreign corporation affords a target for the tax-collector easier to hit than most others, and because the corporation may need, or be forced to put up with, very little compensation for its taxes in the form of public expenditure on infrastructure and other public services.

Beyond this additional tax revenue, benefits to the host country depend on the inability of the investing corporation to capture all the social benefits from its investment, that is they depend on the generation of 'spillovers' of various kinds. In theoretical terms, such spillovers involve a reduction of prices or improvement of product quality for consumers, or an increase in wages and the prices of other local inputs into the production process. More concretely, Caves suggests two possibly important sources of gain to the host country. The first is the training of labour which then becomes available to the economy generally. This will occur if the firm finances the training (rather than the workers financing it through an apprenticeship scheme), and if it over-provides training in relation to its actual needs for skills, as it is particularly likely to do if it is starting a new type of operation in a developing country. The second is productivity gains in domestic firms induced by the behaviour of the foreign firm's subsidiary.

Such gains may result from the migration to domestic firms of executive talent developed in the foreign firm; efforts by the foreign firm to educate its suppliers in such matters as quality control and production flow management, and its customers in the efficient use of its product; and the stimulus to better management of the domestic firms provided by the competition of the foreigner. (These points conflict with the frequent

---

[9] See Johnson, 'The Efficiency and Welfare Implications of the International Corporation', also Caves, loc. cit. The following paragraphs draw extensively on Caves's formulation of the analysis.

assertions that foreign firms enter the market in order to cartelise it, and that their entry somehow suppresses domestic entrepreneurship; the probabilities, however, seem to be on Caves's side.) Caves also argues, plausibly, that such training and industrial spillovers for the host country are unlikely to be matched by losses of spillovers to the home country from the investment's not having been made there; and that they are far less likely to accrue from 'vertical' than from 'horizontal' direct foreign investment, with the exception that 'vertical' investment may have to pay abnormally high wages to attract local labour to inaccessible resource-extraction locations.

The foregoing arguments imply both that there are likely to be significant gains to a host country from direct foreign investment in it, and that these gains are secured at no cost to the country whose corporations are doing the investing—apart, of course, from the loss of profits-tax revenue by the home to the host country. As regards this last, Caves notes that since profits tax rates are more or less the same in most countries, the allocation of capital is not distorted from a globally efficient pattern by the existence of profits taxes. However, it will be distorted by fiscal attractions to direct foreign investment provided by tariffs or other fiscal incentives. Caves also notes that any other way of handling conflicting national claims to the taxation of profits would probably produce chaos.

The analysis rests on a marginal approach to the impact of direct foreign investment on the home and host countries. One would expect a significant and sustained inflow of foreign direct investment to have the end result of raising real wages and real incomes in the host countries, as a consequence on the one hand of the associated increase in the overall capital-to-labour ratio, and on the other hand of the fact that knowledge cannot be permanently monopolised but ultimately becomes a free good. This expectation is subject to the proviso that potential increases in real income are not simply absorbed by a faster rate of increase of population. One would also expect, again on a non-marginal basis, that the outflow of capital and knowledge to the less advanced and less developed parts of the world would have adverse consequences for the real wages of labour in the advanced-country sources of direct foreign investment. There is thus a fairly solid theoretical basis for concern on the part of labour groups in the advanced countries about the implications for them of large-scale outflows of direct foreign investment, a basis which can be disputed only on the doubtful grounds either that the foreigners would otherwise have raised the capital and invented the knowledge themselves, or that the direct foreign investment has such a powerful catalytic effect in energising the indigenous potentialities for economic growth that the losses to home labour from relatively less capital per head and loss of monopoly in the exploitation of knowledge are more than compensated for.

The foregoing discussion of the issues of economic theory involved in direct foreign investment has been conducted in terms of the effects of such investment on 'real' economic equilibrium. Much of the public discussion of it, however, has been conducted in terms of the balance-of-payments effects. The position taken here is that concern about balance-of-payments reflects the propensity on the part of both the major source-countries of direct foreign investment (specifically the United States, and the United Kingdom up to 1967), and many of the recipient countries (including Canada in the late 1950s and early 1960s, and many developing countries) to adhere stubbornly to an overvalued exchange rate. It also reflects the propensity of government economists to concern themselves with financial flows of investment and the remittance of earnings, without proper recognition of the real investment processes by which investments create the productive capacity to earn profits and pay dividends. It may be noted that adherence to an overvalued exchange rate itself creates artificial incentives both to invest abroad, for home country corporations, and to remit earnings rather than reinvest them, for corporations investing in countries with overvalued currencies.

Home Country Issues

As mentioned in the previous section, the most obvious economic problem for the home country involved in direct foreign investment by its corporations is the loss of revenue from profits tax on the earnings of their capital and know-how. This loss, however, has not been an issue in the United States, the major source of direct foreign investment, presumably because tax revenue is not a significant problem in the world's richest country and also because through most of the post-World War II period the United States has been anxious to encourage foreign investment by its corporations as a contribution to postwar economic reconstruction and to economic development. Nor has it been an important issue in the United Kingdom, which is both a recipient and a source of direct foreign investment, though the calculations of the Reddaway Report[10] took it into account and in so doing aroused some criticism for failing to allow for the offsetting saving on the cost of public provision of overhead services for private industry.

In both countries, the chief reason for concern about corporate direct foreign investment has been its contribution or asserted contribution to the country's balance-of-payments deficit. In the United Kingdom this concern led to changes in corporate profits tax legislation. In the United States it led first to 'voluntary' and then to mandatory controls over cor-

[10] W. B. Reddaway *et al.*, *Effects of U.K. Direct Investment Overseas: Final Report*, University of Cambridge, Department of Applied Economics, Occasional Paper No. 15 (Cambridge: Cambridge University Press, 1968).

porate financial practices, designed to minimise the foreign exchange drain on the United States balance of payments. These controls evoked protests, particularly from Canada, about United States government interference with the operations of Canadian subsidiaries of United States corporations, the production of Canadian guidelines for good behaviour on the part of foreign enterprises in Canada, and a continuing and mounting Canadian concern about United States subsidiaries in Canada. They also evoked protests from the American business community, and a series of controversial efforts to measure the immediate and longer-run impacts of direct foreign investment on the United States balance of payments, including the impact effect of the investment itself, the longer-run effects in stimulating and/or replacing United States exports, and the building up of earnings remittances over the course of time.

As argued in the previous section, concern about the balance-of-payments implications of direct foreign investment stemmed from the maintenance of an overvalued exchange rate, in the United Kingdom until November 1967 and in the United States to the present time. In terms of the pure theory of international monetary disequilibrium, it is very difficult to establish a case for the effectiveness of controls on foreign investment as a means of correcting a deficit associated with currency overvaluation, even if the controls are effective in restricting the particular financial transactions at which they are aimed. The only really persuasive argument for using them is that currency overvaluation stimulates foreign investments that would not appear profitable if the exchange rate were correctly valued. But in that case establishment of an appropriate currency valuation would be a superior policy to maintenance of an overvalued rate coupled with investment controls designed to prevent the inefficient allocation consequences of overvaluation.

In the heyday of the last historical era of massive private foreign investment, the era based on the export of British capital to the rest of the world through the London capital market, the view emerged in British socialist and labour circles that these capital exports were diverting capital from investment in British industry and hence from the improvement of the welfare of the British worker. This view gained ground in the conditions of mass unemployment of the interwar period, and was to some extent responsible for the imposition of capital issues control in the 1930s after the suspension of the gold standard. It continues to be an influence on left-wing British thinking about direct foreign investment by British corporations, and more generally the international role of the City of London.

In recent years, and to an important extent as a consequence of the overvaluation of the United States dollar, very similar criticisms of direct foreign investment by American corporations have come increasingly to be voiced by the American labour movement. The American unions' criticisms focus on two major issues. The first is the 'export of jobs' implicit in direct foreign investment. In part this complaint reflects the overvaluation of the dollar and the absence of a firm governmental commitment to a full employment policy; in part, however, it reflects a more fundamental realisation that unions in the United States have been enabled to raise wages to their present high levels by the relative abundance of capital in the United States and the country's leadership in advanced technology industries, both of which advantages, but especially the latter, are now being eroded by the process of direct foreign investment by American corporations in lower-wage countries. The second point of criticism concerns the implications for collective bargaining of the emerging world of 'multinational production'; the argument is that multinational production enables employers to bring in 'scab imports' to reduce the losses to themselves consequent on a domestic strike, and to threaten to expand production abroad and even close down domestic production facilities unless unions moderate their wage and other demands. The result of these criticisms has been a series of proposals, some quite unrealistic, for controlling and slowing down direct foreign investment by United States corporations.

By contrast, the unions in the United Kingdom, while also concerned about the operations of the multinational corporation, have tended to be content with pressing for more information about their activities and for the general desirability of surveillance and international control.

The issues just discussed are essentially economic in nature. It should be noted, however (somewhat in anticipation of the next section), that while much of the concern about direct foreign investment in host countries revolves around the infringement of national sovereignty through political intervention by the home country government in the affairs of its corporations' subsidiaries in the host countries, the home country itself suffers a gradual erosion of sovereignty through the evolution of its national corporations into international, transnational, or multinational corporations. This is not merely a matter of the difficulty of governmental policing of the manifold overseas operations of corporate subsidiaries; it is much more a matter of gradual change in the attitudes of corporation executives towards, and loss of their respect for, the politicians and officials of national governments—including their own—as their horizons expand to comprise the international economy as the sphere of their operations, and they become impatient of those whose vision and responsibilities are limited to the territorial domain of a particular national state.

Host Country Issues

The subsidiaries of foreign-based corporations tend to be viewed with considerable suspicion in host countries, just as the local branches of national corporations were viewed with considerable suspicion in an earlier era which witnessed the rise of the national corporation in competition with the local corporation or family business. Indeed, most of the contemporary criticisms of the economic behaviour of the national subsidiaries of foreign corporations can be found in the historical records, novels, and plays about the economic and social consequences of the intrusion of a branch of a national corporation into a small but apparently prosperous and socially well-integrated local community. There are the same complaints that the local wealthy are not welcomed into partnership in management and profits, local talent is not preferred over rival aspirants to jobs, and potential local suppliers are not preferred over competitors elsewhere. The only difference, though it is an important one, is that the government to which the national firm was subservient was also the national government of the local community, however remote and however resented, whereas the international corporation owes allegiance to a government other than (and in addition to) the government of the nation in which its subsidiary operates. Even this difference, in the period of emergence of the national corporation, was frequently more a difference of degree than of kind. And there is some doubt as to how serious the conflicts between national sovereignties inherent in the dual responsibilities of international corporations to home and host governments really are. Nevertheless, it is necessary in discussing host country issues associated with corporate direct foreign investment to distinguish between issues concerning the economic behaviour of foreign subsidiaries and issues concerning the exercise of sovereignty by the home government over the foreign operations of subsidiaries of its national corporations.

Complaints about and criticisms of the presumed or potential economic behaviour of the domestic subsidiaries of foreign corporations—the distinction between actual and potential is not usually drawn very carefully, though it is important for policy—may touch on any or all aspects of corporate activity, and tend to focus on behaviour relevant to the current concerns of national policymakers. These concerns tend to be of two major types. The first is improvement in the balance of payments, which implies a policy emphasis on export promotion and import substitution. The second is growth and improved efficiency of the domestic economy, which implies policy emphasis on a variety of aspects of industrial activity that policymakers consider critical to the objective, such as participation by residents in ownership and top management, and the conduct of research and development activity domestically. It may be observed in passing that the fundamental theory of balance-of-payments adjustment does not suggest that microeconomic policies aimed at export promotion and import substitution will be effective by themselves in remedying a balance-of-payments deficit, since this typically requires some combination of deflation and devaluation; and also that political ideas of what it takes to make industry flourish are frequently derived by imitative magic rather than by economic analysis.

Concern about the performance of American subsidiaries in Canada has been active for a longer time, and has raised a broader range of issues, than parallel concern in other countries. An early interview study sponsored by the Canadian-American Committee[11] selected six aspects of subsidiaries' behaviour that appeared to provoke the most irritation in Canada. The main points of criticism involved were: refusal to sell equity shares in the subsidiary to the Canadian public; insufficient 'Canadianisation' of personnel; publication of insufficient financial data; marketing and purchasing policies that discriminated against exports and in favour of imports from United States suppliers; insufficient domestic research; and centralisation of philanthropic activities in the American parent's head office.

Some of these issues are specific to Canada, and reflect the opinions of particular vested interest groups. All raise issues of both empirical fact and theoretical interpretation too complex to enter into in this chapter. It may be recorded, however, that Canadian radical opinion (partly in response to the findings of empirical research) has tended subsequently to narrow its specific criticisms down to the alleged failure of United States subsidiaries to purchase a sufficient proportion of its supplies locally, while broadening its general attack into the allegation that the presence of the subsidiaries has suppressed the development of indigenous Canadian entrepreneurship.[12] Meanwhile, Canadian policy has been developing along the lines of requiring more detailed information, establishing guidelines for foreign direct investment, and reserving certain sectors of Canadian economic activity (especially financial) for Canadian-owned or controlled enterprises.

While a detailed analysis of issues pertaining to the economic behaviour of the subsidiaries of international corporations is beyond the scope of this chapter,[13] casual observation of Canadian, British, and other public opinion suggests that public opinion is likely to be particularly aroused about four major issues. One is the issue of public disclosure of financial information, associated with the suspicion that subsidiaries make excess profits and/or evade their fair share of taxes by paying excessive transfer

[11] John Lindeman and Donald Armstrong, *Policies and Practices of U.S. Subsidiaries in Canada* (Washington and Montreal, The Canadian-American Committee of the National Planning Association and the Private Planning Association of Canada, 1960).

[12] See, for example, C. W. Gonick, 'Foreign Ownership and Political Decay', pp. 43-74 in Ian Lumsden (ed.), *Close the 49th Parallel Etc.: The Americanization of Canada* (Toronto: University of Toronto Press, 1970).

[13] A useful and carefully dispassionate discussion of the issues raised by American investment in the United Kingdom is presented in M. D. Steuer, *American Capital and Free Trade: Effects of Integration* (London: The Trade Policy Research Centre, 1969).

prices on purchases from their foreign affiliates or charging too little on sales to them.

A second issue is local research and development expenditure, which has come to be identified as vital to industrial competitiveness and supremacy. This issue raises the question of the character of knowledge as a public good, and the wastes involved in replicating its production or producing it on too small a scale. It also raises the question of efficient use of a country's scarce supplies of qualified scientists and engineers.

A third issue concerns foreign takeovers of domestic enterprises, which seem to excite public alarm. The facts that takeovers offer a capital gain to resident owners that they could not otherwise enjoy, and also that entry into the domestic market by a foreign competitor via takeover rather than establishment of new production facilities gives no indication of whether he intends to act competitively or monopolistically, are usually ignored.

A fourth issue derives from the widely-held notion that there are 'key sectors' or 'commanding heights' in the economy that must be preserved, in whole or at least in part, for resident (national) firms. Unfortunately, economic analysis offers no guidance to the identification of such key sectors, if indeed they exist. Hence the 'commanding heights' are likely to be defined by vested interests or by political symbolism.

Issues arising, not from the economic behaviour of subsidiaries, but from the exercise of sovereignty by the government of the home country over the subsidiaries in conflict with the sovereign claims of the host country, have been most keenly felt in Canada. The main sources of resentment have been on the one hand the 'extraterritorial' application of United States antitrust law, union law, and laws relating to exports to communist countries by United States subsidiaries in Canada, and on the other hand the application of United States balance-of-payments guidelines to the financial operations of such subsidiaries. Other countries do not seem to have been concerned about the extraterritoriality issue, especially as regards exports to communist countries, presumably because the presence of national firms capable of undertaking the business has made the issue an empty one. Nor have they objected strongly to the balance-of-payments guidelines, presumably because they have resented the United States deficit sufficiently strongly to tolerate infringements of their sovereignty by United States balance-of-payments policy.

Issues Special to Developing Countries

While all of the issues discussed in the previous section might arise in connection with direct foreign investment in the developing countries, certain special issues or versions of general issues are particularly likely to arise in that context.

For one thing, the typical developing country is small in relation to the

international corporate giants mainly involved in direct foreign investment, and its expertise in negotiating with foreign corporations is likely
to be extremely limited in comparison with what the corporation can
bring to bear. Hence there is likely to be both suspicion on the part of
government officials that they have been cozened into accepting a bargain
too favourable to the corporation, with a resulting tendency to hector and
harass the corporation subsequently, and suspicion on the part of public
opinion that the government has 'sold out' to the foreign capitalists. Mis-
understanding, confusion, and acrimony on this score are likely to be
enhanced by the popular failure to appreciate two facts about the corporation in the context of a developing country. The first is that the profits of
the corporation are to a substantial degree a return on its past investments
in the generation of productive knowledge, and should not be regarded
simply as a return on the capital invested in the particular local production facility. The second is that the corporation is a competitive profit-
seeking institution and not a government with the powers of taxation, and
therefore cannot be expected to assume the responsibility for promoting
development in the same way as a development plan undertakes that
responsibility. As outlined above, the contribution of direct foreign investment to development is incidental to the purpose of making profits—
though it may nevertheless be important. In consequence, development by
means of direct foreign investment is likely to be highly uneven and
sector-specific—though there is the consolation that profits taxes on
foreign capital and industrial knowledge will provide revenue for the
development plan.[14]

The problems of negotiating with the international corporations are
likely to be especially acute when, as is the case in many developing
countries, the interest of the corporations is in the exploitation of natural
resources rather than in the establishment of domestic manufacturing
facilities. The problem here is to determine an appropriate rent, or an
appropriate depletion allowance, in the face of a highly uncertain future
market situation and under strong pressures to secure an immediate and
large revenue for the government to devote to development programs. The
typical outcome is a bargain that is repeatedly and acrimoniously re-
negotiated in favour of the government.

For fairly well-known reasons, developing countries are also likely to
be particularly concerned with the balance-of-payments aspects of direct
foreign investment. This particular concern stems largely from the
official habit, already referred to, of concentrating on financial flows to the
neglect of the real investment and production phenomena underlying
them. If the exchange rate and the domestic economy are properly

[14] For a fuller discussion, see my 'The Multinational Corporation as a Development Agent', *The Columbia Journal of World Business*, Vol. 5, No. 3, May-June
1970, pp. 25-30.

managed, the increase in output provided by the investment should provide the real resources for servicing it. It has, in fact, frequently been pointed out that direct equity investment is superior to portfolio investment from a balance-of-payments point of view precisely because the servicing payments due are geared to the current profitability of the investment financed by the foreign capital. However, where the foreign direct investment has been attracted by protection or fiscal incentives, the profits earned may not be matched by a genuine contribution to increased output, and the servicing drain on the balance of payments constitutes a real burden on the economy. Such a situation, though, should be ascribed to governmental error in providing socially undesirable incentives to foreign direct investment, rather than blamed on the foreign corporation *per se*.

International Policy Issues

The rapid growth of the operations of the international corporation, and the conflicts of interest that have appeared on the one hand between national governments and foreign corporations operating in their territory, and on the other hand between the claims of national sovereignty of the host and home governments, have led a number of observers to remark on the fact that while there exists an established international agency—the General Agreement on Tariffs and Trade—for the policing of international trade practices and the arbitration of trade disputes between nations, no comparable international authority exists for the regulation of relations between corporations and governments and the arbitration of conflicts of sovereignty over the corporation among nations. Proposals have been put forward, both in business and in academic circles, that such an international authority should be established and properly empowered.[15] However, as C. P. Kindleberger has noted with some surprise, there seems to be little conviction of the need for such an agency among those most practically concerned with the problems involved, the international lawyers, one at least of whom has taken the view that conflicts of jurisdiction are in fact less common than is generally supposed, and can be resolved within the framework of existing institutions.[16] There is also some question of whether the rise of the international corporation and of international business is as powerful a challenge to the nation-state as both its enthusiasts and its critics have made it out to be.[17] Nevertheless, the growth of interest in and support

[15] For example, C. P. Kindleberger, *American Business Abroad* (New Haven and London: Yale University Press, 1969), pp. 206-7.

[16] Kindleberger, *The International Corporation*, pp. 5-7, in reference to Seymour J. Rubin, 'The International Firm and the National Jurisdiction', pp. 179-204 in the volume.

[17] Kenneth N. Waltz, 'The Myth of National Interdependence', in Kindleberger, *The International Corporation*, pp. 205-23.

for the idea, and the inauguration of research into the problem under a variety of auspices, suggest that it will eventually emerge as a practical issue in international economic policy.

Comments and Discussion

RYUTARO KOMIYA opened the discussion: I wish to make two points relating to the positive analysis in the second section of Johnson's paper.

One is concerned with the association of vertical or horizontal integration with oligopoly, product-differentiation, and monopolistic tendencies. I would argue that although monopolistic motives are sometimes important in vertical integration, vertical integration itself has nothing to do with oligopoly or monopolistic competition, and that the same is true of horizontal integration. The existing theory of monopoly, oligopoly, product differentiation, or the theory of perfect competition is basically a static theory which assumes stationary conditions. But a firm in the actual world operates in a dynamic environment, where things are changing constantly, and some of the more important factors leading to vertical integration have dynamic aspects. I name a few of them: first, hedging and speculating; second, communication of information; third, planning and co-ordination; fourth, saving on marketing costs. Take two simple cases of vertical integration. One is integration of mining, smelting or refining and fabricating or making of metals. The second is an owner-occupied house; that is integration of ownership, management of production and consumption of housing. For example, vertical integration may be for the purpose of hedging. When you rent a house, in some cases there will be separate ownership and management and rentals may change from year to year; but when you own a house you do not have to worry about short-run changes. In other words, vertical integration reduces uncertainty in a changing world. Or conversely, you might be speculating, because it is not asserted that vertical integration is always profitable or useful in these cases, but it may be more efficient and more profitable when you think you, as a consumer of these products, know the housing situation of a city better than others. Similar incentives may induce refining or smelting companies to integrate mining.

Vertical integration may be for the purpose of facilitating the communication of information, which is an essentially dynamic element in the operation of a firm. One needs constant flows of information only when one is making decisions from time to time in a changing world. In a static world one does not need more than minimal information. The static theory of vertical integration neglects this aspect. It neglects also the planning and co-ordination aspects. If you own a house, you can expand the house or modify rooms as your family size changes or as children grow up. When you rent a house, you have to persuade the landlord or you have to move to another house when such a need arises.

As I said before, I do not deny monopolistic motives in some cases of vertical integration—in fact I agree that they may be an important factor. But it is a mistake to consider that vertical integration is in itself associated with oligopoly or monopoly. If that is the case, every owner of a house who lives in it is an oligopolist. It seems to me that vertical integration is perfectly compatible with workable competition. Workable competition here means approximation of marginal cost by price, and absence of excessive profits, both in the long run.

The second point I would like to make is that the industry pattern of direct investment is not closely related to national comparative advantage or disadvantage based upon factor endowments. This is clear in cases of the vertical integration type investment: for example, most British or Japanese oil companies producing crude oil in the Middle East. And it is clear when an infant industry, in which a country only has national comparative advantage in the long run, is developed by foreign direct investment initially. An example is the Japanese electrical machinery industry in prewar years. Or if we go back to the early history of Japanese industrial development, there are quite a few other cases in which foreign firms started an infant industry in Japan.

Direct investment (as I argue in Chapter 6) is based upon managerial, technological, marketing knowledge and experience, so that it is only loosely related to factor endowments or comparative advantage. If a country accumulates knowledge and experience to run a company in a certain field efficiently, accumulated knowledge may be used through direct investment in industries in which the host country has comparative advantage.

Johnson replied that he agreed with the points made by Komiya but wondered whether they were matters of semantics rather than substance. He said that his own dissatisfaction with the product differentiation explanation which Caves advances for foreign investments arises from these dynamic considerations associated with the problem of knowledge. To a specific question regarding expansion in employment or higher wages which result from an increased demand for labour Johnson replied that what he wanted to point out in that part of his argument was that one can think of theoretical cases in which direct foreign investment makes no difference to the welfare of the local population at all. What was assumed in the argument was that the direct investment draws factors from other local markets in such a way that prices are not affected, wages are not affected, and the profits are repatriated. Then there is no change but the name of the company doing the business. If imports are replaced and exports can be reduced there may be no change in employment as factors are drawn from the export into the import-replacement activity.

Subsequent discussion of Johnson's paper focused on two issues: the problem of defining foreign investment and the effects of defensive or oligopolistically motivated foreign investment.

It was agreed to confine discussion to the issue of direct foreign investment, although one participant was interested in taking up some of the problems associated with international portfolio investment. To some, Johnson's definition of direct foreign investment in terms of majority ownership or control appeared to present problems. It was observed, for example, that it might not encompass what commonly passes for foreign investment in Japan where minority equity participation is normal. One participant noted that authors of the country studies, reported in later chapters, had observed no consensus with respect to the treatment of foreign borrowings, and he wondered at the logic behind including or excluding outside credits alongside equity interest. It was also pointed out, conversely, that in some cases, credit arrangements by majority-owned foreign firms within host countries allowed substantial control, over investment decisions or supply decisions, for the host government or host-country firms. Another participant thought it useful to identify foreign investment in terms of the foreign assumption of risks associated with undertaking the investment. It was suggested, however, that the reason for concentrating on direct investment was because of an interest in the peculiar significance of capital flows which are directly associated, in a package deal, with the transfer of technology and management. There, neither the question of risk nor the extent to which control may be limited or extended by the terms of borrowing, seems so directly relevant. A Japanese participant suggested that the OECD definition of direct capital flows, which includes minority equity and long-term credit from the parent firm, had justification in terms of Johnson's definition since, even with minority equity, there can be effective control, and long-term credit may strengthen control. In any case, it is difficult to fix on one decisive cut-off point, since control is not easily quantifiable.

An American participant questioned the lack of attention given to 'defensive investment' which acts to reproduce, in the host country, the same oligopolistically competitive situation that exists in industrial capital exporting countries, only at more cost in terms of efficiency. In the host country, the effect is to fragment small sized industries into smaller sized foreign units producing at high cost levels. There are eight refrigerator companies in Canada of inefficient size. The automobile industries in Argentina and Australia are similarly fragmented. Profits for most of these industries are below normal, although there are some external economies to the investor in so far as his 'unprofitable' investment is designed to protect future profit. In such cases there may be real waste. There is evidence that some countries in Latin America are trying to do something about the problem by encouraging dominant producers—Fiat motor cars in Argentina, Ford in Brazil, Renault in Colombia, and so on.

Other participants noted that market fragmentation was commonly associated with tariff protection and competition-restricting domestic policies, and wondered whether it was likely to be common in their absence. It was pointed out, however, that oligopolistic behaviour could result in production under losses for a considerable period in the expectation of future profits. The petroleum industries in Singapore and Japan were cited as examples. Both examples were questioned. Johnson went on to ask what, in any case, both examples were good examples of, because established trade theory suggests that dumping does not hurt, but rather benefits a country provided it continues. In the present context, the availability of foreign capital operating at a loss, for whatever purposes, is likely to be beneficial to the host country unless its use involves wastefully expensive production, and wastefully expensive production only results where there are tariffs or other inefficient domestic policies.

It was further argued that fragmentation of markets can occur in the absence of tariffs in either of two situations, one where there is any kind of barrier to trade—transport costs may come into that category as well as tariffs—and the other where there is the possibility of such a barrier. Johnson's argument that there is no loss from fragmentation was queried on the ground that, whilst there may be no loss in the short term, there could be long-term dynamic losses arising from the fact that many small companies may pre-empt the opportunity for development of a larger more profitable and, therefore, more rapidly growing company. An example may be the compressed air equipment industry in Australia which has, in fact, been protected by a tariff, but which is likely to have been fragmented anyway by the presence of four or five foreign firms, all of them small, all of them making losses, and all of them pre-empting the opportunity for the growth of anything remotely like the Swedish Atlas Copco in Australia.

Another participant said that it should not be taken for granted that foreign investors who appeared to be taking losses in relatively small developing markets were in fact always taking losses. Transfer pricing, excessive charges for technical assistance and royalties could distort the true profit picture of foreign firms. A recent study in Colombia revealed considerable anomalies of this type. Of course, these depended on the taxation and institutional framework within the host country too.

Johnson warned that it was important to isolate the effects of foreign investment *per se* from the effects of tariff and 'developmental' policies. The latter may or may not be beneficial. Especially in developing countries, where foreign firms, because of organisational and technical know-how, will frequently be the first encouraged to enter industrial production, it is important to distinguish the consequences of domestic policies. If the policies have unforeseen side-effects or are misdirected, the foreign firm is often, but usually wrongly blamed. It is necessary to keep clear what are the consequences of this kind of economic policy no matter who does the investing, foreign or domestic firms.

A final comment drew out three elements in the second part of the discussion: the effects of tariffs on foreign firm behaviour; the effects of oligopolistic activity; and the effects of foreign versus domestic activity. It seemed that consideration of the first two elements left little for discussion in the third. Oligopolistic activity covers a whole range of business behaviour, including product differentiation and investment behaviour in a dynamic situation. In industries such as chemicals, for example, where the opportunities for product differentiation through advertising are limited, excessive investment occurs in a rapidly growing market to ensure future market share and profits. That is the kind of oligopolistic investment behaviour about which several participants were concerned. There may well be an interrelationship between these effects and the effects of tariffs. Nonetheless, it appeared, from all the empirical evidence to date, that tariffs and misplaced economic policies are a major cause of the inefficiencies that result from over-investment in small markets.

2 United States Investment Abroad[1]

STEPHEN HYMER

The statistical evidence on foreign investment can hardly bear the weight of the policy proposals and value judgments all of us make, but it is mounting in quality and quantity and it is possible to isolate a few important features with reasonable confidence. This chapter presents a number of such empirical characteristics and draws out some of the value implications for present and future problems.[2]

The underlying framework of my essay can be summarised in the following equation describing the amount of United States direct investment in a country:

$$D = \Sigma a_i (1 - b_i) K_i$$

where D is total United States direct investment in a given country,

         a_i is the share of assets in industry i owned by American subsidiaries,

         b_i is the proportion of a subsidiary's assets financed locally,

         K_i is the capital stock of industry i.

According to this equation, variations in United States direct investment from country to country can be attributed to variations in one of three

[1] The hypothesis in this chapter is based on my doctoral dissertation, The International Operations of National Firms, submitted to the Massachusetts Institute of Technology in May 1960. An attempt is made to bring empirical evidence contained in the thesis up to date using the material in the *U.S. Business Investments in Foreign Countries: Census of 1957* (Washington: Government Printing Office, 1960) (hereafter *Census of 1957*) and the *Foreign Business Investments in the United States, Census of 1959* (Washington: Government Printing Office, 1962) (hereafter *Census of 1959*), as well as the many important empirical and critical studies published since 1960. Unfortunately the *Census of 1966* had still not been released at the time of writing (except for some preliminary results on Latin America contained in the report by the Council for Latin America).

[2] The empirical material used here is illustrative rather than exhaustive. We are now reaching the point where full scaled econometric analysis will be possible for many hypotheses previously evaluated only in qualitative terms. The accompanying data indicate some relations which can be tested. In some cases, where data are not available but soon could be, an attempt is made to suggest lines of approach.

19

factors. The first, *the industrial organisation factor*, is represented by a_i, the American market share in each industry in the foreign country. This share is determined by oligopolistic competition and depends upon the strength of American firms, the strength of foreign competitors, and the accidents of oligopolistic rivalry. For most industries the a_is are zero, but in a few industries they are high on a world wide basis.

The second factor, the *international finance factor*, represented by $(1 - b_i)$, is the parent firm's financial share in its subsidiary's assets. This ratio depends mainly upon the state of the capital market in the host country and on political factors, though it is to some extent related to specific characteristics of the industry involved. Lastly, the volume of United States direct investment in a country depends upon the *composition of its industry*, a factor represented by the K_is, the vector of capital stocks in each industry. To a large extent, the amount of direct investment in a given country depends upon whether that country happens to have those industries with which direct investment tends to be associated or whether it has industries where the value of a_i tends to be low. This in turn is heavily dependent on the industrialisation strategy of the government.

I want to try to use existing materials to study some of the characteristics of D, a_i, b_i, and K_i through time as best I can and to relate them to other magnitudes. It should be noted, however, that by and large these quantities are not themselves the main objects of concern but are intermediaries in a more complex chain. At the deepest level, what concerns people is the degree of participation in the shaping and sharing of values. These include not only economic wealth, our primary focus of attention, but also power, wellbeing, enlightenment, skill, rectitude, affection, and respect, to follow Harold Laswell's categories.[3] However, the connections between the empirical parameters of direct foreign investment and these values is not one upon which we can agree as easily as we can upon the 'facts'.

Another important feature to bear in mind is that, scientifically (econometrically) speaking, it is not proper to separate *economic* analysis from *political* analysis when interpreting data. The coefficients a_i, b_i, and K_i are not determined by economic forces alone. The effect of government in determining the size of specific industries, the amount a firm can borrow, and the share of the United States is obvious. Equally important, the size of a_i, b_i, and K_i affects government policy either through its effects on taxes or through its effect on interest groups pressuring the government. An increase in a_i, for example, may cause national firms either to pressure the government to curb American expansion or give American firms more of a stake and more say in determining policy. To ignore this

---

[3] Harold P. Laswell and Abraham Kaplan, *Power and Society* (New Haven: Yale University Press, 1950).

relationship is to run the danger of interpreting a reduced form equation as a structural equation with consequent errors in prediction and policy.[4]

Historical Perspective

Direct investment has a very long history (see Table 2.1). Most United States multinational firms began their international forays a long time ago,

Table 2.1 Expansion of United States multinational corporations through time

	In all areas	Canada	Latin America	Europe	Southern dominions	Asia and other Africa
(a) Number of companies operating a foreign subsidiary						
1901	23	6	3	22	2	0
1913	47	27	9	37	8	4
1919	74	54	16	45	14	8
1929	123	92	36	95	34	23
1939	153	123	72	116	63	33
1945	158	128	93	120	69	33
1957	183	167	155	160	105	83
1967	186	174	182	185	154	158
(b) Number of companies operating a foreign manufacturing subsidiary						
1901	18	5	3	16	1	0
1913	39	24	6	26	3	1
1919	64	48	10	30	7	4
1929	110	79	24	76	20	15
1939	135	102	56	96	44	18
1945	138	107	73	96	50	17
1957	174	142	131	144	85	61
1967	185	161	171	183	135	134

Source: J. W. Vaupel and J. P. Curhan, *The Making of Multinational Enterprise* (Boston: Harvard University Press, 1968), p. 69.

often before the Depression, sometimes before World War I. Some of the most important firms can trace the beginning of their foreign activities to before 1900. By 1914, the United States had $US2½ billion in direct

[4] This point is developed more fully in Stephen Hymer and Stephen Resnick, 'International Trade and Uneven Development', in J. Bhagwati *et al.* (eds.), *Trade, Balance of Payments and Growth: Papers in International Economics in Honour of Charles P. Kindleberger*, Amsterdam, 1971. See also H. G. Johnson, 'A Theoretical Model of Economic Nationalism in New and Developing States', *Political Science Quarterly*, Vol. 80, June 1965, and Albert Breton, 'The Economics of Nationalism', *The Journal of Political Economy*, Vol. 72, No. 4, August 1964 for articles which integrate political and economic equations in the analysis of foreign investment.

investment. Thus, what seems to be a new phenomenon to a receiving country is often an old practice from the point of view of the firm.[5]

Corporations do not grow old and die. They are, as Harry Johnson has put it, like California Redwoods, with perpetual life, and this is reflected in their international operations. There is little tendency for the activities of foreign enterprise to decline through time and their share of the market to fall. Instead their subsidiaries in each country, once established, tend to grow in step with that industry in that country except where interrupted by extraordinary events like war. When dealing with an international corporation, we are dealing with a long-run problem.[6]

Historical accident plays an important role in determining the market share of particular firms in a particular country. An old example contrasting the meat industry and the tobacco industry can help illustrate this important feature.[7] In the nineteenth century the United States exported meat to Great Britain and Europe. The advent of refrigerated shipping

---

[5] Other evidence on the venerability of foreign investment is as follows: the *Census of 1957* showed that 65 per cent of total investment is concentrated in plants which were established before 1946 (p. 99). Since few plants were established during either the depression or the war, most of these plants must have started before 1930. This is confirmed in the *Direct Private Foreign Investments of the United States: Census of 1950* (Washington: U.S. Government Printing Office, 1953) which found that almost 60 per cent of 1950 investment was in plants established before 1930 (p. 50). In the United Kingdom, fully one-half of the employment in United States controlled enterprises in 1953 was in firms established before 1914: John H. Dunning, *American Investment in British Manufacturing Industry* (London: George Allen and Unwin, 1958), p. 95. In Australia, Brash found over half of the 1962 employment in his sample of American firms began operations before 1929, mainly between 1920 and 1929: Donald T. Brash, *American Investment in Australian Industry* (Canberra: Australian National University Press, 1966). Two-thirds began before 1939. In New Zealand, Deane found 34 per cent of its 1965 employment of respondent companies from all countries to be in firms established before 1930, 50 per cent before 1939: R. S. Deane, *Foreign Investment in New Zealand Manufacturing* (Wellington: Sweet and Maxwell, 1970). These statistics refer to the date on which the branch plant began operations. The relevant concept is the date the *parent firm* first went abroad. If data were available on this basis, they would indicate a much smaller percentage of investment being accounted for by new entrants. See also the case histories reported in Cleona Lewis, *America's Stake in International Investments* (Washington, D.C.: Brookings Institution, 1938); H. Marshall, F. A. Southard and K. Taylor, *Canadian-American Industry* (New Haven: Yale University Press, 1936); D. M. Phelps, *Migration of Industry to South America* (New York: McGraw-Hill, 1936); and F. A. Southard, *American Industry in Europe* (Boston: Houghton Mifflin Co., 1931). In this last work, Southard was able to trace the origins of many firms back to the late nineteenth century. Direct investment by foreigners in the United States appears also to be in old, well-established subsidiaries. Of the $US6 billion of direct investment in the United States in 1959, almost 80 per cent was established before 1941 (*Census of 1959*).

[6] In Canada, for example, the share of foreign firms has shown no tendency to fall and is increasing: Dominion Bureau of Statistics, *Canada's International Investment Position, 1926-1954* (Ottawa: Queens Printer, 1958) and *Foreign Ownership and the Structure of Canadian Industry* (Ottawa: Queens Printer, 1968). For England, only a very slight decline, helped by the war, was found by Dunning in his investigation of the trend in the American share of British industry (Dunning, op. cit., p. 184); of the 115 firms questioned, only 15 claimed their share decreased; 63 firms reported an increase and 37 no change.

[7] L. Corey, *Meat and Man* (New York: The Viking Press, 1950), pp. 202-6. On tobacco see Dunning, op. cit., pp. 30-1.

made it economical for Europe to switch its imports from the United States to Latin America. Both British and American firms established meat packing plants in Latin America. A bitter battle resulted but firms of both countries remained in the industry.

Contrast this with the tobacco case where the invasion of the British tobacco industry by American capital was met by amalgamations of British firms, a period of cut-throat competition, and a market sharing agreement which kept the American tobacco out of Britain, British capital out of America, and established a joint venture to handle third markets. Later, as part of an antitrust decree, American Tobacco was forced to divest itself of its share of the British-American Tobacco Company. Similarly, in the chemical industry, a low level of direct investment in Europe by American firms and a high reliance on licensing reflects the particular form of oligopoly collusion reached in that industry characterised by large firms on both sides of the Atlantic. Also, the joint venture between Imperial Chemical and Dupont in Canada was broken up by an antitrust decree.

Wars have also been an important factor determining market shares. In the United States, in contrast to the general pattern, firms formerly owned by foreigners have in some industries given way to local firms. But many of these were special cases resulting from the war, when German subsidiaries were seized, and some British firms sold to meet exchange requirements of the United Kingdom. Some of the British firms later bought back their interests.

Thus we can observe a wide variety of historical patterns. In one industry firms may divide the world into spheres of interest, with, say, American firms restricting themselves to Latin America, European firms to Asia and Africa, and all competing with Canada. In another industry, firms may co-operate more closely and establish joint ventures to operate in regions outside their home countries. In still other industries, the firms may compete instead of collude and each establish branch plants in most foreign countries. It is not possible to specify *a priori* which of the many permutations and combinations will be chosen; the indeterminacy of oligopoly theory reflects itself in the indeterminacy of direct investment and there is great difficulty in predicting the a_is with any degree of accuracy.

But the system underlying direct investment tends to be characterised by positive feedback and a structure, once established, tends to reproduce itself. This underlines the importance of initial positions in determining future profits and explains in part the emphasis placed by businessmen on market position rather than profitability in determining their investment strategy (this can also be used as an argument for government restrictions, that is, the infant *firm* argument for protection).

It would be quite wrong, though, to project the past pattern into the

Table 2.2   Scale of United States business in foreign countries   ($US billion except where noted)

	All foreign subsidiaries				Subsidiaries in Latin America				Comparable data for United States 1962-3			
					All industries		Manufacturing			Largest 50 firms	Next 50 firms	Largest 200 firms
	1950	1957	1966	1970	1957	1966	1957	1966	All cor-porations			
U.S. investment	11.8	25.3	54.8	70-75	6.6	11.4	1.2	3.3				165.3
Total assets	22.2	42.5		12.0	7.2	12.9	2.3	6.5	291.0	136.2		
Sales		38.1		120-150	4.0	6.7	.7	2.1	420.3	25%	9%	42%
Value added		16.0		40-50	.8	1.2	.319	.475	191.9	25%	8%	41%
Employment (millions)		3.2		5-6					17.0	19%	6%	31%
Wages and salaries		6.7	5.7						99.7	24%	8%	39%
Earnings	2.0	3.6			1.3	2.5	.354	1.147	19.3	11.1		13.0

Source: Cols. 1-3: *Census of 1950, Census of 1957,* and *Survey of Current Business,* October 1969.
Value added for foreign subsidiaries obtained by subtracting materials, supplies and services purchased from total costs.
Cols. 5-8: *Census of 1957* and preliminary results of *Census of 1966* as reported by the Council for Latin America (1970).
Cols. 9-12: U.S. Congress *Economic Concentration,* Hearings before the Subcommittee on Antitrust and Monopoly, May-June 1965 (U.S. Government Printing Office, Washington, 1965), Part I, p. 5 and p. 1894, Part II, pp. 113-14. Total assets and earnings refer to 1962 rather than 1963. Total earnings (profit after tax) were available on a quarterly basis and were multiplied by four. They refer to earnings of manufacturing corporations only. The figure for Sales ($US420.3 billion) refers to value of shipments.

future. We seem now to be witnessing a major upheaval. Market patterns, sometimes set early in the century, remained stable until the fifties, but now radical shifts are occurring in the structure of the international economy, and many industries are characterised by intense oligopolistic competition between firms of different nations. During the next few years, we may expect shifts and fluctuations in the pattern of market shares; but if the past is any criterion, we may hazard the guess that a new pattern will emerge which will remain stable for another long period. The European situation seems to have begun already to work towards stabilisation in terms of market shares; but in Eastern Europe, Asia, Africa and Latin America, the battle is probably just about to begin.

The Rapid Growth of United States Business Abroad

Adequate data on the degree to which United States corporations have penetrated foreign markets are not available but the aggregate investment of American corporations in all foreign countries is very large. At present it totals $US70-75 billion and in recent years it has grown on the order of $US5-7 billion annually (see Table 2.2). These numbers, it should be

Table 2.3   Measures of penetration by multinational corporations for Canada, Australia and New Zealand (per cent)

	Canada All industries		Large firms	Australia	New Zealand
	1945	1954	1961		
Fixed assets					
Land and buildings				6.9	25
Plant and machinery				10.2	35
Value of output	20	30	49	7.0	26
Value added	20	29	47	—	26
Employment	16	21	44	5.1	20
Salaries and wages	—	—	42	—	—
Profits	18	25	—	—	—
Establishments	1.3	2.0	37	—	5
Replacement to					
Land and buildings				14.8	
Plant and machinery				13.1	

Source: Canada: Dominion Bureau of Statistics, *Canada's International Investment Position 1926-1954*; Gideon Rosenbluth, 'Foreign Control and Industrial Concentration', *Report for the Task Force on the Structure of Canadian Industry* (mimeo, 1967). Large firms refers to manufacturing establishments belonging to entrepreneurs with capital investment of more than $25 million in Canada. Australia: Donald T. Brash, *American Investment in Australian Industry*. Data refer to United States firms responding to his questionnaire. New Zealand: R. S. Deane, *Foreign Investment in New Zealand Manufacturing*. Data for all foreign firms.

noted, represent only the capital invested by the American parent in its foreign subsidiary and not the total assets under its control. The total assets of American corporations operating abroad are much larger than the capital invested and probably equal $US110 billion at book value. American corporations, on the average, are able to borrow 40 per cent of their subsidiaries' capital requirements locally in the country of operation.

The foreign penetration of United States industry differs considerably from country to country. In Canada and some underdeveloped countries, foreign investment represents a very large amount of the capital stock. In the rest of the world the American share is considerably lower. In Europe it is still small, relatively speaking, but as it is associated with dynamic industries, it is growing rapidly and of considerable importance. In Japan, it is less than one per cent.

The question is how big is big? To what should we compare foreign investment in order to evaluate its importance; to national income, aggregate capital stock and employment, or to the value of these variables in

Table 2.4   Expenditures by United States companies on plant and equipment in the United States and abroad ($US billion)

Year	In United States	Abroad	Ratio of foreign to domestic
1957	18.2	4.8	26
1958	13.8	4.1	30
1959	14.1	3.7	26
1960	16.4	3.8	23
1961	15.6	4.1	26
1962	16.5	4.6	28
1963	17.5	5.1	29
1964	20.7	6.1	29
1965	24.9	7.4	30
1966	29.8	8.6	30
1967	30.2	9.2	37
1968	30.0	9.4	31
1969	33.6	11.4	34
By industry for 1966			
Food	1.440	0.205	
Paper and pulp	1.460	0.271	
Chemicals	2.960	1.159	
Rubber	0.430	0.188	
Printing	1.802	0.463	
Machines	2.990	0.765	
Electrical machines	1.120	0.265	
Transport equipment	2.990	1.119	
Mining and petroleum	5.910	3.553	

Source: Survey of Current Business, September 1965, September 1966, January 1970, March 1970.

the manufacturing sector alone, or in selected industries within manufacturing?

In general the subsidiaries of multinational corporations are larger than average, more capital intensive, and pay higher wages than those of the host country. Their share of capital and profits therefore usually exceeds their share of output which in turn exceeds their share in employment (see Table 2.3 for some examples). On the other hand, the subsidiaries of United States multinational corporations have less capital per man than their parents and pay lower wages; the foreign share in employment of multinational corporations thus exceeds their foreign share of output or profits.

There is room for a vast number of indicators depending upon the purposes, theory and biases of the observer. However, since direct foreign investment is growing more rapidly than most other economic series, whatever ratio is chosen, the critical point where a quantitative change becomes a qualitative change is likely to be reached fairly shortly, if present trends continue. The examples that follow are indicative.

First, the $US6 billion of value added by all United States foreign business in 1957 was only about 13 per cent of the total United States national income generated in mining and manufacturing that year (about $US120 billion); but whereas foreign activity probably tripled between 1957 and the present, activity in the United States only doubled (see Table 2.4). Plant and equipment expenditure by United States business abroad was about one-quarter of domestic expenditure in 1957 and rose to about one-third by 1969. These ratios are much higher in certain industries.

Secondly, Table 2.5, which compares United States firms abroad with *Fortune*'s 500 largest United States industrial corporations and 100 (or 200) largest non-American corporations, shows that American industry abroad is by itself equal to the industrial sector of a sizeable country and that it is expanding rapidly relative to its parent firms. To large American firms, foreign operations are of considerable importance and growing rapidly.

Thirdly, whereas United States production abroad grew at about 10 per cent per year over the last twenty years, United States exports grew at only 5.4 per cent, indicating a dramatic shift in United States corporate strategy for meeting the challenge of the world market.

Fourthly, and finally, we should note the growing importance of manufacturing, and, in particular, its rapid rate of growth in Latin America, perhaps a portent for the future of other developing countries (see Table 2.6).

What happens if these trends are projected into the future? Judd Polk, for example, taking into account all United States investment abroad and all foreign investment in the United States and elsewhere, estimates that

Table 2.5   Total sales, assets, income, and employees of the industrial corporations on the *Fortune* list

	500 largest United States firms[a]				100 or 200 largest non-United States firms[a]				Foreign subsidiaries of United States firms[a]					
	Sales	Assets	Income	Employees	Sales	Assets	Income	Employees	Sales	Assets	Book value of United States investment	Income	Employees	Value added
1957	188.3	148.8	11.6	9,078	55.2	42.6	2.5	4,800	38.1	42.5	25.4	3.6	3,200	16
1958	176.8	154.4	9.6	8,523	51.6	47.2	2.2	5,000			27.4	3.0		
1959	197.4	168.5	12.0	9,052	55.2	53.1	2.5	5,200			29.8	3.2		
1960	204.7	176.2	11.6	9,179	62.7	60.1	2.9	5,700			31.8	3.6		
1961	209.2	186.8	11.6	9,266	67.8	67.0	2.8	6,000			34.7	3.8		
1962	229.0	197.0	13.4	9,652	98.4	102.9	3.8	8,893			37.3	4.2		
1963	245.1	208.7	14.8	9,966	108.3	114.2	4.1	9,249			40.7	4.6		
1964	266.5	224.7	17.3	10,464	121.2	131.3	4.6	9,804			44.5	5.0		
1965	298.1	251.7	20.1	11,279	130.8	143.4	5.1	9,853			49.5	5.5		
1966	332.6	282.1	22.1	12,307	143.1	159.1	5.2	9,962			54.8	5.7		
1967	358.9	216.9	21.4	13,079	155.1	171.3	5.5	10,113			59.5	6.0		
1968											64.8	7.0		

[a]Value of sales, assets and income in $US billion; numbers of employees in thousands.

Sources: Fortune Magazine, Census of 1957, and *Survey of Current Business Statistics.*

Table 2.6 Growth of United States foreign investment

Year	Value of direct investment at year's end ($US billion)	Earnings ($US '000)	Manu-facturing investment	Latin America Total ($US billion)	Manu-facturing ($US billion)
1950	11.8	1,766	3.8	3.6	.781
1951	13.0	2,236			
1952	14.7	2,327			
1953	16.3	2,258			
1954	17.6	2,398			
1955	19.4	2,878			
1956	22.5	3,298			
1957	25.4	3,561	8.0	8.6	1.3
1958	27.4	3,014			
1959	29.8	3,241			
1960	31.8	3,566	11.0	8.4	1.5
1961	34.7	3,815	12.0	9.2	1.7
1962	37.3	4,325	13.2	9.5	1.9
1963	40.7	4,587	14.9	9.9	2.2
1964	44.5	5,077	16.9	10.3	2.5
1965	49.5	5,460	19.3	10.9	2.9
1966	54.8	5,702	22.1	11.5	3.3
1967	59.5	6,034	24.2	12.0	3.6
1968	64.8	7,010	26.4	13.0	4.0

Sources: Survey of Current Business (various issues), *Census of 1950,* and *Census of 1957.*

the internationalised production associated with that investment is about one-quarter of the total world product.[8] To obtain this rate, he assumes that two dollars' worth of international products is associated with a dollar's worth of direct investment, and less for other kinds of investment. According to Table 2.5 this is not unreasonable for sales but it is too high for value added. On the assumption that the internationalised sector grows at 8 per cent and the non-internationalised sector at 4 per cent, international production will account for 50 per cent of the total world production by the year 2005 and 80 per cent by the year 2040.[9]

In sum, the growth of the United States investments has been very rapid (10 per cent per year from 1950 to 1970). At this rate it doubles every seven years. When projected over the next thirty or fifty years the repercussions of this rate of growth are very large. What are the prospects that it will be sustained? Economic conditions, that is, the size of market and state of competition are favourable. The world market for products

[8] Rates of growth estimated by Judd Polk, Irene W. Meisler, and Laurence A. Viet, *United States Production Abroad and the Balance of Payments* (New York: National Industrial Conference Board, 1966).
[9] Judd Polk, 'Internationalization; A Production Explosion and a Political Challenge', *Business Abroad*, Vol. 95, No. 2, February 1970.

associated with multinational corporations (consumer durables, other items for the mass middle class market, plus key producers' durables) is expanding rapidly. Important competitors in other countries are ready to take advantage of these markets if United States firms do not. Pressure to continue to invest abroad is thus high.

Political forces are a different matter. They tend to exert a resisting pressure likely to turn the exponential expansion of the last twenty years into an S-shaped Lorenz curve. The question is when the turning points will come and how.

The problem as John Powers of the Chas. Pfizer Corporation has put it is that 'practice is ahead of theory and policy'.[10] Multinational corporations in their everyday business practice are connecting consumers and producers on a world-wide basis and creating a new world structure. This will require correspondingly radical changes in the legal, political and ideological framework if it is to be sustained. Therefore, the multinational corporations will have to mobilise political power to bring about these changes, or it will not be able to continue growing as in the past. Can they do so?

As a headline to George Ball's now famous argument that corporations are modern while nation states are old-fashioned institutions rooted in archaic concepts, *Business Week* (17 February 1968) wrote: 'For a worldwide enterprise, national boundaries are drawn in fading ink'. The task of the multinational corporations is to convince nation states including the United States to accept a greater degree of interdependence; to surrender a wide variety of traditional policy instruments—tariffs, balance of payments controls, and probably monetary and fiscal policy; to sacrifice certain sectors of their economy to the interests of the multinational sector; and to accept the cost of protecting and maintaining a system of international private property.

The positive attitude of most nation states towards multinational corporations during the last twenty years may not be a good indicator of future practice. Multinational corporations, because of their favourable position (large size, wide horizons and proximity to new technology) and the favourable environment (the initial large gold reserves of the United States, the formation of the Common Market, the small size of foreign investment), were in the vanguard of the revolution in world economic structure. The next round is likely to be characterised by increased emphasis on politics rather than economics and a much less free hand for business. The conflict is not so much between nationalism and internationalism, as the supporters of the multinational corporations like to put it; or between corporations and nation states, as others prefer; but between groups of people within corporations and nation states struggling

[10] John Powers, *The Multinational Company* (New York: Pfizer Public Relations Department, 1967).

over who decides what and who gets what—that is, between large corporations over their share of the world market, between big business which is internationally mobile and small business and labour which are not, between the middle classes of different countries over managerial positions, between high-wage labour in one country and low-wage labour in another, and between excluded groups in each country and their elites in that country.

Continued expansion of foreign investment will intensify some of these conflicts. In the case of the United States, for example, it has made the economy more open and difficult to manage and cleavages have already appeared between the interests of international investors and the rest of the domestic economy over taxation, balance of payments policy, extra-territoriality, and foreign aid. Multinational corporations want lower taxation on foreign income and freedom from anti-trust and other regulations. They want the United States to adjust its balance of payments through deflation or import control rather than foreign investment, and they want lower tariffs on some goods to permit an expansion of certain cheap-labour imports to the United States, and they want foreign aid to complement their foreign investment. Given the present economic and political tensions in the United States, it is far from certain that multinational corporations will be able to form the alliance necessary to overcome resistances to their expansion.

If multinationalisation provided quick rewards perhaps it could be done. But United States foreign investment is often defensive rather than offensive: that is, to protect an existing position rather than to capture a rich new market. Moreover, the gradual erosion of traditional monetary, fiscal and other policy instruments before new supranational ones are built, may create a gap in government effectiveness which could lead to a loss of national income and perhaps even a serious economic crisis. Finally the cost of protecting international private property from expropriation is rising and will continue to rise, since, as I argue below, a system of multinational corporations holds little promise for promoting widespread participation and its benefits are largely restricted to a minority of population, in the world as a whole and within the United States itself.

The above analysis is speculative and controversial. The important point is to raise, *as a scientific issue*, the question of whether foreign investment will continue to expand—something which involves political analysis as well as economic analysis. Much work needs to be done in this direction. Our work is only half done when we analyse the effect of foreign investment on income and its distribution without looking at the political strength and reactions of the various groups affected. The practice of multinational corporations with regard to countries can perhaps serve as a model.

Dupont is one company that is making a stab in the direction of formally measuring environmental uncertainty, basically as a tool for capital budgeting decisions. The project is still in the research stage, but essentially the idea is to try to derive estimates of the potential of a foreign market, which is, of course, affected by economic conditions. The state of the economy in turn, is partly a function of the fiscal and monetary policies the foreign government adopts. Policy decisions depend on the real economic forces, and on the attitudes of various interest groups in the country, and on the degree to which the government listens to these groups.

In the fiscal and monetary part of their broad economic model, the Dupont researchers have identified fifteen to twenty interest groups per country, from small land-owners to private bankers. Each interest group has a 'latent influence' which depends on its size and educational level and the group's power to make its feelings felt. This influence, subjectively measured, is multiplied by an estimate of 'group cohesiveness': that is, how likely the group is to mobilize its full resources on any particular issue. The product is a measure of 'potential influence'. This in turn must be multiplied by a factor representing the government's receptivity to each influence group.[11]

The Growth of Non-American Multinational Corporations

Much less is known about non-American direct foreign investment than about American. According to OECD-DAC data (Table 2.7) it is about 60 per cent the size of United States direct investment, whereas total manufacturing production outside the United States, excluding socialist countries, is about equal to that of the United States and total exports of

Table 2.7   Book value of direct foreign investment by major countries, 1966 ($US billion)

Investing country	All foreign investment	Foreign investment in underdeveloped countries
United States	54.6	16.8
United Kingdom	16.0	6.2
France	4.0	2.1
Germany	2.5	0.9
Sweden	0.8	0.161
Canada	3.2	0.534
Japan	1.0	0.605
Total[a]	89.6	30.0

[a] Includes countries not listed separately.

Source: Based on OECD-DAC data and Sidney E. Rolfe, *The International Corporation* (New York: International Chamber of Commerce, 1969).

[11] Stanford Rose, 'The Rewarding Strategies of Multinationalism', *Fortune*, 15 September 1968, p. 105.

manufacturing by the United States are only about one-quarter of world exports of manufactures, although some investment and exports of other countries arise from the operations of American multinational corporations.[12]

The rate of growth of non-American direct investment is difficult to ascertain with precision. Investment by foreign firms in the United States grew slowly during the fifties and early sixties but, in recent years, has been averaging almost 10 per cent (from $US9.0 billion in 1966 to $US 9.9 billion in 1967, and $US 10.8 billion in 1968). There are reasons to expect an increased emphasis on foreign investment by European and Japanese firms in the future. Their strategy of expanding through exports rather than investment becomes increasingly difficult as they saturate markets. Their capability to invest will increase as they grow in size[13] and develop more modern systems of business administration. Lastly, the loss by the United States of its gold reserves will work to remove the asymmetries in government policy which in past years discouraged outward investment by non-American firms.

In addition to Europe and Japan, one must speculate what Russia will do. Her exports are increasing. How long will it be before she finds it desirable or necessary to set up local assembly and distribution facilities in order to service her markets?

Increased direct foreign investment by non-American enterprises is both competitive and complementary to the expansion of United States investment. As European and Japanese firms exploit their particular advantages, the hegemonic position of American corporations will be reduced. These advantages include: greater flexibility in dealing with Russia and China; certain special relations with former colonies; special experience in utilising cheap labour in the case of Japan; greater flexibility with regard to joint ventures, management contracts, and the like; and less of an association with United States domestic political problems. These firms could provide a formidable challenge to United States firms, just as they did in the sixties through growth in production and exports. Leading non-American firms grew faster than American firms from 1957 to 1962 and at about the same rate from 1962 to 1967. Japanese firms grew much faster throughout the period.[14]

The complementary side to the growth of non-American firms can be

[12] A. Maizels, *Industrial Growth and World Trade* (Cambridge: Cambridge University Press, 1963), pp. 23, 85, 430, 431.

[13] Gilles Bertin of the University of Rennes is conducting an econometric study of the propensity to invest abroad. His preliminary findings seem to indicate a sharp positive (discontinuous) relation to size and a general upward shift in the curve for European firms in recent years.

[14] See S. Hymer and R. Rowthorn, 'Multinational Corporations and International Oligopoly: The Non-American Challenge', in C. P. Kindleberger, *The International Corporation*, for evidence on the growth of American and non-American firms and for the basis of the next paragraph.

illustrated by a simple model (used in collaboration with Robert Row-thorn):

$$S_1 = a_{11}Y_1 + a_{12}Y_{12} + a_{13}Y_{13}$$
$$S_2 = a_{21}Y_1 + a_{21}Y_{21} + a_{23}Y_{13}$$

where S_i is the total size of large firms in country i, Y_i is total production in country i, and a_{ij} refers to the market share of firms from country i in country j. The subscript *1* refers to the United States, *2* refers to Europe and Japan and *3* refers to other countries.

At present the non-American share of the United States market (a_{21}) is very small. It is possible for the overall growth of American and non-American firms to be roughly equal (thus maintaining present oligopoly balance) and for both kinds of firms to expand faster abroad than at home if European firms become more multinational by increasing a_{21} and a_{23} while American firms increase a_{11} and a_{13}.

This would tend to equalise $(a_{11}, a_{12},$ and $a_{13})$ on the one hand, and $(a_{21}, a_{22},$ and $a_{23})$ on the other. The world would come more and more to resemble the United States market where each of the large firms is spread into every market and roughly speaking has the same share in each sub-market as it does in the total.

The stability properties from such investment come from two sources. In the first place, the relative growth rates of firms of different countries come less and less to depend on differences in the growth of individual markets, that is, the ratio S_1/S_2 becomes independent of Y_1, Y_2 and Y_3. This permits oligopoly equilibrium with constant market shares in the large, independent of differential rates of growth in different countries.

In the second place, increased multinationalisation on the part of European and Japanese firms would give them an increased stake in a world of free capital movements. This enhances the political leverage of American multinational corporations and helps them to mobilise governments around the world for the task of reforming the world economy in the direction they desire. The close association between national firms and their national economy would be broken as well as their dependence on particular national governments. In the extreme, all multinational firms would tend to pressure all governments in similar directions.

Such a state, however, is still very much in the future. Inter-penetration of European and United States firms is well advanced but Japanese enter-prises (and Russian) are outside this system and still closely tied to national governments. Similarly, the nascent capitalists of underdeveloped countries are closely tied to their governments. The critical point has not been reached, though the rapid development of the international com-munications system which will give multinational corporations the power to reach 500 or 700 million consumers at one blow, may soon give them the decisive edge.

Association with a Few Large Firms

Though many firms have some international operations, the number of important investors is relatively small. Fifty American firms, each with foreign investment of over $US100 million (in 1957) accounted for nearly 60 per cent of all United States direct investment abroad. The next fifty largest investors accounted for another 10 per cent. Ninety per cent of all United States direct investment is accounted for by 300 firms (see Table 2.8). To this must be added a dozen or so large European and Canadian concerns that qualify as multinational corporations.

Given the major expansion of foreign investment since 1957, the number of large foreign investors must have increased and the distribution may have become less skewed. We shall know better when the results of the 1966 census are published. However, it is unlikely that this expansion has changed the fact that the largest part of direct foreign investment is accounted for by a relatively small number of firms in an even smaller number of industries.[15]

The large size of the multinational corporation is a major feature of all discussions. They are described as 'giants' or 'mastodons'. They are large relative to their markets and large relative to the governments with which they deal. The parent firms occupy a dominant position in the United States economy and feature prominently in the list of the 200 largest firms that account for over half of the value in industry in the American economy. The subsidiaries are often amongst the largest firms in the countries in which they operate.

Table 2.8 United States direct foreign investment by size of investment

Value of direct investment by size classes	Number of firms All industries	Manufacturing	Percentage of total Industries	Manufacturing
$US100 million and over	45	15	57	35
$US50-100 million	51	24	14	18
$US25-50 million	67	40	9	17
$US10-25 million	126	64	8	11
$US5-10 million	166	89	5	7
Total	455	232	93	88

Source: Census of 1957, Table 55, p. 144.

[15] The data reported for Sweden in Rolfe, op. cit., p. 175 show that twenty-one companies account for 80 per cent of total sales of foreign subsidiaries; the largest of these, SKF, accounts for one-quarter, and the five largest account for almost 50 per cent.

Direct investment tends to be associated with oligopolistic industries. The major investors are dominant producers in industries where a few firms account for a large part of industry output.

Table 2.9 classifies the major United States direct investors in manufacturing industries by the level of concentration of their industries and presents evidence for the United States. Approximately 40 per cent of these firms are in industries where the concentration ratio is greater than 75 per cent (a detailed list of the industries in each category is found in Table 2.10). For the United States as a whole the corresponding figure is much lower; only 8 per cent of the total value of shipments occur in industries where the concentration is higher than 75 per cent. Note that firms have been classified according to their major product, while their direct investments are often restricted to one or two specialities where the firm has particular advantages and where concentration is much higher; a better industry definition would, I suggest, show an even stronger association.

Still the best and most detailed study of the association of foreign investment with concentration is that of John Dunning, undertaken in

Table 2.9   Distribution of major foreign investors in manufacturing by market structure compared to all United States industry

Market structure: concentration ratios for 4 largest companies	Major foreign investors		All U.S. industry	
	No. of firms	Percentage total no. of firms	No. of industries	Percentage total value of shipments
75 to 100%	32	44	40	8
50 to 74%	11	15	101	17
25 to 49%	28	39	157	35
less than 25%	1	1	136	40
Total	72	99	434	100

Source: The Distribution of American Industries by Concentration ratio is taken from U.S. Senate *Concentration in American Industry*, Report of the Subcommittee on Antitrust and Monopoly pursuant to S. Res 57 (85th Congress), Table 17, p. 23. The data on major investors were obtained from Annual Reports. It was possible from this source to trace about 92 of the major foreign investors in manufacturing (Food, Paper, Chemicals, Metals, Machinery, Automotive and Electrical, and Other). A more complete analysis would now be possible using the data collected by the Harvard Business School and in the report of Bruck and Lees. Though there is some uncertainty surrounding certain of these firms, probably at worst no more than five are wrongly included. These firms were classified into industries which were then grouped according to concentration level. Twenty of these firms were in industries for which it was difficult to assign concentration ratios: general food products, general chemicals, metals, electrical equipment, paper products. For some of these industries concentration ratios are probably low; however, the foreign investments may well be in specialised segments more concentrated than the average. See Table 2.10 for a more detailed listing.

Table 2.10 Distribution of major manufacturing foreign investors by market structure (detailed listing)

Less than 25% concentration	25-49% concentration	50-74% concentration	70-100% concentration	Unclassified
Construction and mining machinery 1	Meat products 4	Biscuits and crackers 1	Cereal breakfast foods 2	Chemicals 5
	Dairy products 2	Corn wet milling 1	Chewing gum 2	Metals 1
	Canned fruits and vegetables 3	Abrasives 1	Flavouring syrups for soft drinks 3	Food 2
	Flour and meal 1	Asbestos 1	Hard surface floor coverings 1	Paper products 9
	Cement 1	Photographic equipment 1	Tyres and inner tubes 5	Electrical machinery 3
	Refractories 1	Cleaning and polishing soaps and glycerine 2	Flat glass 1	
	Surgical appliances 1	Plumbing fixtures 2	Tobacco 1	
	Mattresses and bed springs 1	Elevators and escalators 1	Aluminium 1	
	Medicinal chemical and pharmaceutical preparations 6	Vacuum cleaners 1	Tin cans and other tinware 2	
	Paints and varnishes 1		Razors and razor blades 1	
	Tractors and farm machinery 5		Computing machines and typewriters 4	
	Oil field machinery and tools 1		Sewing machines 1	
	Printing trade equipment and machinery 1		Shoe machinery 1	
			Motor vehicles 6	
			Locomotives and parts 1	
Total 1	28	11	32	20

Source: See Table 2.9.

1957. Dunning's classification is reproduced as Table 2.11. *Nearly every branch plant is an industry where it is the dominant producer or one of a small number of producers.* As Dunning concluded, 'three-quarters of the employment in the United States affiliated firms is concentrated in industries where the five largest competitors supply 80 per cent or more of the total output'. Dunning's rough measure of the importance of the American subsidiaries in their industries, though not as systematic as one would wish, is nonetheless clear: American subsidiaries have a very high share in these highly concentrated industries.[16]

Evidence from other countries, though available only in less convenient form, confirms the finding that direct investment is associated with oligopolistic industries.[17]

Table 2.11   Distribution of American-owned enterprises in United Kingdom by market structure

	Number of enterprises	Number of employees
Group A—U.S. firm the dominant producer	12	32,000
Group B—U.S. firm one or more of a small number of strong producers	136	200,000
Group C—U.S. firm one of a number of producers of modest size	57	14,000
Total	205	246,000

Source: Dunning, *American Investment in British Manufacturing Industry*, pp. 156-7. Dunning believes the 205 firms in his sample account for between 90 and 95 per cent of the total labour force of the United States financial and manufacturing units in the United Kingdom. This presentation underestimates the monopolistic characteristics of the industries; the Group C category contains proprietary medicines, beauty and toilet preparations, and foundation garments, which are industries where brand names are very important.

[16] Dunning, op. cit., pp. 60-78.

[17] Maureen Brunt (Statement on Australia in *International Antitrust*, United States: Hearings before the Subcommittee on Antitrust and Monopoly, April and June 1966) in her testimony before the Senate, for example, noted: 'It is striking to observe that characteristically these industries which are dominated by foreign firms are all highly concentrated industries' (p. 263) and 'almost invariably the foreign firm in Australia operates in a highly oligopolistic market setting'. She recorded that in 1964, 41 of the 100 largest mining and manufacturing companies were foreign subsidiaries or affiliates (p. 263). Brash's survey of American firms also provides evidence of this for Australia. A similar pattern was found by Deane, op. cit., in New Zealand.

Official publications in Canada show that half of the United States investment is in industries where the American share is 50 per cent or more (Dominion Bureau of Statistics, *Canada's International Investment Position, 1926-1954*, pp. 4292-3). This underestimates the extent of high concentration.

In Europe, too, we know from Southard's study, *American Industry in Europe* (Boston: Houghton Mifflin Co., 1931) that industries in which American investment is prominent were characterised by a high degree of concentration.

A number of important implications follow from these characteristics. First, the large size of multinational corporations implies an interaction between them and the government quite different from the traditional view, which pictures a large state acting on a plane above business. Large corporations, because of their cohesiveness, their access to information and modern technology, their world-wide network of communication, and their long time perspectives, often act alongside the state or above it. In theory, the corporation is a person operating under the sovereignty of the state. In practice, the actual power of many national governments, relative to multinational corporations, is more like that of city governments than sovereign states.

Table 2.12 Industrial distribution of foreign investment[a]

	1950		1962		1959	
	Foreign investment of United States companies	Ratio of foreign investment to total assets	Foreign sales of United States companies	Percentage distribution of sales of all corporations in the United States	Foreign business in the United States	
					Investment	Sales
20 Food	483	4.0	3,410	15.5	931	2,299
20 Paper and allied	378	8.4	1,180	2.0		
28 Chemicals	513	5.3	4,400	7.9	465	891
Drugs	—	—		1.2		
Other	—	—		6.7		
29 Petroleum	3,390	19.4	n.a.	8.9	1,184	n.a.
30 Rubber	182	8.9	1,332	2.5		
33 Primary metals						
34 Fabricated metals	385	2.1	2,053	12.5	125	276
35 Machinery						
except electric	420	4.4	3,359	7.6	275	432
36 Electrical machinery	386	8.2	3,571	8.6	83	289
37 Transportation						
equipment			6,680	13.5		
Aircraft	—	—		3.7		
Motor vehicles and parts	485	6.1				
Other				9.5		
All other manufactures	599	2.4	2,938		592	944

[a] Industry definitions not exactly comparable.

Sources: Cols. 1-2, *Census of 1950* and FTC-SEC *Quarterly Industrial Financial Reports*, First Quarter 1950.
Cols. 3-4, *Survey of Current Business* and FTC-SEC *Quarterly Industrial Financial Reports* as reproduced in Gruber, Mehta, and Vernon, 'The R & D Factor', p. 24.
Cols. 5-6, *Census of 1959.*

Second, a dichotomy of interest often exists between those firms which have large investments and those which do not. Arguments framed in terms of protecting the national interest are often the rationalisation of national capital attempting to protect itself from the competition of international capital. Similarly, much of the talk about 'one world' and 'le defi international' should be viewed as an ideological banner for the few, but important, firms with international strategies.

This cleavage shows up in many ways. One of them is the debate over balance of payments adjustment. Those firms which cannot invest abroad want help in exporting to meet the challenge of international competition. Those firms which can invest argue about the virtue of locating production where it is 'efficient' and adjusting the local economy accordingly.

This cleavage, it should be noted, does not increase but diminishes with the growth of foreign investment. Small businesses can be divided into three types: those in direct conflict with multinational corporations, those in symbiotic relation as suppliers or distributors, and those which are unaffected. The first group is often destroyed by competition. It is soon out of the picture, unless it acts quickly, as far as political or economic power is concerned. The interest of the second group basically lies in promoting multinational corporations, despite conflict over how rewards are to be shared. The third group of capital also tends to become increasingly favourable to multinational corporations as the advantages it derives from an open international economy become clear, that is, the opportunity to trade and the ability to protect its wealth. In a closed system of economy, national capital is constantly in fear of expropriation and capital controls. When the national economy becomes integrated into an open international system, Swiss Bank accounts become less necessary, as small capital is sheltered by the umbrella of a multinational corporate system emphasising the rights of international private property.

Association with Special Industries

Multinational corporations tend to be concentrated in a few industries with special characteristics.[18] Table 2.12 shows the industrial distribution of direct investment by American firms and the direct investment in the United States by foreign firms. The great bulk of the investment is in 'heavy' industry rather than light, that is, in industries characterised by large firms, high capital intensity, advanced technology and differentiated products. Gruber, Mehta and Vernon found little association with capital

[18] See W. Gruber, P. Mehta, and R. Vernon, 'The R & D Factor in International Trade and International Investment of United States Industries', *Journal of Political Economy*, Vol. 75, February 1967; R. E. Caves, 'International Corporations: The Industrial Economics of Foreign Investment', *Economica*, Vol. 48, No. 149, February 1971; Raymond Vernon, 'International Investment and International Trade in the Product Cycle', *Quarterly Journal of Economics*, Vol. 80, May 1966; and Raymond Vernon, 'Future of the Multinational Enterprise', in Kindleberger, *The International Corporation*.

intensity. However, they restricted their definition to fixed capital (as measured by depreciation and net fixed assets) and not variable capital. Often the strength of the modern firm stems from its ability to advance wages to skilled personnel for long-term developments. Because these are treated as current costs, profits and investment are underestimated. A more detailed analysis within two digit categories would show foreign investment to be concentrated in speciality industries; and that, within firms, foreign investment usually does not cover the full product range but is concentrated in lines where the firm is particularly strong (see Table 2.10).

A full explanation of the factors which determine whether an industry has foreign investment or not is still lacking but the existing studies point to three features: firstly, there must be some kind of barrier to entry in the industry (technological, economies of scale, or differentiated products) so that local firms cannot compete with profits below a level which compensates the multinational corporation for the extra costs of operating in a foreign country and integrating geographically dispersed operation; secondly, it must be advantageous to produce locally rather than export from a single production centre (this depends upon tariffs, the size of the market, and the threat of local competition); and, thirdly, the firm must find it more profitable to exploit the foreign advantage through direct investment rather than licensing. Hence a technological lead is not a sufficient explanation of foreign investment. One must also explain why the technology is not sold like other commodities. The answer usually lies in the marketing characteristics of the advantage, that is, the difficulty of extracting full quasi-rent where markets are imperfect.

Non-American multinational corporations tend to be in the same kind of industries as American corporations. Perhaps the most intriguing characteristic of direct investment is the number of cases of foreign companies which have branch plants in the United States in the *very same* industries that American firms have branch plants abroad. Table 2.13 lists fourteen important industries in which American firms have large foreign investments, and where one of the major firms operating in the United States is a branch plant of a foreign firm. This cross-investment shows that American direct investment cannot be explained simply in terms of better access to capital, better entrepreneurship, better technology or higher profits abroad, since the flow takes place in two directions. Analysis of oligopolistic bargaining strategy is, however, helpful; it is not unusual for leading oligopolists to establish inroads into their competitor's home territory to strengthen their position; cross-investment may be a reflection of this tactic on the international level.

The industries associated with multinational corporations tend to grow more rapidly than aggregate national income. This suggests a steady increase of direct investment in Western Europe and the growing importance of the Eastern European market. It also implies that the developing countries offer a more important market than might at first seem the case. Development programs over the decades have created in many countries a large urban proletariat, a considerable increase in the stock of education, a nascent industrial capitalist class, the beginnings of a physical infra-structure suitable for manufacturing, and an expanded modernised government sector. These elements are likely to grow rapidly in the next decades, given the level of past and existing government programs. Though many problems remain, rapid industrialisation is indicated. Since the strategy of most countries is to stress the expansion of the small privileged 'modern' sector rather than the development of the lower two-thirds of the population, demand will shift more and more in the direction of consumer durables and brand name products (processed food, drugs and medicines, cosmetics, etc.)—that is, towards the mass middle-class market.

These markets are important to the American multinational corporations since the marginal costs of serving them are low (the costs of product development and marketing knowledge is a fixed cost). Not to fill them would open spaces for rival multinational firms or lead to the emergence of serious local competition which could eventually threaten the home market in developed countries. The motives for direct investment are thus both offensive and defensive—the seeking out of new sources of profit, and protection from future attack.

Table 2.13   Examples of cross-investment

Industry in which United States has major investments	Foreign-controlled firm operating in United States
1. Concentrated milk	Nestle
2. Soft drinks	Orange Crush
3. Biscuits	Westons
4. Paper	Bowater
5. Pharmaceuticals	BASF, Bayer, Hoechst, Ciba
6. Soap	Lever Brothers
7. Petroleum	Shell
8. Tyres and tubes	Dunlop
9. Aluminium	Pechiny
10. Farm machinery	Massey-Harris-Ferguson
11. Business machines	Olivetti, Moore, Philips
12. Sewing machines	Necchi
13. Automotive parts	Bosch
14. Fountain pens	Bic, Waterman

Source: A fuller list of American subsidiaries in the United States, unfortunately without any index of the scale of operations, is found in Appendix A. of S. Rolfe and W. Damm, *The Multinational Corporation in the World Economy* (New York: Praeger, 1970), pp. 131-67.

In making a foreign investment the strategy of the firm is to maximise the return on its advantage while consolidating its ability for self-sustained growth. This involves getting control of marketing facilities through advertising, or dealer networks, and continuous heavy expenditure on product development to maintain high barriers to entry. Smaller firms can often do better than the large firms at one point of the product cycle. The large corporation gains its strength by planning and co-ordinating over the whole product cycle, and absorbing successful small firms when they reach a certain stage in their growth. Given the revolution in communications and the rapid growth of industry abroad, the product cycle comes more and more to include the stage of foreign marketing and production as well. Hence, the importance to large American firms of free capital movements and free entry to new markets if they are to maintain their world share.

From the point of view of the United States, the ability of its firms to innovate continuously and to spread their advantages widely has considerable importance. In 1908, Alfred Marshall analysed the problem of the then dominant economic power as follows:

England will not be able to hold her own against other nations by the mere sedulous practice of familiar processes. These are being reduced to such mechanical routine by her own, and still more by American ingenuity that an Englishman's labour in them will not continue long to count for very much more than that of an equally energetic man of a more backward race. Of course, the Englishman has access to relatively larger and cheaper stores of capital than anyone else, but his advantage in this respect has diminished, is diminishing, and must continue to diminish; and it is not to be reckoned on as a very important element in the future. England's place among the nations in the future must depend on the extent to which she retains industrial leadership. She cannot be *the* leader, but she may be *a* leader.

The economic significance of industrial leadership generally is most clearly illustrated just now by the leadership which France, or rather Paris, has in many commodities which are on the border-line between art and luxury. New Parisian goods are sold at high prices in London and Berlin for a short time, and then good imitations of them are made in large quantities and sold at relatively low prices. But by that time Paris, which had earned high wages and profits by making them to sell at scarcity prices, is already at work on other things which will soon be limited in a like way. Sixty years ago England had this leadership in most branches of industry. The finished commodities, and still more, the implements of production, to which her manufacturers were giving their chief attention in any one year, were those which would be occupying the attention of the more progressive of Western nations two or three years later, and of the rest from five to twenty years later. It was inevitable that she should cede much of that leadership to the great land which attracts alert minds of all nations to sharpen their inventive and resourceful faculties by impact on one another. It was inevitable that she should yield a little of it to that land of great industrial traditions which yoked science in the service of man with unrivalled energy. It was not inevitable that she should lose so much of it as she has done.[19]

The United States is now in a similar position to Great Britain. Its great strength in innovation and organisation cannot be denied. But a striking feature of recent decades is the narrowing of lead-times and the shortening of the product cycle. Direct foreign investment provides one way of meeting this challenge.

Note that this new international division of labour implies a continued dependence on the part of underdeveloped countries as they specialise in the later stages of the product cycle. Direct investment thus has a dual aspect: it brings capital, technology and managerial skill, but it centralises the means for producing capital, technology and organising ability. The relationship between the developed and underdeveloped countries may become like the relationship between major and minor cities, the one continuously innovating and dispersing activity to surrounding areas, the other having continuously to adjust to changes in the centre. The gap could then remain permanent as the relationship between leader and lagger is reproduced through the vehicle of corporate control.

Capital

The structure of international ownership and control varies considerably as firms choose between many devices for international operations: licensing agreements, management contracts, minority interest, joint ventures, or wholly-owned branch plants. Within any one system, the degree of control can vary from complete centralisation to a great degree of local autonomy.

For the United States there seems to be a strong preference for the wholly-owned subsidiary, although this may be changing. At the time of the last United States census of foreign investments, ownership of foreign branch plants or subsidiaries was 95 per cent or more in 75 per cent of the cases of American investments.[20] A similar pattern is found for foreign investment in the United States: 76 per cent of the foreign invest-

---

[19] Quoted by S. H. Frankel in 'Industrialisation of Agricultural Countries and the Possibilities of a New International Division of Labour', *Economic Journal*, June-September 1943. Frankel deals with the challenge of new countries, especially Japan. His article contains other citations in the same vein, for example, by Loveday who, in 1931, said: 'The future lies with the countries whose whole economic organisation is most mobile, with those which have the imagination to foresee future needs.'

[20] Three-quarters of the employment of Brash's sample of United States subsidiaries in Australia was in firms 100 per cent owned (p. 64). Deane found 63 per cent of the foreign subsidiaries in New Zealand completely owned (p. 24).

ment in the United States was owned 95 per cent or more and 20 per cent was owned between 50 and 95 per cent.

The basic pattern of financing direct investment is illustrated in Tables 2.14 and 2.15. Multinational corporations make a sharp distinction between equity and non-equity capital. The parent company's share of equity capital in foreign subsidiaries averages 85 per cent while the share of non-equity capital is only 25 per cent. On average, firms finance only about 8 per cent of total assets through equity securities, in contrast to about 31 per cent in the form of creditor capital.

This pattern of finance is as true for corporations investing in the United States as it is for American corporations investing abroad, suggesting that it is a feature of the multinational corporation in general and not the particular countries in question.

The high share of equity securities can to some extent be explained by the imperatives of global profit maximisation. The multinational corpora-

Table 2.14   United States and foreign patterns of financing direct investments

	Direct investment by United States in foreign countries (1957) (per cent)			Direct investment by foreigners in the United States (1959) (per cent)		
	Equity capital	Debtor capital	All capital	Equity capital	Debtor capital	All capital
United States share	86	25	61	14	81	50
Non-United States share	14	75	39	86	19	50
	100	100	100	100	100	100

Sources: Census of 1957 and *Foreign Business Investments in the United States.*

Table 2.15   Financing of United States foreign subsidiaries

Area	Percentage of liabilities held by U.S. parent	Percentage of net worth held by U.S. parent	Percentage of total assets held by U.S. parent
All areas	25	86	61
Canada	37	79	62
Latin America	25	93	69
Western hemisphere	17	87	65
Europe	11	84	46
Africa	24	81	52
Asia	13	94	62
Oceania	29	84	53

Source: Census of 1957, p. 108.

tion is a substitute for the market as a method of co-ordinating decisions in different countries. It centralises control in order to take advantage of the effects of decisions in one country on profits in another. Local shareholders interested only in local profits would ignore externalities and frustrate this goal.

We may state the argument more precisely as follows. Direct investment occurs because the profits of an enterprise in one country Π_1, are dependent on the profits of an enterprise in another country, Π_2, that is,

(1) $\Pi_1 = F(\Pi_2).$

To maximise global profits $(\Pi_1 + \Pi_2)$ the following must hold:

(2) $\dfrac{\partial \Pi_1}{\partial \Pi_2} = -1.$

But if the parent firm owns only λ (less than 100) per cent of the enterprise in country 2, it will maximise $(\Pi_1 + \lambda\Pi_2)$, by setting

(3) $\dfrac{\partial \Pi_1}{\partial \Pi_2} = -\lambda$

which only partially exploits global interdependence. For example, concentration of production in a low-cost partially-owned subsidiary, rather than a high-cost fully-owned one might increase total profits, but the firm shares the gains in profits in one country with local shareholders, while it stands the loss in the other alone. A corollary of this is that a local investor might be reluctant to participate in a venture with an international firm which has the power to siphon off profits to one of its wholly owned subsidiaries located elsewhere.

A similar problem arises in the case of vertical integration, for example, the selling of a patent. The real marginal cost of using the patent is zero. To maximise global profits, the branch plants should produce where its marginal revenue product also equals zero. But how will profits be allocated between enterprises? If there are local shareholders in the foreign country, the profits accruing to the branch plant must be separated from the profits of the parent firm. To do so, some price must be used to value the patent. But if a price is charged, managers, attempting to maximise profits of the branch plant, will economise on the use of the patent accordingly. Production will be restricted and total profits lowered.

The usefulness of complete ownership as a device for appropriating externalities and maximising joint profits constrains the financial flexibility of multinational corporations. No matter how cheap capital is in a given country, there is a disadvantage to selling equity securities because of the distortions introduced by local partners. However, this applies only if one assumes firms try to maximise profits legally belonging to shareholders in the home country. An alternative assumption is that firms view all dividends, including those paid to shareholders in the home country, as a cost of borrowing and attempt to maximise retained earnings. Letting d_1 and d_2 be dividends paid in country *1* and *2* respectively, the firm maximises $(\Pi_1 + \Pi_2 - d_1 - d_2)$ instead of $(\Pi_1 - \lambda\Pi_2)$ as above. Provided dividends in each country do not depend on profits earned in that country, that is, provided they depend only on total profits and the conditions prevailing in the capital market in each country, equity securities introduce no distortion in the production decision of the type described above.[21] In the future, it may be increasingly possible for firms to do this in practice by issuing European or Latin American equity securities, for example, and declaring dividends and profits in such a way as to minimise borrowing.

Once the equity constraint is fulfilled, the firm is free to choose between capital markets according to relative interest rates. However, their behaviour appears paradoxical at first sight. We find American subsidiaries in Europe borrowing 80 per cent of their non-equity needs in Europe, while at the same time European subsidiaries in America also borrow 80 per cent of their needs in America. It appears therefore that to Americans capital is cheaper in Europe, while to Europeans it is cheaper in America. Moreover, American firms seem to find capital cheaper abroad in nearly all instances of direct investment, for in every country they borrow something locally and almost never finance completely from the American sources (Table 2.15). Yet America is usually thought of as a source of cheap capital. One would expect that large American firms, with easy access to the American capital market and branch plants scattered throughout the world, would be anxious to act as a financial intermediary investing as much as possible in subsidiaries abroad and lending to unaffiliated foreign enterprises as well.

One reason for not doing this may be that firms have nationality and tend to calculate profits in terms of the currency in which they pay dividends. When comparing the costs of borrowing at home to the cost of borrowing abroad, the firm must add a risk premium to the home interest rate and in the usual case this will outweigh the difference in interest rates. If r equals the capital costs of borrowing in America, r' the capital cost of borrowing abroad, and t the risk premium, the firm bases its decision to borrow on whether

$$r + t \gtreqless r'$$

because international arbitrage will ensure that the interest rates in two countries do not differ by more than the cost of professional arbitrage. Letting a equal this cost, then $(r + a)$ will be equal to or greater than r' and $(r + t)$ will be greater than $(r + a)$. The primary occupations of firms with direct foreign investments are mining, manufacturing, or distribution, and not finance: in the difficult act of arbitrage they are likely to be at a comparative disadvantage relative to the banks and other financial

[21] I am grateful to Edith Penrose for this point.

institutions which specialise in these activities. Some large international firms, at a given point of time, may have better facilities for transferring capital between two countries than financial firms, but by and large the division of labour can be expected to apply here as elsewhere.[22]

The same principles will of course apply to firms investing in the United States. They too should borrow locally and avoid taking a position. Thus, to a multinational firm, the question of where capital is cheapest is not simply a question of prevailing interest rates in various countries, but also its own vantage point. There is a sort of relativistic effect, as firms facing the same world structure of interest rates add different risk premiums.

Thus, multinational corporations do not necessarily move from where it is abundant to where it is scarce since, within an industry, capital will flow from the parent to the subsidiary. At the turn of the century, for example, Europe had cheap capital, and America was technologically dynamic; portfolio investment flowed from Europe to America but direct investment flowed from America to Europe. Interest rates affect the size of the flow but they may have a perverse effect. Cheap capital in a country may attract equity capital because of the greater leverage it permits.

If capital markets were perfect, the direction and the amount of direct investment would be of no importance. In the above example, for instance, the outflow of direct investment from the United States would raise interest rates in New York and cause a compensating inflow of capital from Europe until interest rates were again equalised. The method of financing the branch plant would determine the gross flows of capital but not the net flows and would have no effect on overall distribution.

The financing practice of firms may be changing. In addition, as foreign investment grows, creating a world climate favourable to multinational corporations, more and more companies including smaller ones may expand international operations. Many of these will use management contracts or licences to avoid the difficulties of establishing a wholly owned subsidiary. In addition, larger companies may also show greater ingenuity in devising new forms of international associations which maximise rent on their particular advantage but allow more local participation in other areas. This has the advantage of creating local political allies and also has cost advantages. The small local firms typically pay lower wages and can gain certain concessions from government, thus lowering their cost and prices. The large firms can specialise more and more on software, that is, their organising and marketing ability, and shift the burden of owning the hardware, that is, fixed capital, and managing labour to outsiders. Large Japanese firms to some extent follow this practice and it

---

[22] Borrowing costs change this model but little. As they are a rising function of the quantity borrowed, the supply curve of capital is tilted upwards. This has two effects, the substitution effect encouraging firms to finance a greater proportion from home, and the scale effect discouraging investment in the country where capital is expensive because of low overall profitabilities.

has been prescribed for American business abroad by Daniel Parker, for example, who stresses the difference between certain key operations which the multinational corporations must control, and the production of inputs (which he calls industrial infrastructure), which they can give over to local business.

> The multinational corporation has assets, tangible and intangible, and they will not come into a market if doing so involves a dilution of their equity. For instance, the arrow clip on this Parker Pen—it enhances not one whit the writing capability *per se* of this pen, but we have found that it produces confidence in the mind of the buyer, even to the extent that people in less-developed parts of the world who are illiterate seek to buy the cap only, without the writing part, to use the arrow clip as a symbol. In this manner, an important part of Parker's assets is not just being able to make superior writing instruments, but the share of mind that we have in the markets of the world. We will not come in and share ownership with local nationals on the basis of balance sheet costs. Multinationalism, be it European or Japanese or American, involves similar principles—the values that go beyond the *pro forma* balance sheets of a proposed local national company. Such sharing is unlikely and illogical. But each such endeavour can be benefited from and needs industrial infrastructure. The nationality of the source of supply is an unimportant matter. This is where the external economies' opportunity really is, where the local national opportunity really lies.

Labour

The employment associated with direct investment will not be known until the results of the 1966 census are published. In 1957, when direct investment was only about one-third of its 1970 level, the number of people employed in foreign countries by United States business firms was

Table 2.16 Employment and wages in United States business abroad, 1957

	Wages and salaries ($US billion)	Employees (000s)	Average compensation per employee (dollars per year)			
			All industries	Manu-facturing	Mining and smelting	Petroleum
All areas	6.9	3,200	2,100	2,100	1,800	3,200
Canada	2.6	670	3,900	4,000	3,600	6,000
Latin America	1.4	950	1,400	1,100	1,500	5,000
Europe	2.0	1,080	1,800	1,600	. . a	2,100
Africa	0.1	100	1,200	1,400	550	2,200
Asia	0.4	240	1,500	1,000	. . a	2,200
International	0.2	20	2,100	2,100	. . a	2,200

a Number of firms not large enough to be representative.
Source: Census of 1957.

3.2 million (1957 census). Employment must have grown more slowly than capital since then, but a figure of 5 or 6 million does not seem unreasonable. For Latin America excluding Cuba the preliminary results of the 1966 census indicate that employment rose 50 per cent from 1957 to 1966 while direct investment doubled (Table 2.1).

The area distribution of foreign employment, wages, and compensation per employee in various countries is shown in Table 2.16. In general wages are lower abroad than at home but are higher than average for the host country, in part because the subsidiaries are larger and more capital intensive than other firms and in part because of political vulnerability. Wages are particularly high for the few employed in highly capital intensive petroleum production.

The number of Americans sent abroad to work in the subsidiaries in American multinational corporations is small—about 1 per cent concentrated in higher posts (see Table 2.17). At first sight this would seem to indicate a high degree of local participation. In fact it does not since levels of decision-making are not specified. A company can offset pressure to hire nationals for top management posts by downgrading the functions of the office and centralising control.

To indicate the kinds of data we require on the structure of employment, we refer to the management literature on corporative administrative structures and span of control.[23] In the version presented by Simon, for example, it is assumed that each executive can supervise n employees and that the ratio of wages at any level of the hierarchy to the one below is b. Since this model is used only for illustrative purposes, the many complications involved will not be discussed. This leads to an employment pyramid as depicted in Table 2.18.

Location theory suggests that while employment at lower levels will be spread throughout the world rather widely, executives at higher levels will tend to be concentrated in a few locations in the home country.

---

[23] On the levels of authority within the corporations see: Herbert A. Simon, 'The Compensation of Executives', *Sociometry*, March 1957; Norman H. Martin, 'The Levels of Management and Their Mental Demands', in *Industrial Man, Businessmen, and Business Organizations* (New York: Harper Bros, 1959); William M. Evan, 'Indices of the Hierarchical Structure of Industrial Organizations', *Management Science*, April 1963; M. F. Hall, 'Communication Within Organizations', *Journal of Management Studies*, February 1965; J. H. Horne and Tom Lupton, 'The Work Activities of Middle Managers: An Exploratory Study', *Journal of Management Studies*, Vol. 2, No. 1, February 1965; John Dearden, 'Timespan in Management Control', *Financial Executive*, August 1968; Robert E. Thompson, 'Span of Control Conceptions and Misconceptions', in *Emerging Concepts in Management* (London: Macmillan Co., 1969); Thomas L. Whisler, 'Measuring Centralization of Control in Business Organizations', in W. W. Cooper *et al.* (eds.), *New Perspectives in Organizational Research* (New York: John Wiley & Sons, Inc., 1964); and Hans B. Thorelli, 'Salary Span of Control—A Study in Executive Pay', *Journal of Management Studies*, October 1965. This last work is a study of executive pay in Sears Roebuck's Latin American branches. Thorelli found that a large part of the variation could be explained by the executive's level in the overall corporate hierarchy and the total wage bill of all employees under him.

The main argument can be summarised briefly as follows. Increased division of labour within the corporation which accompanies the growth of the corporation increases productivity and the variety of tasks the organisation can accomplish. If all employees do the same thing, the range of their combined activity is limited; if each employee is assigned to one of n tasks, then m employees can jointly accomplish mn different activities. This would result in chaos if it was not co-ordinated. Hence increased differentiation and subdivision require elaborate organs of integration at higher levels.

For this complex hierarchical system to work, the organisation must develop efficient vertical communications so that their information flows

Table 2.17 Employment structure of United States business abroad

	United States business abroad 1957		United States business in Latin America (excluding Cuba) 1966	
	Total	Sent from U.S.	Total	Sent from U.S.
Managers technical and professional	178,000	14,000	1,600 31,000	1,200 800
Other salaried wage earners	1,251,000	5,000	136,000 292,000	— —
Total	1,942,000	19,000	475,000	2,000
Estimated grand total	3,200,000			

Source: Census of 1957, p. 22, and report of the Council for Latin America (1970).

Table 2.18 International corporate structure

Levels of corporate hierarchy	Number of persons	Salary per person	Share of employees located in the U.S.	Nationality and class
Executive level 1	1	b^6w	100%	Mostly American and
Executive level 2	n	b^5w	very high	upper middle class
Executive level 3	n^2	b^4w		
Executive level 4	n^3	b^3w	(declining)	(increasingly heterogeneous)
Executive level 5	n^4	b^2w		
Executive level 6	n^5	bw		
Operatives	n^6	w	50% (?)	Many races and nationalities

Source: See text.

up and orders flow down easily. It must also have strong lateral communications at the higher levels so that decisions will be co-ordinated and integrated. But for lower levels it is usually necessary to restrict lateral communications to eliminate noise and to prevent the lower echelons from organising themselves in opposition to the higher ones.

The general pattern therefore is that the higher one goes in the hierarchy, the greater the need for lateral communication. At the highest levels, continuous face to face contact and a large measure of common understanding are necessary. Hence the need for a common background and a common meeting place.

This applies to communications between business enterprises as well as within business enterprise. Corporations differ greatly in the geographical distribution of their operatives, depending upon the industry—specific pull of men, markets, and raw materials; but they tend to locate co-ordinating offices in the same major cities in order to benefit from common communications networks, specialised personnel and other infrastructure. The higher levels, where strategy is made, tend to be even more concentrated geographically. It is almost true that nearly every major corporation in the United States must have its general office in New York or else maintain a large proportion of its higher personnel there if it is to operate effectively in the capital market, be in touch with the media, and have access to the pool of specialised knowledge and services concentrated there.

In sum, the growth of firms involves a double movement; expansion or spread at the bottom, concentration at the top. Local firms differ from national firms in the location of top executives as well as in the scope of operations. The local firm is directed locally; national firms are controlled from the strategic metropolis. Similarly, national firms differ from multinational firms not only in the geographical scope of their operations but also in where their strategy is made. Multinational corporations are connected to the world's major financial capitals and linked to each other by a variety of special networks. National firms do not move in these circles.

This means that the international distribution of high level employment will depend crucially upon the degree to which economic activity is organised multinationally or nationally. A world dominated by multinational corporations would tend to concentrate higher level decision-makers in a few centres in the advanced world. Other places would conduct only intermediate or lower level activity and would have a correspondingly truncated employment structure.[24] In addition, nationality at higher levels would tend to be more homogeneous (that is, upper- and

[24] See R. M. Haig, 'Toward an Understanding of the Metropolis', *Quarterly Journal of Economics*, February 1926, and R. D. McKenzie, 'The Concept of Dominance and World Organisation', *American Journal of Sociology*, Vol. 33, July 1927 for an analysis of the hierarchy of cities.

middle-class European) than at the bottom where people of all races and nationalities are represented. This is still true in the United States where conditions of upward mobility are most favourable.

Stratification along these lines would have important political consequences. Unfortunately the data are poor and we are very much in the dark about this aspect of multinational corporations. Surveys showing the following type of data for employees of multinational corporations are badly needed if we are to begin evaluating the impact of a world of free capital movement:

> salary structure, which would indicate status within the organisation better than job title;
> level of decision-making which could be defined in terms of the amount of money the person was authorised to spend, the time span of discretion, authority for promoting subordinates, etc.;
> nationality, which would include educational and class background; geographic location including per cent of time spent in various countries, and amount of travel.

The meagre data currently at hand hardly confront the issue.

Comments and Discussion

BRUCE WILKINSON opened the discussion: It may be useful to re-organise and summarise the main features of the paper, thereby pin-pointing the various issues warranting either elaboration or discussion.

First, there was a review of the expansion of United States business abroad and of foreign firms in the United States and elsewhere.

Secondly, evidence is offered that direct investment appears to be concentrated in relatively few industries, and suggestions are made about the characteristics which encourage this investment, namely: barriers to entry such as scale economies, technology and product differentiation; and advantages to local production over export or licensing generally hinge on the strategy of preventing erosion of market position in oligopolistic markets and on the desire to extract full quasi-rents when markets are imperfect. These features are in turn used to help explain the cross-investment nature of so much international direct investment.

Statistical evidence of the great size and high concentration ratios of these multinational corporations is also presented, accompanied by the observation that the corporate power often exceeds that of the governments of the countries in which they operate.

Projections, or perhaps hypotheses, are formulated so that the recent rates of expansion of direct investment, if continued for some decades, would imply almost complete dominance of multinational corporations in world production and trade and the centralisation of top level managerial and organisational abilities in a very few key centres throughout the western world.

Finally, speculation occurs as to whether this expansion will continue, given, on the one hand, the increasing economic and hence political power of those large firms and, on the other, the growing resistance by governments concerned with the rapid encroachment of the multinational corporations into almost every realm of governmental and private decision-making.

This speculation about the future of the multinational firm *vis-à-vis* the nation state, together with the economic implications thereof, is clearly the main theme of Hymer's chapter, occurring again and again throughout. Hymer's own position on what this outcome might be (or perhaps should be) is much less clear, however.

In spite of the fairly favourable governmental attitude to multinational firms in the past, he foresees a tighter official hand on business in the future as objections are raised to these giants by small businesses not mobile internationally, as firms operating internationally erode traditional monetary and other national governmental policy instruments without supranational substitutes being developed to replace them, and as it becomes clearer that the benefits of multinational corporations go to a few groups only in the United States, and the rest of the world, and generally not to the developing nations, and result in increased centralisation of control in a small elite group located in but a few centres on the earth. These, then, are the types of hypotheses upon which he bases his view that the multinational corporation may be thwarted greatly in its future development.

Yet he also indicates that these business giants are undertaking research to identify the various resistance groups they have to confront, and estimate the cohesiveness of these groups and the extent of the influence they may wield with governments. The implication is that the corporations will in due course be able to act to counter the influence of these groups.

He also argues that as European and Japanese multinational firms expand, some stability in their overall world market shares may be achieved and, in turn, together they can pressure governments and the world economy into change as they desire. Even if the market share stability is not reached, and one may well question that it would occur in the way outlined, joint action by multinational firms from various home countries could presumably still occur.

Again, he hypothesises that the division between large firms investing internationally and small firms which do not will lessen. Those small businesses in similar production lines which object to the international approach will soon be competed out of operation unless they too join on the international bandwagon. The remaining firms will come to support the multinational firms either because they are suppliers to them, or simply because the freeing of the international economy brings prosperity and lessens fears of expropriation and controls.

Finally, at the same time as he submits that there will be increased concentration of key operations in a few people in only a few locations (which may bring resentments and government interference) he also hypothesises that the big firms through new licensing arrangements and the farming-out of production of many inputs to local firms will enable more participation by the smaller business thereby gaining their support and, in general, keeping the natives from getting too restless. He also appears to support the view that such increased local participation through supplying inputs provides new opportunities for achieving external economies by the individual nations and thereby forestalling unfavourable government action toward multinational firms. It is not clear to me how this last hypothesis is expected to work in actual practice.

In brief, Hymer has built up two contrary sets of hypotheses about the future development and role of multinational firms, the one set leading to the view that they will continue their rapid growth and eventually attain an overwhelming significance in world affairs, undisciplined by nation states, the other set suggesting that growth will be stifled by a hostile governmental environment. The validity and relative importance of them only can be determined by empirical investigation and even then probably in an *ex post* way.

As Hymer has indicated, the truth will probably lie somewhere between these extremes. There may be, for example, greater governmental participation in multinational firms through a variety of techniques. One is legislation by host countries designed to prevent actual or anticipated actions by foreign firms regarding transfer pricing, exporting, research and development behaviour viewed as detrimental to national interests. Or there might be more joint ventures between government and industry of the British Petroleum or Panartic Oils type, or even government ownership of a firm with international operations as with the Canadian Polymer Corporations.

The view was expressed in Chapter 1 that foreign direct investment inflows or outflows should not be restricted for balance of payments reasons, but rather that the investment should be free and that the exchange rate adjust as necessary for balance of payments purposes. I would agree with the view that direct investment flows should be freed, but I would go further to suggest that investment in foreign equities by official government agencies may be a way of reducing the need for exchange rate changes as well as accomplishing other objectives of nation states. There is insufficient time to develop the argument fully here but a brief comment may be useful.

To illustrate, where multinational firms fail to provide opportunities for foreigners to share directly in the benefits of their growth in any substantial way through share issuance by their subsidiaries, governments (particularly of surplus developed countries) may use their reserves directly or through a wholly-owned subsidiary to buy shares of the parent firms on the stock exchanges of the home country, at the same time sterilising, when necessary, by means of usual central banking policies, the effect of the initial surpluses on the domestic money supply. In the present world situation, such purchases by surplus countries, if of sufficient magnitude, would both alleviate the United States balance of payments problem and reduce the need for possible revaluation by surplus countries. Also the recent freeing of the Canadian rate to float upward to avoid an embarrassment of foreign exchange riches at a time of temporary domestic anti-inflationary measures would have been unnecessary. This view would of course be unacceptable to advocates of flexible exchange rates, but for those who endorse a fixed system it may be worth examining further.

Hymer was then asked whether he saw developments in world industrial structure to be similar to those which took place in the United States prior to the antitrust movement. If this were so, could there not emerge some American-type equilibrium on a world scale, with large corporations competing in world markets but with their market shares held in check? Hymer said that the analogy was appropriate but that, to him, this implied no Utopian vision.

There was one comment on Professor Wilkinson's plan for the investment of monetary reserves by recipients of direct foreign investment in the stock of foreign corporations. The political brilliance of Professor Wilkinson's scheme was not questioned, but the economic benefit was. The essence of the Wilkinson plan seemed to be that foreign stock could be bought up with balance of payments surpluses generated by capital inflow. The problem was that the capital inflow would generate inflationary pressures and, with the purchase of foreign stock, there would be no transfer of real resources to offset them. There seemed little benefit in foreign investment without some transfer of real resources. Wilkinson explained that his interest here was in developed surplus countries, like Germany, Japan, Canada or Australia, and that the inflow of real resources may not be so crucial to them. Moreover, he saw no reason why the central banks involved could not neutralise any inflationary pressures in the normal way. He suggested that buying a share in multinational firms might well be a superior alternative, in many cases, to trying to develop your own.

A number of participants questioned some of the premises upon which Hymer's projections of the increasingly dominant role of multinational corporations were based.

First, it was argued by some that the communications revolution did not of necessity imply increasing concentration in decision centres. Indeed, the disutilities of living in the metropolis were more and more apparent, and the development of sophisticated communications systems no longer made it necessary. Seen in this perspective, the potential national and international loci of control in international companies would not appear so monolithic. Further, industrial concentration has probably not increased markedly in the United States, and it may have fallen in Europe, although the absolute size of industrial enterprises may have increased. In Europe, concentration has declined partly in consequence of the growth of new multinational corporations. The prospect of increased industrial concentration and power—the central theme of Hymer's thesis—did not, therefore, appear so overwhelming.

Second, the growth of alternative power centres, inspired by still-pervasive 'nationalistic' interests, was pointed to as a constraint on the economic and political power of established multinational corporations. On the one hand, there was disagreement with Hymer's assertion that the participation of local interests was undesirable from the viewpoint of the multinational corporation. Local interests may 'introduce distortions' but they also have the advantage of providing various types of 'local knowledge'. On the other hand, the vision of international collusion on a gigantic scale between large business interests in the United States, Western Europe, Japan and elsewhere seemed fanciful because of the strength of nationalistic interests. Pressures from both directions were unlikely to produce the Kafkaesque solutions which Hymer imagined, one participant concluded.

Third, an Australian participant, comparing Hymer's work with that of the great speculators like Orwell, saw political influence by multinational corporations as a relatively minor problem. Whilst admitting the different position of smaller nation-states, he suggested that in a country like Australia where there had been a good deal of investment by the largest multinational corporations, there was surprisingly little evidence of influence on government policy decision-making. It is clear that foreign corporations are much more frightened than domestic corporations and the wide range of domestic pressure groups of using domestic political channels. They adopt a relatively timid approach precisely because they are afraid of political reaction, and precisely because they have most to fear from nationalistic xenophobic counter-pressures. Others supported this view, one suggesting that the origins of Hymer's analysis were peculiar to the scene on the American continent. Elsewhere, the United States corporation is not so dominant, nor are governments so reluctant to assert their interests in an environment where there is competition between American, Japanese, European and other corporations. An Asian participant added that conflict surely arose between directives from corporation headquarters and the laws of the host country but that Cuba, and many less extreme cases, offered considerable encouragement to sovereign behaviour by governments.

Hymer agreed that modern communications systems make it possible to avoid centralisation and that the multinational corporation was not a technological necessity, but felt that communications systems were, in fact, being exploited asymmetrically. He also agreed with the substance of the three criticisms above, but warned that his work did not aim to predict, just to project. He stressed that there were two sides to every trend projected and that he would not presume to judge their resolution. What he had aimed to do was to specify the contradictions rather than predict or prescribe the outcome—although he had his own ideas about what would constitute a better world. He was grateful that Wilkinson had pointed out so clearly that his chapter contained certain things like facts, certain things like hypotheses, and certain things like speculations. Like McLuhan, he had tried to be cool. He urged everybody to continue filling in their own probability estimates.

3 Problems of Host Countries

A. E. SAFARIAN

The chapter title indicates that this could be a formidable subject, and for this reason I want to concentrate on a few key issues.[1] In particular, I suggest that the inadequacy of the theory of direct foreign investment has meant that some conclusions on economic welfare, both negative and positive, may have been drawn too readily. Some of the macro effects seem clearer, although our understanding of several key questions about the nature of the inputs involved is still unsatisfactory. Finally, I will suggest that policy responses have little to do with questions of the known effects on economic welfare, but rather are the result of political questions, including here questions of the distribution of the gains from economic growth.

It should be emphasised that my comments apply only to direct investment between the more developed countries. The case of less developed countries presents both economic and political issues which do not arise, or do not arise in the same way, in the more developed countries.

Transaction Costs and the Multinational Firm

Let me begin by outlining a few ideas about the reasons for organising production in the framework of the firm.[2] We know that joint undertakings are frequently a source of conflict for the parties involved, the problem being that the value of the assets of one of the parties is dependent on actions taken by other parties. The problem can be understood by reference to the costs of transaction. This term has been used in various ways to refer to the costs of effecting exchange. We will use it to refer to

[1] The first section of this chapter relies heavily on research under way with my colleague John McManus, which will be published eventually in longer form.
[2] This line of thought draws on the early work of R. H. Coase, 'The Nature of the Firm', *Economica*, Vol. 4, November 1937, and 'The Problem of Social Cost', *Journal of Law and Economics*, Vol. 3, October 1960, as well as the recent contributions by Steven N. S. Cheung and others.

those costs of obtaining efficient production that could be avoided if it were possible to centralise effectively the ownership of all the resources engaged in a particular productive activity. More specifically, transaction costs within a jointly-conducted production process are those which must be incurred in order that each participant take full account of his actions on production cost. In such a joint activity an owner of labour services, for example, might reduce his effort if the costs are less than his gains. Some of the effects will be incurred by other resource owners, who must then incur costs to constrain the effects of this on their resources. Many other similar types of interdependence can be cited, such as the effect one owner of a resource may have on the rate of depreciation of another's resource, or the effect one resource owner may have on the quality of overall output. It is this cost of constraining individual behaviour within joint undertakings that we call transaction costs.

Put somewhat differently, some actions by individuals do not evoke automatic reactions from others who are affected thereby. Such externalities mean that the reciprocity which exists through the medium of exchange is missing because transaction costs are so high as to rule out certain kinds of exchange. If reciprocal exchange is prohibitively expensive, opportunities will exist for some individuals to gain at the expense of others.

One can use these concepts to classify the types of organisation for joint activity which are best designed to maximise the wealth of all the participants. In some cases, the price mechanism provides sufficient constraint to lead all parties to act individually so that there is an efficient outcome for the group. Where necessary, moreover, contract can be used not merely to effect an exchange but also to constrain the opportunities for one of the parties to gain at the expense of the others involved.

These devices may be insufficient as interdependence grows, whether because of increasing complementarity, complexity of activity, or number of participants. As a result, for some activities there can develop a large difference between attainable factor costs and the minimum level of costs obtainable with zero transaction costs.

The firm might, of course, confine its co-ordinating role to those aspects of interdependence which are not effectively constrained by prices and contracts. The difficulty would be that individual owners of resources, constrained in some dimensions but not others, would direct their maximising efforts to the latter. Thus, in varying degrees, the firm supersedes price mechanisms and individual contract in so far as activity within the group is concerned. While this form of constraint reduces the losses due to externalities, it can lead to other losses because of the removal of incentives for efficient behaviour.

What has all this to do with the multinational corporation and the issues for host countries? Both the theory of why foreign direct investment takes place, and some welfare aspects, can be extended by application of this line of thought.[3] On motivation, what has to be explained is the fact that foreign direct investment is much more common in some types of industries than in others. This suggests that some activities in a country are more dependent than others on occasions taken abroad, and will tend to be constrained in ways already discussed. Where transaction costs are low, the price mechanism and international trade can constrain, at the margin, the damage which foreign parties will impose. Where transaction costs make the price mechanism too costly, independent firms in different countries can enter into contracts, such as licensing arrangements. But in some internationally-joint activities the property rights cannot be easily transferred or are too costly to constrain by contract. It may be very difficult to state what each party to the contract must do, or to ascertain during the contract whether the terms were fulfilled. Large external effects will persist, which can be reduced by organising a single binational or multinational firm.

The multinational firm will be chosen to organise production if the sum of the values of two or more interdependent, autonomous firms in two or more countries is less than the sum of their values if their actions are co-ordinated (at least in part) by fiat rather than by prices and contracts. Note that many activities in different countries which are interdependent can be most cheaply co-ordinated by prices and contracts, in the sense that internationally centralised resource management would involve losses in excess of gains from eliminating prices and contracts.

Let us illustrate the kinds of interdependence which will create a potential for gain by establishing multinational firms. Industries in different countries are often interdependent because of communications spill-overs. This is particularly significant between Canada and the United States for reasons of proximity and cultural similarities. A firm in the United States which advertises, for example, with a view to maximising its wealth in the United States often creates a demand for its product in Canada. It can exploit that demand by export, except that in secondary manufactures this is often prevented by barriers to trade. It might exploit that demand by a contractual arrangement with an independent Canadian

---

[3] We should draw attention to the early work of Stephen Hymer, The International Operations of National Firms, in which he emphasises the imperfection of market competition in the advantages of the foreign parent as the principal motive for the establishment of foreign subsidiaries. More recently he has commented on some of the other implications of Coase's work. See also C. P. Kindleberger's work, such as *American Business Abroad*, Chapter 1, for analysis along similar lines. R. E. Caves has recently used the capture of quasi-rents to explain direct investment, and generally extended the analysis of effects by applying industrial organisation theory. See his 'Foreign Investment, Trade and Industrial Growth', *The Royer Lectures*, University of California, Berkeley, December 1969, and 'International Corporations', *Economica*, February 1971.

firm, assuming that transaction costs between the two are absent or can be constrained at low cost. Franchise arrangements are one typical example. But consider an advertising campaign designed to assist continual product development, as in the automobile industry. An independent Canadian producer would have considerable difficulty in forming a contract to constrain his dependence on the advertising of the United States firm. The Canadian firm might wish to stipulate the advertising effort in the United States, the types of media in which the advertising was placed, its regional impact, the aspects of the product to be emphasised, and so on. The autonomous maximising behaviour of the United States firm and the Canadian firm are not automatically consistent. As the contribution of the advertising of the United States firm to the Canadian producer's value becomes more costly to constrain by contract, the Canadian firm will have a higher value as a subsidiary than as an autonomous firm. It becomes more efficient to co-ordinate these resources, to some extent at least, rather than rely solely on prices and/or contracts.

Other dimensions of interdependence can be cited which lead to multi-national firms. One which has received some emphasis is monopoly and monopsony power, for the firm with market power exerts pecuniary external effects upon other firms. The concentration ratio might be another, in the sense that the higher the concentration ratio within the industry in one or both countries the greater will be the gains to an individual firm from an international extension of its control.

Let us turn, however, to consider some of the welfare implications of this approach. Our first point must be a reference to the literature on gains from trade. This literature indicates that, if countries have different technologies or if there are other constraints that prevent factor price equalisation, foreign investment will change the host country's factor endowment so as to increase (but not maximise) its real income. An optimal policy of interference can be developed for international flows of goods and capital.[4] Such an approach, however, rules out by assumption the existence of transaction costs. The analysis would be identical for both portfolio and direct investment only if capital imports always occurred with direct investment and if the causes of the two types of foreign investment were the same—neither of which is the case. To put it briefly, only those capital inflows that are a function of the host country's rate of return will necessarily create a higher real income. But foreign direct investment is not a function of the host country's rate of return. Therefore, its effects on a receiving country's industrial mix, hence on its

---

[4] See particularly the contributions of Murray Kemp, for example, 'The Gain from International Trade and Investment: A Neo-Heckscher-Ohlin Approach', *American Economic Review*, September 1966, and R. W. Jones, 'International Capital Movements and the Theory of Tariffs and Trade', *Quarterly Journal of Economics*, February 1967.

terms of trade and real income, are unpredictable by a gains-from-trade model.[5]

A second problem which prevents an *a priori* analysis of the gains from direct investment is that some of the kinds of interdependence which lead to it appear to be closely involved with market power. We have not pursued the relation between transaction costs and concentration here, but one cause of concentration may be the exploitation of resources which cannot be exchanged between independent firms except at high cost. Foreign control of domestic resources, in brief, may in some cases be a way of limiting competition from potential rivals in world markets, or of extracting monopoly rents in domestic markets.

Finally, note that transaction costs are defined here only as the costs of enforcing the terms of a contractual agreement, and the multinational firm is regarded as a way of reducing or eliminating such costs. One should not conclude that the reduction of transaction costs is necessarily a benefit to the economy. For transaction costs as used here are not synonymous with social costs. Transaction costs are not unavoidable. A change in the concentration of ownership of particular resources, for example, could lower transaction costs by reducing the number of contracts necessary to combine complementary resources in production. We do not know what the social costs of this action are, however, unless we are prepared to state what effect the implied change in the distribution of income has had on social cost.

For these reasons, general conclusions about the welfare effects of foreign direct investment do not seem possible with this analysis. Foreign subsidiaries may certainly have advantages, but it does not follow that these will necessarily benefit the economy. These conclusions on welfare effects have been put negatively, but it is important to note that they are in fact neutral. My conclusion, in brief, is that there is no economic basis for having a *general* policy towards foreign direct investment in so far as the approach to this point is concerned.

Reaping the Gains from Foreign Investment

Macro effects and some more dynamic elements of the foreign direct investment process have been considered more extensively in the literature, hence my comments will be brief.

The most general point is that if direct investment is accompanied by

[5] Suppose the production functions of two countries differ so that free trade does not equalise factor prices internationally. If the country with the higher rate of return permits free international flows of portfolio capital, factor prices will be equalised in the two countries. This will be to the mutual advantage of both countries if the same commodity is relatively capital-intensive in both countries. But foreign direct investment need not, *a priori*, increase the output of capital-intensive industries. It could raise the output of relatively labour-intensive industries in spite of the relatively high rate of return in the host country.

capital import, this is likely to raise the income of the host country.[6] The volume of capital increases, hence the wage rate rises. The return on capital falls, but this is a transfer to domestic labour. Where there is significant foreign ownership to begin with, the loss may be to foreign rather than domestic capital owners. One important source of gain is the taxes levied on the profits of foreign enterprise. The extent to which the tax gain is realised depends, of course, on the success of the public authorities in collecting an appropriate share of the revenue generated by the subsidiary's activity. This is not an easy undertaking given the existence of transfer pricing in multinational companies designed in part to minimise global tax costs, and given the frequent difficulty of determining what an arm's length price should be for unique products traded between related parties. In addition, part of the potential tax gain may be passed back to the foreign owner in order to attract the investment. These types of problems are likely to be particularly acute in a federal form of government in which the constituent states or provinces have significant powers in developing manufacturing or resource industries, in which they compete for investment, and in which the federal co-ordinating power is weak.

These and other possible qualifications to the gains from direct investment clearly reflect a failure on the part of the domestic authorities to pursue appropriate policies with respect to the inflow. One can envisage situations where such policies, plus inappropriate macro policy (including exchange rate policy) actually reduce total capital formation, or lead to balance of payments problems in servicing the foreign debt. But one can also envisage situations where inappropriate macro policies create similar types of problems without any recourse to foreign investment. There seems little point in ascribing to foreign investment what are clearly problems in public policy responses to such investment.

Another key point involves the extent to which we can attribute external economies to foreign ownership as such. This implies that nationality of control leads to an activity being conducted more intensively or differently than would otherwise be the case. Both the analytical and empirical studies of foreign direct investment frequently emphasise such external economies as an important gain from it.[7] No doubt there are many external economies which can be generated by a foreign subsidiary. How these should be assessed in analysing the benefits of foreign direct investment depends on three points. First, are these external effects

---

[6] See especially G. D. A. McDougall, 'The Benefits and Costs of Private Foreign Investments from Abroad: A Theoretical Approach', *Economic Record*, March 1960, and Donald T. Brash, *American Investment in Australian Industry*, Chapter 11.

[7] See, for example, McDougall, loc. cit., p. 193; E. Penrose, 'Foreign Investment and the Growth of the Firm', *Economic Journal*, Vol. 66, No. 220, June 1956, p. 233; and three empirical studies, John H. Dunning, *American Investment in British Manufacturing Industry*, Donald T. Brash, op. cit., and A. E. Safarian, *Foreign Ownership of Canadian Industry* (Canada: McGraw-Hill of Canada, 1966).

peculiar to foreign direct investment or would domestic capital which replaced it generate such effects? Second, apart from any tax benefit on investment, residents of a country gain only to the extent that such benefits are passed on in lower consumer prices or higher factor prices, rather than remaining with the foreign firm. Third, what is the best form of access to such technology from the viewpoint of national welfare?

These and related issues have recently been examined by Johnson in the framework of the welfare economics of technological and managerial knowledge as an input.[8] Some research strongly suggests that direct investment can often be identified with comparative advantage in the production of new commercial knowledge in some national markets, along with its subsequent application in others.[9] It suggests, in brief, that neither the industry nor the associated external economies could be duplicated elsewhere in such cases at the same time and cost. This raises the question of infant industry protection to nationally-owned firms against direct foreign investment. As Johnson notes, this argument rests on the assumption that there are social benefits from investment in creating new knowledge which cannot be captured by the firm which invests in knowledge, and that these are greater for domestically-owned firms than a foreign-owned firm. Assuming one can accept this proposition, it does not follow that optimal policy would be to restrict the activity of foreign direct investment.[10] This overlooks, for example, the incentive to inefficiency which protection itself offers. Moreover, in some industries it might involve lower costs to acquire the knowledge through licensing or partnership arrangements. There is, finally, an important dilemma in the creation or development of new knowledge in that incentives to investment are usually necessary for its production, on the one hand, but the knowledge which is thereby created should optimally be made available to all users without charge. In other words, outright purchase by the state for general use might be superior to any of the alternatives just noted in such cases. If that seems an extreme or impracticable position, one might consider whether countries—especially those with low incomes—which are net recipients of large amounts of new knowledge from direct investment or other means are wise in adhering to patent systems which encourage maximum payment of monopoly rents.

These few comments do not by any means exhaust the more dynamic aspects of this issue. The main problem is that social scientists know rather little about some key determinants of the creation and/or applica-

8 See Harry G. Johnson, 'The Efficiency and Welfare Implications of the International Corporation' in Charles P. Kindleberger (ed.), *The International Corporation*.
9 See Raymond Vernon, 'International Investment and International Trade in the Product Cycle', *Quarterly Journal of Economics*, May 1966, pp. 190-207.
10 These points are discussed more fully in Johnson, loc. cit., especially pp. 36 and 51-3.

tion of knowledge. One has only to consider the scant and erratic attention given to entrepreneurial-organisational-managerial roles in much of formal economic theory and measurement. While generally doubtful of infant-industry arguments for protecting nationals against the competition of foreign investment, I have sometimes wondered if relatively small and nondiscriminatory changes in tax or expenditure items, or much more important changes in institutional arrangements and attitudes, might not remove severe impediments to the efficiency of these (and hence other) inputs and to their knowledge-creating and using capacities. The Canadian historical context might be a suggestive one for such an examination, in terms of such factors as the effect of tariff and anti-combines and other policies in limiting competition, the historic official restrictions on merchant-banking roles (or even equity participation) for many of the major financial institutions, the linguistic and social barriers to attaining managerial roles for significant portions of the population, and the under-investment in those educational skills most closely related to growth.

National Interests and Foreign Investment Policies

The main arguments which have been used to suggest restrictions on foreign direct investment in developed host countries rest on political premises. Some of these are essentially non-economic in character, although not devoid of links with economic nationalism. Arguments based on military technology, or on preserving cultural differences through domestic ownership of communications media, fall into this category.

The case for protectionist policies toward direct investment, as a political force, extends well beyond this type of argument. Before proceeding to these arguments, it should be noted that any economic benefits from direct investment are themselves not devoid of positive political effects, depending on how well policy options are exercised. For example, a larger economic base or higher per capita income is an important aspect of the increase in choices really available to a country, which in turn is an important aspect of policy.

Let us turn to the arguments which see national independence as threatened by foreign equity capital. In one sense all specialisation and exchange, or economic integration, involve a surrender of independence in the sense that they may limit or complicate the exercise of some forms of domestic policy. There is an economic gain involved, however. Some recent work suggests that the mobility of capital internationally does not so much alter the host country's ability to pursue independent stabilisation policies as it does the mix of monetary-fiscal policies which can most effectively achieve domestic stabilisation goals.[11] And the 'problem' for

[11] See R. E. Caves and G. L. Reuber, *Canadian Economic Policy and the Impact of International Capital Flows* (Private Planning Association of Canada and University of Toronto Press, 1969).

domestic policy may in fact be a challenge to operate it more intelligently, as with the overvaluation of the Canadian dollar in the late fifties and early sixties.

But more specific arguments have received more prominence. Two deserve particular mention. One is the temptation for the government in whose national jurisdiction the parent company is located to implement certain policies by exercising power over foreign subsidiaries. In extreme cases this becomes a straightforward example of extraterritorial extension of domestic law or regulation, as with the attempts by United States authorities to prohibit or control the trade of foreign subsidiaries with certain communist countries. Somewhat similar effects have resulted from the balance-of-payments guidelines and the external application of antitrust policies by the United States. For the host country this involves an erosion of its sovereignty in that foreign laws or regulations take precedence over domestic for its residents.

Clearly there is a conflict of interest here between sovereign states with different policy approaches, rather than between the government of the host country and the subsidiary or the parent. The optimal solution to such conflicts might be intergovernmental negotiation and perhaps formal agreement on how to resolve the more explicit cases.[12] In the meantime such conflicts lend support to those who regard direct investment as undermining independence, and in some countries are a major force behind restrictive policies towards such investment.

The other issue arises from the effects on income distribution. The political response to foreign investment depends on the effect on private groups in the host country, and this is uneven. I think this helps explain why it is difficult often to achieve consensus on policy. In Canada, for example, the present controversy over direct investment has been maintained for a decade and a half while as yet producing only *ad hoc* policy responses.[13] It may help also to explain some of the types of policies which are offered, particularly those designed to prevent competition with certain groups or to secure some of the monopoly rents for domestic investors.

There are various approaches to the question of the income distribution effects of direct foreign investment. The most convincing overall long-term result, in my view, is that the real wage rate will rise given the addition

---

[12] Unilateral decisions by the foreign government to desist in the practice, or various forms of countervailing policy by the host country, are inferior solutions since they leave the principle undisturbed. For a discussion of this issue in the Canadian context, see the report of the Task Force on Foreign Ownership, *Foreign Ownership and the Structure of Canadian Industry* (Privy Council Office, Ottawa, 1968), especially pp. 295-346 and Conclusions.

[13] Admittedly the intensity of the controversy has varied a good deal, apparently in response to such factors as economic conditions (inversely related) and the incidence of other types of difficulties with the United States (positively related). I doubt whether there is much relation to the serious research findings on the subject, regardless of their conclusions.

of capital and the spread of technology.[14] These gains, of course, might be taken in terms of population increase or employment opportunity, depending on policy on such matters as immigration and the extent to which technology is labour-saving. The effects on domestic capital are more varied—although, as suggested earlier, total capital formation should rise barring perverse macro policies in response to capital inflow. We have already noted the effect in terms of lowering the rate of return of domestic or other foreign firms—though the motive for direct investment, as noted earlier, is not the rate of return as such. To put it differently, competitive firms may lose given higher wage rates or lower market prices or a reduced market share, unless any external economies accompanying direct investment compensate them. Complementary firms gain. In circumstances where these competitive effects are not the probable ones but entry to an industry is barred for a time, potential domestic entrants lose in other ways. In addition, the discussion in the first section suggests that the value of the subsidiary to domestic owners is less than that to the parent. The latter is therefore unlikely to favour a share issue for the subsidiary's stock, or, if you wish, to share any monopoly rents with local investors. The effects on the demand for senior personnel are also not clear. Foreign investment increases the scope for employing such persons both directly and, in some cases, as a means to entering affiliates abroad. What is also visible in the host country, however, is that some significant portion of the senior positions in the subsidiary are filled by nationals of the parent country.[15]

All of this is productive of significant group differences in views on the effects of direct investment. The question is how these differences are reconciled to yield agreed policies. One answer has been supplied by research on nationalism as a collective consumption good.[16] This set of ideas suggests that the benefits from investment in nationalism are both general and particular. The general benefits accrue to all those who derive psychic income from investment in nationalism, while the more tangible benefits accrue to those who benefit directly—by way of higher real income or better jobs—from investment in nationalism. Policy then

[14] See the references above to McDougall and Brash. It has been suggested that, given tariff protection to build a protected manufacturing sector, the inflow of foreign industrial capital will redistribute income from resource rents to labour. See R. E. Caves, 'International Corporations', *Economica*, February 1971, p. 42, and the reference there to a forthcoming article by R. W. Jones.

[15] This varies a good deal, of course. The proportion is quite low for United States owned subsidiaries in Australia and the United Kingdom, considerably higher for Canada, presumably reflecting such factors as distance and salary differentials relative to positions in the parent firm.

[16] See Albert Breton, 'The Economics of Nationalism', *Journal of Political Economy*, Vol. 72, No. 4, August 1964, pp. 376-86, and H. G. Johnson, 'A Theoretical Model of Nationalism in New and Developing States', *Political Science Quarterly*, June 1965, pp. 169-85. One may suggest that the latter title could be interpreted in a too restrictive manner in describing the types of states with such propensities.

becomes less concerned with raising income than with distributing it. The reconciliation of conflicting group interests can be brought about by persuading those who lose real income in the process that their psychic income has risen. If my conclusion above is correct on the income distribution effects of direct investment, such policies normally involve a redistribution of real income from lower to upper classes.

I need hardly add that national feeling can serve better ends than this particular form of protection for special groups, and that national investment can yield higher real income where social and private costs or returns diverge. Nevertheless, the theory just noted does help explain the persistence of certain types of policies with respect to direct investment.[17]

Conclusions

Our conclusion using the transaction cost approach was that a *general* policy on foreign direct investment could not be defended in terms of economic welfare. If capital import is involved there are likely to be benefits to real income (including tax revenue here). Where direct investment reflects superior knowledge whose benefits cannot be retained by the firm, and which are not available as cheaply and as soon by other techniques, further gains are possible.

The above analysis also implies that a sophisticated policy of discrimination by industry might enhance any gains from direct investment.[18] This seems difficult with present analysis and data, and one might be pessimistic about its acceptability in view of the kinds of political considerations described above. There is also scope for research on alternative methods of access to knowledge from abroad, in the hope that in some cases lesser-cost techniques can be encouraged.

The extension of foreign law or regulation to host countries through subsidiaries seems to me to be of a different order. Unless resolved, this will lead to increasing regulation of such firms and also to increasingly serious confrontations between nation-states as multinational corporations

[17] One such policy in Canada is that foreign-controlled subsidiaries be required, or given incentives, to issue what are non-controlling blocks of shares to Canadian investors. This proposal was first advanced by a Royal Commission in the late fifties. It was implemented through mild tax incentives in the federal budget of 1963 to subsidiaries issuing at least 25 per cent of their equity. The policy survived (admittedly as a second-best proposal) in the recommendations of a task force, several of whose members might not generally have been thought to be overly sympathetic to small shareholder capitalism. It was recently advanced (raised to the 51 per cent level but still leaving effective control with the parent) by a committee of the House of Commons whose chairman is reported to have stated that: 'For all we know right now it could involve a massive misallocation of capital'. It appears to be a good example of a proposal which has some symbolic value, which would benefit investor interests, but whose general economic effects are mainly doubtful or negative.

[18] Caves has suggested, for example, that external economies are less likely to accompany direct investment in natural resources and rents are larger. He adds, however, that there is great uncertainty about the rents to be derived in advance of the development of the resource. See Caves, loc. cit., pp. 42-4.

spread—whatever their national origin may be. Many of the other problems ascribed to foreign direct investment seem to me more directly attributable to the failure to implement stabilisation-growth policies and appropriate tax policies. The fear of foreign investment also reflects the failure to develop adequate policies to control the effects of large corporations, wherever owned.

Two final points: first, my own reading of the overall empirical results to date is somewhat more optimistic than this consideration of analytical possibilities might suggest. Studies of the performance of the foreign-owned firms, in terms of their competitive and other effects, have mainly yielded results which are at least neutral and often positive in comparison with resident-owned firms. Second, I have limited myself to a narrow interpretation of the national interest. Ultimately, domestic policy in this as in other respects depends on one's view of the kind of international setting for trade, investment and other flows which will be most conducive to a country's interests. If that view favours a significant degree of specialisation and exchange, then one should take this into account in assessing how the national interest may be affected by policies on direct investment.

Comments and Discussion

HEINZ ARNDT opened the discussion: Safarian's subject could be interpreted in two senses: first, the problems of the costs to the host country in a cost-benefit analysis of private investment; second, the problems faced by the host country in trying to minimise these costs or maximise the benefits. It may be useful to attempt to classify the first group of costs as they appear in Safarian's chapter and in quite a number of others presented in this book.

There are, first, the strictly economic ones. These seem to reduce to two: those which arise from high costs of capital, or of the package of capital-management-technology, in cases where the foreign investor manages to secure a monopolistic position of some sort; and those (partly overlapping with the former) which arise, as Safarian has pointed out, basically from short-sighted or inadequate policies in the host country. The latter include protectionist policies and subsidies from which the foreign investors derive quasi-rents, excessive tax concessions which reduce the host country's share in the profits of foreign investors, and the various ways in which these profits are allowed to be surreptitiously minimised by transfer pricing and similar devices.

Secondly, there are what might be called the political costs to the host country. Among them is the extraterritoriality problem where governments of capital-exporting countries try to impose their policies on the subsidiaries of their own companies and therefore indirectly on the government of the host country. Sadli also refers in a later chapter to pressures liable to be exerted on developing countries in favour of foreign investors through the leverage of foreign aid. There are, finally, all the issues raised by Hymer, the risks of domination of small national states by large multinational corporations.

Thirdly, there are what one might call the still wider social effects alleged by some critics, effects on income distribution within the host country, the possible displacement of domestic entrepreneurs by foreign firms and possible alliances between international and national capital, as Marxists see them.

Safarian comments on most of these points, though he does not deal with them all systematically. In the first section, he tries to see how far the concept of transaction costs helps us understand why direct investment (as contrasted with other international capital movements) takes place at all. It is my impression that, although he begins by saying this may help to throw light on the welfare aspects, he ends with an agnostic conclusion: it does not appear to settle welfare aspects at all, though it may be useful in positive analysis.

He then takes up some of what he calls dynamic aspects. He refers to inappropriate domestic policies, such as protectionist policies, by which host countries have unduly reduced the benefits or increased the costs of foreign investment to themselves. Wionczek, in Chapter 12, concedes this point in relation to Mexico but goes on to suggest a number of reasons why the blame attaches, after all, to the foreign investors or at least to the process of foreign investment.

Safarian also refers to the external economies yielded by foreign investment in the host country, but he does not pursue this further and instead takes up the opposite case where domestic firms are said to generate external economies which might provide the basis for infant industry protection. In this connection he makes a very puzzling suggestion, questioning the wisdom of less developed countries in accepting the international patent system. Is he really suggesting that they should follow the Soviet example?

Finally, Safarian takes up a number of political aspects. First, on the extraterritoriality problem I agree with other commentators that this seems to have affected Canada a good deal more than other countries. I cannot recall a single instance where it has even been alleged that this has been a serious factor in Australia. Secondly, he mentions, very much in passing, possible adverse effects of foreign investment on domestic income distribution, a point which is given very much more prominence in Hymer's chapter. Thirdly, he touches on potential conflict of interest between the foreign parent company and its local subsidiary which, in his view, lies behind the reluctance of some of the parent companies to permit local equity participation. I should have thought that there are other aspects to this question that might well have been brought out. Those who worry about foreign control often seem inadequately aware of the fact that minority equity participation simply increases the extent of foreign control per dollar invested, while insistence on majority local equity participation is liable to have a considerable deterrent effect. A much more convincing argument for minority equity participation is the 'mutual education' effect. The executives of foreign companies can learn something from local people on their boards (such as the expertise they often possess in dealing with the local government agencies) while similarly there is quite a strong case, particularly in less developed countries, for local equity participation, in other words for joint ventures, as a way of providing technical assistance in managerial and entrepreneurial skills.

Finally, Safarian refers to the role of economic nationalism and to the suggestion that economic nationalism may be regarded as a collective consumption good. Formally, this is unexceptionable. But the same is true also of such forms of hysteria as anti-communism, anti-colonialism, anti-capitalism, anti-semitism and so on. All the economist can really do— Professor Kindleberger in his chapter has some rather important and sensible things to say on this—is to inform the public and the politicians about the economic costs of indulging in this particular form of 'collective consumption'.

Thereafter, discussion of Safarian's chapter was directed at four main issues: alternative approaches to the transfer of industrial knowledge; the role of foreign investment in generating external economies; the problem of incorporating political objectives into economic analysis; and the special problems of investment policies under a federal system.

Safarian took up Arndt's question about his approach to the ownership of knowledge. He said that, elsewhere, Johnson had explained different approaches to patents law, and other institutionalised knowledge rights, by observing that where the creation of knowledge is costly, to compensate the innovator, temporary monopoly rights over knowledge were granted. The sale of those rights spreads the benefits of knowledge creation throughout the community and erodes the monopoly position of its creator until it becomes virtually a public good. For a small country, one which is not in the knowledge producing business significantly and one which has no prospect of making money on its knowledge from sales of it to foreign investors, it may not be sensible to draft automatically the kind of monopoly privilege, through the patent system for example, which is granted in more developed countries. It may well be quite rational to adopt a quite different approach to knowledge rights at different stages of development.

One participant queried Safarian's observation that, in their external economic effects, foreign and domestic firms may substitute for each other. He argued that strong external effects were commonly associated with foreign investment because the foreign investment package embodied some technological or managerial advance which was transmitted to the host community. Rather than look upon foreign and domestic investment as substitutes in this respect, he considered it more profitable to ask what additional external effects foreign investment would yield. He added that frequently, of course, there will be no access to new technology except through direct investment.

Safarian replied that he had intended simply to suggest that domestic firms need be no different from foreign firms in their external effects. Some firms can internalise the benefits of special knowledge, from others the effects will spill over to the rest of the economy. These external effects are not peculiar to foreign investment. More importantly, the question of whether direct investment is the only form of access depends, as the analysis in the paper suggests, upon whether the transaction costs are very substantial. Safarian went on to say that generalisation was difficult, however. Work by Baranson, Vernon and others in which an attempt was being made to look at the economic and political benefits and costs of various types of licensing arrangements from within joint ventures through to wholly-owned direct investment seemed interesting and promising. Different types of access to knowledge is probably desirable in different cases. In some cases it may well be better for the state to acquire the knowledge, in others direct investment was clearly the best way. Another participant added that, when we look across the whole range of knowledge transfers, there is a very sharp distinction in all countries between agriculture and industry, with states investing in, acquiring, and disseminating knowledge so that the suggestion that the state is sometimes well placed to buy and distribute knowledge is not all that strange. It is the practice in agriculture: the question is whether in manufacturing industry there are cases where this alternative might not be preferable to the acquisition of knowledge through private enterprise channels.

On the question of nationalism as a public good, it was suggested that the aim of those who invented this approach to policy analysis—and in this Johnson admitted some complicity—was not to justify the various unjustifiable 'isms'. It was to try to explain the role of these phenomena (such as nationalism, commitment to industrialisation for the sake of industrialisation, or nationalist protectionism) which do not fit into a theory of political behaviour based upon the assumption of rationality in the pursuit of economic benefits, in limiting the process of economic choice.

Finally, several participants drew attention to the disadvantages of federalism in the competition for foreign resources. Playfordism (so called after a particular Australian premier) reduces the public sector's return on investment and encourages the misallocation of domestic resources in this, as well as other, connections. Canadian provincial and Australian state governments evidenced this behaviour. The misallocation of resources in the Australian chemical industry, together with the creation of wasteful excess capacity, was cited as a particularly unfortunate example.

4 Direct Foreign Investment and Economic Development

CHARLES P. KINDLEBERGER

In an effort to narrow and simplify the scope of this chapter, I shall deal only with the relations between host countries and foreign firms specialising in primary products for export. This leaves out consideration of the home country and the problems of investment in import-competing manufactures. The former could readily be added by extension of the technique; the latter by its modification, some suggestions toward which are indicated along the way at particular points.

This chapter offers no real discussion of historical wrongs. For the most part they are assumed to exist, most probably objectively, but certainly in the perception of the officials and public of the host country. The facts in many cases will be cloudy or difficult to interpret. In the International Petroleum case in Peru, for example, the country and the company differ about the title to land which Peru deeded in 1826, after independence, to one of its citizens, and whether this title legitimately included mineral rights, about the lease which I.P.C. obtained from the British owner in 1914, and about the legitimacy of the international arbitration to which Peru agreed, after some British arm-twisting, in 1922. The facts are complex and debatable; the emotions to which they give rise are not. And there are numerous cases of outright 'exploitation'. Diaz Alejandro contrasts the carpet-baggers who invaded Cuba and especially the Isle of Pines after 1898 to buy up sugar land, with the moratorium on new foreign investment in Germany after World War II, imposed until after monetary reform and the beginnings of reconstruction.[1]

Where an original bargain is lop-sided owing to ignorance on the side of the citizens or government of the host country, the moral history is even more debatable. Is it wrong to take advantage of advanced technology or wider access to information so long as there is no misrepresentation, no wrongful obtaining of inside information, no bribery, corruption, gun-

[1] See Carlos F. Diaz Alejandro, 'Direct Foreign Investment in Latin America', in Kindleberger (ed.), *The International Corporation*, p. 321.

boats, or strong-arm tactics? Is the advanced foreigner under any obligation to share his knowledge and technology with owners of natural resources prior to fixing the terms of a concession? In many instances, of course, there is no knowledge of oil or ore deposits, but only a suspicion of their existence; such investment is risky. But suppose the foreigner had a monopoly of the technology, so that there was no other way to obtain it other than by making a deal with him, and suppose the proposition was risky *ex ante*, but paid off *ex post*. Is that exploitation? Is it possible to have situations which were not exploitative *ex ante* but are properly regarded so *ex post*?

In economics, bygones are bygones. The past is forgotten when it produces no income. Historical wrongs, however, may well have payoffs. They produce streams of income for political figures or political parties, and may easily produce a payoff for a country in xenophobic cohesion. Social and political cohesion which is tolerant of similar units on the same or higher and lower levels is likely to be considered superior to that based on antipathy. But the latter may be better than none. Social and political cohesion based on isolationism or xenophobia may be a consumption good which can substitute for real income in the welfare function of a country,[2] or it may even be a producer's good, which spurs a people on to greater productive efforts or more saving, and incentive for the effort needed for development. It may keep masses quiet while unequal income distribution stimulates capital formation and growth. Compare the Mexican formula for development as expressed by a cynic: 'Revolutionary slogans and high profits'.

The present values of the title are, of course, present discounted values. A foreign firm will undertake investment when the present discounted value (PDV) of the stream of income envisaged exceeds that of costs, which are largely but by no means solely current, both calculated at some appropriate discount rate. But a given foreign investment has a present discounted value for the host country, as well as for the firm undertaking it. It would be possible to calculate PDVs for various political and social elements in the host country on a disaggregated basis. More than this, there will be alternative present discounted values of a given investment for a host country, depending upon different regulations or different rates of tax. In particular, there will be a different value for the investment depending upon whether it is operated by the foreign firm under non-discriminatory national treatment, or if it be nationalised, which under international law presumably calls for compensation. The question in all these cases is what to include in the stream of income and what in the stream of costs. This is the subject of the present chapter. The discussion

2 See Albert Breton, 'The Economics of Nationalism', *Journal of Political Economy*, August 1964.

is not mathematical, although it makes use of three simple equations simply to organise the discussion of the costs and benefits to different players in the non-zero sum game of direct investment in less developed countries, and to the same player with different strategies. The models are extremely simple, and would have to be modified probably for different primary products such as tin in Bolivia or Malaysia, oil in Venezuela or Indonesia, bananas in Central America, or tea in India or Ceylon. Changes would be especially required, as already noted, if the models were to be applied to import-competing manufactures.

The Variables

New investment is undertaken or not undertaken on the basis of a simple formula for capitalising a stream of income. In perpetuity, where the income is constant, it is expressed as

$$(1) \qquad\qquad C = \frac{I}{r}$$

where C is the capitalised value of the investment, I is the annual income on it in perpetuity, and r is the normal rate of profit expressed in per cent per year.[3] If C, the value of the asset, exceeds C', the value of the stream of costs by some normal proportion, the investment will be undertaken; if not, not. In what follows the I is disaggregated into various elements, which are viewed from three vantage points: that of the foreign investor (f), that of the home country (h), but under two different circumstances, one when the investment is operated by a foreign investor (h_f) and one when it is nationalised (h_{nat}).

The three formulations permit three comparisons: first, the value of a given investment to the foreign investor and to the home country; second, the value of the investment to the host country in foreign ownership and after nationalisation; and third, the value of the investment to the foreign investor and to the host country, when the latter operates it itself. These three comparisons address three issues in the literature: the distribution of the gains from foreign investment;[4] the appeal of confiscation of foreign investment by a developing country;[5] and the theory of direct investment.

---

[3] We disregard below the complications introduced by an irregular time profile of earnings, which of course is the normal expectation.

[4] For the Prebisch contribution, see Economic Commission for Latin America, United Nations, *The Economic Development of Latin America and its Principal Problems* (New York, 1950) and *Economic Survey of Latin America, 1949* (New York, 1951). See also H. W. Singer, 'The Distribution of Gains Between Investing and Borrowing Countries', *American Economic Review*, Vol. 40, No. 2, May 1950, pp. 473-85, reprinted in American Economics Association, *Readings in International Economics* (Homewood, Illinois: Irwin, 1967).

[5] Martin Bronfenbrenner, 'The Appeal of Confiscation in Economic Development', *Economic Development and Cultural Change*, Vol. 3, No. 3, April 1955, pp. 201-18.

Three Identities

The present discounted values may be approximated by three identities as follows:

$$(2) \quad C_f = \frac{(S_f - w_f L - r_f K - T_h - G_f)z}{D_f}$$

$$(3) \quad C_{h_f} = \frac{T_h + (w_f - w_h)L - G_h + EE_{G_f} + EE_f + N_f}{D_h}$$

$$(4) \quad C_{h_{nat}} = \frac{S_h - w_h - r_h K - pRDM - G_h - A + EE_h + N_n}{D_h}$$

Where C is the present discounted value of an investment,

         S is annual sales,

         L is labour required by the project,

         T is annual taxes paid by the project over time,

         K is capital stock,

         G is the annual cost of services provided by government or government investments,

         RDM is foreign technology and management,

         EE is external economies,

         A is annual compensation payments over a long period,

         N is satisfaction from national ownership (n) or dissatisfaction because of foreign ownership (f), normalised as an annual return on a public good or evil,

         D is the discount rate in per cent per annum,

         p is the price of foreign technology and management per year,

         w is the annual wage rate,

         r is the rate of return on capital in per cent per annum,

         z is an element of political risk where $1 > z > 0$, and 1 represents no risk and 0 represents a certainty of loss owing to political factors.

Marketing

First compare S_f and S_h, the sales of output of a particular investment in foreign hands, and after nationalisation. Under well-functioning international markets and perfect competition, $S_f = S_h$. The nature of the ownership would be a matter of indifference to sales. But this is by no means the only outcome. Many observers in less developed countries, such as Prebisch, and most Marxist and strongly left observers, believe that S_h under nationalisation would exceed S_f, because of the overcoming of monopsony. Julien, for example, or Magdoff claim that United States firms pay low prices but get large amounts of needed raw materials at high profits.[6] Presumably when S is decomposed into PQ, Q may be high, but P is unduly low. With different ownership Q might remain the same or decline slightly, while P would rise by more than Q declined to raise total S. Or the typical Canadian fear is that an American company which owned a high-cost mine in the United States and a low-cost one in Canada might be cut back in depression according not to economic, but to political considerations—how much more unpleasant it would find unemployment in Montana than in British Columbia, for example. Under these circumstances, $S_h > S_f$ and, other things equal, a shift to Canadian ownership would improve Canadian and world welfare.

This is by no means the only possibility, however. The theory of direct investment postulates that the foreign investor must have an advantage over the domestic investor in order to overcome the disadvantages of operating in a foreign culture and at a distance from its decision centre. One of the possible advantages, especially relevant in bulky primary products like oil and iron ore that are costly to ship and store, is that a vertically-integrated company can sometimes co-ordinate different stages of production more efficiently than a system of disaggregated markets. Production, shipment, processing and distribution must be articulated with some precision, if it is expensive to have excess supplies or gaps in supply at separate stages. This may require an overall directing brain which the disaggregated market, with separate decision-making at each stage, does not provide. Long-term contracts are a partial substitute for this vertical integration, but raise awkward questions of dependence at times of renegotiation and renewal.

There is an element of monopsony here, to be sure. Highly efficient units at a given stage may be unwilling to operate independently for fear of being cut off from sources of supply or potential marketing outlets by an oligopolistic industrial structure. Once vertical integration enters an industry with only a small advantage, it tends to spread with little or no economic justification. But the economic efficiency of co-ordinated operations in different stages of production, where there are economies to be gained from such co-ordination, must mean that there are many cases where $S_f > S_h$. This seems to me to be the explanation of why Japanese ownership is appropriate in Australian iron mines, why Hirschman may be wrong in recommending blanket divestment of foreign investment in Latin America and to support Adelman's position that the large international oil companies will still find a place when and if they have been

---

[6] Claude Julien, *L'Empire américain* (Paris: Grasset, 1968); Harry Magdoff, *The Age of Imperialism: The Economics of U.S. Foreign Policy* (New York: Modern Reader Paperbacks, 1969), p. 207.

pushed out of producing areas, and when the consuming and producing countries have failed any longer to hold up the price of world oil.[7]

The foreign company's advantage over local enterprise may lie in marketing even without the economies or co-ordination just outlined. These economies are probably not important in copper, but both in Zambia and in Chile arrangements for government acquisition of 51 per cent ownership of producing mines have provided for management and sales by the foreign firm. In the case of Sociedad Minera El Teniente, S.A., before nationalisation, the Chilean government owned 51 per cent and the Kennecott Copper Corporation (through the Braden Copper Company) 49 per cent, but Kennecott had a contract with the board of directors—a majority appointed by the Chilean government—to manage the operations of the mine and 'an Advisory Sales Contract that calls for our advising the Board on market conditions, pricing and related matters'.[8] Where the marketing company has a special advantage, it must be presumed that the marketing fee includes a rent on its scarcity. But in complex bargaining situations of this sort, where there is no competitive standard, it would be difficult to measure such rent.

There is no clear indication where $S_f = S_h$ exceeds or falls short of it. Anything can happen. Circumstances alter cases. There is every reason to examine the circumstances of a particular case and arrive at a judgment as to the extent of real economies of market and of monopsony power, both that which can be evaded, and that which cannot.

Labour Costs

In the enclave case, where the foreign company brings in workers from the home country, or even, as in the guano industry in Peru a hundred years ago, from China, L must be subdivided into L_h and L_f and possibly L_f into L_{home} and $L_{contract}$.[9] Disregarding these cases, however, we may focus on the rent which local labour, L, may earn under foreign investment. This is $(w_f - w_h)L$ in (3) and is positive though not always sizeable. This increases domestic purchasing power, and thus has local benefits. It may also have costs of creating a dual economy and disincentives for ordinary labour to work at occupations outside the foreign investment sector, as opposed to waiting for a job in that sector.

[7] See Albert O. Hirschman, *How to Divest in Latin America, and Why* (Princeton, N.J.: International Finance Section Princeton University, No. 76, November 1969); and M. A. Adelman, 'The Multinational Corporation in World Petroleum', in Kindleberger (ed.), op. cit., pp. 227-41, especially 241.

[8] See C. D. Michaelson, 'Joint Mining Ventures Abroad: New Concepts for a New Era', the 1969 D. C. Jackling Award Lecture, American Institute of Mining, Metallurgical and Petroleum Engineers, Washington, D.C., 19 February 1969. See also the similar arrangements between Zambia and the Roan Selection Trust, set out in the Statement by the Chairman, Sir Ronald L. Prain, accompanying the *Roan Selection Trust Ltd. Annual Report* for 1969.

[9] See J. Levin, *The Export Economy* (Cambridge: Harvard University Press, 1960).

If the shadow price of domestic labour is zero, the total $w_f L$ is a gain for the less developed country in (3), but the dual economy complications are more serious. If labour unions organise and push up the discriminatory wage paid by foreign investors, the external economies in training from the foreign investment may be reduced as more home-country labour is brought in, or more foreign capital to substitute for domestic labour.

Capital Costs

Typically one can expect $r_f < r_h$. This is another element of monopoly. One theory of direct investment asserts that ploughed-back profits are the cheapest form of savings, and need to earn only slightly more than the government bond rate in the home country to make it worthwhile for the corporation to expand rather than to pay out earnings to its stockholders. Where continued expansion in its home market is likely to cut prices and profits, a company may go abroad and expand in a non-competing area. Under this theory, a firm need not earn more abroad than at home to undertake foreign investments, or more abroad than its local competitors, so long as it earns more than the long-term government bond rate at home and is able to avoid depressing home profits. To the extent the theory applies at all, it is more relevant to direct investment in manufacturing than to primary production.

Even if we reject the cost-of-capital theory of direct investment, however, it is likely that $r_f < r_h$. This is the original basis for thinking that direct investment belongs to the theory of capital movements, rather than to—the present view—oligopoly theory. With separated capital markets, and no other distinct advantage in technology, management and the like, direct investment would flow, like portfolio capital, from capital-rich to capital-poor countries. Only with capital markets perfectly joined, and perfectly competitive, with $r_h = r_f$ for all kinds of borrowers does the cost of capital become irrelevant to direct investment. The basis for thinking $r_f < r_h$ is either that capital markets are imperfectly joined, or that they are not perfectly competitive so that larger and better known firms have an advantage over smaller and less well known borrowers. In this latter circumstance, the foreign firm may have an advantage in borrowing at a cheaper rate than host-country enterprise, even in the host-country capital market. I understand that McKinnon and Shaw are exploring the infant-industry aspects of capital markets in less developed countries, to test the hypothesis that learning-by-doing is strong in them, and that there is merit in discriminating against borrowing by foreign firms on the ground that this inhibits the step-by-step development of a flourishing capital market, vital to development.

A fortiori the foreign firm has an advantage over the enterprise of the less developed country when it comes to borrowing in the capital market of the developed country, especially when the borrowing record of the less developed country is complicated by past defaults or rolling over of debts.

Technology and Management

There is no counterpart for $pRDM$ in identity (2), which expresses the present value of the investment to the foreign firm. This is because it is assumed that the costs of research and development, and management, including market management, are sunk, and that incremental costs of extending these services to a particular foreign investment are negligible. This will not always be true, of course, particularly in instances where it is necessary to modify the technology appropriate to developed countries before it can be used in less developed situations. In addition, in the long run, the company may feel it necessary to spread its overhead evenly over all operations. R & D could be regarded as an investment on which the company had to earn a return in every use. In this case it could be included with K on which the company wanted a return of r_f or with equity on which it required D_f. The question whether foreign subsidiaries are charged management fees, or whether these are lumped with profits and taxed, may turn on such questions as whether a given subsidiary is a joint venture or 100 per cent owned. It may be necessary in some cases, therefore, to allow for a $pRDM_f$ which is distinct from $pRDM_h$.

Whether $pRDM_f$ is zero or positive, however, it is likely to be lower than $pRDM_h$. Local entrepreneurs in less developed countries who need technology or management services, including marketing, may be expected to pay for them at competitive and not monopoly prices, that is, when they can get the R & D and management services at all. Many firms in developed countries choose to invest abroad rather than license because they protect their proprietary interest in the technology inviolate by not renting it out, and because the market for technology does not squeeze out the last bit of rent available, as direct investment may do. Much technology is available on licence, of course, and there is a border-line where the decision to license or not is a close one. Moreover, new technology can be produced to order by specialised research firms, though results cannot be guaranteed and the services are said to be expensive. A local firm in a less developed country may find it sufficient to hire management consulting services rather than employ foreign enterprise full time. Nonetheless, there is likely to be a higher cost, or less service, in research, development and management when a firm is owned locally than when it is foreign.

Government Expenditure

G_h is provided by the host country; G_f is the annual cost of economic overhead capital of the sort usually provided by government which the foreign investor may be required to contribute, in a few cases of large companies investing in fairly primitive economies. Aramco's construction of ports and railroads in Saudi Arabia would be one example; or the United Fruit Company's initial investment in the Central American railroad. For the host country, this G_f may pay external economies (EE), but in most cases G_f serves primarily the interests of the foreign investor. Where it is a railroad such as that from Ras Tenura to Mecca, built by Aramco for the Saudi Arabian government with little or no benefit to the company, it is evidently in lieu of taxes, and could be consolidated with T_h.

G_h is government expenditure which the host government must undertake to make the foreign investment viable. It is assumed to have no external economies or to be net of external economies. It is unlikely to be a net benefit, rather than a cost, although it might be that unanticipated external economies made the *ex ante* result positive, rather than negative. In any case it is assumed to be no different before or after nationalisation.

Taxes

Taxes raise a particular problem of the time profile because of the shift of bargaining power from a time before a foreign investment is installed until after it is fully developed. Before a concession is granted the weight of bargaining power is largely on the side of the company. Countries grant tax concessions to compete for potential investments, although they are urged by such economists as Bhagwati, Diaz Alejandro and Rosenstein-Rodan to form cartels and limit the erosion of contract terms. Once the investment has been made, however, the balance shifts. The increase in levels of taxation is most clearly seen in petroleum where small royalties per barrel gave way to income-tax schemes, taxing corporate profits at levels which mounted from 25 to 50 and finally as high as 75 per cent, followed by calculating income on the basis of posted rather than actual prices and of hypothetical rather than realised income. The Organization of Petroleum Exporting Countries insists on the legitimacy of contract renegotiation, not unknown in Anglo-Saxon practice when the circumstances prevailing at the time of the original contract have drastically changed. Such renegotiation when no objective circumstance has changed other than bargaining power raises subtle questions of legality to which an economist has nothing to contribute.

Taxes on oil companies in the Middle East have risen from $US1 billion in 1960 to $US6 billion in 1969. I know of no data on other primary products such as tin in Malaysia and Indonesia, iron ore in Africa, Latin America and most recently Australia, copper in Africa and Chile. It is evident, however, that the variability of profits with export prices is an important qualification to Raul Prebisch's controversial view that the long-run terms of trade tend to turn against primary producers.

Such terms of trade on merchandise account fail adequately to measure the distribution of welfare between the industrial-investing country and the primary-producing host. For this purpose we need what have been called variously the terms of trade on returned value[10] or the terms of trade on current account with the rate of profit earned by investor, which had been declining, shown as an offset to the decline of export commodity prices.[11]

Note that the capacity of less developed countries to tax is fairly well developed when they confront a few large raw-material producers but less so in import-competing lines. In the former case, they are not inhibited by the requirement of national treatment, and can tax directly, and indirectly through other means such as multiple exchange rates, up to the limits of the companies' reserve price at which they will pull out. It is important not to go too far. The rate of tax and the definition of what is income are both largely in the control of the host country. In import-competing industry, however, it is not so clear. There is growing evidence that some (a few? many?) foreign investors require their subsidiaries to buy equipment, components and raw materials from an international subsidiary and charge higher than competitive prices. The purpose is to transfer profits from one jurisdiction to another, often a Panamanian or Bahaman based tax haven, in order to minimise taxes. The opportunities for this sort of manipulation are evidently less in raw-material production, where the bulk of the value added, apart from profit, is locally produced, than in import-competing manufacture. The remedy lies not in forbidding foreign investment so much as reducing tariffs on the final product and in increasing the sophistication of tax officials so that they will be in a better position to define the income on which taxes are levied.

Taxes are the main benefit to the less developed country from foreign investment in primary production. The rent to domestic labour and external economies, while interesting in particular cases, are typically less significant than the level of taxation. Here the host country wants high taxes on old investments where its bargaining power is strong, and low for new investments it hopes to entice. Case-by-case tax determination, or a discriminating monopoly, is the optimum strategy for such a less developed country but is generally excluded by the nature of competition and the legal principle of non-discrimination. Cartels to prevent competitive tax concessions, already referred to, are hardly proof against the real divergence of interests of rival countries seeking a single investment. But the national payoff to better training in tax law and fiscal economics is probably high.

[10] See Markos Mamalakis and Clark W. Reynolds, *Essays on the Chilean Economy* (Homewood, Illinois: Irwin, 1965).
[11] See C. P. Kindleberger, *The Terms of Trade: A European Case Study* (New York: The Technology Press and John Wiley, 1956), pp. 18ff.

External Economies and Diseconomies

EE are external economies and diseconomies. They fall into three categories: EE_{G_f}, the benefits to the local economy from economic and social overhead investment undertaken by the foreign firm and which may be taken to be positive; EE_f and EE_h, which are the external economies, positive and negative, from the foreign investment itself, and from its nationalisation. The external economies may include Hirschman-type linkages which stimulate the growth process, training effects, including those in technology and management which reduce dependence on foreign investment, change the bargaining position and enable the host country over time to command an increasing share of the rent. It is assumed that all external economies accrue to the host country and none to the foreign firm, although this may not be true where the investor's advantage lies in his capacity to achieve economies of scale by articullating production in several markets. This last is more likely to be the case in import-competing manufacture—as for example, the articulation of Ford production in Britain, Belgium, and Germany—than in raw-material production. The enhanced benefit to the producer from vertical integration over competitive markets at separate stages of raw-material production has already been treated in the difference between S_f and S_h.

EE_h may well be negative if the country's credit standing is affected by its action in nationalising particular foreign-owned property. The Peruvian government, for example, has taken two full-page advertisements in the *New York Times* in an attempt to persuade investors that the trouble with the International Petroleum Company and the nationalisation of certain Grace agricultural properties did not alter its policy of welcoming foreign investment.[12] These advertisements emphasise the continued investment programs of I.T.T. and the South Andean Copper Company, although the first involves some disinvestment and there is evidence elsewhere in the press that the second represents a reluctant decision to keep on investing for fear of losing the substantial assets already accumulated. Any loss owing to the invoking of the Hickenlooper amendment or similar retaliation would be included under EE_h. EE_h differs from EE_f in two respects, therefore. While certain economies such as linkages are identical whether the investment is foreign or domestic operated, some training and management economies may be smaller with domestic operation, and some diseconomies may ensue from nationalisation.

EE_h has a somewhat asymmetrical quality. A reputation attractive to foreign investors is difficult to build, easy to lose. An individual investor may be exasperating in the way he transgresses local law, extracts exorbitant profits and the like, but he enjoys the protection against penalty that the local government wants to maintain a 'good climate for foreign

---

12 *New York Times*, 28 September and 16 November 1969.

investment'. With growing sophistication in the investment process on the side of investors and governments, however, it will ultimately be possible to deal with separate cases on their merits without concern for these externalities.

Amortisation

Where foreign investments are bought up locally as in Chile, Ecuador, Bolivia, Peru in Latin America and Tanzania and Zambia in Africa, there may or may not be compensation. The doctrine asserted by the United States in the Mexican Eagle case is that compensation should be 'prompt, adequate, and effective', which means the capital value of the assets, payable immediately in convertible foreign exchange. In the event this doctrine, which requires a payment to the owners equal to D_f, has been watered down. Payment is usually made on an annual basis, often in kind in the product of the investment.

The formula for discounting a perpetual stream of incomes does not properly apply to a flow of compensation payments for a stipulated period. Where the period is a long one, and the discount rate is high, however, the difference is negligible. In many cases, host country and firm abandon all pretence of using present discounted values for estimating payments due, but rather adopt the fiction that a dollar tomorrow is the same as a dollar today. The practice is widespread in international debt negotiations of moving this year's debt service, which, say, Ghana or Indonesia cannot pay, forward to follow the last scheduled payment without regarding the debtor as in default. The present value of the payment may decline as much as 90 or 95 per cent in these cases, depending upon the rate of discount applied. Creditors' consortia adopt this fiction, in defiance of the economic doctrine that bygones are bygones, because they are fearful that default and readjustment of principal may be infectious. By the same token, firms which are bought out by eminent domain and paid the nominal value of asset ceded, but over time and without interest, and their governments, accede in the arrangement for inability to do better. But the economist should recognise that in these cases while

$$\Sigma A = PDV(S_t - w_f L - r_f K - T_h - G_t),$$
$$PDV(A) < \Sigma A$$

Risk

Ex post, of course

$$PDV(A) = PDV[(S_t - w_f L - r_f K - T_h - G_h)z]$$

where z is the risk of nationalisation. But z must be calculated *ex ante* before a company can judge whether to undertake a given investment. Operationally, the *ex post* value is of limited importance.

Note that it would be possible to include z with D_f, the foreign rate of discount. It is better to separate it out, however, so as to indicate that a given firm has one rate of discount for all investments, but different risks attaching to those in separate countries.

Nationalism

N, the satisfaction which a country gets from national ownership (N_h) or the dissatisfaction that it feels from foreign control over its resources (N_f) takes us again to the contribution of Albert Breton in 'The Economics of Nationalism'. Presumably N_f is negative and N_h positive, that is, there is shame or unease from having domestic real assets owned and controlled from abroad, for reasons of group solidarity and xenophobia; and pride and satisfaction from domestic control. The values of N_f and N_h, expressed as negative or positive flows of income per year, depend upon: first, the extent of foreign ownership, with N_f being larger, the larger the proportion of total enterprise controlled from abroad; second, the degree of development, with both N_f and N_h being larger for less developed and smaller for more developed countries per unit of foreign or domestic control, however measured; and third, the history of past investment, with N_h being larger the longer and more lurid the record of historic wrong-doing by foreign investors.

N_h may be positive for a country as a whole but negative for certain local groups of politicians and businessmen who work with foreign investors. Thus Franz Fanon believes it insufficient to nationalise foreign investment; it must be socialised as well.[13] On the other hand, the positive value of N_h may be small for the country as a whole, and do little to reduce the situation of inequality in which $C_{h_f} > C_{h_{nat}} - N_h$ but N_h is of great importance to particular politicians and even business competitors. Thus, N_f and N_h, aggregated and disaggregated, are important political variables in many less developed countries and developed countries as well. The economist is perhaps in no position to measure them in a numeraire which enables them to be used to calculate C_{h_f} and $C_{h_{nat}}$, in (3) and (4), except by revealed preference.

Discount Rates

D, the rate at which streams of income are discounted to capitalise them, differs from r, the rate of interest on bonds, by virtue of business risks. z applies to political risks. Whether risks of foreign exchange control belong in D or z is a matter of indifference. As noted, z could be included in D, but is not. The borderline is hazy.

In a riskless world, $z = 1$ and $r = D$. But in a classic world with a given state of the arts, economic men, modest government, no externalities, and competition, so that $S_f = S_h$, $w_f = w_h$, $r_f = r_h$, if there was still risk, D_f would probably be lower than D_h because of better capacity of

[13] Franz Fanon, *The Wretched of the Earth* (New York: Grove Press, 1965).

some businessmen in some countries to manage business risk. This bears on the theory that direct investment arises from differences in the capacity of businessmen in different countries rather than any other advantage. In this classic world, $C_{f_{nat}}$ would be less than C_f and foreign investment would be desirable from the standpoint of world welfare.

D_h does not enter into the comparison between (3) and (4) since it is the same in both cases, and so should play no part in any decision to nationalise a foreign investment. The difficulty is likely to arise when the host country is disaggregated and certain groups apply a high rate of discount to the negative items in (4), that is, to the need to pay for foreign capital, research and management, and to the losses from discouraging future investments. In these cases, political and business leaders presumably apply one rate of discount to the positive item S_h and N_h, and a different and higher discount to the offsets. In these conditions, nationalisation of foreign investment is irresistible.

Conclusion

A comparison of (2) and (3), between C_f and C_{h_f}, addresses the question of the division of benefits between the investing and the host country. This is the issue raised by Prebisch and Singer more than twenty years ago. The distributional question has a number of asymmetries where a gain or loss for one is not necessarily a loss or a gain for the other for several reasons, because of z, perceived risk, which is less than 1 for the investing country but does not raise the return to the host; external economies for the host country, with no cost to the investor; because of N_f which poses a political cost for the host but with no evident benefit for the home country;[14] and because even an equally divided stream of benefits would be discounted at different rates.

I have already suggested that C_f and C_h have both been growing, but C_{h_f} at a faster rate than C_f in oil, and probably other areas such as iron ore, bauxite, copper as well. More data are needed.

Comparison of (3) and (4), C_{h_f} and $C_{h_{nat}}$ poses Bronfenbrenner's problem of the appeal of nationalisation. It is assumed that, in most cases, the difference between all items but the last in the numerator on the right-hand side will be larger in (3) than in (4), and positive, so that apart from N_f and N_h, C_{h_f} would be larger than $C_{h_{nat}}$. This is especially the case if the external diseconomy from confiscation ($EE_h < 0$) is substantial, but is almost certainly the case otherwise. The critical issue is political. As noted, N_f is negative and N_h positive. They are not necessarily equal; they doubtless differ from country to country, in absolute value, and they may have different time profiles. It is likely that in a

---

[14] This presumes that there is no offsetting pride in foreign direct investments in the home country akin to the pride which countries derived from colonies. Some critics who believe in neo-colonialism and neo-imperialism may dispute this.

country which feels strongly politically about foreign investment—perhaps by reason of historic wrongs—the pain of foreign ownership ($N_f < 0$) is likely to stay high over a long time, albeit rising to periodic heights from time to time when the foreign corporations come into the news; whereas after nationalisation, N_h, which is positive, will have a high value for only a short time and will thereafter decline. This may account for the willingness of some countries, such as Ghana, with a new government, to restore foreign ownership and management after nationalisation.

Comparison of (2) and (4), the value of a given project in foreign and in domestic ownership, can be used without any hint of nationalisation to illustrate the theory of foreign direct investment. Leave A, EE_h and N_h out of (4), A because it is zero, EE_h and N_h since they may be presumed small. Normally S_f will exceed S_h, and $r_f K$ will be less than $r_h K$. $pRDM$, moreover, is a negative item in (4) not found in (2). The only advantage for C_h is cheaper labour.

With development, to be sure, S_h will approach S_f and even surpass it as it contains substantial monopsony elements, $r_h K$ will approach $r_f K$ as the country's credit standing improves, and $pRDM$ will decline towards zero as doing leads to learning. The equations leave out the disadvantage at which the foreign investor works by virtue of the strangeness of the culture and the decision from the decision centre. But if the time profile of returns in (4) changes through time, the discounting formula must be altered. The weight that future higher returns contribute to the present discounted value of the investment in national ownership then depends heavily on D_h. When it matures, the infant industry must pay for its care in childhood.

Comments and Discussion

MIGUEL WIONCZEK opened the discussion: Anyone cognisant of the international debate about the distribution of gains from foreign private investment between capital exporters and host countries would agree with one of Kindleberger's major theses that once *both* economic and political factors are considered, the distributional question has a number of asymmetric characteristics of a non-zero sum situation. I refer to Kindleberger's observations on p. 77 and agree that additional work along the lines suggested in the paper might throw considerable light upon the nature of the increasing number of conflicts between private foreign investors and developing countries, particularly in respect to the sectors whose domestic control is viewed, in the light of historical experience, as of particular economic *and* political importance for future development. Kindleberger's paper strongly intimates that political economy rather than neo-classical economic theory should be applied as a tool of analysis to these situations.

In Kindleberger's presentation of the variables involved one point does not seem convincing. He claims that incremental costs of extending the availability of the existing stock of technology and management to a particular new foreign investment *are not* negligible, contrary to contentions of many writers in the developing countries. Furthermore, he shows sympathy for a proposition that 'the company may feel it necessary to spread its [R & D] overhead evenly over all operations'. Pioneering field studies in respect to the transfer of technology through foreign private investment in Latin America strongly suggest, however, that, first, additional expenditures of foreign investment on adapting technology to local conditions *are* negligible and in many cases nil, and, second, pricing of technology transfers aims not at spreading more evenly its costs but—under conditions of monopolistic technology control—at maximising profits to the parent system, while proving to the host country that accounted profits of a subsidiary are 'less than reasonable'. This behaviour creates a superficially strong case for additional fiscal and other incentives for foreign investment, incentives that in the words of one commentator amount in many situations to impressive and unnecessary 'give ways'.

One would suspect that Kindleberger's position is highly influenced by his exposure to the characteristics of capital *cum* technology flows from the United States to Western Europe. There, as Dunning has recently noted:

> The share of U.S. investment in Europe's industries is still small but strongly concentrated in the research-intensive and growth sectors. This implies a strong technological impact . . .[15]

This is not the case of Latin America, where the share of United States investments in manufacturing is very large. Moreover, they are concentrated in industries with constant or stagnant technology. The host countries could easily acquire such technology from sources other than international corporations, if only they had the necessary institutional framework for its absorption and adaptation. Here I find myself sympathetic with the Hirschman proposition that the unduly large presence of foreign private capital in Latin American countries diminishes rather than fosters the development of local technological and managerial skills.

It seems, furthermore, that when talking about risks of foreign direct investment in the developing countries Kindleberger takes them too literally. The situation in Latin America, for example, where presumably risks of nationalisation, expropriation, etc., are higher than elsewhere, suggests some degree of exaggeration in this respect. Except in Mexico (1938), in Cuba (1959-60), and Chile (1971) the takeover of foreign

[15] John H. Dunning, 'Technology, United States Investment, and European Economic Growth' in Kindleberger (ed.), *The International Corporation*, p. 173.

properties in that part of the world did not, on the whole, affect adversely economic interests of the foreign investors. The same is most probably true about recent takeovers of foreign mining properties in Congo and Zambia. If one leaves aside an *opéra comique* type of conflict such as the I.P.C. case in Peru (1968), one is left with the impression that most takeovers in Latin America—particularly in public utilities and mining sectors—represented the *quid pro quo* between economic gains of foreign parties and political gains of the host countries.

Kindleberger's observation about a number of asymmetries related to the distribution of gains from a foreign investment act applies as well to the exit of foreign investors, at least in Latin America. First, there are strong reasons to believe that the departure of foreign companies from public utilities and their more or less simultaneous entry into Latin American manufacturing represents a gain rather than a loss for foreign capital. Second, one is also tempted to think that the so-called conflicts in the Latin American extractive industries may represent economic gains for 'nationalised' foreign companies. It has still to be proven that as long as the international marketing of output is left in foreign hands, the solution of conflict through the earlier Chilean-type nationalisation of mining represents economic loss to former owners. Multinational mining corporations may, in fact, gain from the so-called nationalisation if they receive fair (or more than fair) compensation as it happened, among others, in Chile and Congo. It may well be in the long-term interest of these corporations to be forced into joint mining ventures with the host countries. The compensation may just release capital funds and managerial skills needed for starting new more profitable mining ventures elsewhere.

This would be particularly true if one were to take into consideration dynamic world-wide changes in the availability of industrial primary commodities. There is growing evidence to the effect that we are witnessing a major revolution in that respect, comparable only to the opening of the riches of American continent to the advanced world by Spanish and Portuguese in the sixteenth and seventeenth centuries, and the discovery of African and Middle East mineral resources by European colonial powers between 1870 and 1914. The most recent mineral discoveries in Australia, West Africa and the Arctic areas indicate that we have left— presumably for a long time ahead—the natural resources scarcity world of Adam Smith, Ricardo and Malthus. What is scarce today is technology and managerial skills and not natural resources. Because of the asymmetries of the world communication and information system (see Chapter 2), underdeveloped host countries are hardly aware of this new situation. Not only do they act under traditional assumptions, but they are inefficiently equipped for negotiations with multinational mining firms. These last, on the other hand, endowed with access to the global communication system, can behave more rationally. In dynamic supply conditions their strategy calls for constant shifting sources of supply to new areas where no political complications or risks are present or perceived.

How does all this affect Latin America? It is quite probable that the changing world natural resources picture together with the presence of nationalist pressures will shortly make Latin America into a residual supplier of mineral commodities to industrial countries. Since, first, inward-directed import-substitution industrialisation programs do not seem to be working as expected, and, second, economic modernisation and increased productive efficiency through intraregional division of labour within the framework of regional integration of the LAFTA type encounters growing obstacles, the outcome may well be the achievement of domestic control over extractive industries accompanied by industrial stagnation. Such a situation would be a poor substitute for accelerated growth through expansion of traditional mineral exports *cum* efficient regional industrialisation.

The alternative to running risks of secular stagnation might be to negotiate new agreements with foreign mining corporations, aimed at increased tax yield and increased domestic value added in this sector, for the purpose of using government proceeds from the mining sector to strengthen in all sectors of the economy the capacity for absorption and creation of the scarcest production factor—technology and managerial skills, that is, creating non-physical infrastructure needed for efficient industrialisation.

Whether such strategy is politically feasible in Latin America remains an open question. As Johnson aptly put it, we economists propose and politicians dispose. This happens all over the world but even more so in the underdeveloped societies.

Some participants were interested in the practical application of Kindleberger's scheme of analysis. One asked whether it would be possible to measure N_n, the nationalistic effects, or EE, the external economies effects. What kind of measure could be used to reveal the price of nationalism? Another suggested that, instead of writing N into the equations as if it were a known quantity, it might be better to put it the other way round and calculate the cost, for example, of the benefits foregone by nationalisation. N would become the variable, the magnitude of which you try to measure. Kindleberger said that he suspected that N could be quantified by elimination: having looked at all the things that can be measured, the cost of nationalism could be calculated in terms of what is lost or the cost of what is obtained for the shame, or whatever it is, of having foreign control. As for the second point, he said that, whilst the procedure was quite legitimate, he had been really trying to address himself to the theoretical question, and would prefer to leave the manipulation of the equations to others.

One participant wondered whether the arguments once put forward by Bronfenbrenner about nationalisation implied that it did not pay to nationalise unless there was an element of confiscation. On the confirmation that, if C_f in equation (2) equalled A in equation (4), there would be no gain from nationalisation, he went on. In most cases of nationalisation, the argument was about how much confiscation was involved. This was always difficult also because of the several ways of valuing assets. However, the fact is that the confiscation element inevitably affects the terms of access to foreign investment in the future. If you nationalise at one point, and decide that you want foreign investment later, or you nationalise one sector and decide that foreign investment is still desirable in other sectors, terms of access will be tougher. Kindleberger illustrated the external economies effects of nationalism with reference to Peru. There the investment climate has been affected by an act of nationalisation in one sector. The response by foreign investors does not involve any conspiratorial political or business reaction. But the unconsciously parallel action of creditors and bankers in New York has dried up access to foreign investment. Reference was also made to the way in which the Chinese communists never confiscated any foreign enterprise. They bought foreign assets out at very low prices, having made it impossible by regulation to operate without substantial losses. It seemed that that sort of behaviour was not more generally practised because of its costs in terms of the effect on investment climate mentioned above.

Another questioner raised the problem of disaggregation of streams of benefits over time or across groups. He felt that many of the problems had been avoided by assuming a constant stream of benefits in the comparison in Kindleberger's equations. For example, nationalisation might mean lower productivity immediately but higher productivity later, or more to some groups than to others. Professor Kindleberger agreed fully and referred to the same line of argument in his paper. But he thought it useful to begin the analysis in these terms so that the relationship could be specified more clearly.

Discussion of Kindleberger's paper, as well as Wionczek's commentary, turned finally to the issue of resource investment in developing countries. An American participant elaborated a 'wasting asset' view of foreign investment in the mineral resources of developing countries. Faced with political uncertainties and the possibility of expropriation, investors in resource developments could be seen as having a powerful motivation towards extraction of the rents as quickly as possible and search and movement elsewhere.

An Australian participant thought that this view of resource development reflected circumstances on the American continent but not in other places. A more common problem, it was suggested, was that foreign investors did not carry through investment rapidly enough. They monopolised resource development through extensive leaseholdings and were treated to generous investment incentives. In many parts of the world, it seems more likely that the host's own interests in foreign investment will be dissipated in incentives than that company interests will face nationalisation. Bougainville Copper was cited as an example where tax incentives were unnecessarily extended to the resource developers. Not only in Australasia, but also in Asia and Africa, the situation facing the foreign investor was quite unlike that in Latin America. At the same time, these observations were felt to be compatible with Wionczek's comments about the market position of resource producers. Another Australian participant thought that the Bougainville case may have had another side to it: there is a tax holiday but in the longer run the investing company will pay a higher taxation rate than the rate generally prevailing in Papua-New Guinea. Taxation holidays may have some rationale if the uncertainties mentioned by the earlier commentator were significant.

Wionczek drew attention to another aspect of the problem of resource-oriented investment, related to the asymmetrical nature of the communications system. He noted the ignorance in Africa and Latin America of mining developments in Australia and the advantages of mining companies in negotiations under these circumstances. Whilst he felt that attempts to form cartels in international resource markets were generally unwise and unlikely to succeed, association between producers could have considerable advantage in the form of information exchange. He also questioned the use of the confiscation alternative in resource development where some of the profitability depends on marketing.

In his summary remarks, Kindleberger agreed with those who had stressed the competitive nature of world resources markets. He remarked that Venezuela had done brilliantly in 1957 in selling the capital value of its oil concessions for $US700 million, but those who had bought them certainly had not gained anything by the sale. The Organisation for Petroleum Exporting Countries hung together miraculously and, from time to time, there was a coincidence of interests, but basically they were very competitive. He thought it unlikely that cartelisation of resources markets would be effective. He added that the problem of too many incentives would not be solved easily—if it has not been solved within federal Canada and Australia, how much more difficult is the problem, say, between Burma and Indonesia. His conclusion was that new entrants would have it tough in this non-zero sum game of foreign investment in resources development.

5 United States Investment in Australia, Canada, and New Zealand

DONALD T. BRASH

Direct foreign investment has had an enormous impact on the development of Australia, of Canada, and of New Zealand. The purpose of this chapter is to look at the American component in that investment and, in the light of the latest evidence from all three countries, to discuss some of its costs and benefits.[1]

The importance of United States direct investment is, of course, very different in the three countries (see Table 5.1). Canada has long been the largest single recipient of American capital, and by the end of 1968, the book value of United States direct investment in Canada had reached $US19,488 million—slightly larger than United States direct investment in the whole of Europe and equivalent to 30.1 per cent of the world-wide total.[2] For Canada, direct investment from the United States made up 81.8 per cent of the foreign direct investment from all countries at the end of 1966,[3] while in 1963 United States residents controlled 46.2 per cent of all the capital employed in Canadian manufacturing, 52.0 per cent of that in mining, and 63.2 per cent of that in petroleum and natural gas. Within the manufacturing sector, United States control was particularly high in automobiles and parts (97.4 per cent), rubber (90.3 per cent), electrical apparatus (66.3 per cent) and chemicals (54.4 per cent).[4]

United States direct investment has been important in Australia too, though significantly less so than in Canada. By the end of 1968, it had reached $US2,645 million—a figure exceeded only by Canada, the

---

[1] The author was, at the time of writing, on the staff of the International Bank for Reconstruction and Development, Washington, D.C. The Bank is in no way responsible for any of the views expressed.

[2] U.S. Department of Commerce, *Survey of Current Business*, October 1969, p. 28.

[3] Dominion Bureau of Statistics, *Quarterly Estimates of the Canadian Balance of International Payments*, Third Quarter 1969, p. 27.

[4] Dominion Bureau of Statistics, *The Canadian Balance of International Payments 1963, 1964 and 1965 and International Investment Position*, p. 128. Data for a more recent year were not available at the time of writing.

Table 5.1 Book value of United States investment in Australia, Canada, and New Zealand, by sector, 1950-68 ($US million)

	Australia				Canada					New Zealand		
	Manu-facturing	Mining and smelting	Other[a]	Total	Manu-facturing	Mining and smelting	Petroleum	Other	Total	Manu-facturing	Other[a]	Total
1950	98	11	92	201	1,897	334	418	930	3,579	9	16	25
1951	127	12	116	255	2,009	406	563	992	3,969	11	20	31
1952	151	14	143	308	2,303	564	719	1,055	4,641	11	26	37
1953	172	15	137	324	2,540	698	941	1,170	5,349	12	22	34
1954	201	20	168	389	2,777	822	1,165	1,279	6,043	15	25	40
1955	240	25	227	492	3,093	904	1,381	1,383	6,761	18	24	42
1956	268	29	248	545	3,526	1,002	1,759	1,508	7,795	19	29	48
1957[b]	297	22	264	583	3,924	856	2,016	1,973	8,769	17	31	48
1958	350	22	283	655	4,164	938	2,293	2,075	9,470	16	34	50
1959	399	27	316	742	4,565	1,089	2,467	2,189	10,310	15	39	54
1960	476	33	347	856	4,827	1,325	2,664	2,363	11,179	18	35	53
1961	506	36	415	957	5,076	1,367	2,828	2,331	11,602	18	46	64
1962	582	46	469	1,097	5,312	1,489	2,875	2,457	12,133	32	53	85
1963	687	82	505	1,274	5,761	1,549	3,134	2,600	13,044	36	62	98
1964	810	100	565	1,475	6,198	1,713	3,196	2,748	13,855	n.a.	n.a.	n.a.
1965	893	161	625	1,679	6,872	1,851	3,356	3,239	15,318	n.a.	n.a.	n.a.
1966	1,000	251	672	1,923	7,692	2,089	3,608	3,628	17,017	n.a.	n.a.	n.a.
1967	1,262	320	778	2,360	8,095	2,342	3,819	3,842	18,097	n.a.	n.a.	n.a.
1968	1,418	365	862	2,645	8,546	2,636	4,088	4,219	19,488	n.a.	n.a.	n.a.

[a] Mainly investment in the petroleum sector, for which separate data are not available for most years.

[b] Data for years prior to 1957 are based on the 1950 investment census, with reported annual changes carried forward. Data for years from 1957 on are based on the 1957 investment census.

Sources: United States Department of Commerce, *Balance of Payments Statistical Supplement, Revised Edition,* 1963, and *Survey of Current Business,* various issues, except that data for Australia for 1961 and 1962 were supplied directly by the Department.

United Kingdom, and West Germany—but this was equivalent to only 4.1 per cent of the world-wide total of United States direct investment.[5] Australian statistics do not permit a direct comparison between the accumulated book value of United States direct investment and that of direct investment from other countries. A survey published by the Australian Department of Trade and Industry in 1966, and relating for the most part to 1965, suggested that United States direct investment was about 39.6 per cent of the total accumulated direct investment in the manufacturing sector, somewhat smaller than the United Kingdom share (50.1 per cent).[6] But all the evidence suggests that this position is changing rapidly. For the seven years 1962/63-1968/69, United States direct investment in Australia made up 49.7 per cent of the total new investment, compared with a British share of only 37.5 per cent.[7] The value of manufacturing production 'apportioned to' United States direct investment rose from 7.5 per cent to 9.4 per cent of the total between 1962/63 and 1966/67, a much sharper increase than that achieved by British capital (from 10.2 per cent to 10.8 per cent).[8] In mining, the shift in relative importance has been even more dramatic: in that sector, the value of production 'apportioned to' United States direct investment rose from 9.2 per cent to 18.5 per cent of the total between 1963 and 1967, compared with a rise from 16.3 per cent to 19.2 per cent for British capital.[9] Beyond manufacturing and mining, American companies have long been important in the petroleum sector, and are rapidly assuming importance in such diverse fields as merchant banking and land improvement.[10]

By contrast, United States direct investment in New Zealand has been very small—both absolutely and even in relation to the New Zealand economy. The United States Department of Commerce no longer publishes data for United States investment in New Zealand separately, but when they last did so, for 1963, it totalled only $US98 million, or 0.24 per cent of the world-wide total.[11] Deane found that, even in the New

[5] *Survey of Current Business*, October 1969, p. 28.

[6] Department of Trade and Industry, *Directory of Overseas Investment in Australian Manufacturing Industry*, Canberra, 1966, p. ix.

[7] Commonwealth Bureau of Census and Statistics, *Annual Bulletin of Overseas Investment*, Canberra, 1968-9, p. 11. Note that the United States share quoted actually includes a small amount of 'Canadian' investment; most of this is in reality United States investment through a Canadian subsidiary in the motor vehicles industry.

[8] Commonwealth Bureau of Census and Statistics, *Overseas Participation in Australian Manufacturing Industry: 1962-63 and 1966-67. Part I, Overseas Ownership*, Canberra, p. 9.

[9] Commonwealth Bureau of Census and Statistics, *Overseas Participation in Australian Mining Industry: 1967*, Canberra, p. 13.

[10] American interests appear to be especially active in the northern section of the Northern Territory, where they are reported to hold about 50 per cent of the entire area on long-term lease.

[11] United States Department of Commerce, *Survey of Current Business*, August 1964, p. 10.

Zealand manufacturing sector—where, with the petroleum sector, United States capital is best represented—the value of production in establishments controlled by United States companies was only 14.4 per cent of the total for the whole sector, in 1963/64. While the production of United States-controlled establishments rose by 111 per cent between 1955/56 and 1963/64, this was significantly less than the increase recorded for the foreign sector as a whole (169 per cent) and little above the expansion of all New Zealand manufacturing (90 per cent).[12] Most of the major companies which one immediately associates with United States foreign investment are represented in New Zealand, but the manufacturing operations of many of them are either very small (e.g. Kraft, I.B.M.) or are sub-contracted to other companies (e.g. Goodyear, Kelloggs, Johnson & Johnson).[13]

Recognition of the benefits of foreign direct investment is widespread in all the countries under review. In Australia, the Prime Minister himself saw fit to state publicly late in 1969 that:

> The importance to Australia of a strong and continuing inflow of overseas capital has never been questioned by my Government . . . Without it, it would have been impossible for us to develop as quickly as history demands we must. Our immigration programme would have been restricted. Import replacement and a growing independence of many overseas commodities would have been curtailed, and we would not have grown the industrial muscles we need. This overseas flow of investment has developed resources which were previously unutilised, contributed to the sustained growth in our export income, and raised the general level of efficiency and real incomes in many sectors of the economy. It confers great benefits on us, and it is essential that it should continue.[14]

Similar views are prevalent in both Canada and New Zealand.

And yet in the last decade all three countries have taken measures of one kind or another to exercise specific controls over some aspects of the behaviour of foreign companies or to reduce dependence on foreign capital. In Canada, there have long been some areas of the economy from which foreign investment is debarred, but a period of intensifying effort to reduce the spread of foreign ownership seems to have begun in 1958.[15] In that year, applicants for radio and television licences were required to be Canadian citizens. Two years later, tax incentives were introduced to stimulate Canadian investment in local enterprises. In

---

[12] R. S. Deane, *Foreign Investment in New Zealand Manufacturing*, pp. 471-3.
[13] Ibid., pp. 103-52.
[14] Parliamentary statement by Prime Minister John Gorton in the House of Representatives, Canberra, on 16 September 1969.
[15] Most of the information in this and immediately following paragraphs is based on the Report of the Task Force on the Structure of Canadian Industry, *Foreign Ownership and the Structure of Canadian Industry*, 1968, pp. 383-8.

1961, the government increased its support of the Industrial Develop-ment Bank to enable it to make funds available to Canadian companies which might otherwise sell equity to foreign companies. The following year, measures designed to increase financial disclosure by all larger companies and to encourage research activities in Canada were intro-duced.

In 1963, special depreciation provisions were offered to any company engaged in manufacturing or processing in Canada provided that at least 25 per cent of its equity was owned by Canadians and that 25 per cent of its directors were resident in Canada. Any company meeting those con-ditions, and with shares listed on a Canadian stock exchange, was also subject to a reduced rate of withholding tax on dividends to foreigners. The same year, exemption from Canadian withholding tax on bond interest was granted to certain types of foreign financial institutions to encourage foreign capital into Canadian bonds rather than Canadian equity.

In 1964 and 1965, measures were introduced to inhibit foreign invest-ment in Canadian newspapers and financial institutions. (It is germane to the present discussion that the law to prevent foreign ownership of Canadian banks was introduced as a direct result of the transfer of a rather small bank (the Mercantile Bank) from Dutch to American control in 1963.) In 1966, interest payments on all bonds issued by public authorities were exempted from the withholding tax in a further attempt to increase the attractiveness of Canadian debt instruments.

In 1967, the government issued its 'guiding principles of good corpor-ate behaviour' for Canadian subsidiaries of foreign companies shortly after the United States government introduced its balance of payments guidelines for United States companies investing abroad. The Canadian guiding principles do not have the force of law: rather they are a set of 'desirable objectives'. But they cover not merely the dividend policies of foreign subsidiaries (the most obvious response to the United States guidelines) but also a whole range of other corporate policies including those on procurement, exports, intra-company pricing, employment, ownership, disclosure and research.

In 1970, following an attempt by an American-controlled company to acquire a controlling interest in a large Canadian uranium mine (Denison Mines Ltd), the government moved to prevent individual foreign corpora-tions acquiring more than 10 per cent of the equity of such companies, and re-activated a previous proposal to create a Canada Development Corporation. The latter would be designed to check the spread of foreign ownership by itself buying the equity of Canadian companies threatened by foreign acquisition.

The shift in Australian policy towards foreign investment dates from about the mid-sixties. Foreign companies have long been excluded from radio and television, and for many years have not been permitted to establish new banks. Public opinion, and even many pronouncements by government leaders, have long expressed a preference that foreign subsidiaries should employ Australians wherever possible, share ownership with Australians, and be free from parental restriction on their export activities. But it appears that the first time the government brought real pressure to bear in these areas—at least since the Labor government of the forties—was in 1964, when the Minister for Territories indicated that there must be provision for Australian participation in any proposal to develop the bauxite deposits at Gove Peninsula. Following introduction of the United States guidelines in 1965, the government requested that the Reserve Bank be consulted before overseas companies (or Australian companies with a substantial foreign shareholding) complete plans to borrow in Australia, and in September 1969, when the government clarified its policy in this area, it was made very clear that the level of Australian ownership was to be a major determinant of the amount of borrowing to be allowed.

The government has also taken measures to increase the availability of capital to locally-owned enterprises which might otherwise be tempted to sell ownership and control to foreigners. It gave financial backing to the Australian Resources Development Bank when it was established in 1967, and has set up the Australian Industrial Development Corporation. In announcing the government's intention to establish the latter, the Prime Minister himself indicated that 'its objective would be . . . to substitute fixed-interest borrowing abroad for some of the overseas money at present supplied in return for a surrender of Australian equity'.[16]

To reduce the likelihood that existing Australian companies will be acquired by foreign corporations, the government asked the Australian stock exchanges late in 1968 to modify their listing requirements to allow companies to amend their Articles of Association to ensure 'that control of the company, exercised through the voting power of the shareholders, remains in Australian hands'.[17] The following month the stock exchanges agreed to the request.

For New Zealand, it is impossible for the outsider to be sure when policy on foreign direct investment began to change. This is because the most important single change in policy, that concerning the desirability of having foreign subsidiaries share ownership with local investors, was reflected not in a change in the law but rather in pressures exerted by the Department of Industries and Commerce in connection with its control of import licences. That this policy dates back to at least the

---

[16] *Australian Financial Review*, 12 February 1970.
[17] Press Release by the Prime Minister's Department, No. 96/1968, 5 December 1968.

early sixties is known.[18] Deane suggests that it may have begun in 1958, 'when the intensification of import controls gave [the government] a powerful persuasive tool'.[19]

In 1964, the government gazetted the Overseas Takeovers Regulations giving it authority to vet all acquisitions of New Zealand companies by foreign interests and to prevent those deemed contrary to the national interest. The following year, the government introduced the News Media Ownership Act, making it illegal for overseas ownership to exceed 20 per cent of the equity in any company engaged in broadcasting (including television) or newspaper publishing. Authority to control capital issues also gives the government enormous powers and as of today it is 'impossible for a foreign company to invest in New Zealand, take over a local enterprise, or raise funds on the domestic capital market without the consent of government'.[20] These controls apply also to New Zealand companies. Such even-handed impartiality cannot be said to apply to the government's latest legislative move in the field, however—the Companies Amendment Act of 1969. This requires only those private companies with an overseas shareholding of 25 per cent or more to yield up their annual accounts to the Registrar of Overseas Companies, for all to inspect.

Any attempt to provide a complete explanation of why policy towards foreign investment has hardened in all three countries over the last decade would require a detailed analysis of the political situation in each of them. This is beyond the scope of this chapter. But clearly a major part of the explanation is that an important body of opinion in all of these countries has perceived what it believes to be significant costs of foreign investment, and it is these which will be the focus of our attention. The perception of these costs differs in the three countries, but all those which have been the subject of major debate in any of them will be discussed. Some can no longer be taken seriously.

Profitability

This appears not to have been an important concern for Canadians for quite a period, nor for the Australians since early in the sixties. It was, however, of considerable concern to Australians during the fifties, and continues to be of some concern to New Zealanders.[21] In part this Australasian concern has stemmed from an almost unbelievably unsophisticated

[18] During a survey of American subsidiaries in Australia in 1963, I was told by one executive that his company maintained a policy of retaining complete American ownership in all its subsidiaries throughout the world. Only in New Zealand had the parent company been compelled to modify that policy.
[19] Deane, op. cit., p. 70.
[20] Ibid., p. 6.
[21] See, for example, H. W. Arndt, 'Overseas Borrowing—the New Model', *Economic Record*, August 1957, especially pp. 250-1, and Deane, op. cit., pp. 335ff.

Table 5.2 Net earnings of United States direct investment in Australia, Canada, and New Zealand, by sector, 1950-68 ($US million)

	Australia				Canada					New Zealand		
	Manu-facturing	Mining and smelting	Other[a]	Total	Manu-facturing	Mining and smelting	Petroleum	Other	Total	Manu-facturing	Other[a]	Total
1950	22	1	5	28	301	52	17	75	445	2	1	3
1951	28	2	6	36	268	68	3	81	420	2	2	4
1952	24	3	7	34	297	54	12	96	459	2	2	4
1953	40	2	14	56	337	44	14	107	502	2	4	6
1954	49	6	10	65	296	57	10	125	488	4	2	6
1955	51	3	13	67	363	86	39	129	617	5	2	7
1956	42	5	17	64	398	97	91	159	745	4	3	7
1957	56	5	20	81	342	70	112	129	653	4	4	8
1958	64	2	24	90	349	37	57	126	569	4	5	9
1959	70	6	26	102	438	67	74	134	713	4	5	9
1960	75	8	18	101	398	88	98	134	718	7	4	11
1961	59	8	10	77	360	96	114	156	726	7	6	13
1962	94	5	13	112	460	97	121	147	825	8	6	14
1963	105	8	14	127	525	127	149	147	948	9	8	17
1964	114	10	−3	121	565	191	170	180	1,106	n.a.	n.a.	n.a.
1965	108	10	8	126	606	198	183	222	1,209	n.a.	n.a.	n.a.
1966	107	18	21	146	628	191	196	222	1,237	n.a.	n.a.	n.a.
1967	119	20	12	151	613	240	207	267	1,327	n.a.	n.a.	n.a.
1968	141	33	19	193	672	285	243	278	1,478	n.a.	n.a.	n.a.

[a] Mainly the petroleum sector, for which separate data are not available for most years.

Sources: United States Department of Commerce, *Balance of Payments Statistical Supplement, Revised Edition*, 1963, and *Survey of Current Business*, various issues.

way of measuring profitability, at least in the popular financial press: it is still almost universal practice to express company profitability in terms of profit as a percentage of the par value of the ordinary share capital, a concept which would be laughed out of court if even suggested in North America. Because foreign subsidiaries usually see no good reason to 'capitalise' their reinvested profits—or indeed even much of their initial investment[22]—their share capital is often a very small fraction of total shareholders' investment. In this situation, foreign companies earning quite modest profits on shareholders' equity are portrayed as earning 'excessive' profits.[23]

How profitable has United States direct investment in fact been in these three countries? The figures in Tables 5.2 and 5.3 are based on information provided to the United States Department of Commerce. They do not, of course, provide a completely satisfactory measure of profitability. They express net profits as a percentage of book value of investment, and so on that score tend to overstate 'true' profitability. On the other hand, they omit payments of interest, royalties, technical assistance and other fees to the parent company. They take no account of the possibility that intra-firm pricing policies have had a significant impact on subsidiary profitability. But all the evidence suggests that the inclusion of other types of income accruing to the parent company would not substantially alter the impression created by the table,[24] and, to anticipate our later discussion of intra-firm pricing, it seems likely that this may have been a significant factor leading to understatement of profits only in the petroleum sector of Australia and New Zealand.

At any event, the figures in Table 5.3, summarised in Table 5.4, suggest that United States direct investment in Canada has earned only modest profits over the last two decades. There has been some improvement in the profitability of investment in the petroleum sector, but this has been offset by a gradual decline in the profitability of investment in manufacturing.

In Australia, the profitability of United States investment was high in the early fifties but has been declining fairly steadily ever since. In part,

[22] There are in fact significant tax advantages to the parent company in *not* capitalising much of its investment in a foreign subsidiary.

[23] For examples, see Donald T. Brash, *American Investment in Australian Industry*, p. 4.

[24] In New Zealand, R. S. Deane found that, of 30 United States enterprises operating in the New Zealand manufacturing sector in 1964/65, 21 were paying either a management fee or a royalty to their parent company; in 1963/64, the ratio was the same. But the magnitude of these payments was apparently not large: though he does not give separate details for United States investment, he shows that total management fees and royalties paid by all foreign enterprises in New Zealand manufacturing amounted to only 17.9 per cent of foreign investment's net earnings in manufacturing in 1963/64, only 11.9 per cent in 1964/65 (Deane, op. cit., pp. 490-3). For Australia, I found that taking fees, royalties, and interest into account raised the net return to United States parent companies from 7.9 per cent to 9.2 per cent in 1961/62 (Brash, op. cit., pp. 260-1).

Table 5.3 Net earnings as percentage of book value of United States direct investment at end of previous year in Australia, Canada, and New Zealand, by sector, 1951-68 (per cent)

	Australia				Canada					New Zealand[b]		
	Manu-facturing	Mining and smelting	Other[a]	Total	Manu-facturing	Mining and smelting	Petroleum	Other	Total	Manu-facturing	Other[a]	Total
1951	28.6	18.2	6.5	17.9	14.1	20.4	0.7	8.7	11.7	22.2	12.5	16.0
1952	18.9	25.0	6.0	13.3	14.8	13.3	2.1	9.7	11.6	18.2	10.0	12.9
1953	26.5	14.3	9.8	18.2	14.6	7.8	1.9	10.1	10.8	18.2	15.4	16.2
1954	28.5	40.0	7.3	20.1	11.7	8.2	1.1	10.7	9.1	33.3	9.1	17.6
1955	25.4	15.0	7.7	17.2	13.1	10.5	3.3	10.1	10.2	33.3	8.0	17.5
1956	17.5	20.0	7.5	13.0	12.9	10.7	6.6	11.5	11.0	22.2	12.5	16.7
1957	20.9	17.2	8.1	14.9	9.7	7.0	6.4	8.6	8.4	21.1	13.8	16.7
1958	21.5	9.1	9.1	15.4	8.9	4.3	2.8	6.4	6.5	23.5	16.1	18.8
1959	20.0	27.3	9.2	15.6	10.5	7.1	3.2	6.5	7.5	25.0	14.7	18.0
1960	18.8	29.6	5.7	13.6	8.7	8.1	4.0	6.1	7.0	46.7	10.3	20.4
1961	12.4	24.2	2.9	9.0	7.5	7.2	4.3	6.6	6.5	38.9	17.1	24.5
1962	18.6	13.9	3.1	11.7	9.1	7.1	4.3	6.3	7.1	44.4	13.0	21.9
1963	18.0	17.4	3.0	11.6	9.9	8.5	5.2	6.0	7.8	28.1	15.1	20.0
1964	16.6	12.2	-0.6	9.5	9.8	12.3	5.4	6.9	8.5	n.a.	n.a.	n.a.
1965	13.3	10.0	1.4	8.5	9.8	11.6	5.7	8.1	8.7	n.a.	n.a.	n.a.
1966	12.0	11.2	3.4	8.7	9.1	10.3	5.8	6.9	8.1	n.a.	n.a.	n.a.
1967	11.9	8.0	1.8	7.9	8.0	11.5	5.7	7.4	7.8	n.a.	n.a.	n.a.
1968	11.2	10.3	2.4	8.2	8.3	12.2	6.4	7.2	8.2	n.a.	n.a.	n.a.

[a] Mainly the petroleum sector, for which separate data are not available for most years.

[b] Expressing profit rates in New Zealand to one decimal place suggests an accuracy which is in fact somewhat spurious for two reasons. First, the absolute levels of investment and net earnings are low, and since they are rounded in the source documents to the nearest million dollars, the error introduced is significant. Secondly, the United States Department of Commerce believes that some United States companies report their investment and earnings in New Zealand as part of their Australian operations: this is why separate New Zealand figures have not been published by the Department since those for 1963.

Source: Derived from Tables 5.1 and 5.2.

this may be the result of special circumstances—the long gestation period on much of the enormous recent investment in mining, and the unprofitability of investment in petroleum as a result of the intra-firm pricing policies of firms in that industry. The declining profitability in those sectors will almost certainly be reversed in the early seventies as recently discovered ore bodies, and reserves of oil and gas, come into full production. But the decline in the profitability of United States investment in the manufacturing sector seems genuine: Australian statistics suggest that this decline was checked in 1969, but it seems unlikely that it will be quickly reversed in any major way.[25]

In New Zealand the picture is very different. Profitability was high in the early fifties and became even higher in the late fifties and early sixties. Investment in manufacturing became particularly profitable. Unfortunately the United States Department of Commerce has not published separate information on New Zealand since that for 1963, but it can be inferred from data published by the New Zealand Department of Statistics that the profitability of United States investment, though declining somewhat, remained high until at least 1966.[26] About that time, however, profitability fell very sharply—indeed, in the year ended March 1968, the net earnings of United States-affiliated companies operating in New Zealand were, in total, negative. To judge from the industrial breakdown of the earnings of all foreign investment in New Zealand, this extraordinary reversal was probably in part the result of a temporary decline in the fortunes of a small number of United States companies in gasoline retailing and motor vehicle assembly, but in part also it almost certainly represented a more general decline in profitability that year.

What does high profitability mean in any case? In a competitive environment, it presumably means that the company concerned is meeting a demand more effectively than its competitors. With free entry to the industry, it tends to be a temporary phenomenon. And the experience of Australia and New Zealand with United States investment in no way contradicts this. In Australia, profitability was particularly high in the early part of the fifties precisely because competition within industries where United States investment was important (for example, motor

[25] To a surprising extent, the decline in the profitability of aggregate United States investment in Australian manufacturing reflects the decline in the profitability of General Motors-Holden's. GMH's investment in Australia made up about one-quarter of all United States investment in Australian manufacturing in 1958, and earned an after-tax profit of 31 per cent. A decade later, GMH's investment had declined to one-sixth of the total and earned only 11 per cent. (Data supplied by GMH compared with statistics published by the United States Department of Commerce.)

[26] Department of Statistics, *Report on the Balance of Payments for the year 1967-68*, 1968.

Table 5.4 Net earnings as percentage of book value of direct investment by sector, 1951-5 to 1966-8 (per cent)

	Australia				Canada					New Zealand		
	Manu-facturing	Mining and smelting	Other	Total	Manu-facturing	Mining and smelting	Petroleum	Other	Total	Manu-facturing	Other	Total
1951-55	25.6	22.5	7.5	17.3	13.7	12.0	1.8	9.9	10.7	25.0	11.0	16.0
1956-60	19.7	20.6	7.9	14.5	10.1	7.4	4.6	7.8	8.1	27.7	13.5	18.1
1961-65	15.8	15.5	2.0	10.1	9.2	9.3	5.0	7.7	7.7	37.1[a]	15.1[a]	22.1[a]
1966-68	11.7	9.8	2.5	8.3	8.5	11.3	6.0	7.2	8.0	n.a.	n.a.	n.a.

[a] 1961-3 only.

Source: Table 5.3.

vehicles) had been substantially reduced as a result of import and exchange controls. Protection against imports was maintained, albeit in different and perhaps somewhat reduced form, in the sixties, but by then heavy investments by new producers (often American themselves) had eroded much of the profitability of the early arrivals. In New Zealand, the intensification of import controls in the late fifties must almost certainly bear an important part of the blame for the increase in profitability of United States investment at that time, while the small size of the market and the less-than-enthusiastic official welcome given to new foreign investors made it less likely that this situation would be broken by increased domestic competition. It is of enormous significance that the high profitability of United States investment in New Zealand was abruptly terminated when demand and supply were brought more closely into line by deflation and devaluation in 1967. Where appropriate policies towards the balance of payments and new foreign investment are followed, it is highly unlikely that 'excessive profitability' will long be a problem.

The Balance of Payments

No other aspect of foreign investment has been so widely misunderstood as its impact on the balance of payments of the recipient country. The commonest fallacy is that which first appeared in carefully argued form in an article by J. Knapp in 1957,[27] in which he 'measured' foreign investment's real contribution to the resources available to the host country by the simple expedient of subtracting remitted profits and dividends from capital inflow. The Canadian literature seems to be relatively free of this kind of argument, but it has been widely used in both Australia and New Zealand.[28]

Sometimes the argument appears in more sophisticated form, in what might be called the 'Streeten dilemma'. In several recent papers Streeten has argued that, since foreign investment must grow at a rate above the rate of return on foreign investment if profit remittances are not to exceed new capital inflow (Domar's 1950 argument), and since the rate of return on the existing foreign capital stock is almost certainly greater than the rate of growth of the host economy, the host country faces a choice between, on the one hand, a slow rate of growth of foreign investment—consequent balance of payments problems; and, on the other, a more rapid rate of growth of foreign investment—and increasing alienation of the country's

[27] J. Knapp, 'Capital Exports and Growth', *Economic Journal*, Vol. 67, No. 432, September 1957.
[28] See E. L. Wheelwright, 'Overseas Investment in Australia', in Alex Hunter (ed.), *The Economics of Australian Industry* (Melbourne: Melbourne University Press, 1963), pp. 145-6, and, for example, W. Rosenberg, 'Capital Imports and Growth—the Case of New Zealand', *Economic Journal*, Vol. 71, March 1961.

capital stock to foreigners.[29] This line of thinking was no doubt in the minds of the authors of the Vernon Report in Australia when they noted, in discussing the relationship between new capital inflow and profit remittances, that 'once an economy has a substantial body of overseas investment, it is in a sense "on the tiger's back" '.[30]

But of course the Streeten dilemma only makes sense if one concedes that the effect of foreign investment on the balance of payments can be measured in terms of profit remittances and capital inflow; if one concedes, in other words, that the operation of the foreign-financed capacity makes absolutely no difference to the rates of growth of imports and exports. It should not have been necessary to argue since Alfred Kahn published his reply to J. J. Polak in 1951[31] that, as long as the output of foreign investment is not purchased in an inflationary manner, the sale of this output makes available an increased supply of exportables, reduces expenditure on imports, and/or frees resources in home-trade sectors for employment in international-trade sectors. Provided, therefore, that the economy has capacity to move resources from one sector to another without excessive cost, foreign investment cannot of itself create a balance of payments problem for the host economy even if it is highly profitable and is concentrated in sectors not directly related to the production of exports or import-substitutes.[32]

In fact, most United States direct investment in all three countries has been in sectors having a very direct impact on the balance of payments. Probably the only significant activity of United States companies which has not had an immediate impact on the balance of payments of these countries has been gasoline distribution though perhaps, in Canada, the operations of American-controlled financial institutions also qualify for this category. This predominant emphasis on international-trade sectors would make it difficult to argue that the operation of United States-owned companies has been detrimental to the balance of payments of Australia, Canada and New Zealand even if these countries had no capacity for inter-sectoral resource movement.

---

[29] See, for example, Paul Streeten, 'New Approaches to Private Overseas Investment for Development', paper presented to Bellagio Conference, October 1967; 'The Contribution of Private Overseas Investment to Development', paper presented to Columbia University Conference on International Economic Development, February 1970.

[30] Commonwealth of Australia, *Report of the Committee of Economic Enquiry*, May 1965, Vol. I, pp. 283-4. To be fair, it should also be noted that the authors of the report added the qualification, 'unless the trade balance is improving sufficiently to meet the additional income payable overseas'. But that they saw the dilemma in very much the way Streeten does is clear later in the report (see especially p. 293).

[31] Alfred E. Kahn, 'Investment Criteria in Development Programs', *Quarterly Journal of Economics*, Vol. 65, No. 38, February 1951, especially pp. 42-4.

[32] This subject is more fully discussed in many places. See, for example, Gerald M. Meier, *International Trade and Development* (New York: Harper and Row, 1963), pp. 109-11.

Ownership

The desire that American-controlled companies should share ownership with local investors is, as already noted, widely felt in Australia, Canada, and New Zealand. At present, relatively few United States companies are prepared to gratify that desire. In Australia, a recent survey of 208 American-affiliated companies in the manufacturing sector revealed that 60 per cent were wholly American in ownership (and these represented 78 per cent of the total employment of the companies surveyed). In Canada, 74 per cent of a survey population of 221 were wholly American. In New Zealand 84 per cent of a population of 55 were wholly American in ownership (this number represented 91 per cent of the total employment of the American-affiliated companies surveyed).[33] And, it should be noted, this prevalence of the wholly-American subsidiary obtains despite a quite perceptible trend, at least in Australia[34] and New Zealand,[35] for newly established subsidiaries to invite some local shareholders into partnership.

But in what sense should this pattern be regarded as a 'cost' of United States investment? Three principal reasons have been advanced for the view that it is desirable that foreign-affiliated companies invite local investors into partnership, and none of them is very well based. One concerns the question of control. There appears to be a widespread belief that a company in which local shareholders have an equity interest will be more amenable to the national interest than will a wholly foreign company. In theory (and very often in practice), however, a minority local equity merely extends *foreign* control over *local* resources, and not *vice versa*. Indeed, even where the local equity is in a majority, foreign control will be substantially unimpaired if the local shareholding is widely dispersed or if the company is heavily dependent on the foreign affiliate for markets or technology.

Sometimes, it must be conceded, a local shareholding does result in greater weight being given to local interests in the company's decision-making process. Safarian found, for example, that companies with a Canadian shareholding had a Canadian president, and directors resident in Canada, much more frequently than did wholly American companies. A similar pattern has been detected in Australia, and, for all foreign-affiliated companies, in New Zealand.[36] But there is no consistent evidence suggesting that companies with a local equity participation export a larger percentage of their output,[37] for example, or in other ways

[33] See Brash, op. cit., p. 63; Safarian, *Foreign Ownership of Canadian Industry*, p. 223; Deane, op. cit., p. 80.
[34] Brash, op. cit., pp. 61-3.
[35] Deane, op. cit., compare Tables 4-9 and A. 4-4.
[36] See Safarian, op. cit., pp. 260-2; Brash, op. cit., pp. 105-6; Deane, op. cit., pp. 163-72.
[37] Safarian, op. cit., pp. 259-62; Brash, op. cit., pp. 231-3; Deane, op. cit., pp. 327-31.

behave more closely in line with national aspirations. Indeed, in some respects companies with a local equity participation probably behave in ways which are *less* in line with national aspirations than do wholly foreign companies: wholly foreign companies may tend to pursue a more conservative dividend policy than do jointly-owned companies, for example.[38]

A second reason advanced in favour of having foreign-affiliated companies share ownership is that a local equity participation will reduce the future cost of remitting profits in foreign exchange. This is perfectly true, of course, but what is almost invariably ignored by proponents of this view is that, if the local equity is purchased at a fair market price—a price which, in other words, reflects the market's expectations of the future earnings of the company—the *immediate* cost of purchasing the local interest in terms of capital outflow (or capital inflow foregone) is merely a reflection of the discounted present value of the *future* profit outflow averted. Only if the market's expectations prove to have been unduly pessimistic will the host country's balance of payments benefit from a policy of pressuring foreign-affiliated companies to share ownership. At least in Australia and New Zealand, the market seems more prone to over-estimate the future profitability of American-affiliated companies, and in this situation sharing ownership with locals is detrimental rather than beneficial to the balance of payments.

A third argument in favour of persuading foreign-affiliated companies to share ownership is that, by pursuing a policy of holding all equity abroad, foreign companies undesirably restrict the development of a local capital market. This matter has been of particular concern in Canada and has been mentioned in New Zealand also.[39] There appear to be two somewhat different issues here. One is that, because foreign-controlled companies do not make equities available for purchase by local investors, the latter tend to buy foreign securities. This may be true, but in itself it hardly seems a valid reason for concern because the capital outflow which would be averted by providing more securities for local purchase would presumably be offset by capital repatriation (or absence of capital inflow) on the part of the foreign-controlled companies. The second is that, with a relatively small total volume of transactions on the local market, the ability of the market to mobilise capital for the local entrepreneurs of the future is limited. This may be a valid argument for developing countries but hardly for the countries here discussed, all of which already have an established network of financial institutions and a widespread custom of equity investment. It is also open to question

---

[38] Brash, op. cit., pp. 95-8; Deane, op. cit., pp. 345ff.
[39] See, for example, Task Force Report, *Foreign Ownership and the Structure of Canadian Industry*, pp. 39, 277-93; Z. Frankel, *New Zealand Overseas Borrowing* (Wellington: New Zealand Institute of Economic Research, 1968), p. 77.

whether making available for purchase shares in the local subsidiary of a General Motors or a Union Carbide really does accustom local investors to providing the risk capital for a budding Henry Ford or a John D. Rockefeller.

A supplementary reason sometimes advanced for persuading foreign companies to share ownership is that such a policy is likely to lead to their disclosure of more financial information about their operations.[40] But as Deane has noted,[41] sharing equity with locals is no guarantee of disclosure and, since the 'first-best' alternative of amending company legislation to compel more complete disclosure is so readily available (and has, in fact, already been used by all three countries in varying degrees), there seems little reason to use the 'second-best'.

To be set against these dubious benefits of pressuring foreign companies to share ownership, moreover, are certain specific costs. One is the fact that some foreign companies prefer not to invest than to share ownership. It is unlikely that the relatively gentle persuasion currently exerted by the Australian and Canadian governments on this point has had much deterrent effect. But Deane gives some vivid illustrations of the cost which New Zealand has incurred because of its insistence on getting a share of the equity whenever possible. Because of the limited accessibility of Deane's work, it is worth quoting two of his examples at length:

> In the first example firm X, one of the most efficient of those visited, applied for an import licence to enable it to produce a material and sell it in New Zealand for 70 per cent of its landed cost at the time. The import saving was estimated at $60,000 per annum. The Department of Industries and Commerce viewed the project favourably except for the fact that X was 100 per cent foreign owned. The department stated that the import saving was secondary to the local participation question, and that a licence would be granted if a New Zealand interest was made available. The parent refused to cooperate. As a result the project fell through. . . .
> [Another] example involved a New Zealand company, A, which set up a joint 50-50 subsidiary, B, with a foreign partner, C. The latter was required particularly to assist with technical knowledge. Another foreign company then proceeded to take up a 50 per cent interest in A. The next licence application for development of B's activities was turned down solely on the basis of a foreign interest in B which was considered by officials to be excessive. Directly and indirectly it amounted to about 75 per cent. Realising the futility of the position, C offered to sell its holding in B to A. The import licences then became available, although A lost the benefit of its association with C.[42]

[40] See, for example, Task Force Report, p. 412.
[41] Deane, op. cit., p. 92.
[42] Ibid., pp. 98-9.

Even where compulsion to share ownership does not deter a foreign company from making an investment, it is likely to restrict somewhat the host country's access to the technology of the parent company because of the latter's fear that local partners will pirate its know-how. A tendency of this kind has been detected both in New Zealand and in Australia.[43]

A local shareholding may have two opposing influences on the extent of restrictions on a subsidiary's freedom to export. On the one hand, there may be a beneficial impact because of possible parent company reluctance to arouse resentment amongst local shareholders and because United States antitrust laws probably make it more difficult to formalise such restrictions with a partially-owned subsidiary. On the other hand, the parent company has a much stronger incentive to restrict the export freedom of a partially-owned affiliate than a wholly-owned. The empirical evidence is inconclusive but suggests that the presence of a local equity interest is indeed associated with a reduced freedom to export.[44]

Finally there is an intangible but possibly quite significant cost: it is almost certainly *more* difficult, and not less, for a government to treat a jointly-owned company rationally. My own knowledge of the Canadian scene is not sufficient for me to illustrate this argument from Canadian experience, but there seems plenty of support for this thesis in Australasia. It seems relevant, for example, that many of the foreign-controlled companies in both Australia and New Zealand which have invited domestic residents into partnership also depend on a high level of protection from imports. The Australian government's decision to continue providing a special subsidy for domestic oil production—estimated by Alex Hunter[45] at 20 per cent even after the reduction in price to the 'import parity' level in September 1970—may well have been influenced by the fact that Australia's largest and most widely-held company holds a 50 per cent interest (with Standard Oil of New Jersey) in the most important oil field now in production.

Local Borrowing. In contrast to the general desire that foreign-owned companies invite local equity capital into partnership, there is some resentment when the same companies raise fixed-interest capital locally. This resentment has focused especially on United States subsidiaries since the balance of payments guidelines of the United States government urged United States companies to finance abroad as much of their foreign investment program as possible.

In principle, this is a reasonable concern and the measures taken by the Australian government to exercise some control over the local

---

[43] Ibid., pp. 101, 248; Brash, op. cit., p. 138.

[44] Brash, op. cit., pp. 231-4; Deane, op. cit., pp. 317-30; W. P. Hogan, 'British Manufacturing Subsidiaries in Australia and Export Franchises', paper presented to the Economic Society of Australia and New Zealand, New South Wales Branch, September 1965.

[45] *Australian Financial Review*, 26 March 1970.

borrowing of foreign subsidiaries in 1965, systematised in 1969, are well justified. Where domestic companies find themselves at a substantial disadvantage *vis-à-vis* foreign subsidiaries simply by virtue of the world-wide reputation of the latter, some countervailing interference with the market mechanism seems quite appropriate.

In practice, of course, local borrowing appears to have been only a minor source of funds for United States companies operating in Canada and Australasia, at least before the United States balance of payments guidelines were promulgated in the mid-sixties. Safarian found that, of 188 American-affiliated companies which answered this question in his survey, 134 (or 71 per cent) derived no funds from Canadian sources during the decade of the fifties. A further 23 (12 per cent) derived less than 25 per cent of their funds from Canadian sources. Since some of the companies which raised capital in Canada presumably did so by stock issues, debt financing was obviously of minor significance for the over-whelming majority of the companies surveyed. In Deane's survey, only 25 per cent of American-owned respondents had any long-term liability outstanding to New Zealand creditors in 1965: this compares with a figure of 37 per cent for British-affiliated companies, 65 per cent for Australian-affiliated companies, and 73 per cent for a group of New Zealand-owned public companies. (Deane also found that jointly-owned companies were more likely to borrow long-term funds in New Zealand than wholly foreign companies.) As a proportion of the total book value of the American-affiliated companies operating in New Zealand in 1965, long-term liabilities to New Zealand creditors amounted to only 9.4 per cent. In my own survey of American-affiliated companies in the Australian manufacturing sector, long-term liabilities to Australian creditors amounted to only 7.3 per cent of the book value of the 101 companies which provided information on this point. Again, wholly American companies (4.5 per cent) were less dependent on Australian credit than were jointly-owned (13.6 per cent). Two out of every five American-affiliated companies had some long-term liability outstanding to an Australian creditor, but in most cases the actual amount was very small.[46] Certainly, American-affiliated companies, especially in the mining sector, have recently made some very substantial borrowings on the Australian market, but at least in the well-publicised cases the local borrowings have been but a small fraction of the foreign borrowings.

Management and Research. Another alleged cost of foreign invest-ment is the supposed failure of foreign-affiliated companies to afford employment opportunities to local managers and scientists.

This is only partly a concern for employment opportunities as such. In the case of management, it reflects also the belief that if foreign-affiliated

[46] See Safarian, op. cit., p. 238; Deane, op. cit., pp. 201ff., 446-51; Brash, op. cit., pp. 81-4.

companies are managed locally, they are more likely to behave in ways consistent with national aspirations. There may be an additional interest in the new techniques which can be learnt in the employ of a foreign-affiliated company. These are valid sentiments, but certain qualifications need to be borne in mind before deciding on the conclusions they suggest.

To begin with, the evidence that local management is either better aware of, or more likely to act on, the national interest than foreign management is by no means conclusive.[47] It is not without significance that the best known example of an aggressively 'Australian outlook' in the management of American-affiliated companies in Australia is that of Mr L. J. Hartnett, managing director of General Motors-Holden's during part of the thirties and forties. Hartnett was appointed to manage the company by the American parent and had never lived in Australia before (he was actually British by birth). Since the performance of management, whatever its nationality, is likely to be judged by the growth and development of the subsidiary, the difference in actual behaviour between managers who are foreign and those who are local is often small. Secondly, the acquisition of new skills by local management is in many cases facilitated rather than impeded by the presence of foreign executives. This is especially true when the foreign executives regard themselves as responsible for the subsidiary only temporarily and actively train local personnel to take their places.

In any case, the number of American personnel employed in affiliated companies is small in both Canada and Australasia. In 1962, a survey of 138 foreign-affiliated corporations in Canada (most of them American-owned) with assets of at least $US25 million revealed that of a total of 1,003 senior officers resident in Canada, only 235 were foreign nationals.[48] In the same year, my own survey in Australia showed that 105 American-affiliated companies, employing a total of nearly 82,000 people, employed fewer than 200 Americans. Less than half the latter number held executive positions in Australia. Sixty-three of the companies, 60 per cent of the sample, neither employed an American nor had an American director resident in Australia in 1962.[49] In Deane's survey in the mid-sixties, 80 per cent of the managing directors of the 20 American-affiliated companies in his sample were New Zealanders. In 65 per cent of the companies, no personnel from the parent company were employed at all. As a proportion of total company employment, Americans amounted to less than 0.25 per cent.[50]

The employment of local scientists is desired also for reasons only partly connected with concern for the employment opportunities of

[47] See, for example, Brash, op. cit., pp. 107-8.
[48] Quoted by Safarian, op. cit., p. 54.
[49] Brash, op. cit., pp. 107-8.
[50] Deane, op. cit., pp. 166-7, 170-1.

scientists. There is the additional feeling that it is a 'good thing' to have as much research done locally as possible. The reasons for this view are usually not articulated and, even when they are, there is usually little consideration given to the most appropriate location for this research. There might well be some national advantage if foreign subsidiaries did *not* themselves tap the supply of scientific personnel, leaving this resource available for locally-controlled companies.[51]

But in any case, as with the employment of local management, there is considerable evidence that American-affiliated companies do as much research as locally-owned companies—possibly even more than local companies. In Canada, Safarian found that exactly the same proportion of foreign-affiliated (mainly American-affiliated) companies were conducting research in Canada as in his control group of Canadian-owned companies. He noted moreover that the research programs of the two sets of companies conducting research were broadly similar in nature. He concluded that 'roughly the same proportion engage in research-development but the non-resident firms do more of it'.[52]

And despite some pre-election publicity given in 1969 to the closing of research departments in Australian companies acquired by American investors, a similar situation almost certainly prevails in Australia. In my own survey, the main determinants of where an American-affiliated company was conducting research seemed to have been its size and age. There was no clear indication that jointly-owned companies conducted any more research than did wholly American ones and, to judge from the relative number of chemists, draftsmen, laboratory and other research staff employed, it appeared quite possible that the American-affiliated companies as a group did more research and development work than did Australian companies.

Deane found that 11 out of 20 American-affiliated respondents in his survey conducted some research in New Zealand, though in at least 5 of these cases the research was of 'a limited nature only'. He also discovered that, in common with other foreign-affiliated companies, they employed significantly more people in the 'professional and technical' category (a category distinguished from those engaged in management and administration) than did New Zealand industry generally, thus at least suggesting the possibility that they conduct more research than do New Zealand companies. Evidence from the United Kingdom lends weight to this view that American-affiliated subsidiaries often do more research locally than do their nationally owned counterparts.[53]

[51] For fuller discussion, see John H. Dunning and Max Steuer, 'The Effects of United States Direct Investment in Britain on British Technology', *Moorgate and Wall Street*, Autumn 1969, especially pp. 17-19.
[52] Safarian, op. cit., pp. 280-2.
[53] See Brash, op. cit., pp. 147-54; Deane, op. cit., pp. 259ff., Dunning and Steuer, loc. cit., p. 23.

Intra-firm Pricing. Still another concern, albeit one confined to the more sophisticated, is that American subsidiaries evade local taxes by over-pricing imports from, and under-pricing exports to, their parents. Even if American-affiliated companies were successful in evading virtually all taxes in this way, the host country would still be better off than without the American investment, of course, since without the investment it would have gained *no* tax revenues on the relevant production. But in principle such evasion is one way in which the benefit of foreign investment can be reduced, so it is a legitimate concern.

The problem is potentially more serious on the import side than on the export for two reasons. First, while many American-affiliated firms purchase a high proportion of their total imports from their foreign parents, the percentage of exports sold to the parent is typically lower. Thus, in Canada, in 1965, a survey of 266 of the larger foreign-affiliated firms revealed that about 70 per cent of all foreign purchases were from affiliates, whereas only about 50 per cent of foreign sales went to them. In Australia, 91 per cent of the imports of 76 American-based companies surveyed in 1961/62 came from, or through, foreign affiliates: no information is available on the importance of export sales to affiliates at that time, but it is certain to be now very much lower than the ratio on the import side because of the enormous recent growth in exports of minerals to non-affiliated customers in Japan. In New Zealand, the ratio of imports purchased from affiliated companies is high while both the absolute total of exports and the share going to affiliates is low.[54] Secondly, while imports purchased from affiliates tend to be components and semi-manufactured items of almost infinite variety, exports to affiliates more often tend to be relatively standardised raw materials. Establishing a 'fair market price' is easy for neither category of transaction, but is surely relatively simpler for the latter. This eases the problem of tax authorities in policing the prices of export transactions.

What evidence is there that American-affiliated companies do pay more than a 'fair market price' for materials purchased from their affiliates? Not much. In Canada, one-half of a population of 192 firms surveyed by Safarian in 1959 believed that affiliation had had no effect, or a very limited one, on the nature, source, and cost of materials. A further forty companies stated that 'affiliation led to joint purchases with the parent, contacts with suppliers, and other effects. The common characteristic of all of these was that they were explicitly described as helping the subsidiary in its purchasing programmes'.[55] Most of the balance indicated that, while affiliation led to significant purchases from

---

[54] See Task Force Report, p. 202; see also Safarian, op. cit., pp. 123, 151-3; Brash, op. cit., p. 211; Deane, op. cit., pp. 232, 325, 328.
[55] Safarian, op. cit., p. 162.

the parent firm itself, the subsidiary was in fact free to secure supplies elsewhere if it was to the subsidiary's advantage to do so.

In Australia, sixty-four American-affiliated manufacturing companies (including most of the large ones) gave me classifiable information on the prices paid for purchases from affiliates in 1962. In nine cases, the local executives felt the prices paid were considerably below the world price for similar goods—indeed, in one case the Australian Customs Department refused to accept the invoice valuation as the true valuation for duty purposes. Another forty-nine companies felt the prices paid were closely in line with or slightly below world prices, often because they were able to take advantage of the volume discounts obtained on the bulk purchases of their parent companies. Only nine companies felt they were being charged excessively high prices by their United States affiliate, and even this relatively small number includes companies where there was some doubt that the local company could, in fact, have purchased more cheaply from other sources because of patent restrictions.[56]

In New Zealand, Deane found that virtually all the foreign-affiliated companies in the manufacturing sector claimed complete freedom in the determination of their importing policies. Many respondents claimed that, because of the need to use their limited import licences to the best possible advantage, they simply could not afford to buy from affiliated sources unless these were fully competitive. Of fifteen American-affiliated respondents, four claimed to buy no imports from affiliated sources, four said that the question of price was irrelevant because no source outside the group was available, five claimed that affiliated sources were cheaper than alternative sources, and none claimed that purchases from affiliates were more expensive than those from other sources.[57]

On the other hand, the surveys quoted in Australasia specifically did not include the local subsidiaries of American oil companies, and both quoted some evidence that these companies may have paid above 'world market prices' for their imports of crude oil after market prices began to fall significantly below posted prices in the late fifties. But in both countries the most significant items of evidence quoted were tax assessments above those indicated by the company's own estimate of its profits.[58] It seems unlikely that, with alert tax authorities in all three host countries, significant tax evasion occurs through over-pricing of imports from affiliates.

Nor is this surprising. The incentive to 'load' import prices must be weak in both Canada and Australasia, especially since United States legislation in the early sixties made the use of 'tax-havens' more difficult.

---

[56] Brash, op. cit., pp. 215-18.
[57] Deane, op. cit., pp. 226-32.
[58] Brash, op. cit., pp. 218-20; Deane, op. cit., p. 236.

Company tax rates in all three countries are broadly similar to those in the United States, and in practice there are no exchange restrictions on the remittance abroad of company profits. In New Zealand, quantitative import controls produce an important incentive *not* to overstate prices.

Though the evidence is scanty, the same happy situation almost certainly obtains in the pricing of exports to foreign affiliates. Indeed, Kindleberger quotes the authors of the Canadian Task Force Report as believing that Canada may get higher prices for its exports of raw materials when they are sold by monopolistic foreign-affiliated companies than would be the case if Canadian companies were to sell them independently.[59]

Restrictions on Exports. An issue which has generated considerable concern about the costs of foreign investment, especially in Australasia, is the suspicion that foreign parent companies restrict the export freedom of their subsidiaries. There is concern that, since foreign companies often tend to be concentrated in the sectors which nationalists regard as the host country's best prospects for future export growth, these restrictions significantly impede the country's development prospects.

There can be no doubt that many American parent companies do place such restrictions on the export freedom of their subsidiaries in Canada and Australasia. Safarian found that seventeen of the American-controlled companies he surveyed in Canada—13 per cent of the classifiable responses—felt that their American affiliation had an unfavourable effect on the volume of their exports, while Deane found that half of the American-affiliated companies in his New Zealand survey were subjected to export restrictions, most of them severe (limitation to the Pacific islands only). In Australia, my own survey revealed that 76 per cent of the American-affiliated respondents suffered under some geographical restriction on exports, and some of the remainder were restricted in other ways (price, packaging, etc.).[60]

But often such restrictions are not very relevant in practice because of high local production costs:[61] in other words, the view of the nationalist ignores the fact that many of the American-affiliated companies, in all three of the countries under discussion, were induced to invest only by actual or promised import protection. To expect these companies to export soon after establishment is therefore highly unrealistic.

It is interesting to note in this connection that the larger the local subsidiary—and therefore presumably the more internationally competitive—the less important do parental restrictions on export freedom appear to be. Safarian found, for example, that the great majority of the

---

[59] C. P. Kindleberger, *American Business Abroad*, p. 111.
[60] See Safarian, op. cit., p. 136; Deane, op. cit., pp. 322-3; Brash, op. cit., pp. 228-9.
[61] See, for example, Brash, op. cit., p. 223; Deane, op. cit., p. 327.

American-affiliated companies in Canada which felt their affiliation to be a negative factor on their export performance had assets of less than $US5 million.[62] In my own survey in Australia there was often the same thing, varying with the length of time the subsidiary had been established. Thus, while only 23 per cent of the forty-seven companies which had been established five years or less had exports of at least 1 per cent of sales in 1962, 57 per cent of the forty-six established for more than five years attained such a level of exports in that year.[63]

It is also highly relevant that the *actual* export performance of American-affiliated companies is, at least in Canada and Australia, as good as that of locally-owned companies, and may even be somewhat better than that of locally-owned companies as a result of their foreign affiliation. Safarian has noted that:

> Export from Canada originating with these [American-affiliated companies] accounted for about 50 per cent of total Canadian exports of manufactures (including pulp and paper) in 1957, while for petroleum and other minerals and metals combined the proportion was over 85 per cent. These proportions are higher than the proportion of capital invested in Canadian industry which was owned and controlled by residents of the United States at that time . . . These estimates suggest that, on an aggregative basis, the American-owned sector of the industries involved is more oriented to exports than are the other sectors.[64]

While recognising that such aggregative statistics are open to a number of objections, Safarian observed that his own data, which focused on frequency distributions rather than aggregates, suggested that the overall effect of foreign affiliation on export performance was 'either non-existent or favourable except for a small minority of cases'. He also found that the number of a company's foreign affiliates had, if anything, a positive rather than a negative effect on its export orientation.[65]

In my own Australian survey, I did not compare the export performance of American-affiliated companies with that of a control group of locally-owned companies, so that my conclusions mean less than do Safarian's. But it was very clear that, while a few companies would have exported more had it not been for parental restriction, others derived important benefits first from the fact that those restrictions themselves often gave the Australian affiliate an exclusive market right in nearby areas; and secondly from the extensive network of affiliated sales outlets to which they had access. While the ninety-three respondent companies accounted for only 6.5 per cent of total Australian manufacturing produc-

---

[62] Safarian, op. cit., p. 136; see also p. 120.
[63] Brash, op. cit., pp. 223-4, 232.
[64] Safarian, op. cit., pp. 119-20.
[65] Ibid., pp. 128, 137.

tion in 1961/62, they together accounted for 10.2 per cent of the value of Australian manufactured exports that year.[66]

In Deane's New Zealand survey, foreign-affiliated manufacturing companies as a group had a poor export record in absolute terms, but compared very favourably with locally-owned manufacturing companies. American-affiliated companies compared unfavourably with other foreign-affiliated companies but, since they apparently had a marginally greater degree of freedom from parental export restriction than most other foreign-affiliated companies, this fact was probably the result primarily of the uncompetitive nature of the New Zealand operations of American corporations.[67]

Over the long term, the length of which will vary depending primarily on the economic life of plant and equipment in the industry in question, it would be irrational for a profit-maximising parent firm to restrict the output of its foreign subsidiaries unless tax differentials, governmental restrictions on profit remittance, or local shareholders were important factors distorting the decision.[68]

And, in fact, the evidence suggests that, over the long term, firms do tend to behave rationally. The writer encountered one American company which, after buying out the non-affiliated shareholders in one of its Australian subsidiaries, doubled the capacity of the Australian plant, closed the plant of another affiliate in the United Kingdom, and commenced exporting the output of the Australian plant to the United Kingdom, Canada and Japan.[69] Another American company, producing fastening equipment, purchased a controlling interest in an Australian company primarily in order to scale down its own production of a certain item of construction equipment in favour of imports from the Australian affiliate. Safarian notes that in 1963 the Studebaker Corporation closed its United States automobile operations entirely, and 'switched its production for the United States and overseas markets to its Canadian plant, where lower manufacturing costs and favourable tariff and currency arrangements prevailed'.[70] At present, most of the Mavericks and Hornets (small cars made by the Ford Company and American Motors Corporation respectively) sold in North America are made in Canada.[71]

Takeovers. Concern about foreign investment is rarely more intense than when a large foreign corporation acquires control of a previously locally-owned company. There are some valid reasons for this concern: in particular, such takeovers may, in certain circumstances, be objected to

[66] Brash, op. cit., pp. 222, 227, 230.
[67] Deane, op. cit., pp. 314-31.
[68] For a fuller discussion, see Irving Brecher and S. S. Reisman, *Canada-United States Economic Relations* (Ottawa: Royal Commission on Canada's Economic Prospects, 1957), pp. 140-5.
[69] Brash, op. cit., p. 233.
[70] Safarian, op. cit., p. 116n.
[71] *The Economist*, 21 February 1970, p. 52.

on 'infant firm' grounds, or on the grounds that they have an adverse effect on the competitive structure of the industry in question. Both these arguments receive further examination below. Here it is necessary to note that most of the popular resentment against foreign acquisitions of domestic corporations has nothing to do with economic rationality at all.

That concern for the level of competition is not one of the factors motivating resentment against takeovers has perhaps never been more dramatically illustrated than when the Australian subsidiary of Nabisco attempted to acquire Swallow and Ariell Ltd in 1964. The latter was a small Australian-owned firm which had not earned a profit since 1961. Its attempted acquisition by Nabisco sparked a prolonged battle for the company between Nabisco, on the one hand, and the Australian Biscuit Company Pty Ltd on the other. Australian public opinion, at least as reflected in newspaper editorials and correspondence, was strongly behind the locally-owned Australian Biscuit Company in the struggle, despite the fact that Australian Biscuit was a closely-held family company which stood to raise its estimated market share from an already dominant 70 per cent to 80 per cent by the acquisition.

Most commonly the popular objection to foreign takeovers is simply an objection to what is seen as a 'mere' transfer of the ownership and control of assets built up, often over many years, by local effort. It ignores the obvious desire of local shareholders to sell these assets, presumably because their rate of discount is different from that of the foreign corporation or, more likely, because the profits they expect from the company under continued local ownership are different from those expected by the foreign corporation when it is in control.

In other words, foreign takeovers rarely involve a 'mere' transfer of ownership. Not infrequently they involve the acquisition and rehabilitation of companies on the verge of collapse: Reuber and Roseman, in their analysis of the takeover of Canadian companies between 1945 and 1961, found that 43.5 per cent of Canadian mining companies acquired by foreign corporations in that period were making a loss before acquisition, and the same applied to 17.9 per cent of acquired companies in the manufacturing sector.[72] In Australia also, many of the largest acquisitions have been of Australian companies in serious financial difficulties. Where the acquired company is operating successfully, takeover frequently means major expansion in its operations and very often complete renovation of its operating methods.[73]

In any case, Canadian evidence suggests that takeovers have been quantitatively a rather unimportant part of United States direct investment. Even after adjusting for price changes, Reuber and Roseman found

---

[72] Grant L. Reuber and Frank Roseman, *The Take-Over of Canadian Firms, 1945-61: An Empirical Analysis* (Ottawa: Queens Printer, 1969).
[73] Brash, op. cit., pp. 55-6, 127.

that the value of the assets of firms acquired by foreigners (mainly American corporations) between 1945 and 1961 represented only 12.3 per cent of the value of the total assets controlled by foreigners in the Canadian manufacturing sector in 1962, and corresponding figures for other sectors were even lower (5.9 per cent for trade, 1.7 per cent for mining, and 0.02 per cent for finance).[74] Official Canadian statistics show that, while sixty Canadian concerns fell under United States control in the years 1962-4, ninety-three others moved out of United States control during the same period.[75] Despite their strong position in the Canadian economy, United States firms acquired substantially fewer companies in Canada than did local firms over the period 1945-61 (416 as compared with 1,183); as a proportion of the total number of Canadian-owned companies, United States acquisitions were entirely negligible.[76] It is also relevant to our later discussion of the impact of foreign investment on the competitive structure of industry that only some 27 per cent of the foreign acquisitions in Canada in 1945-61 were aimed at the takeover of a direct competitor.[77]

So far, we have been examining various alleged costs of United States investment and have dismissed all of them as either theoretically fallacious or empirically of little practical importance in Canada, Australia and New Zealand. But there remain two allegations which are less easily disposed of. One is the 'infant firm' argument against foreign investment and the other is an argument based on foreign investment's effect on the structure of industry.

The Infant Firm Argument. It is not disputed that foreign-affiliated companies often have important advantages *vis-à-vis* domestic companies —better technical and managerial know-how, greater access to both product and factor markets, more widely known brandnames—and some, most recently Albert Hirschman,[78] have argued that therefore foreign investment, while beneficial to domestic residents in the short run, actually harms the recipient country in the longer run because of the stultifying effect which this competition has on the development of local enterprise. The argument is often extended to take into account the probability of declining costs (through learning effects as well as external economies), and a justification for restricting the inflow of foreign investment is built on grounds parallel to the infant industry case in tariff

74 Reuber and Roseman, op. cit.
75 Dominion Bureau of Statistics, *The Canadian Balance of International Payments 1963, 1964 and 1965 and International Investment Position*, p. 74.
76 Reuber and Roseman, op. cit., p. 32. The Report of the Task Force on the Structure of Canadian Industry also conceded that, at least in the manufacturing sector, the amount of merger activity accounted for by United States-controlled companies has been lower than their importance in that sector would suggest (p. 147).
77 Reuber and Roseman, op. cit., pp. 85-7.
78 Albert O. Hirschman, *How to Divest in Latin America, and Why.*

theory. In Hirschman's view the climate for foreign investment 'ought to turn from attractive at an early stage of development to much less inviting in some middle stretch',[79] when domestic resources of entrepreneurs and skilled manpower are likely to be able to fill the gaps left by a decline in the importance of foreign investment. There seems little doubt that, as indicated earlier, such a change in the climate is actually occurring in both Canada and Australasia, though whether it will go as far as Hirschman would like is open to doubt.

The problem with the infant firm argument, of course, is that it is impossible to refute conclusively. One can never be sure how a country would have developed had it moved decisively to check the inflow of foreign capital at some relatively early stage. Hirschman himself concedes this point.[80] It is certainly not reasonable, as some polemicists do, to deduce generally applicable principles from, say, the Japanese policy on foreign investment and that country's growth experience.

There is also something slightly paradoxical about the Hirschman view that countries should attract foreign capital at an early stage of development and repatriate that capital at a later stage. If Hirschman is right—and foreign investment, by providing such a complete package of skills and resources, tends to preclude the development of local skills and initiative—it is not immediately clear either why countries should welcome capital at any stage of development or why, having welcomed it, they have unutilised talent 'waiting in the wings' by the time they reach a middle stage of development.

Even where foreign investment is of great importance in the economy, moreover, countries which have reached a relatively advanced stage of development appear to have abundant opportunities for local initiative and entrepreneurship. That this is so is surely attested to by the many thousands of locally-owned enterprises in both Canada and Australasia, many, to be sure, small in relation to the subsidiaries of foreign corporations but many others powerful corporations by any standard and often themselves investing abroad. (In Canada, Alcan Aluminium, Massey-Ferguson, Hiram Walker, and International Nickel spring to mind, and in Australia B.H.P., A.C.I., C.S.R. and such aggressive smaller companies as Repco and Kiwi International. New Zealand has long had insurance companies with an international orientation, and manufacturing companies such as U.E.B. are now looking in the same direction.)

The survival of such local companies, despite a historically generous welcome to foreign investment in all three countries, should really cause no surprise, for, while foreign investment presumably does affect the prospects of some entrepreneurs adversely, it benefits those of others both through 'linkage' and demonstration effects. On these grounds alone,

[79] Ibid., p. 6.
[80] Ibid.

therefore, the infant-firm argument against foreign investment seems dubious.

Perhaps even more important, foreign investment is likely to benefit domestic incomes now, whereas the growth of domestic companies which might occur in its absence is likely to produce equivalent benefit only after a lag. (Experience in Australia and New Zealand suggests that that lag might be considerable, at least in the more sophisticated industries. One thinks of the vain attempts of the Australian government to induce A.C.I. to undertake the Australian manufacture of motor vehicle engines in 1939;[81] or the spectacular collapse in the early sixties of the locally owned McKendrick Glass Manufacturing Co. Ltd in New Zealand, despite a government assurance that the company could have 80 per cent of the New Zealand market, low rental land, and a leased factory.)[82] Because of this lag, it will often be found that the economic 'benefits' of restricting the inflow of foreign investment, when appropriately discounted, are in fact non-existent or negative. Indeed, this will almost inevitably be true when it is recalled that what is being compared is, on the one hand, the discounted present social value of an investment when it is made by local citizens; with, on the other hand, the discounted present social value of that investment when made by foreigners, *plus* the discounted present social value of the investment of the local capital thereby released in the next most profitable avenue.[83]

Structural Effects. Another serious allegation against foreign investment has been well stated by Stephen Hymer:

> The operation of foreign ownership decreases the number of firms in the world and tends to encourage imperfectly competitive behaviour. In general, imperfect competition reduces economic welfare because it decreases the efficiency with which resources . . . are allocated. Prices facing consumers tend to be higher than they would otherwise be and consumers tend to be made worse off.[84]

There can be little doubt that foreign investment does tend to reduce the number of firms in the world. There is abundant evidence that the industries where it is most important are those characterised by a high degree of concentration.[85] But for precisely the reason that foreign investment usually brings the firms of different nations into more intense com-

[81] Brash, op. cit., p. 290.

[82] Deane, op. cit., pp. 129-30.

[83] Donald T. Brash, 'Australia as Host to the International Corporation', in C. P. Kindleberger (ed.), *The International Corporation*, pp. 312-13.

[84] Stephen Hymer, 'Direct Foreign Investment and the National Economic Interest', in Peter Russell (ed.), *Nationalism in Canada* (publisher's name not known), 1966, p. 194.

[85] Deane, op. cit., pp. 300-5; Hunter (ed.), op. cit., p. 7; Task Force Report, pp. 141-4.

petition with each other, it does not, as Hymer himself recognises,[86] *necessarily* reduce the overall level of competition. Five or six multinational corporations are likely to generate at least as much competition as 15 or 20 companies if the latter are primarily domestic in orientation and are spread two or three to each industrial nation.

In accusing foreign investment of encouraging imperfectly competitive behaviour, its critics often implicitly assume that in the absence of foreign investment a condition approximating that of perfect competition would prevail—or, at least, a condition more nearly approximating perfect competition. Because of the enormous importance of economies of scale in virtually all of the industries where foreign investment is significant, however, this is clearly an unrealistic assumption, especially in the relatively small economies of Canada and Australasia.

Very often, from a national point of view, the most likely alternative to three or four admittedly imperfectly competitive foreign-affiliated companies is not perfect competition but monopoly. Thus, it was not until Rothmans of Pall Mall (of Britain) and Philip Morris (of the United States) invaded the Australian cigarette market in the mid-fifties that the almost total monopoly of the British Tobacco Co. (Australia) Ltd in that market was broken. It required the intervention of Colgate-Palmolive to break the virtual monopoly which Unilever Australia had enjoyed in the Australian soap flake and detergent market until 1960. And there appears to be no prospect of B.H.P.'s monopoly of the Australian steel market being broken before the (rumoured) intervention of a powerful foreign steel group.

These examples, and others which could be quoted, suggest that, while foreign investment may decrease the potential for worldwide competition by reducing the number of independent companies in the world industry, it frequently acts as a spur to competition within the individual host country. In most industries, moreover, countries still retain the option of reducing tariffs (or abolishing import quotas) if foreign investment threatens to raise prices by reducing competition.

The real danger of foreign investment to the structure of industry in some countries, far from being its reduction of competitive forces, may be its tendency to fragment industry undesirably. As I have suggested elsewhere, it appears that often

> the combination of almost any actual or potential barrier to trade with the oligopolistic nature of most of the industries in which foreign investment is important tends to produce a great proliferation of small-scale foreign-owned units, without any real prospect of rationalisation or consolidation . . . If the units were domestically owned,

[86] Stephen Hymer, 'The Efficiency (Contradictions) of Multinational Corporations', *American Economic Review*, Vol. 60, No. 2, May 1970, p. 443.

one could expect market forces to bring about consolidation over a period; when they are owned by large internationally competing corporations, this is highly unlikely. Faulty tariff policy is partly to blame for this situation in many cases, but even a country pursuing an exemplary tariff policy may encounter the problem.[87]

There is little doubt that examples exist of this tendency in Canada, though they may be less glaring than those in Australasia because of the absolutely larger Canadian economy. In Australia, the motor vehicle industry is a good example of the problem: the subsidiaries of five or six international corporations, the larger ones making acceptable profits, the smaller ones barely breaking even or making losses, all operating at below the most efficient production runs, and almost all dependent on continued protection from imports. The reduction of that protection would certainly reduce the profits of the companies in the industry and might even induce a few to leave the industry. But the substantial investment made by the others, coupled with the risk that trade barriers would be re-erected in the future, would keep at least three or four in the industry for a substantial period. The emergence of one internationally competitive producer, which would soon be possible on the basis of the Australian motor vehicle market, would be unlikely. Other examples abound in such different industries as chemicals and compressed air equipment.

In New Zealand, the day after Comalco (jointly owned by Kaiser Aluminum and Conzinc Riotinto Australia) announced it would spend more than $US10 million to process aluminium in New Zealand, Alcan New Zealand announced a $US6.5 million expansion program designed to maintain its lead in the fabrication of aluminium in that country.[88] In 1963, when a local affiliate of the Von Kohorn Universal Corporation of California announced its intention to begin nylon production in New Zealand, an affiliate of the British firm I.C.I. immediately announced its intention to do the same.[89] In neither industry is there room for two producers of competitive size, and in the nylon industry it is doubtful if there is even room for one. New Zealand's import quotas must bear part of the blame for this situation, but so also must foreign investment.

Finally, we come to the less exclusively economic costs of American investment. An economist is clearly not competent to analyse these in detail, but some comments are necessary for the sake of completeness.

One of the alleged costs of foreign investment is that it complicates further the already complex task of economic management.[90] There is undoubtedly some truth in this. The fact that a foreign subsidiary some-

---

[87] Brash, 'Australia as Host', p. 317.
[88] *Australian Financial Review*, 24 April 1970.
[89] Deane, op. cit., pp. 114-15.
[90] See, for example, Hymer, 'The Efficiency (Contradictions) of Multinational Corporations', p. 447.

times has access to effectively limitless resources from its parent clearly reduces the impact of changes in domestic monetary policy. And the need to adjust the current account of the balance of payments to fluctuations in the level of capital inflow adds another dimension to balance of payments management. But the argument can easily be exaggerated. Part of the effect of monetary policy after all is through its impact on the psychological climate of the business community and, if this is bleak as a result of a tight monetary policy, the foreign affiliate is unlikely to feel a strong incentive to tap the resources of its parent even when these are available. Fiscal policy retains its full efficacy in any case. As for the balance of payments, to an important extent the current account adjusts automatically to a change in the rate of capital inflow.[91] Any additional adjustments required are no different in kind than those required to adjust to, say, a change in export prices.

Another cost of foreign investment, it is argued, is simply that of 'foreign control' of the economy. Sometimes this concern is focused, rightly or wrongly, on foreign ownership of the 'commanding heights of the economy'—banking, transportation, telecommunications, steel, news media. In fact, United States investment is not important in these key sectors in either Australia or New Zealand, and other foreign investment is important only in banking. In Canada, a United States company has a major, though non-controlling interest in telecommunications, but United States companies have only a small stake in banking, transportation, steel, and news media.

In both Canada and Australia, however, many other important industries are substantially American owned. At first sight, the extent of 'American control' over these economies is therefore substantial also. Certainly many investment decisions affecting Canada and Australia are taken in Detroit and New York rather than in Toronto and Sydney. But as long as the markets of Canada and Australia remain actually or potentially distinct from that of the United States, American subsidiaries will normally behave in substantially the same manner as do locally-owned companies. This is particularly true in import-replacing manufacturing industries, presumably because the governments of both Australia and Canada have regulated and taxed the flow of imports very much more often than they have that of exports. As long as both countries

---

[91] Caves and Reuber have produced evidence suggesting that the Canadian current account balance adjusts rather well to exogenous changes in the inflow of direct investment under 'average conditions' (Caves and Reuber, *Canadian Economic Policy and the Impact of International Capital Flows*, pp. 40-1). The New Zealand Department of Statistics long ago noted that, for that country, there seemed to be an inverse correlation between the volume of direct investment and the size of the current account balance, a decrease in that balance (an increase in the deficit) frequently coinciding with an increase in the inflow of direct investment and vice versa (Donald T. Brash, *New Zealand's Debt Servicing Capacity* (Christchurch: University of Canterbury, 1964, pp. 19-20)).

retain basically free enterprise economies, important investment decisions will continue to give the appearance of being made in the United States. As long as both countries remain sovereign states, however, with control over their own monetary and fiscal policy, tariffs, sales taxes, export taxes, consumer credit regulations, mining regulations and all the rest, the essential decisions will continue to be made in Ottawa and Canberra.[92]

Is there not a threat to the sovereignty of all countries in receipt of American private investment from the fact that American-owned companies abroad are regarded as being subject to American law by the United States government? This problem of extraterritoriality has given rise to conflicts between the United States and countries in receipt of American investment over three main issues. The first has been over antitrust law; the second, exporting to communist countries; and the third, United States balance of payments safeguards.

It would be idle to deny that in all three areas the United States has attempted to control the behaviour of American-owned companies incorporated and legally resident in foreign countries. It will be difficult to make a lasting improvement in the political climate for United States capital abroad until the United States government renounces its right to exercise such control. But that granted, it is easy to exaggerate the practical significance of the extraterritoriality issue, at least for Canada and Australasia.

To begin with, the extraterritorial extension of United States antitrust law has had some clear advantages for all three countries. In the absence of vigorous domestic legislation to inhibit restrictive trade practices, the extension of United States antitrust law is known to have broken monopolies and prevented acquisitions in Canada,[93] and to have reduced participation in industry pricing agreements and deterred parent company restrictions on export freedom in Australia.[94] In the case of Canada, moreover, the United States government has entered into an informal bilateral agreement with the Canadian government designed to reduce the tension caused by the extension of its antitrust laws into Canada.

United States control on exports to communist countries, especially severe on exports to mainland China and to Cuba, would probably have had a rather limited practical impact on total exports even had it been rigidly enforced. In practice it has not been possible to enforce the law

---

[92] See also Donald T. Brash, 'American Investment and Australian Sovereignty', in Richard Preston (ed.), *Contemporary Australia* (Durham: Duke University Commonwealth Studies Center, 1969), pp. 547-8, 550-2.

[93] See I. A. Litvak and C. J. Maule, 'Conflict Resolution and Extraterritoriality', *Journal of Conflict Resolution*, September 1969, especially pp. 315-16. These writers note that 'an exhaustive study . . . has failed to uncover any detrimental economic effects in Canada when United States court decisions affect the ownership and structure of Canadian industries'.

[94] Brash, *American Investment in Australian Industry*, pp. 190-1, 226.

rigidly, at least on United States-affiliated companies in Australia.[95] Perhaps in recognition of this, perhaps in an attempt to improve relations with both China and the countries where American-affiliated companies operate, the United States government partially lifted its controls on what United States foreign subsidiaries could export to mainland China in December 1969.[96]

As far as the United States balance of payments safeguards are concerned, Canada was exempted from the more objectionable provisions (though only after a substantial outflow of funds to the United States),[97] and Australia promptly took apparently effective action to combat their effects. In New Zealand, the government has long exercised control over capital raised by locally incorporated companies. Deane asserts that the possibility that a company is raising capital in New Zealand primarily to repay a foreign debt is explicitly examined in the exercise of this control.[98]

How should we assess the cultural and more intangible political impact of American investment? Many of these are extraordinarily difficult to analyse. Is the Americanisation of the Canadian way of life the result of American investment, for example, or the result of the fact that most Canadians can watch American television, listen to American radio, see American movies, and read American magazines and newspapers as easily as they can Canadian? One could well argue that it is the very fact that Canadians are so familiar with American products through these media, coupled with Canadian tariff policy, that makes investment in Canada so attractive to American corporations.

It is clear that United States investment does act as a vehicle for the spread of American culture in a broad sense, though its precise role is impossible to establish. It presumably also has some bearing on the foreign policies of the host countries, but this is even more difficult to establish: Canada, Australia and New Zealand have so many more obvious reasons for being closely allied with the United States that it is being unbelievably naïve to imagine that it is the presence of United States capital which is the primary explanation of their policies. Indeed, in Australia's case, it is partly the desire to strengthen its alliance with the United States which explains that country's past unqualified welcome to United States investment.

What, then, is the balance? For Australia and Canada, there can be

[95] Ibid., p. 230. It may well have been possible to exercise tighter control on subsidiaries in Canada because of their proximity; see Litvak and Maule, loc. cit., pp. 309-14.
[96] Foreign subsidiaries of United States corporations are now free to sell non-strategic goods to mainland China without prior United States Department of Commerce authorisation provided that these goods contain no parts or materials of United States origin and embody no unpublished United States technology. Where components of technology of United States origin are involved, authorisation is still required, but may be granted for quite a wide range of goods.
[97] See Litvak and Maule, loc. cit., pp. 317-18; also Safarian, op. cit., pp. 253-6.
[98] Deane, op. cit., p. 213.

little doubt that United States investment has been of enormous net benefit. It is almost impossible to imagine the Canadian economy without
American investment. After many years of substantial capital inflow,
Canada's balance of international indebtedness is now substantially less,
in relation to GNP, than in many periods in the past.[99] Interest and dividends due to foreign investors as a percentage of total Canadian export
earnings have also been declining in recent years.[1] Both indicators at
least suggest that capital inflow has given Canada a stronger economy, an
economy with the capacity, if Canada so chooses, to be less dependent on
foreign capital than formerly. It is surely significant that the report of the
Task Force on the Structure of Canadian Industry, which is often critical
of the role of United States investment, nevertheless recommends that one
of the main functions of a special agency to co-ordinate Canadian policies
on foreign investment should be to 'facilitate the entry of new multinational firms'.[2]

Australia also has derived great benefit from United States investment
—the enormous exports of minerals are currently the most spectacular
example, but the impact of United States capital on the manufacturing
sector is only marginally less exciting. The gain from the investment by
General Motors-Holden's alone would perhaps be enough to vindicate
Australia's past 'open-door' policy towards United States capital.[3]

Only in New Zealand must there remain real doubt about whether
United States investment has made a net contribution or not. There has
apparently been nothing comparable in New Zealand to the 'G.M.H.
effect' in Australia while the combination of heavy protection, market
fragmentation, and excessive demand has emasculated the benefits one
could otherwise have expected. Blame for the heavy protection and
excessive demand must, of course, lie not with United States investment
but with the New Zealand government.

Comments and Discussion

RODERICK DEANE opened the discussion: It is, I suppose, an inevitable
problem that one runs the risk of preaching to the converted. Accordingly, one should perhaps not be surprised that Brash seems to have
assumed that the benefits of foreign investment need not be spelt out in
as much detail as the so-called costs. After all, it is the costs which the
critics also concentrate upon, and Brash has done a good job of placing

[99] In 1964, Canada's net external indebtedness was equivalent to 42.4 per cent
of GNP, as compared with 100 per cent in 1926. (I. A. Litvak and C. J. Maule,
'Foreign Investment in Canada', in Litvak and Maule (eds.), *Foreign Investment:
The Experience of Host Countries* (New York: Praeger, 1970), p. 79).

[1] 'As a percentage of sales of goods and services abroad [interest and dividends
due foreign investors] have fallen from 16 per cent in the late 1920's and 25 per
cent in the 1930's to 9 per cent in 1957-65.' Task Force Report, p. 252.

[2] Ibid., p. 396.

[3] See, for example, Brash, *American Investment in Australian Industry*, pp. 197-
202.

the popular disadvantages in their appropriate empirical and theoretical context. But the job could possibly have been made a little easier if a more positive bias had been adopted. In particular, I should have liked to see some analysis of the effects of foreign investment along orthodox lines: that the decision by a foreigner to invest abroad is a decision to make available to the host country additional resources; that these claims may be over additional tangible resources, in the form of the capital inflow, or intangible factors, such as the various accompanying managerial and technical skills; and that direct investment, in constituting an addition to domestic savings, enables a host country to attain a given future stand-ard of living with a lower current sacrifice in terms of consumption fore-gone. Of course, the increment to income generated by direct overseas investment will be shared between foreign residents and domestic income earners. As for the latter, one thinks of taxation gains and the benefits derived from any external economies resulting from foreign investment. In at least some of these cases, and particularly in respect of the dis-semination of new techniques, skills and know-how, there has been a considerable body of evidence accumulated, especially on a case study basis. Brash might have spent a little more time setting the advantages against the costs, especially given the inadequacy of some of the critics' argument in respect of the claimed disadvantages.

My second major general impression is the superficial surprise a lay-man may record in reaction to what he may consider to be substantial inconsistencies in policymaking. Brash demonstrates clearly and logi-cally that many of the objections raised against foreign investment are of little substance. Furthermore, he employs a wide range of empirical information to refute many of the nationalists' claims. Much of the data used are now five to ten years old. Even given the lags one must expect in the policymaking arena, the rational expectation might have been for some easing in the official (and, probably, public) doubts about overseas capital devouring the countries under discussion. Yet, in fact, the position is quite the reverse. As the weight of evidence favouring direct investment builds up, so too do policies seem to be hardening. The empirical re-searcher is left pondering the futility of his efforts.

As Brash rightly emphasises, political and social considerations are just as important as the often misunderstood economic implications of a capital inflow. And given the persistence of the high levels of protection Brash mentions, officials and governments *must* be liable to disillusion-ment if they expect trade barriers to stimulate the growth and develop-ment of viable domestically owned and operated industrial sectors when in fact they seem to do more to encourage the rapid expansion of foreign-owned enterprises. Again, despite the evidence, the nationalist's ideal world continues to remain a good distance away from the reality he can manage to achieve by his direct controls. A similar situation prevails on the balance of payments front: it must always be easier to blame the so-called 'foreign capitalist' for one's problems than to face the inadequacy of one's own monetary and fiscal policies.

In a competitive environment, the benefits of overseas investment, implicit rather than explicit in Brash's chapter, can normally be expected to outweigh the costs, given that many of the latter may be relatively un-important. In other words, host countries should worry less over ques-tions of local share participation, foreign 'control' and 'domination', employment of too many non-residents, 'stifling' of local research and the associated 'undue' dependence on foreign know-how, 'excessive' profits (other than where elements of monopoly profits exist), 'over-priced' imports, too much domestic loan-raising by foreigners, onerous restrictions on exports, and so on. Instead the concern of host govern-ments should be biased towards problems pertinent to the whole economy, and not simply to the foreign-owned sector. The maximisation of gains from foreign capital is to be achieved in a similar way to the maximisation of benefits from domestic investment. This implies more attention to industrialisation policies generally, systems of protection, the nature of domestic market structures, overall monetary and fiscal man-agement, and the appropriateness of a country's foreign exchange rate.

Turning for a moment from the general to the particular, I must challenge Brash on a couple of points. First, I would question the blessing he gives to the Australian guidelines policy under which local borrowing by foreign companies requires official sanction. Voluntary controls of this type are discriminatory in more than one sense and suggest, yet again, that bureaucrats can do the job of funds allocation more efficiently than the market system. I remain unconvinced on this score. Not only are foreign companies discriminated against *vis-à-vis* domestic firms, but also co-operative foreign enterprises are discriminated against relative to those companies which fail to seek official approval for their Australian fund-raising operations. In Australia I imagine an example of the problems involved in this sort of policy would be in the finance company area, where presumably many firms must simply ignore the guidelines. In New Zealand, the matter is handled on the basis of the government's unfortunate philosophy that direct controls should be all-pervasive, and it has legislated accordingly. Some would feel this is even more objectionable than a voluntary program. New Zealand's repu-tation for favouring direct controls is obviously such that many assume everyone and everything is subject to them. Brash has erred slightly in that New Zealand-owned enterprises are not subject to Capital Issues Control. Finally, on the question of local borrowing, it seems that again the concern is primarily a reflection of inadequate host and home country policies in broader areas, especially those in respect of interest rates and exchange rates.

On the question of foreign control and local share participation, I would offer two observations. I agree that often the concern over foreign control is an irrelevant one given that the foreign enterprise cannot operate in a vacuum. Local rules and regulations must be observed. But, despite my own claim in the New Zealand study Brash mentions, where I suggested local share participation was usually little more than a sop to political nationalism, I must concede the possibility of conflicts of interests, some of which can be serious. In New Zealand, for instance, this has been a relevant argument in respect of at least one large company engaged primarily in exporting where it is quite clear that expansion in recent years has been inhibited by a foreign majority shareholding. But whether one or two such examples constitute a generalised case for local participation at all costs is quite another matter of course.

I guess these comments can be appropriately summed up with a point Brash made in his Australian study: the question is not so much whether foreign investment is good or bad; rather it is whether host countries are pursuing the sort of policies which will ensure the maximisation of the net benefits from a capital inflow, and this of course is where the doubts must exist. This raises the question of the usefulness of generalised conclusions, such as those Brash draws, when theory suggests the need to judge individual cases on their merits in any environment which is characterised by imperfect competition.

Subsequent discussion ranged over a number of issues including the justification for foreign investment guidelines; the origins of the Japanese approach to the foreign investment package; the role of foreign investment in resources development; the gain from foreign investment to Australia in postwar years; the appropriateness of foreign technology to local factor proportions; balance of payments problems; and the taxation problem posed by intra-company pricing.

Brash's defence of the Australian guidelines policy on foreign investment was attacked on two grounds. On the one hand, it was suggested that the problem of unfair access by large well-known international companies to the capital market could best be dealt with by the establishment of an institution such as the Australian Industries Development Corporation which could compete effectively on the international capital market for funds to be channelled to local firms. On the other hand, it was argued that foreign investment guidelines were not justified as a distortion-correcting measure when capital exporting countries imposed sanctions on capital export and encouraged borrowing in host country capital markets. From the recipient's viewpoint, it remained best to allow foreign firms to borrow wherever and as cheaply as they could. Brash said that, in his paper, he was not referring to the ability of Australian firms to borrow on the international capital market: rather it was the possibility that the sheer scale of borrowing by very large multinational corporations could so drain a small national capital market that local investors with no direct access to the international market could be starved of funds.

A Japanese participant contrasted the relatively favourable attitudes in Australia, Canada, and New Zealand to the cautious attitudes towards foreign investment in Japan. He and others felt that the contrast was explainable partly in terms of the easier social and cultural communication between these countries and the major capital exporters, so that xenophobic reaction was less pronounced, relative to Japan; and partly in terms of the different structure of actual or potential investment. Much of the investment in Australia, Canada, and New Zealand was in resource development, whereas, in Japan, it was potentially directed into import substituting manufacturing activity. In Japan, therefore, there was more concern that foreign investment might come to dominate import-competing industries without generating necessary development of exports. The automobile and computer industries were cited as problem cases. An Australian participant noted that there was significant foreign investment in import-competing industry in Australia, Canada, and New Zealand and similar concern about export development but without the same effect as in Japan. He suggested that there was another more obvious reason why Japan has been so hesitant about foreign investment, namely the protectionism of local manufacturing interests and the fear of direct foreign competition in a carefully protected domestic market.

This last comment led to the observation that the significant difference between Japan and other recipients of foreign investment is the presence in Japan of well established entrepreneurial resources. In consequence, Japan had the option of disaggregating the capital-technology-management package, of buying foreign technology separately, and of adapting it to local needs. The option does not exist over a wide range of economic activity for other host countries.

An American participant wondered why foreign investment was required for resource development projects in Australia and Canada, since it seemed unlikely that there was a lack of managerial or entrepreneurial capacity for these activities, and both countries were very creditworthy. In the case of developing mineral resources for export to Japan, there was also a guaranteed market and stable price conditions. Is there something amiss with the Australian capital market? Is there, indeed, a lack of entrepreneurship in the minerals extraction field? Or is it that Australians are nice easy-going people who do not like being hard-nosed and prefer to hire that talent from the United States?

Several factors were adduced to explain the role of foreign investment in the extractive industries in Australia and Canada. First, some resources were extremely costly to prove and market initially, and this required large amounts of risk capital. Iron ore was probably not such a case in Australia, despite the early marketing risks, but oil may have been. Next, there are economies in vertically integrated operations across national boundaries because of communications and information costs. Iron ore developments in the fifties in Canada were quoted as a case where production and exports were built on the market link established through a multinational corporation. An Australian participant developed this point with reference to the marketing arrangements and information systems within groups like Conzinc Riotinto of Australia or the Rio Tinto group. He also pointed out that, in mining, much of the ownership was British and Australian. The technology was well known and the management was largely Australian. This prompted the comment from another American participant that, although he could not be sure about Australians, he felt that perhaps Canadians were not such easy-going people if their record in the management of multinational corporations could be taken as evidence. The role of Australians and Canadians in the management of multinational corporations raises the question of why this management capacity has been directed into these particular channels.

One participant asked the counter-factual question: what would Australia's growth and industrial performance have been like if the Australian government had adopted a closed-door policy towards foreign investment in the postwar period? It was suggested that the motor car and electronics industries may well have developed more efficiently through concentration in Australian-owned firms rather than as they did, fragmented by foreign ownership. Several participants queried this approach to the problem and the evidence on which it was based. Brash said that all the evidence he had gathered suggested that the GMH venture involved significant technology import and capital import. It was true that GMH obtained a substantial overdraft to finance the Holden project, but it comprised only 10-15 per cent of the company's total assets. Could these factors have been obtained more cheaply? A.C.I. and other Australian firms certainly did not respond to the government incentives to manufacture a motor car in Australia at that time.

Other issues raised included the appropriateness of the foreign investor's technology to local conditions, a point which was related to the place of American investment in Japan in the early postwar period, and investment by Australia in smaller scale manufacturing ventures in South-East Asia now.

Most participants agreed that the balance of payments problems were not of great magnitude, although they could not be dismissed entirely. The particular argument which Brash used, namely that balance of payments issues were not a concern provided that the economy had the capacity to move resources from one sector to another without excessive cost seemed, to at least one participant, to beg the question.

Finally, some felt the problem that intra-firm pricing posed for taxation authorities was greater than Brash had suggested. The long litigation over the Shell case in Australia was one example. The problem was that, frequently, there was no appropriate benchmark whereby to measure the appropriateness of prices and, therefore, the declared tax burden. Brash agreed that this was a problem but suggested that the taxation authorities, in Australia for example, were in a strong position. He also agreed that, whilst export franchises may not in fact limit exports too severely, there was a strong case for pressing their elimination.

6 Direct Foreign Investment in Postwar Japan[1]

RYUTARO KOMIYA

Information and statistics are much more abundant in Japan than in most other countries,[2] and this is true of information on various aspects of foreign direct investment into Japan. A major source of information on foreign-owned enterprise in Japan is an annual census taken (since 1967) on foreign-owned corporations conducted by the Ministry of International Trade and Industry (MITI). An earlier study published in 1964 by MITI, another one published in 1965 by Nihon Keizai Chōsa Kyōgikai [Japan Economic Research Council], and the annual *Yearbooks on Foreign Investment into Japan* [*Gaishi Dōnyū Nenkan*] are also highly useful. The first section of this chapter is based mainly upon these publications.

Foreign-Owned Enterprise in Japan

There are relatively few foreign-owned enterprises operating in Japan. The most detailed census on foreign-owned enterprises identified 611 foreign-owned corporations in 1967. In 1969, questionnaires were collected from 665 firms.[3] The coverage is almost complete, since the

[1] Financial support from the Tokyo Centre for Economic Research is gratefully acknowledged.

[2] See H. H. Hedberg, *The Japanese Challenge* (German language edition) (Stockholm: Bonnier, 1969).

[3] A study in 1965 by Nihon Keizai Chōsa Kyōgikai (Japan Economic Research Council) gives a somewhat smaller total. A check of the list of foreign-owned companies attached to this study and that of the MITI census for 1969 reveals that the difference is primarily due to a more complete coverage of very small firms, particularly in trade, by the MITI census.

Compare the number of foreign-owned corporations in Japan with those in other countries: there were more than 4,000 companies, with foreign participation in West Germany (Deutsche Bundesbank *Monthly Report*, May 1969). Even in Sweden, which was not influenced much by the upsurge of American direct investment in Europe since 1960, because of its secluded position and the smallness of its population, 377 permits for establishing *new* foreign enterprises were issued by the central bank during the three years 1964 to 1966 (*Yearbook of Sveriges Riksbank*, Vol. LIX).

Japanese government keeps track of foreign direct investment through foreign exchange regulations. The census does not cover independent proprietors of foreign nationality operating in Japan, but they are by and large insignificant.

The MITI census definition of a foreign-owned corporation is based upon 15 per cent or more foreign ownership for 1967, and 20 per cent or more for 1969. It covers only companies incorporated in Japan, and does not include branch offices or agencies of foreign corporations.

These foreign-owned enterprises were classified into three categories: about 30 per cent are 'pure' foreign, that is, companies with 100 per cent foreign ownership, most of which are small, and 60 per cent are 'joint ventures', that is, companies newly set up under contracts between Japanese and foreign parent companies. Slightly less than half of the 'joint ventures' are on a 50-50 basis. The rest are 'foreign-participation' companies, where foreigners have come to own a part (more than 15 or 20 per cent) of Japanese indigenous companies.

Most of these firms are small. In 1967, only 38 had more than 1,000 employees, 149 had capital between ¥100 million and ¥1 billion, 44 between ¥1 billion and ¥10 billion, and 7 had capital of more than ¥10 billion. In comparison, there were altogether 4,400 companies with capital between ¥100 million and ¥1 billion, and 950 with capital more than ¥1 billion, in Japan in 1967 (not including those in finance and insurance).

The foreign-owned enterprise is a relatively new phenomenon in Japan. Of 454 companies from which questionnaires were collected in 1967, 307 were established after 1961, 71 between 1956 and 1960, 51 between 1945 and 1955. Only 25 of them dated from prewar years. This means that in 1955 there were only 70 or 80 foreign-owned corporations in Japan.

Only few foreign enterprises overcame distance, cultural and linguistic barriers, and nationalistic attitudes of the government and people, to establish themselves in Japan before 1940. Moreover, some corporations which were first established with foreign participation have been naturalised; that is, the proportion of foreign ownership has diminished or even disappeared. This is partly due to government policies encouraging naturalisation. Also, as Japanese gained managerial experience and technical expertise, foreign ownership gradually lost its *raison d'être*. Nowadays there are quite a few such 'naturalised' corporations: Toshiba (a General Electric partner), Nihon Electric (Standard Electric), Fuji Electric (Siemens), Mitsubishi Electric (Westinghouse), Toyo Electric (English Electric), Nihon Victor (RCA Victor), Nihon Columbia (Columbia), Sumitomo Rubber (Dunlop), Yokohama Rubber (Goodrich), and Nihon Sheet Glass (Libbey Owens). Today these are all leading Japanese companies in their respective fields, and the average Japanese would not know that they were originally set up with a high degree of foreign participation.

On the other hand, although inward foreign direct investment is a relatively new phenomenon in Japan, it is not correct to think that inward direct investment is increasing rapidly at a constant and high rate. Table 6.1 indicates that the increase in the number of permits or the number of new companies established is not quite matched by the increase in the amount of investment. Apparently, many smaller foreign-owned companies have been established recently, or many permits for smaller amounts (say for additional stock issues) have been granted.

Foreign-owned corporations in Japan are predominantly American. Of 653 corporations for which 'nationality' is known in 1969, about two-thirds (405 companies) are American,[4] followed by Swiss (50 companies), German (35), British (35) and French (21). European countries altogether account for 182 companies (28 per cent). This is in contrast to the prewar situation, where Europe accounted for more than half the foreign firms in Japan.[5]

Table 6.1   Inward direct investment into Japan, 1955-69

	Inward direct investment in balance of payments statistics (IMF)[a] ($US million)	Equity capital obtained by foreign direct investors[b]	
		No. of permits issued	Amount authorised ($US million)
1955	6	9	2.3
1956	16	23	5.4
1957	32	22	7.2
1958	12	18	3.6
1959	18	21	14.5
1960	6	34	31.5
1961	44	41	40.2
1962	45	43	22.6
1963	88	92	42.7
1964	83	125	30.6
1965	47	106	44.6
1966	30	142	39.8
1967	45	169	29.8
1968	76	194	52.7
1969	72		

[a] Based upon IMF method, but does not include earnings reinvested.
[b] Authorisation under the *Gaishi-ho* [Law on Foreign Capital]. Does not cover the so-called 'yen-basis' investment. Figures are for fiscal years (April to March).

Source: Bank of Japan, *Monthly Bulletin of Balance of Payments Statistics* (various issues).

[4] This under-represents American nationality, since some of the Swiss, Canadian, Venezuelan, or Panamanian companies are in fact American.
[5] Similarly, of patents and know-how bought by Japanese firms 65 per cent (in terms of number of permits issued) are from American firms, whereas in prewar years America accounted for approximately 40 per cent and Germany 20 per cent.

Looking at it from the other side, in 1969, of the top 200 American manufacturing corporations in the *Fortune* list, 78 had subsidiaries (with more than 20 per cent participation) in Japan, although some subsidiaries were not in operation (for example, Nihon Ford) or insignificant. On the other hand, of the top 100 manufacturing corporations outside of the United States, 18 were Japanese, and only 14 of the rest (82) had subsidiaries in Japan.

Relative Share and Industry Pattern. How large is the share of foreign-owned corporations in the Japanese industry and trade, relative to Japanese indigenous companies? Table 6.2 gives two series of estimates for the relative share of foreign-owned companies in all Japanese corporations in terms of sales, profit after tax, total assets owned, net worth, and employment. Figures without parentheses are those for 127 companies which include almost all of the larger foreign-owned companies and are estimated to account for 81 per cent of the total sales of all (653) foreign-owned enterprises (with 20 per cent or more foreign ownership) in 1968, while figures in parentheses are for a more complete sample of 454 companies (with 15 per cent or more foreign ownership).

Table 6.2   Shares of foreign-owned corporations in sales, profit and assets in all Japanese corporations[a]

	1963	1964	1965	1966	1967	1968
All industries						
		1.3	1.4	1.4	1.4	1.4
Sales	(1.6)	(1.6)	(1.6)	(1.7)		
		1.3	2.5	2.2	2.4	3.0
Profit after tax	(2.4)	(1.7)	(3.0)	(2.7)		
		1.8	1.9	1.9	1.9	1.9
Assets	(2.3)	(2.3)	(2.4)	(2.3)		
Net worth	(3.0)	(3.0)	(3.2)	(3.2)		
Employees					0.4	0.5
Manufacturing						
		2.5	2.5	2.8	2.8	2.8
Sales	(3.0)	(3.0)	(3.2)	(3.3)		
		2.6	3.8	3.4	3.5	4.4
Profit after tax	(3.2)	(2.8)	(4.4)	(3.7)		
		3.1	3.2	3.4	3.4	3.6
Assets	(3.6)	(3.8)	(3.9)	(4.0)		
Net worth	(4.0)	(4.1)	(4.5)	(4.7)		
Employees					1.1	1.2

[a]Figures without parentheses are for 127 companies (published in April, *1970 Report*), and those in parentheses are for 454 companies (published in *1968 Report*). For a fuller explanation see text.

Sources: MITI Census, 1968 and April 1970 Reports.

Table 6.2 shows that the share of foreign-owned corporations, taken as a whole, is very small: they account for 1 to 3 per cent for all industries, and 2.5 to 4 per cent for manufacturing, depending on years and on how their share is measured. Their share has been increasing since 1963, but not too rapidly. The share in employment is disproportionately low, reflecting their operations in less labour-intensive and more capital-intensive industries (petroleum, chemicals, etc.). Table 6.2 also shows that they are on average more profitable than Japanese corporations in terms of the ratio of net profit to sales. This is because they operate in relatively capital-intensive fields where the 'turn-over ratio', the ratio of sales to total assets, is low. But they are less profitable than Japanese corporations in terms of net return on equity, which is perhaps a more meaningful measure of profitability. Apparently the ratio of net worth to total assets of foreign-owned corporations is higher than that of Japanese corporations, but not very much.

Lower profitability of foreign-owned than indigenous enterprises might be somewhat surprising. This is partly due to low profit rates in petroleum and rubber, two industries which account for about one-third of foreign direct investment in Japan (see Table 6.4).

Now consider the share of foreign-owned corporations in individual industries, given in Table 6.3. Foreign-owned corporations account for more than 10 per cent of total industry sales only in petroleum and rubber.

In petroleum, most of the leading refining companies are foreign-owned and operate on a 50-50 basis. The 50 per cent foreign-owned companies account for slightly more than half output in terms of the volume of refining. Exceptions are Idemitsu, which is owned by a

Table 6.3   Japan: shares of foreign-owned corporations[a] in sales for selected industries, 1964-8

Industry	1964	1965	1966	1967	1968
Foods	0.5	0.6	0.7	0.9	0.9
Chemicals	3.3	3.7	3.8	3.9	4.3
Medicines	6.2	6.7	7.4	8.4	8.0
Petroleum	62.2	60.0	58.5	59.6	58.8
Rubber	17.6	17.7	18.8	18.6	19.2
Non-ferrous metals	4.0	4.8	4.8	4.4	6.0
Machinery	4.2	4.4	5.7	5.1	5.7
Electrical machinery	2.5	2.4	2.9	3.3	3.2
All manufacturing (including others)	2.5	2.5	2.8	2.8	2.3
All industry	1.3	1.4	1.4	1.4	1.4

[a] 127 corporations. See footnote to Table 6.2 and text.

Source: MITI Census, April 1970.

Japanese family, highly successful and the leader in the volume of refining, and Maruzen, in which Union Oil (United States) is a minority (32 per cent) shareholder. MITI's policy towards energy supply in the postwar years has been to limit foreign ownership in petroleum refining to no more than 50 per cent while allowing 100 per cent ownership in marketing (as with Esso, Mobil and Shell), and also to encourage Japanese indigenous refiners. But most of the indigenous refiners except Idemitsu have been rather unsuccessful. In any case, the industry has tended to suffer from excessive investment, overcapacity and low profits, in recent years.

In rubber, the leading firm, Bridgestone, is indigenous (although Goodyear now owns 5 per cent) and highly profitable, while foreign companies own minority shares of the much less profitable followers: Yokohama (Goodrich owns 33.6 per cent), Sumitomo (Dunlop owned 100 per cent until 1959, and now owns 43.7 per cent), Otsu Tire (Firestone, 24 per cent) and Nitto Tire (U.S. Rubber, 25 per cent).

In chemicals, the majority of larger foreign-owned corporations are 'joint ventures'. Typically, in order to produce certain chemicals using patents and know-how owned by a foreign parent company within Japan, a joint-venture company with a Japanese chemical company is set up on a 50-50 basis (or with less than 50 per cent foreign ownership). This is partly a result of MITI's policy: foreign companies have generally been requested to seek a more than 50 per cent Japanese participation. The initiative, however, is taken more often by the Japanese side rather than from the foreign. There are many 100 per cent foreign-owned enterprises, but most of them are either very small or set up on the so-called 'yen basis' or perhaps a combination of both.

In medicines, 32 American, 14 Swiss, 13 German and several other world-famous pharmaceutical firms have subsidiaries in Japan, which produce patented products under licences from the parents. The share of foreign-owned corporations is about 10 per cent, but if only patented medicines are considered, the share is much higher.

The situation in machinery and in electrical machinery is more or less similar, except that in these industries, and particularly in the latter, foreign direct investment in Japan was already substantial before the war. As already mentioned, however, many companies which were originally established with a high degree of foreign participation have been 'naturalised'. Most of the larger companies in the Japanese electrical machinery industry operating since prewar years such as Toshiba, Mitsubishi, Fuji Electric, Nihon Electric, and Sumitomo, are naturalised. Notable exceptions are Hitachi and Matsushita. The latter was small in prewar years. Nihon Victor (established in 1927) and Nihon Columbia (1910) in musical records and stereo equipment were both established as 100 per cent subsidiaries originally but were completely naturalised in the 1930s: the former is now in the Matsushita group, and the latter in the Hitachi group. Both of them, especially the former, have been highly successful in the postwar years. Today in this field there are only three more than 50 per cent foreign-owned companies of any significance, all of which were established in prewar years: namely, Nihon I.B.M. (with capital of ¥19 billion in 1969, and 100 per cent foreign-owned), Nihon National Cash Register (¥5 billion, 70 per cent), and Toyo Otis Elevator (¥1.8 billion, 80 per cent).

The share of Nihon I.B.M. in Japan's electronic computer industry is about 40 per cent, by purchasers' expenditure between 1957 and 1964. A small part of this is domestically produced machines. Sperry Rand follows, with a share of about 16 per cent (no domestic production). The six Japanese indigenous firms comprise less than 40 per cent. The share of Japanese firms has been rising and perhaps passed 50 per cent recently. Protective government policy including import restrictions is an important factor behind this. But so far the success of Japanese firms has been mainly in smaller and medium type machines, and amongst the larger variety I.B.M. is still predominant.

Petroleum and chemicals (including medicines) account for approximately a quarter each of the total foreign direct investment in Japan, and electrical, transportation and other machinery accounts for another

Table 6.4   Japan: Foreign direct investment inflows[a] by industry, 1949-67

Industry	Number of permits issued	Total amount authorised ($US million)
Electrical machinery	102	28.9
Transportation machinery	24	25.6
Other machinery	242	26.9
Metals	48	22.7
Chemicals	178	87.8
Textiles	34	2.4
Petroleum	45	96.9
Rubber and leather	24	15.0
Construction	8	0.5
Glass, stone, clay and ceramics	24	7.0
Transportation and communication	20	0.6
Warehousing	1	0.0
Commerce	176	10.9
Service industries	34	0.9
Food manufacturing	22	6.5
Others	48	11.4
Total	1,013	334.1

[a] Does not include the 'yen-basis' investment.

Source: *Yearbook of Inward Foreign Direct Investment and Technology* [*Gaishi Donyū Nenkan*], 1968-9, pp. 188-9.

quarter: these five industries together account for about 80 per cent of the total (see Table 6.4).

Motives. In the 1967 census, the 'foreign-participation' companies and the Japanese-parent companies of the joint venture type foreign-owned companies were asked about their motives in entering the joint ventures or in inviting foreign companies to participate in their management. Out of 327 companies answering the question, 270 (83 per cent) mentioned 'the importation of foreign technology' and 195 mentioned it as the most important motive. 'The use of brands' came next, but was far less important: 129 companies mentioned it but only 25 as the most important motive. The use of brands is in most cases a secondary factor, accompanying new products or new technology. For manufacturing companies the technological incentive is naturally more significant: 229 companies (93 per cent) out of 246 mentioned it and 172 gave it as the most important reason.

On the other hand, foreign companies were asked about their motives for direct investment in Japan. The leading answer is 'growth potentiality of the Japanese market': 326 companies (79 per cent) out of 411 foreign companies mentioned it, and 242 (68) as the most important reason. Next comes 'growth potentiality of the Far Eastern and Asian market, and Japan's advantageous location in the region': 160 (39 per cent) checked it, but only 33 (9 per cent) as the most important factor.

Although a questionnaire survey of motives can be misleading and difficult to interpret, in this case the general pattern is quite clear. Very often these Japanese companies wanted just to purchase know-how and patents, but the foreign companies wanted to have management control, so that joint ventures were set up or foreigners bought into Japanese firms. From the foreigners' point of view, management control is often considered as mandatory or desirable in such a situation, for if just know-how and patents were sold without being accompanied by direct investment, this would, it is feared, simply strengthen Japanese firms as their competitors, not only in Japan or in the Far East but even in their home markets. Also, foreign firms want to share the profit which accrues from the use of new technology in a rapidly growing economy.

Export and Import. A remarkable characteristic of foreign-owned enterprise as compared with indigenous Japanese enterprise is its high degree of dependence on imports. As Table 6.5 shows, usually more than 40 per cent of its purchases of raw materials, parts, and merchandise are imports, and their share in national imports is disproportionately high, relative to their share in sales, in total assets (see Table 6.2) or in exports. Much of this is explained by the imported crude oil of the petroleum industry, but even if petroleum is excluded, the import ratio is believed to be around 25 per cent. Apparently, direct investment into Japan is primarily for the purpose of selling products, which are produced partly or almost wholly abroad, in Japan's domestic market. Investment is not so much aimed at exploiting cheaper labour or other favourable conditions for production in Japan, in order to export to the investors' home and other markets.

It is difficult to ascertain to what extent the poor export performance of foreign-owned enterprises is due to territorial restrictions on exporting. According to a questionnaire study, when a joint venture company is established a clause restricting the destination of export is usually included in the contract between Japanese and foreign parent companies. Of 255 joint venture companies answering the questionnaire, 125 had restrictions on exporting to North America, 118 to Europe, 112 to communist countries, and 82 on exporting to the home country of the parent. Thus, export restriction is widely practised but its character and impact are difficult to ascertain.

Effects on the Balance of Payments. It must not be inferred from the above that foreign direct investment into Japan deteriorates rather than improves Japan's balance of payments in the long run, apart from its initial impact in the year in which it takes place.

Table 6.6 is the balance of payments of foreign-owned enterprises in Japan, carefully prepared from MITI's census returns under certain plausible assumptions. While the table is interesting in itself, it does not reveal the effect of foreign inward direct investment upon Japan's balance of payments. This is because if, for example, foreign oil companies did not come to Japan (or were prohibited from doing so), Japanese indigenous companies would have more or less taken their place and have imported crude oil in much the same quantity. This may be true also of a part of royalties. The state of affairs which would have obtained if foreign-owned enterprises had not come into existence is highly conjectural and uncertain.

Table 6.5   Export and import of foreign-owned corporations in Japan (per cent)

	1963	1964	1965	1966	1967[a]	1968[a]
For foreign-owned enterprises						
Export/Total sales	4.8	5.4	6.5	6.9	6.0	6.8
Import/Total purchases of raw materials, etc.	46.8	45.8	43.2	41.5	39.6	37.9
Shares of foreign-owned in the national total						
Export	2.4	2.5	2.8	3.2		
Import	14.0	15.0	15.5	15.0		

[a] For 127 companies, from the 1969 Census.

Source: MITI Census, 1967: for 454 companies.

A partial equilibrium approach to the issue of direct investment and the balance of payments is misleading. The issue must be analysed by a general equilibrium approach.[6]

Differences and Similarities. There are several ways in which foreign-owned companies differ from indigenous ones. As already mentioned foreign-owned companies are generally new entrants in their respective fields and as such they are Schumpeterian 'innovators' in some aspect of their operation.

First, most of them brought new production technologies into Japan. In most cases, this is the very reason why they established in Japan. On the other hand, they tend to do less R and D within Japan than comparable Japanese indigenous firms, since they can rely on the parent company's R and D.[7]

Second, an example of 'innovation' in marketing is Coca-Cola's direct marketing method. The traditional Japanese retail and wholesale system is very complicated, particularly in the case of textiles, sundries or groceries. Products of a factory often go through several stages of merchanting before reaching retailers. Coca-Cola decided to skip over all this,

Table 6.6   Balance of payments of foreign-owned enterprises in Japan (¥ billion)

	1963	1964	1965	1966
Current account (A = B + C)	(—)277	(—)309	(—)307	(—)344
Commodity trade (B)	(—)251	(—)178	(—)275	(—)307
Export	48	64	87	112
Import	(—)299	(—)342	(—)362	(—)418
Invisibles (C)	(—) 26	(—) 30	(—) 32	(—) 37
Dividends	(—) 10	(—) 12	(—) 12	(—) 12
Interests	(—) 10	(—) 11	(—) 12	(—) 13
Royalties	(—) 7	(—) 7	(—) 8	(—) 12
Long-term capital account (D)	40	26	25	22
Equity capital	24	13	19	14
Bonds	7			
Long-term borrowing	16	13	5	8
Short-term capital account (E)	21	10	1	4
Total[a] (A + D + E)	(—)216	(—)273	(—)281	(—)317
	(11)	(—21)	(—14)	(—8)

[a] Figures in parentheses are the total when enterprises in the petroleum, rubber, and non-ferrous metals industries are excluded.

Source: MITI Census, 1967, pp. 46-7: for 454 companies.

[6] For example, a model of the balance of payments like the one used in Ryutaro Komiya, 'Economic Growth and the Balance of Payments: A Monetary Approach', *Journal of Political Economy*, Vol. 77, January-February 1969, may be used to analyse the effects of a shift in external factors giving rise to a flow of direct investment.

[7] There are of course exceptions. An extreme case is RCA Research Institute (100 per cent owned by RCA) which is engaged only in basic research. Since salaries of researchers are relatively low in Japan, more such direct investment in research establishments may take place in the future.

and to deliver to retailers and outlets directly from factories by its own delivery fleet. This highly successful marketing method is now employed by other foreign-owned and Japanese enterprises. Its impact on Japan's distributive system has been considerable. Another example is modernisation of the service network in construction machinery. Since around 1965, Caterpillar, Koehring, International Harvester and several others have established joint-venture companies in Japan. One of the results of competition is a vast improvement in customer service as well as in product quality.

Third, in finance and personnel management, the differences between foreign-owned and other Japanese companies are noticeable but not great. For example, the ratio of equity (book value) to total assets is very low in postwar Japan by American, European or prewar Japanese standards. It now stands below 20 per cent (the average for all corporations). The equity ratio for foreign-owned companies tends to be higher than the comparable Japanese indigenous firms, but not very much. In Japan, foreign-owned corporations too borrow very heavily from banks and other financial institutions, since this is an accepted and cheap financing method in Japan.

Weekly working hours are a little shorter, and wages are higher, within the foreign-owned (particularly within 100 per cent owned) than within indigenous companies. For example, five days (instead of the traditional five and a half days) is the more prevalent working week among foreign-owned firms. The quantitative differences in this regard, however, are not significant. The so-called *nenkō-joretsu* system is widely practised by Japanese firms. This is a seniority principle in the matter of promotion, and bureaucratic salary schedules are based upon educational backgrounds, age, and the number of years served in the company, instead of individual ability or performance. Also, the employment by a large, respectable firm (or a government ministry, a local government, or a university) is a matter of life-time commitment: once a firm employs a man, it not only keeps him until the age of retirement, but also promotes him and raises his salary in due course. For employees too, it is difficult and unusual to move from one firm to another before the stipulated age of retirement. Recent trends are away from these traditional practices, but the old custom is very difficult to change. Foreign-owned companies largely accept this Japanese custom in their personnel management. Some of the smaller, 100 per cent owned companies try to emphasise personal achievement, but personnel management of larger, well established foreign-owned companies is little different from that of their Japanese competitors. This is a field in which it is very difficult for a single firm to 'innovate'.

Disadvantage for Foreign Direct Investors. The *nenkō-joretsu* system means that there is only a very thin labour market for top or middle managers, engineers and even skilled workers except the market for new high school or university graduates. The companies recruit young personnel and train them within the firm, to fill the posts of top management or chief engineers after twenty or twenty-five years of service in the company.

This system presents a handicap to newcomers, particularly foreigners. Few fresh graduates of leading universities prefer employment in new foreign-owned companies even when offered a high salary, since foreign companies cannot (or so Japanese think) offer security and stability under the *nenkō-joretsu* system. Also, what happens if the foreign investor decides to withdraw, say, after five years?

A 50-50 joint venture is a solution to this difficulty. Necessary personnel at various levels for the new company is provided by the Japanese parent company under the *shukko* [temporary transfer] system. For example, when a young executive of the parent company works in the joint venture company for a certain length of time, he is considered to be within the *nenkō-joretsu* system of the parent company, all his interests being guaranteed. The parent company steps up employment of new graduates and promotion to fill the vacancies due to *shukko*. This is an important reason, quite apart from the government's policy, why the joint-venture type of foreign investment is preferred to 100 per cent ownership.

Foreign and Japanese Managers. The 1967 census of foreign-owned enterprises detailed information on 3,057 directors serving in foreign-owned companies. It shows that 42.9 per cent are those who are 'related' to foreign parent companies, 36.7 per cent are related to the Japanese parent company, and 20.5 per cent are others (Japanese directors serving 'pure foreign', or 'foreign participation'). But it is misleading to think that the management of a foreign-owned company is typically dominated by foreigners.

First, less than one-fifth of 'those related to foreign parents' are non-managing directors who only sit on the board of directors; a majority of Japanese directors are 'inside' directors who execute daily business.

Second, although I have checked only a limited number of cases, my general impression is that a high proportion of foreign-nominated directors is confined mostly to nearly 100 per cent foreign-owned companies, most of which are very small. Most large, well established foreign-owned companies appoint a Japanese as president. Having a foreign president has several disadvantages in doing business in Japan. The majority of directors of such companies are Japanese. For example, in the case of Nihon I.B.M. which is a 'pure foreign' company, the president, executive vice-president and all directors but one are Japanese.

Third, the proportion of foreign-nominated tends to be higher in new companies than in older ones. Once the business is well established, it becomes less urgent to send directors from the home country, who are much more expensive altogether than nationals.

Fourth, a foreign-nominated director does not necessarily have the same nationality as the foreign parent company. He may be recruited from anywhere in the world, and many of them are Japanese.

On the other hand, the proportions of foreign and Japanese managers of a company do not tell much about whether foreigners or Japanese really control the company. Most key decisions may be made by foreign parents even when most directors are Japanese. By and large, such a question often makes little sense. The purpose of the management is to earn profits and grow, whether controlled by foreigners or Japanese, and those who can manage well will dominate the management in the long run.

Frictions. So far there are very few cases of frictions or complaints against foreign-owned enterprises. There is no case like discharging employees by General Motors and Remington Rand in France in 1962, the G. E. Ball case, or a few other cases hotly discussed in Europe some time ago. This is not at all surprising, since the government has so far been highly selective and restrictive.

There are two cases, however, in which, in Japanese opinion, foreign direct investors used unfair, predatory techniques. What happened precisely is not clear, but it is vaguely believed to be as follows. In each case, one large American firm making beds and furniture, and another making floor wax, offered a certain licensing contract to a small, family-owned Japanese company, and at the same time bought minority shareholdings and sent managers. American managers urged the adoption of an expansionary policy, whereby the company ran into financial difficulties. To fill the losses and to continue the expansionary policy, the American parent company proposed an issue of new stocks. The Japanese owner found that he could not but agree, even though he did not have enough money to keep his majority. The American company became the majority owner, and the Japanese family was ousted from the management. The American obtained valuable production and distribution facilities in Japan very cheaply.

Somewhat similar, more well-known cases are those of Honen-Lever and Nichiro-Heinz. Honen and Nichiro, both large Japanese companies in food manufacturing, set up a joint venture in which they had the majority ownership: Honen (55 per cent) with Unilever (45 per cent) in 1964, and Nichiro (51 per cent) with Heinz (49 per cent) in 1965. Afterwards, financial difficulties of the joint ventures and new issues of stocks led to 'takeovers by foreign capitalists'. Unilever obtained 80 per cent in 1967, and Heinz 80 per cent in the same year.

On the other hand, complaints by foreign direct investors against the Japanese government and particularly MITI are widespread and sometimes bitter. But they are almost all concerned with restrictions on new or additional investment, expansion into new fields, or the use of new technology. In other words, the government agencies do not seem to have interfered with foreign-owned companies once they have had their operations authorised. As far as I know there is no case in which a permit was revoked or in which a foreign-owned company was asked to curtail its operation.

Government Policy

There are several sources describing the Japanese government's regulations on foreign direct investment in detail. Most of the more detailed sources are in Japanese, but one published by the OECD is in English.[8] As far as the factual information is concerned, I have little to add to the OECD study, to which readers are referred. Following are some general observations on Japanese government policy towards direct capital inflow.

'Yen-Basis' Investment. In the early postwar period the government's major concern with foreign direct investment seemed to be the balance of payments. Although a foreign investment inflow improves the balance of payments in the year in which it takes place, the government feared, it seems, that payments of dividends and liquidation in later years would be a substantial burden, or a destabilising factor.

In any case, until around 1960, foreign direct investment into Japan was very much limited (see Table 6.1). The future of the Japanese economy was uncertain in the beginning, and in general Japan was little known abroad. Moreover, imports were severely controlled until 'import liberalisation measures' which were taken between 1960 and 1963.[9] Japanese commercial policy before 1960 was to import only what the government considered essential: those raw materials, fuels and machinery which could not be produced in Japan. Under such circumstances, there was little room for direct investment which is heavily dependent on imports.

The government's concern with the balance of payments is reflected in the 'yen-basis' provision adopted from October 1956 to June 1963. Under this provision foreigners were free to establish a company (both 100 per cent owned and partly owned) in Japan or buy newly issued stocks of a company established under this provision, provided that earnings from investment or liquidation proceeds would not be remitted abroad. The earnings or liquidation proceeds should be accumulated and reinvested in yen, within Japan. A few industries such as banking, mining,

8 OECD, *Enquiry into the Regulations and Conditions Governing Certain International Capital Movements in Japan*, Committee for Invisible Transactions, Paris, March 1967.
9 Japan became an Article XI member of GATT in 1963.

electric power, gas and water supply, railway and marine transportation were excepted, but shipbuilding was the only excepted industry within the manufacturing sector.

Apart from those long established since prewar years, most of the large, more than 50 per cent foreign-owned companies such as Nihon I.B.M., Esso (100 per cent), Mobil Oil (100 per cent), Nestle Japan (100 per cent), Nihon Olivetti (100 per cent), Teikoku Oxygen (82 per cent owned by Société L'Air Liquide) were established or expanded (by new stock issues) under this 'yen-basis' provision between 1956 and 1963.

Since foreign exchange dealings for this yen-basis direct investment were automatically authorised by the Bank of Japan, few statistics were compiled of the yen-basis transactions, and some government statistics on inward direct investment do not include them (for example, Table 6.1, columns 2 and 3, and Table 6.4).

As rapid growth of the Japanese economy attracted more and more attention abroad, there was a rush, though small in scale, of foreign enterprises coming to Japan after about 1960. According to a survey undertaken by the government in June 1963 when the yen-basis provision was abolished, there were 289 foreign-owned companies established under that provision as compared with about 150 companies authorised under the *Gaishi-ho* [Law on Foreign Capital] to establish or enter 'foreign-participation' after obtaining individual permits. The latter procedure is necessary when a foreign company buys stocks of already existing Japanese companies, or when the foreign investor wants to remit abroad earnings and liquidation yields freely.

The government and particularly MITI was naturally alarmed and abolished the provision, thereby inviting criticism from foreign governments and the OECD for going backward when the world was endeavouring to advance its effort towards capital liberalisation. The abolition of the provision was urgent from MITI's viewpoint, however. First, when Japan became an Article 8 member of IMF,[10] the remittance of earnings would be liberalised. Then the remaining difference between the yen-basis and *Gaishi-ho* companies would be only in regard to liquidation procedures. But, generally, foreign direct investors have a long time-horizon, and will not invest unless there is a good prospect of profitable business for at least 20 years and possibly for 30 or more years. The restriction on remitting liquidation proceeds is no serious obstacle to foreign direct investors, so long as the country's general economic and political conditions are stable and prosperous. If this is not the case, direct investors shy away whether or not the government guarantees the remittance of liquidation proceeds.

Second, even if the restriction on remittance of earnings and liquidation

[10] This took place in 1964.

proceeds were continued, when imports including invisibles are fully liberalised, foreign investors may be able to repatriate profits and even principal through underinvoicing and overinvoicing. The government can quarrel with the foreign-owned companies on the transfer prices, and tax collectors of some countries do this,[11] but it is cumbersome and is not very effective anyway.

Liberalisation Measures. Since Japan began negotiations to become a member of OECD in 1964, the Japanese government has often been urged by OECD to abolish or reduce restrictions on capital movement and especially on inward direct investment. The United States government and businessmen often requested the Japanese government to change its restrictive policy, which is, in their view, a violation of the Japanese-American Commerce and Navigation Treaty of 1953, and the issue became a regular item in the annual Japanese-United States meeting of Cabinet members after 1965.

Responding to these requests, the Japanese government decided to liberalise inward direct investment gradually, and put into force the 'First Liberalisation Measures' in July 1967 and the 'Second Liberalisation Measures' in February 1969, and prepared the Third Measures for September-October 1970. The essential points of the First Liberalisation Measures are two. First, two groups of 'liberalised industries' are enumerated. In the first group, the government automatically authorises the foreign investor to establish a new joint venture with a Japanese company when the foreign ownership is no more than 50 per cent, unless it is exceptionally harmful to Japan's national interests. There are few other conditions to ensure that the joint-venture company be not dominated by the foreign parent, or that it be not a disguised form of takeover. In the second group, foreign ownership up to 100 per cent is to be authorised.

Second, inward portfolio investments by foreigners in stocks of a Japanese company are automatically authorised up to 20 per cent (15 per cent in a few 'restricted industries' such as banking, electric power, etc.) of the total stocks issued by that company. Purchase by one individual is, however, limited to no more than 7 per cent. Previously these limits were 15 per cent (10 per cent) and 5 per cent respectively.

The Second Liberalisation Measures simply added more industries to the first and second groups of 'liberalised industries' above or reclassified some industries from the first to the second group. The Third Measures follow the same pattern, and raise the limits for portfolio investment.

Thus, liberalisation is concerned with newly establishing a company.

---

[11] Japan's tax agencies do not seem to have bothered foreign-owned companies or themselves much with this. This is because the problem arises mainly in the case of 100 per cent owned subsidiaries, whereas there are few large 100 per cent foreign-owned companies.

Takeovers of, or agreed participation by foreigners in existing Japanese companies are still to be screened case by case as before, although the government promised, in the announcement of the First Liberalisation Measures, more 'flexible' judgment, more simplified procedures, and faster decisions.

Whether the Liberalisation Measures constitute an important step toward liberalisation depends on the number and names of industries included in the two 'liberalised groups'. My view is that the liberalisation policies so far taken, that is, the First and Second Measures, amount to little. The government so far has selected only those industries in which Japanese firms are considered competitively strong enough *vis-à-vis* foreign firms, or where inward direct investment is least likely to take place.[12] From July 1967 when the First Liberalisation Measures were put into force until December 1968, there are just four cases of joint ventures which came under the new provision.[13] All of them are 50-50 owned, there being no instance of a 100 per cent foreign owned company established under the new provision.

The situation will change substantially when the Third Measures are carried into effect. The Third Measures will be far more extensive than the First and Second. Probably only a limited number of industries will remain non-liberalised, and most industries will be included in the first (50 per cent) liberalised group.

Screening of Capital Inflow. So far most inward direct investments into Japan are those which have gone through a case-by-case screening process by the Japanese government. While there is fairly detailed information on cases approved by the government, little is known about applications that were turned down. The OECD study, referred to earlier, cites information from MITI that 453 applications for inward direct investment were filed between April 1962 and March 1966, of which 83.6 per cent were approved, 8.6 per cent were withdrawn, and 7.7 per cent were still under consideration at the end of October 1966. Needless to say, these figures do not tell much. One does not bother to file an application which has no chance of approval. Withdrawals may be due to what amounts to the government's refusal, and those approved may or may not have undergone substantial changes on the 'advice' of the government.

---

[12] When the First Liberalisation Measures were announced, I wrote in a weekly economic periodical (in Japanese) that 'This is not to liberalise ... If it is simply to make a long list of "liberalised industries", why not enumerate *sake* (Japanese rice wine), soya-sauce, *miso* (Japanese bean paste) and what not?' To my surprise, both *sake* brewing and soya-sauce manufacturing were added to the 100 per cent liberalised group in the Second Measures a year later!

[13] According to *Yearbook on Foreign Direct Investment for 1968-69.* The total number of newly established foreign-owned companies (including new 'foreign-participation' companies) given in MITI's census is 49 for July 1967 to June 1968, and 81 for July 1968 to June 1969. Another source gives 18 cases of investment in 'liberalised' industries as compared with 287 cases altogether for the three years 1967 to 1969.

Foreigners often complain that the criteria or standards according to which the Japanese government approves, requests changes to, or turns down applications have never been made clear in an official document,[14] that the reasons of refusal are only vaguely stated orally and not explicitly written down, and that the rules which the government officials use in screening applications and negotiating for changes in applications with applicants have never been explained. It seems to me that, as in many other similar cases with the Japanese government, the officials do not have, or do not know, any firm and precise criteria upon which they themselves are making decisions. There seem to be only vague standards which have been changing over time.

Although there are cases of more than 50 per cent foreign ownership of large companies, such as I.B.M., Nestle, National Cash Register, Esso, Mobil, Shell and some others, they are very few and almost all of them were either established in prewar years or were yen-basis companies. Apart from smaller enterprises, the government approved under the *Gaishi-ho* screening procedure the establishment of few if any large companies which were more than 50 per cent foreign-owned.

It is not correct to say, however, that no more than 50 per cent ownership is the principle to which the Japanese government adheres. As mentioned above, the Liberalisation Measures explicitly designated the 'second group' of liberalised industries, in which foreign ownership of newly established companies up to 100 per cent is automatically approved. But the 'second group' so far has included only those industries where Japanese enterprises are highly competitive in the world market and foreign direct investment in Japan is unlikely, or where firms are small and numerous and foreign control of the industry is most unlikely. Examples of the first type are iron and steel, motorcycles, shipbuilding, pianos, watches, and cement, not to speak of *sake* or soya-sauce. Those of the second type are beauty parlours, barber shops, tourist services, construction consultants.

The principle behind government policy here is, therefore, to limit more than 50 per cent foreign ownership in case possibilities exist for domination of an industry by a few large foreign-owned enterprises.

For the same reason, government policies are intended to protect the existing Japanese managements in various ways. The Liberalisation Measures are concerned only with newly established foreign-owned companies, and takeovers of or 'foreign-participation' in existing Japanese companies continue to be screened case by case as before. There is a clause to guarantee that a new company in the 'liberalised' industries is

---

[14] In a document presented to OECD, the Japanese government mentioned three basic standards applied in screening which are so general and vague as to amount to nothing: namely (a) co-ordination of industrial development, (b) maintenance of full employment, and (c) domestic as well as external financial and monetary equilibrium.

not a disguised form of takeover. Also, when a 50-50 joint-venture company is established in the up to 50 per cent liberalised industry, 50 per cent of the Japanese side must be owned by Japanese companies operating in the same industry, and 30 per cent must be owned by a single Japanese parent.

Strategic Industries. The government's concern with foreign domination has been greatest in the case of 'strategic industries'. A 'strategic industry' means a new, technologically advanced industry where only a very small number of enterprises in the world have succeeded in profitable exploitation of new technological innovations. Automobiles, petroleum, petrochemicals, certain chemicals, electronics in general and particularly computers and integrated circuits, and atomic energy have been considered 'strategic' industries by the government at one time or another in the postwar years. The government is seriously concerned particularly with the situation in which only a few giant enterprises dominate all over the world, as in automobiles or computers.

The government has been eager to promote Japanese-controlled enterprises in these areas, so that Japanese indigenous enterprises can become competitive and share the benefits resulting from rapid technological advances and their growth potential.

Small Business and Business Disruption. Another important element in the government policy towards foreign investment is to protect small business and avoid disorderly conditions in areas hitherto dominated by small- or medium-sized firms. When a plan is made public to set up a large joint venture or a 'pure foreign' company in such an industry, usually small firms in the related industries which are supposed to be adversely affected naturally protest against the plan and request the government to stop or to limit the 'inroad' of foreign capital into Japan. The government has often responded to such a request and taken restrictive measures. Sewing machines, beverages (Coca-Cola), bakery products and other foods, and the retail trade (supermarkets) are examples of industries where this factor has played an important role.

The following are a few typical, recent examples where the Japanese government intervened purposefully. In 1964 Texas Instruments filed an application for establishing a 100 per cent owned subsidiary to produce semi-conductors in Japan. In 1966 MITI advised that approval for the investment would be granted if Texas Instruments agreed to set up a 50-50 joint venture with some Japanese firm instead of a 'pure foreign' subsidiary, to offer to other Japanese producers the patents on integrated circuits owned by Texas Instruments at a reasonable rate of royalties, and to limit the output of integrated circuits for three years after beginning operation. The government intention to promote Japanese 'infant firms' or 'embryo firms' in this area is obvious. The American government sent a letter to the Japanese government protesting that this was a violation of the American-Japanese Commerce and Navigation Treaty. In 1968 Texas Instruments made public its plan to set up a 50-50 joint venture with Sony, and at the same time to license Toshiba, Hitachi, Mitsubishi, and Nihon Electric, and the matter was 'solved'.

In 1968, Borg-Warner and Aishin applied for the establishment of a joint venture in which Borg-Warner was to produce automatic transmissions. Aishin is a subsidiary of Toyota, making automatic transmissions and other parts for Toyota cars. MITI objected to the share Borg-Warner wanted in the joint venture, which was 51 per cent.

When MITI simply delayed decision, Borg-Warner asserted that Aishin's transmission infringed upon Borg-Warner's patent rights. There were rumours that Borg-Warner was going to abandon setting up a subsidiary and to sue Aishin for damages instead. In the meantime, Ford (50 per cent), Nissan (25 per cent), and Toyo-Kogyo (25 per cent) set up a joint venture called Nihon Automatic Transmission to produce automatic transmissions in Japan, which was quickly approved by MITI in December 1969. Nissan cars had been equipped with Borg-Warner transmissions, but they will now use Nihon Automatic Transmissions. Borg-Warner decided to concede, and accepted a 50-50 split. A year and three months after Borg-Warner first applied to establish a subsidiary, MITI approved it on a 50-50 basis.

Fairchild obtained a permit from the Okinawa government for producing integrated circuits in Okinawa in 1969, and recently announced a plan for large-scale production there. This is in anticipation of the retrocession of Okinawa to Japan in 1972. Once established in Okinawa, Fairchild can come to the Japanese mainland after the retrocession.

MITI immediately responded to this move by Fairchild, and according to newspaper reports, notified Fairchild that unless the latter changes its plan MITI will 'retaliate' through import restrictions on Fairchild's integrated circuits and by not allowing Fairchild to license, or to set up joint ventures with, Japanese firms. From MITI's point of view, this is consistent with its earlier attitude toward Texas Instruments. The case is under negotiation.

In December 1969, Nabisco applied to the Japanese government to set up a 50 per cent owned joint venture subsidiary with Yamazaki (40 per cent) and Nichimen (10 per cent): the former is a large bakery and confectionery company while the latter is one of the giant Japanese trading companies. Instead of MITI, the Ministry of Agriculture, which is said to be much more protectionist than MITI, is in charge of the case. In the bakery and confectionery industry there are many small firms, and they strongly oppose this new joint venture. The Ministry of Agriculture is reported to have requested two conditions: first, that Nabisco-Yamazaki shall not use the Nabisco brands before liberalisation of the bakery and confectionery industry, and second, that the ownership shares should change to 45 per cent Nabisco, 45 per cent Yamazaki and 10 per cent Nichimen. Negotiations are now under way.

Regulations on Patent and Know-how Licensing. Closely related to the Japanese government's restrictive policy on inward direct investment is its similar policy on patent and know-how contracts. Almost every such contract licensing Japanese firms to use patents, know-how, or brands owned by foreigners used to go through a case-by-case screening process until June 1968. Since then the Liberalisation Measures were put into force. Contracts on technology in petrochemicals, electronic computers, atomic energy, space and aeronautics, and a few other industries are to be screened as before. Others are automatically approved within a month, 'unless [they have] seriously harmful effects on the Japanese economy'.

The government policy in screening these contracts in recent years is very similar to its policy on direct investment: to protect Japanese firms and to ensure 'orderly' development of the Japanese industries. The criteria explained above fully apply here also.

According to the OECD publication mentioned earlier, from April 1962 to March 1966 the government received 1,968 applications, approved 90.7 per cent, and turned down 4.6 per cent of them. The rest (4.7 per cent) were still under consideration at the end of October 1967.

The government sometimes requests lower rates of royalty or initial payments, amendments to export franchise clauses, or the so-called minimum payments clauses.

The Majority View

Since it strongly influences the Japanese government's policy and businessmen's attitude toward foreign direct investment, a brief explanation of the prevalent majority view of foreign direct investment may be of some help to foreigners.

It is generally believed that the overall strength, called variously 'capital power', financial power, managerial power, 'technological power' or R and D power, of large foreign corporations far surpasses that of their Japanese equivalents. The sheer size of large foreign corporations, particularly multinational or world enterprises, is a source of economies of scale enjoyed only by them. They have great strength in R and D, and the technological gap, as reflected in the R and D expenditure per capita or per employee. So long as there is such a gap in 'capital power' or in R and D, liberalisation of inward direct investment will lead to foreign domination or monopolisation of Japanese industry.

Most serious is a great gap in technology. Until recently, the government's restrictive policy both on direct investment and on patent and know-how contracts has resulted in the establishment of many joint ventures. But when direct investment is liberalised, large foreign enterprises will not be interested in joint ventures but will establish 100 per

cent subsidiaries instead. Japanese firms will be excluded from technological progress, and foreigners will have monopolies based upon patent
rights and technological superiority.

Another weakness of Japanese corporations is a high debt to equity
ratio. This means the firm must pay a large amount of interest even in
depression or recession periods. The average ratio of debt to total assets
for all Japanese corporations has steadily been declining in postwar
years, and now stands below 20 per cent, whereas the ratio for large
foreign corporations is much higher.

Particularly undesirable is a takeover of a Japanese firm by a foreign
firm, since in this case, unlike the case where a new company is established, no immediate increase in employment nor immediate import of
technology takes place, and Japanese control is lost.

There are several other undesirable aspects of foreign direct investment. For one thing, foreign multinational corporations concentrate
research and development in their home countries, whereas Japanese
corporations, even if less efficient in the short run, contribute to technological development in Japan in the long run. Also, the foreign newcomers often practise dumping, disturb 'orderly business conditions', and
lead to the bankruptcy of small enterprises.

It is feared, particularly by government officials, that foreigners may
not co-operate with the Japanese government in its effort to achieve
policy objectives. The government administration in Japan often takes
the form of informal regulations and 'persuasion' which Japanese firms
obey readily. This is because intimate relations with the government pay
in the long run (or disobedience invites retaliation). But foreigners may
not obey, giving rise to difficulties for the government in the administration of policy.

For these reasons, before liberalising inward direct investment, the
overall strength of Japanese firms must be enhanced through 'industrial
reorganisation', that is, mergers and industry-wide co-operation programs, development of 'R and D power', 'structural improvement' of
small business, and so on.

Many government officials, particularly those in MITI, businessmen
and journalists consider liberalisation of inward direct investment as a
sacrifice which Japan must pay for international co-operation or for her
membership in the community of advanced industrialised nations, rather
than a benefit to Japan in itself.

Recently the general climate has gradually been changing somewhat, as
more and more businessmen and others meet Americans and Europeans
and are told that free direct investment is a commonplace in Europe and
elsewhere. Recently *Keizai Dantai Rengokai* [The Council of Economic
Associations], a highly influential organisation which represents the
Japanese business community, issued a statement urging a faster and

more extensive liberalisation policy in the Third Liberalisation Measures. But even in this statement, the emphasis is laid not on the inherent benefits resulting from freedom of direct investment, but on meeting the request of other leading nations and creating a friendly, liberal, and co-operative world amosphere. This is all the more so, in view of rising protectionist tendencies in the United States, as observed in the recent Japanese-American textile issue.

Government officials and businessmen are beginning to pay lip service to the merits of liberalisation of direct investment, but often they behave as if it is desirable in other industries but not in their own (or in industries of which their Ministry or agency is in charge).

The Theory of Direct Investment[15]

From the time of Ricardo to the recent theory of optimum currency areas, domestic mobility and international immobility of factors of production are cited as the critical differences which distinguish the discipline of international economics from the general body of economics, although it is conceded that it is a matter of degree rather than a black and white distinction. But in the case of direct investment, the factor itself moves across the border, so that the classical distinction does not apply.[16]

The reasons why a firm undertakes direct investment across national borders are very similar to those of a firm undertaking direct investment within a country in different regions, markets or industries. The only difference is that the barriers to investors are higher between countries than between regions within a country. Cultural and linguistic barriers, or institutional and legal differences are greater internationally. Exchange risks must also be borne. But in a stable, prosperous, liberalised international economy, the difference between domestic and international investment is small and diminishing.

As a firm grows and accumulates managerial, technological and financial resources, it tries to apply them most profitably to surrounding investment opportunities. It invests abroad since, from the firm's point of view, marginal productivity of scarce managerial and other resources is higher in the long run, when investing abroad rather than domestically.[17]

---

[15] The following sections are based upon my earlier work (in Japanese): Ryutaro Komiya, 'Economics of Liberalisation of Capital Movement', *Economist* (Tokyo), 25 July 1967, and 'Direct Investment and Industrial Policy', in H. Niida and A. Ono (eds.), *Industrial Organisation in Japan* (Tokyo: Iwanami Publishers, 1969), pp. 322-63.

[16] This is true also of capital movement in general and migration. Therefore there has been little in the way of theories analysing the causes and conditions which determine the flow of 'international' capital or migration, as distinct from the general body of economics. The theory of international capital movement so far has been concerned mostly with effects rather than its causes.

[17] Edith T. Penrose, *Theory of the Growth of the Firm* (Oxford: Blackwells, 1959), and 'Foreign Investment and the Growth of the Firm', *Economic Journal*, June 1956.

The growth of a firm and hence direct investment may be in a horizontal or vertical direction, or a firm may grow in a conglomerate way. Whichever the direction of growth, the management must carefully examine the alternative ways of using scarce managerial resources under its control or available in the near future as the firm grows. It puts them to most profitable or most urgently needed purposes.

Looking from the host side, new direct investment in industry is new entry into the field in which direct investment takes place. Thus, the conditions governing foreign direct investment into an industry are similar to those governing new entry. Low profit rates, stagnant demand and artificial barriers discourage both new entry and direct investment, while high profits, growth potential, and particularly investment opportunities which have not been or cannot be exploited by existing firms, attract new entry.

Most new entrants are innovators in the sense of Schumpeter. This is particularly true of foreign companies undertaking new direct investment, since they are endowed with managerial resources quite different from those which domestic firms command.

Once established in the host country, foreign-owned companies gradually become assimilated. Innovations will be followed by other firms, and ex-innovators and ex-followers will become little different from each other in the long run. The behaviour of foreign-owned enterprise is conditioned by market conditions of the host country, and hence will not be much different from their competitors unless there are some specific reasons.

The essential factor of production which moves when direct investment is taking place is managerial resources, rather than capital in the sense of financial funds or real capital goods. Managerial resources here mean managerial, technological, financial, marketing and other knowledge and experience, accumulated and embodied in a company's management and its staff, which enable it to run and expand efficiently and profitably in a particular field.

Take, for example, the Texaco-DEA (Deutsche Erdoel A.G.) case in 1966. Texaco obtained 90 per cent of the stocks of DEA in exchange for its own convertible debentures. Capital in the sense of financial funds or real capital goods did not move at all. By swapping debentures, which is not accompanied by control, for stocks enabling managerial control, Texaco brought into Germany its managerial resources to run DEA.

Financial funds can be raised within the host country, and almost all direct investors do this. Foreign-owned enterprises in Japan generally borrow very heavily from Japanese financial institutions. What is essential in direct investment is management control, and hence managerial resources which enable control, and not capital funds.

Monopoly Questions. Some authors argue that monopolistic or oligopolistic elements are essential for direct investment, or that direct investment is based upon monopolistic advantage.[18] This view is not correct, in my opinion. While I agree that 'to overcome the inherent native advantage of being on the ground, the firm entering from abroad must have some other advantage not shared with its local competitor',[19] such advantage may not be based upon monopoly or market control.

Suppose that a firm which has a factory in one region is going to build a second factory in another region. Does this simple fact imply that the firm is oligopolistic or has some monopolistic advantage? Or when a retailer, a supermarket chain, or a bank opens a new branch in a different part of a city or a region, is it always based upon monopolistic advantage? I think the answer is no, in the ordinary sense of the word 'monopolistic'. A firm having more than one factory, outlet or branch is compatible with non-differentiated products and workable competition.

A great pianist may well travel to many different cities all over the world to play at concerts. One might call him a monopolist, but it is better to say that his advantage is based upon 'natural scarcity', rather than 'contrived scarcity'.

Here is a story of a direct investor, somewhat like such a pianist.

Consider, for example, the trading firm of Frazar and Company which has carried on a business for three generations in the Far East . . . Frazar and Company introduced a series of products into Japan which reads like a roster of American engineering achievements during the period. In 1887 it sold the Japanese their first electric light plant . . . In 1891 it supplied Tokyo's first streetcars . . . E. W. Frazar was given the Ford agency for Japan in 1909. To encourage business, he established a taxi company as well as a drivers' school . . . He became interested in possibilities of fish canning in Japan. This led to the development of the salmon-canning industry . . . In one line after another, business died away as American manufacturers went into direct distribution, or the Japanese learned to copy the product and supply their own needs. Success therefore called for initiative and imagination, and a high degree of flexibility in seeking out new opportunities.[20]

This story illustrates the theory that the direct investor is a Schumpeterian 'innovator', and that his advantage is bound to be temporary, unless he continues to innovate or is supported by 'contrived scarcity', or something else.

---

[18] Stephen H. Hymer, 'Direct Foreign Investment and the National Economic Interest', in Peter Russell (ed.), *Nationalism in Canada*; C. P. Kindleberger, *International Economics* (Homewood, Illinois: Irwin, 1963 and 1968); Kindleberger, *American Business Abroad*.

[19] Kindleberger, *International Economics*, p. 391.

[20] W. W. Lockwood, *The Economic Development of Japan* (Princeton: Princeton University Press, 1955), pp. 329-30.

This is not to deny that a large part of world direct investment today is undertaken by only a small number of huge 'multinational' corporations. Both horizontal and vertical expansion of these giants, domestically and internationally, may be for the purpose of controlling market at home or abroad.

But in terms of the number of firms, most direct investors are not motivated by monopolistic motives: only about one-sixth of more than 600 foreign-owned companies in Japan are related to the giant world enterprises in the *Fortune* list.

Moreover, even such giants are often to be viewed as innovators trying to create some 'natural scarcity' through R and D or new marketing techniques, rather than static monopolists. A and P in the 1930s and 1940s which expanded into many states in the United States should be considered as an innovator rather than a monopolist, operating in rapidly changing, more and more competitive markets.[21] Many large enterprises are expanding into many parts of the world in a similar way, though on a larger scale.[22]

One must, therefore, carefully examine, in each individual case, whether and in what ways direct investment is accompanied by monopolistic factors.

Problems for Policy

When a firm undertakes direct investment abroad, it is because marginal productivity of the firm's managerial resources is higher abroad than at home—or that is what the firm expects. Managerial resources are used more efficiently than when direct investment is prohibited or restricted. Therefore, assuming that no monopolistic or oligopolistic distortions are involved, free direct investment generally improves the world's productive efficiency, and is beneficial both to investing and host countries. Although one can easily construct exceptional cases in which this general conclusion does not hold, most such cases are rather unlikely to eventuate in the context of industrialised countries today.

Generally speaking, direct investment is beneficial to most groups in the host country. Wages, interest rates, and even stock prices will rise when an inflow of direct investment takes place. Consumers will undoubtedly gain, and the tax revenue will increase.

Those who hold similar managerial resources might be hurt. But even here the long-run development effects are important. Consider the following: Japanese musicians have benefited from, rather than been hurt by allowing foreign musicians to visit Japan freely. By prohibiting foreign pianists to visit Japan, Japanese pianists might be able to sell more

[21] M. A. Adelman, *A & P: A Study in Price-Cost Behavior and Public Policy* (Cambridge: Harvard University Press, 1959).
[22] Kindleberger, *American Business Abroad*, pp. 33-5.

concert tickets in the short run, but such a policy will weaken, rather than strengthen them in the long run.

Viewed in this perspective, the Japanese government's policy on inward direct investment has so far been too restrictive as in many other fields of its economic policy. It has probably limited inward direct investment to a level much lower than is optimal. Most of the concerns expressed in the prevalent majority view are analytically incorrect or have little factual relevance.

Particularly, in so far as the size of the foreign investing firm is below a certain limit, say in terms of total assets, restriction on direct investment, whether newly established or takeover, makes little sense.

I am not proposing, however, a completely *laissez-faire* policy. I shall here take up a few of the most relevant issues for Japan in formulating rational government policy on foreign direct investment.

Monopoly. The government must try to avoid extension of monopoly power established abroad, or monopolisation of the domestic market by powerful foreign monopolists. In this area, however, what is most needed is a general anti-monopoly policy, applicable to foreign and indigenous firms alike, and international co-ordination of antitrust policy. Admittedly, what is good anti-monopoly policy is a difficult problem, and international co-operation is more of one.

The Japanese government, particularly MITI, has been applying double standards in this regard. It has tried to limit market control by foreign, multinational giants through regulation of direct investment, particularly of takeovers, but at the same time has been lenient towards mergers, cartels and other monopolistic practices indulged in by large indigenous firms. This is true not only of Japan but also of many other countries.

MITI's policy aim has been to foster 'strong' Japanese firms which can successfully compete with foreign giants in individual fields. For this aim, MITI encouraged 'industrial reorganisation', which means mergers and co-operation among Japanese firms within the same industry. But such a policy is often in conflict with antitrust policy. Also, requiring Japanese firms *in the same industry* to participate when a 50-50 joint venture is set up under the Liberalisation Measures is anti-competitive. This would limit the role of foreign-owned enterprises as 'innovators' in the host country.

The Japanese government officials in charge of economic policy towards industry often emphasise 'maintaining orderly conditions in an industry' or 'establishing a co-operative order in an industry'. This means reducing excessive price competition, temporary or permanent protection of inefficient small business, or co-ordination or allotment of plant and equipment investment to avoid excess capacity, depending on the situation. In any case the government's policy towards industry has tended to be overly protective, favouring existing firms or the most influential ones among them, in disregard of new entrants to the industry and consumers. The government's restrictive attitude towards foreign direct investment is only a reflection of this general protectionist pattern.

On the other hand, although various arguments in favour of or against current United States policy on domestic mergers can be made, Japan should adopt, for the time being, a similar line towards American or other foreign direct investment into Japan. For example, one of the big three American automobile producers can be allowed to establish a subsidiary in Japan but mergers with Japanese automobile companies should be prohibited. This can be done without the current system of screening: the clause on mergers in the Japanese anti-monopoly law suffices, if it is properly reinterpreted.

Also, predatory dumping, large-scale pre-emptive advertising and other monopolising techniques by actual or potential monopolists should be prohibited.

Infant Firm Protection. To protect infant or embryo indigenous firms in 'strategic' industries is a worthwhile policy aim. Two major problems here are, first, how to identify those infants who are likely to be able to stand up on their own in the near future, and second, which policy measures should be used. These are problems of infant industry protection in general, however, not peculiar to direct investment or to international trade. Even in a closed economy with no international trade or investment, protecting an infant firm or industry may be beneficial to economic welfare.

Foreign direct investment often plays an important role in establishing a new industry. A notable example in Japan is the prewar development of the electrical machinery industry mentioned earlier.

Restrictions on foreign direct investment, for example, allowing foreign ownership only up to 50 per cent in a company, or prohibiting foreigners to operate altogether, in such a 'strategic' industry, may be a useful policy tool to encourage development of an infant industry, but not always.

Foreigners who intend to undertake direct investment usually complain that such a restriction is unfair, but arguments whether something is fair or not are often futile. If world-wide equalisation of per capita income is desirable (if not, why offer aid or preferential tariffs?), helping a country to develop an infant industry (assuming it is successful) must be a good thing. The foreign firm at least has a choice of not investing at all in the country requiring 50 per cent participation by local firms.

Moreover, in an industry such as electronic computers, dominated world-wide by one or a few firms, the world should be thankful to the British and Japanese governments and people for efforts to promote new producers at their own cost.

On the other hand, it is obvious that restrictive measures, for example, the 50 per cent rule, interfere with efficiency in the short run. If, within a country, each local government required 50 per cent participation of local firms in plants and branch offices of national firms located within its jurisdiction, national economic efficiency would be impaired. By the same token, almost any form of restriction on foreign direct investment for the purpose of bringing up 'infants' is harmful to efficiency at least in the very short run. Moreover, foreign companies may not come in at all, because of a restriction on ownership or operation and may even go to a near-by country which offers better terms to them. Also there may be better ways of protection. In any case, long-run gains must be weighed against short-run losses, to justify infant industry protection.

Managerial Development. Management is a peculiar kind of productive factor, in that it learns by doing: namely its productivity improves over time simply by being used actively. This is a characteristic shared by other professional activities. Most other factors such as land, financial funds or unskilled labour do not have this characteristic. Even with skilled labour, the rise in productivity from learning-by-doing is very limited. Managers' salaries (and other incomes) in companies of different sizes and at different levels vary approximately in proportion to the range and importance of managerial decisions made. The larger the company, or the higher the level, the higher is a manager's salary. This is because management ability is a scarce factor, and the ability to run a larger organisation efficiently is scarcer.

An effective way to raise the per capita income of a nation, then, is to encourage accumulation of managerial (and also, technological, financial, marketing, etc.) knowledge and experience among its citizens.

Foreign direct investment is often considered as undesirable in the host country, lest foreign-owned companies should dominate industry and foreigners should occupy most of the important managerial positions. Or, even when nationals occupy most positions in the management of subsidiaries as in Japan, important decisions might be made by the management of the parent company which dictates subsidiaries what to do. Concentration in R and D by foreign companies is feared for the same reason.

The reason why a takeover of one of a country's large representative companies by foreigners is viewed as a serious loss is partly sentimental, but may to some extent be justified from the above considerations.

Development of the managerial ability of the citizens of a nation is a very important factor in economic growth, and in some countries it might be a factor to be taken into consideration in formulating policy towards foreign direct investment.

Here again, however, when a country considers restriction of foreign direct investment for this purpose, say, by limiting foreign ownership of companies larger than a certain size below 50 per cent, or by requiring the appointment of nationals to the positions of presidents and directors or the employment of indigenous engineers and scientists, it must weigh long-run gains against obvious short-run losses. Also, it is not the only nor the most important way for the government to encourage managerial development: it can establish graduate business or engineering schools, productivity centres, subsidise retraining programs, provide overseas scholarships for retrainees, organise teams to study management in other countries, offer managerial and other business information, and so forth.

Certain restrictions on foreign direct investment for this reason may be justified in other countries, but they are unwarranted in Japan today, which has experienced most vigorous development of ability to organise, manage and expand complicated business systems. In my view the Japanese government has been overly protective in this regard. Instead of requiring foreign companies to co-operate with Japanese (as in the 50-50 joint venture), they should be encouraged to compete with each other. Except in an infant industry or when the foreign company is an overwhelming monopolist, competition rather than protection will strengthen Japanese managerial ability at this stage of Japan's industrial development.

The current policy on direct investment almost amounts to prohibition of a takeover of existing Japanese companies by foreigners. This is overly protective. A takeover takes place when the invader finds an opportunity to utilise the company's resources more efficiently than present management does. Virtual prohibition of takeovers enables inefficient managements to remain undisturbed. Though it may be uncomfortable for weaker managements, takeovers by foreigners should be liberalised provided that certain rules of takeovers are laid down to ensure fairness and some degree of stability.

Moderation of Sudden Changes. When in an industry in which there are many small firms, the immediate impact of a new, abrupt entry by a technologically superior large firm is expected to be so large as to drive many firms into bankruptcy, government intervention is called for. Such a situation arises more often when the new entrant is a foreign-owned company than when it is an indigenous one, since foreign enterprises are often endowed with quite different technologies or marketing techniques.

In such a case, the government should take 'temporary', not 'permanent' protective measures. For example, the government may request the new entrant to postpone its plan for six months or a year, or to limit its operation in a certain way for the first few years. This will give the small firms concerned time for adjustment. Or the government may give a subsidy or loans for modernising them, provided that the modernisation plan is effective and useful. But these measures should always be only for a limited period of adjustment.

The following policies on direct investment ought to be adopted in Japan.[23] First, direct investment into Japan should generally be liberalised except in technologically 'strategic' industries and perhaps in a few other special fields such as broadcasting or newspapers. Restrictive measures to moderate sudden changes should be only for a limited period.

Secondly, the current Japanese Anti-Monopoly Law should be applied vigorously, possibly with some reinterpretation, to check monopolistic or oligopolistic behaviour of both foreign and Japanese giant corporations. This means, among other things, that takeover of a large Japanese company by a foreign company in the same or related fields should be prohibited.

Thirdly, in spite of what has been said hitherto, the 50-50 principle may not be too bad a rule, under the circumstances: that is, given the prevalent protectionist attitude which is difficult to change quickly. This would facilitate liberalisation of direct investment in which Japanese participate at least 50 per cent except possibly in 'strategic' industries.

Such a policy would be far better than the current case-by-case screening procedure. Its arbitrary, *ad hoc*—from foreigners' point of view—treatment of individual cases irritates and in some cases infuriates foreigners more than anything else. The simple 50-50 principle, with a few restricted areas mentioned above and a few 100 per cent liberalised fields, may be a reasonably good solution.

The government's Third (and Fourth) Liberalisation Measures may come close to this 50-50 principle, as far as newly established companies are concerned. I am suggesting that 'foreign-participation' in, and takeover of, an existing company should also be liberalised.

It needs to be made clear that Japan today does not really need incoming foreign direct investment. Although direct investment generally improves the world's productive efficiency and is beneficial both to hosts and guests, Japan's rate of economic growth has recently been higher than almost any other country's, and will remain so in the near future. The high rate of growth is supported by various factors, and foreign direct investment which has brought new production technologies and has otherwise encouraged innovation in Japan is undoubtedly one of them. But Japan does not have to grow faster than, say, 8 or even 6 per cent. The marginal utility, so to speak, from growing faster than 6 or 8 per cent is very small.

More particularly, plant and equipment investment in the private sector has recently tended to expand too rapidly, giving rise to various kinds of serious imbalance between the private and public sectors. In

---

[23] As already mentioned, mine is a minority view in Japan. Although academic economists are generally more liberal than government officials, businessmen and journalists, they are also much divided. Therefore, the following must not be taken as representing the Japanese view in any way.

Japan today, with a large balance of payment surplus and inflationary pressures, foreign investors are not welcome from a macro point of view. Therefore somewhat restrictive policies on the part of Japan which help to divert direct investment away from Japan towards other parts of the Far East and South-East Asia may well be beneficial to all parties. This would act to cool down Japan's growth and accelerate development in other countries. The business community in investing countries (including Japan) might benefit from a lighter aid burden or from the balanced growth of the area.

Comments and Discussion

HUGH PATRICK opened the discussion: Komiya's paper lucidly describes the limited nature and extent of foreign investment in Japan, traces government policy, disposes of many of the faulty arguments against foreign investment, and provides very balanced judgments. I also find Komiya's liberal attitude very congenial. While he looks at all foreign direct investment in Japan, quite properly his paper deals mainly with United States investment in Japan, since American investment constitutes the dominant foreign share and since the pressures on Japan to liberalise emanate mainly from American-based firms.

Let us make no bones about it. Japan has had one of the most restrictive policies regarding foreign direct investment in the world, certainly the most restrictive among the developed nations. As I think Hymer once pointed out to me, France always talks about keeping foreign investment out and in practice has let it in, while Japan always talks about letting foreign investment in and in practice has kept it out. This comes out quite clearly in Komiya's paper.

The Japanese view as to the ideal terms for foreign direct investment in Japan are clear. They want at most a 50-50 joint venture between a technologically-sophisticated foreign firm and an established Japanese firm in any given industry, with day-to-day management in Japanese hands, but with each side having veto power over basic policy decisions. The operations of the joint enterprise are to be narrowly defined to utilise the specific technology that only the foreign firm can provide, without expanding into other, more standard products which Japan can feasibly produce on other terms. Of course, licence and patent arrangements are preferable to joint ventures, but as a given Japanese industry comes closer to the frontiers of knowledge, the fewer foreign firms it can bargain with and the more it must accept the joint ventures method of obtaining technology. As camouflage, Japan has liberalised to the extent of allowing 100 per cent foreign equity participation in those few industries where foreign firms would be crazy to enter, as Komiya notes.

In mid-August 1970, Japan extended this system of 'liberalised' foreign investment to cover about three-fourths of Japan's industries but, so far as I know, essentially on the terms just outlined. However, there may be some important qualitative changes: joint ventures may be allowed a wider range of operations, and administrative barriers over the associated licensing and royalty arrangements (which have been important in the past) may well be eased.

Many American firms have been very upset at their virtual exclusion from the rapidly growing Japanese market through the combination of tariffs or quotas and restrictions on direct investment. American business-men frequently assume that the rules of the international economic game should include unrestricted foreign direct investment flows. This is at times so fundamental an ideological tenet that the American reaction is emotional and irrational, rather than pragmatic and bargaining. Or per-haps I have been talking to lower-echelon types, and the top executives of multinational firms are very rational in assessing their interests in free international capital markets, as Hymer has suggested in his chapter and its discussion.

Japan is unique in the world in the extent to which it has been able to untie the foreign direct investment package of capital, management and control, and technology. Domestic saving has been so high that foreign capital needs to finance domestic investment have been negligible, and balance-of-payments needs have been adequately met by clever short-term and long-term portfolio borrowing. Good quality, managerial skills and entrepreneurial drive postwar Japan has had in ample supply. The real need has been for foreign technology. This has been imported in immense quantities, but almost entirely through the more than 10,000 licensing and royalty arrangements made with foreign firms.

Komiya suggests that Japan has allowed a somewhat less-than-optimal inflow of foreign direct investment. My own belief in market mechanisms inclines me toward similar views, but my rationality forces me to judge that Japanese policy has been highly efficient in terms of its objectives. Part of the matter lies in the nature of the objectives themselves. Japan has had the economic goals of access to foreign technology, and of obtaining the stimulating impact of foreign competition in those industries which are strong enough to respond to foreign competition positively and creatively without being overwhelmed by it. Evolving conditions suggest that on both grounds Japan will accept foreign equity participation more readily than in the past.

There are broader, less economic, goals which blend importantly in the mix of objectives of Japan's foreign direct investment policy. A strong desire exists to maintain without great change the economic system, and power relationships, between the central government and Japanese big business. These close informal ties are based not just on common educa-tional backgrounds of decision-makers, or on the government bureau-cracy's 'administrative guidance', or on business support of politicians, but also on a very real and substantial overlapping of the governmental and big business concepts of the national interest. Foreign firms tend neither to understand nor to accept this system; they only cause trouble.

More broadly, Japanese have a simple but pervasive and tenacious feeling that they do not want foreigners in control of anything important in Japan. It is a homogeneous society and robust culture, with a real sense of distinction between Japanese and others. To evaluate these broader objectives is to raise fundamental questions as to the desirable nature of the economic system, the sharing of power in society, and indeed how homogeneously 'Japanese' a society Japan wants. These, of course, are questions which can be answered only by Japanese, not by foreigners.

Rather than concluding on this perhaps disquieting note, let me raise two minor quibbles. First, Komiya correctly points out that Japanese managers have risen to very high posts even in foreign-controlled firms, and of course they control most joint ventures. His Nihon I.B.M. example is somewhat extreme, however. He may not be aware that while the president and other senior officers are Japanese, I.B.M. also has located in Tokyo a management company which oversees activities in all of East Asia, including basic policies of Nihon I.B.M. The senior staff positions are virtually all filled by Americans.

Secondly, in his discussion refuting monopolistic advantage as required for foreign direct investment, Komiya quite correctly points to other elements of 'natural scarcity' rather than 'contrived scarcity' such as entrepreneurship and managerial skills. Here he strikes upon themes in the papers of Hymer and others and in our discussions. However, the criterion of percentage of firms 'not motivated by monopolistic motives' provides only a weak test. Granted that five-sixths of foreign direct investors are not so motivated, they are essentially all small firms which individually and in aggregate have little impact on the Japanese economy. What really count are the remaining one-sixth, the 100 or so firms 'related to the giant world enterprises in the *Fortune* list'. They are significant. A better test would consider their share of sales in an industry's total. And it would be useful to examine, in another study, their motivation and behaviour in more detail.

Further discussion of Komiya's chapter was dominated by two questions: first, whether politico-economic trade-offs were important in Japan's ability to preserve fairly restrictive policies towards foreign investment in recent years; and second, to what extent it was desirable and possible for developing countries to emulate Japan's example.

The first question was raised by a North American participant who remarked that the United States had used its political muscle to force a number of countries to accept various agreements under which American firms gained access to investment markets, and asked whether Japan's ability to maintain its position on foreign investment was a direct consequence of the valuation of the political alliance. For example, some evidence suggested that United States aircraft technology had been sold to Japanese producers in exchange for the establishment of an additional air wing by the Japanese government. How far, then, is what is taken for Japanese success in restricting the entry of foreign investment really based on American support, on political grounds, of policies which the United States, on economic grounds, would not normally accept? And to what extent, therefore, is it possible for anyone else to pursue like policies?

Several participants were dubious of the frame of political analysis implied by this question. Some found difficulty in accepting a view that whether a country adopts a liberal or restrictive policy on foreign investment or not is largely determined by its exposure to United States political pressures. The implicit suggestion that the freedom of other countries, in Europe, is so constrained by United States political pressures on this point that the differences in their policies are to be explained by American policy rather than their own policies was criticised.

Later, the actual premise of the question was queried. It was pointed out by Japanese participants and others that, in fact, there had been a lack of American interest in Japanese investment and foreign investment policies until quite recently. The issue was considered of little importance and American attitudes, tacit or otherwise, were conditioned by that circumstance. In the fifties access was open, through re-opening of established operations and 'yen-basis' investments, to American investors, but it was little used. Only in the last five or six years had foreign firms become interested in the potential of investment in Japan, and since then the American government had been putting its economic case forcibly. One Japanese participant suggested that the politico-economic calculus was much more complex than suggested in the original question, and that it was difficult to establish any simple trade-off between investment access and political support. Others insisted that the tenacity of Japan's policies towards foreign investment was more successfully explained by the alliance between Japanese business interests and nationalistic attitudes expressed in government policy.

A participant from a developing country said that, in his experience, the decision-making power on foreign investment lay very much with the host country and the individual foreign corporation. Another participant, with administrative experience in the United States, agreed, although all these decisions were clearly not taken independently of complicated sets of political, sociological, and institutional constraints.

The second question was put by a number of participants in one form or another. In the light of what is known about Japanese experience, should a restrictionist policy towards foreign investment be recommended for developing countries?

Komiya felt that Japan's situation after World War II was quite different from that prevailing in most developing countries. There was a larger industrial experience and wider industrial base in Japan even at that time. He also felt that Japanese policies towards foreign investment had been far too restrictionist. It was pointed out by other participants that Japan had entertained a very liberal approach to foreign investment in the early stages of her economic development, and especially between 1900 and the 1930s, essentially because she wanted technology as rapidly and as cheaply as possible. Few firms were interested in Japan at the time but a number of large British and American companies did establish operations that played an important role in industrial development—in electrical apparatus, machinery, automobiles and other industries like oil refining and rubber manufacture. Both G.M. and Ford had assembly plants in Japan in the 1920s. During the war, these companies were expropriated. After the war, they were offered the alternatives of returning or selling their assets. Many companies did not judge the prospects to justify re-establishment, but I.B.M. and the oil companies were among those which stayed. The history of Japan's experience with foreign investment prompted some to conclude that, up to a certain stage, the process of economic development would be handicapped by restrictionist policies towards foreign investment but that, beyond that stage, more options were open even if continual restriction continued to have substantial economic costs. The work of Baranson on the adoption of the diesel engine in Japan and India—where there was more costly absorption of new technology—led others to a similar conclusion.

Attention was also drawn to the distinction between Komiya's view of the contribution and advantage of direct investment in terms of managerial superiority and Hymer's view in Chapter 2, that oligopolistic practice is its chief advantage.

7 Japanese Investment Abroad[1]

KOICHI HAMADA

Japan is about to emerge as a major capital exporter. Most advanced countries in the world have experienced, during their process of economic development, a transition period from being capital importers to capital exporters. If we look at the balance of payments figures, we can clearly see that Japan is passing through this transition period so far as the overall balance of capital account is concerned. And if we look at only the component, direct investment, we find that Japan is investing abroad slightly more than foreigners are investing in Japan.

Thus, a series of questions naturally arises: What are the trends and composition of Japanese investment abroad? What kind of attitude is taken by the Japanese government towards direct investment abroad? What are the problems facing Japanese firms operating abroad? What is the relationship between direct investment and the process of economic development in Japan as well as in the host countries?

This chapter is designed to answer these questions, quantitatively if possible, and to make a tentative attempt to forecast the future pattern of Japanese direct investment.

[1] The author is very grateful to Mr Yusuke Kashiwagi, Vice-Minister of Finance for International Affairs, and to Mr Yukinori Itō of the Export-Import Bank of Japan for their helpful suggestions. Also he has benefited from discussions with many of his colleagues, especially with Professor Tadashi Kawata and Ryutaro Komiya. The author is solely responsible for the errors remaining and the opinions expressed in this paper. The following material was helpful in the preparation of this essay: Hikaru Aihara, *The Role of Foreign Capital in Asia [Ajia ni okeru gaikukushihon no yakuwari]*' (Tokyo: Asian Economic Research Institute, 1969); Ryutaro Komiya, 'Foreign Investment and Industrial Policies [Chokusetsu tōshi to sangyo seisaku]' in Horoshi Niida and Akira Ono (eds.), *Industrial Organisation in Japan [Nihon no sangyo seisaku]*; Ministry of International Trade and Industry, *Foreign Trade of Japan, 1970* (Tokyo, 1969); Nihon keizai chōsa kyōgikai, *Japanese Firms in Southeast Asia [Tonan Ajia no Nihon kigyo]* (Tokyo, 1969); OECD, *Enquiry into the Regulations and Conditions Governing Certain International Capital Movements in Japan*; Saburo Okita and Takeo Miki, 'Treatment of Foreign Capital — A Case Study for Japan', in J. H. Adler (ed.), *Capital Movements and Economic Development* (New York: Macmillan, 1967); Ryoichi Takagi, *Foreign Investments by Japanese Firms [Nihon kigyō no kaigai shinshutsu]*; and the Export-Import Bank of Japan, *Quarterly News [Yūgin Jōhō]*, March 1969.

Trends in Japanese Investment Abroad

Japan resumed its direct investment abroad around 1951. It was not until
the 1960s, however, that the increase in Japanese direct investment
became noticeable. Recent trends in Japanese direct investment are
shown in Table 7.1. Statistics on the flow of Japanese investment abroad
can be obtained from two sources. One source is the Ministry of Finance
which gives the authorisation to projects proposed under the Foreign
Exchange and Foreign Trade Control Law (1949). The number of projects approved and the scale of projects are reported. The other source is
Balance of Payments Statistics compiled by the Bank of Japan. As can be
imagined, the first figure is usually larger than the second, indicating that
there exists a substantial lag in the actual transfer of funds behind
authorisation.

The flow of direct investment abroad is around 0.3 per cent of GNP,
and the accumulated stock of direct investment is around 1.5 per cent of
GNP. This stock-income ratio is smaller than that of most advanced
countries. But the annual flow of Japanese investment has been growing
at a very high rate. This contrast seems to suggest that Japan is now
catching up rapidly with other advanced countries.

Table 7.1   Annual flow of Japanese direct investment abroad and
foreign investment in Japan ($US million)

Authorisation data			Balance of payments data					
Direct investment abroad			Direct investment abroad		Foreign direct investment in Japan		Current balance	Long-term capital
Fiscal year	No. of projects	Amount	Out-flow	In-come	In-flow	Income pay-ments		
1951-6	295	45						
1957	72	34						
1958	78	65						
1959	123	54						
1960	151	94						
1961	133	164	104	9	47	20	−1,014	53
1962	179	99	62	11	46	22	− 16	203
1963	223	128	125	12	88	25	−1,071	458
1964	194	121	44	12	70	38	29	17
1965	209	157	105	15	51	39	1,049	−553
1966	253	227	101	21	43	44	996	−835
1967	306	232	137	27	37	53	− 331	−740
1968	382	552	228	37	93	80	1,473	− 80
1969	560	647	231	46	56	106	2,065	−640
Total	3,158	2,619	—	—	—	—	—	—

Source: Ministry of Finance and Foreign Department, The Bank of Japan.

Table 7.2 gives the industrial composition of overseas investment at the end of 1969 and Table 7.3 gives its regional distribution at the end of March 1970.[2] A more detailed cross-classification by region and industry is available from data at the end of March 1969 (see Table 7.4).

Before looking further into the detailed cross-classification by regional and industrial distribution, it is worth mentioning that the four largest Japanese investment projects are Arabian Oil, in the neutral zone between Kuwait and Saudi Arabia, Minus Steel in Brazil, Pulp Industry in Alaska, and oil extracting in North Sumatra.

Table 7.4 suggests that Japanese foreign investment has certain characteristics. For the mining industry a large part of investment is concentrated in the Middle East, but if we set aside the Arabian oil project, South-East Asia holds the largest share. As for manufacturing investment, Latin America's share is the largest, and that of South-East Asia and North America are the next. But if we exclude the pulp project in Alaska, South-East Asia and Latin America are the most important areas. For commerce, North America and Europe are the largest recipients. To sum up, manufacturing is important in developing areas like Latin America and South-East Asia, while commerce and other investment (including insurance and banking) are important in the advanced areas.

The breakdown between developing and advanced countries is set out in Table 7.5, where investment is also classified by type. About 59 per cent or more of the foreign investment is undertaken in developing countries. This ratio has been increasing. In 1967, 58 per cent was in developing areas and at the end of 1969 about 61 per cent.

Investment is mostly either in the form of equities purchase or providing credits. In the first case Japanese companies obtain equities of the

Table 7.2   Industrial composition of accumulated direct investment by Japan, end 1969 ($US '000)

	No. of projects	Amount
Manufacturing	1,023	702
Agriculture and forestry	72	45
Fisheries	77	18
Mining	141	667
Construction	20	29
Commerce	844	319
Banking and insurance	74	160
Migration	182	25
Other	226	285
Total	2,659	2,250

Source: Ministry of Finance.

[2] The fiscal year in Japan starts in April and ends in March.

Table 7.3   Geographical distribution of Japanese investment abroad ($US '000)

Fiscal year	North America No.	Value	Latin America No.	Value	Asia No.	Value	Middle East No.	Value	Europe No.	Value	Oceania No.	Value	Africa No.	Value	Total[a] No.	Value
1951-9	142	75,028	143	62,037	200	36,380	10	20,185	69b					3,565b	564	197,158
1960	36	13,236	31	23,274	64	19,163	1	36,015	18					2,307	150	93,998
1961	28	13,822	27	38,578	49	28,434	3	77,889	27					5,495	133	164,205
1962	39	16,370	33	29,016	75	24,048	1	23,996	31					6,095	177	99,424
1963	49	52,666	43	21,192	82	26,311	1	14,671	44					12,656	223	127,424
1964	34	27,360	50	44,212	80	30,373	0	11,539	32					6,985	195	126,470
1965	52	44,119	50	59,009	73	35,703	0	11,420	34					7,198	207	157,186
1966	70	108,617	34	54,659	107	28,772	4	24,836	39					10,223	253	227,107
1967	65	57,117	35	40,643	160	50,741	2	19,866	45					60,608	307	223,976
1968		185,722		41,161		71,437		24,144		156,149		30,633		42,861	c	551,133
1969		131,000		86,000		210,000		99,000		34,000		77,000		10,000	c	668,000
1951-69	738	723,000	526	499,000	1,331	560,000	26	306,000	288	302,000	126	159,000	73	77,000	3,158	2,619,000
Percentage	27.6		19.1		21.0		11.7		11.5		6.1		2.9		100	

a The columns do not add laterally or vertically because the data are incomplete.
b Includes Europe, Oceania, and Africa 1951 to 1967.
c No detail available.

Source: Ministry of Finance.

firms in host countries in return for supplying funds, commodities or know-how. In the second case, Japanese companies lend equipment, patents, or long-term funds to the firms in the host country. This type of investment is also common where there is some restriction by the government in the host countries on the acquiring of equities. 'Direct business activity', including 'obtaining real estate abroad', is a type of foreign investment in which Japanese companies directly operate business without founding a corporation in the host country. This type, although desirable for the parent country, is hardly welcomed by the host country. The Arabian oil project is among the few projects of this type.

The Motives and Performance of Japanese Investment Abroad

Thanks to an exhaustive survey made by the Export-Import Bank of Japan, there is fairly detailed information about the motives and economic performance of Japanese firms abroad.[3] This survey analyses the answers of firms investing abroad to questionnaires which were distributed in July 1968. The objectives of direct investment abroad by manufacturing industries are summarised in Table 7.6, and those by agriculture and forestry, fisheries and mining industries in Table 7.7. Generally, developing exports and sustaining markets are the most important objectives among manufacturing firms. Importing natural resource products is the most important in agriculture, forestry, fisheries and mining.

As compared with the previous survey made in 1965, exporting products to other countries has become more important. This reflects the fact that such investments in manufacturing as are designed to make use of low wages abroad and to export products to Japan or other countries have increased. In East Asia, especially in Formosa, direct investment in textiles, electric machinery and sundries is often of this type. These investment projects are promoted by the existence of a duty-free zone for exports and also by the expectation that preferential duties will be applied to the products of developing countries. This is a noteworthy new development.

The wage rate in Hong Kong is about three-fourths of that in Japan, and that in Formosa is about one-third or one-fourth. Moreover, the labour productivity in Japanese firms in Formosa is reported to be 80 per cent of that in Japan. Under these conditions, it is likely that Japanese investment of this new type will increase. Since the economic relationship between the Republic of Korea and Japan has improved rapidly, the same type of investment has also been increasing in Korea.[4]

---

[3] Export-Import Bank of Japan, *Quarterly News*, March 1969.
[4] Since 1969, Japan has increased its investments in Korea. One joint venture, Sansei-Sanyo Electric Company, specialises in export production under its terms of establishment.

Table 7.4 Japan: outflow and accumulated values, cross-classification for fiscal year 1968 ($US '000)

Industry	North America	Latin America	Asia	Europe	Middle East	Oceania	Africa	Total
Foodstuffs	—	87	3,809	1,246	—	—	1,401	8,542
	1,617	5,996	24,715	5,034	—	1,597	2,350	41,309
Textiles	—	1,657	13,580	279	—	289	—	15,808
	3,000	44,421	46,260	972	—	10,403	926	105,978
Wood and pulp	13,500	—	1,393	—	—	—	2,387	17,280
	122,991	22	4,774	—	—	—	2,437	130,224
Chemicals	466	1,829	2,388	281	—	—	—	4,964
	9,730	5,036	10,170	1,154	—	1,419	212	27,721
Iron and metal	—	111	3,711	16	—	180	—	4,018
	389	62,984	25,338	16	—	2,363	—	91,090
Machinery	—	2,493	3,333	360	—	—	6	6,192
	2,401	32,755	7,307	1,798	—	—	6	44,287
Electric machinery	120	2,530	3,444	—	343	42	50	6,529
	325	10,291	14,124	278	343	652	1,061	27,704
Transportation machinery	—	3,553	159	—	—	—	607	4,319
	10,000	62,953	10,735	3,200	1,000	—	656	88,544
Other	700	318	3,874	359	42	—	311	5,604
	1,195	4,006	25,878	1,765	316	—	346	33,506
Subtotal of Manufacturing	14,786	12,578	35,691	2,541	385	511	4,762	71,254
	151,648	228,464	169,301	14,217	1,659	16,434	7,938	589,711

Agriculture, forestry	1,911 / 3,061	714 / 2,050	8,000 / 28,553	— / 430	— / —	— / —	— / 2,404	10,625 / 36,498
Fisheries	— / 1,840	725 / 6,844	270 / 2,266	34 / 115	— / 143	100 / 837	591 / 1,901	1,720 / 13,946
Mining	30,887 / 78,086	12,207 / 44,600	23,805 / 117,832	— / 366	27,711 / 265,638	42,200 / 42,634	21,872 / 50,571	158,682 / 599,727
Construction	— / 3,785	425 / 21,419	300 / 844	— / —	— / —	— / —	— / —	725 / 26,048
Commerce	105,604 / 231,538	3,592 / 9,814	1,317 / 7,782	6,522 / 15,929	41 / 436	— / 141	2,294 / 5,417	119,370 / 271,057
Others	32,584 / 122,587	10,920 / 100,449	2,054 / 13,868	142,052 / 175,951	7 / 473	50 / 216	1,120 / 1,165	188,737 / 414,709
Total	185,722 / 592,545	41,161 / 413,640	71,437 / 340,446	151,149 / 207,008	28,144 / 268,349	42,881 / 60,262	30,633 / 69,446	551,113 / 1,951,696
Percentage	30.4	21.2	17.4	19.6	13.7	3.1	3.6	100

Source: Ministry of International Trade and Industry.

Table 7.5 Japan: breakdown of direct investment into developing and advanced countries ($US million)

	Developing countries		Advanced countries		Total	
	No. of projects	Amount $US million	No. of projects	Amount $US million	No. of projects	Amount $US million
1968 fiscal year	252	214	119	337	371	551
Equity purchase	214	67	101	137	315	204
Long-term credits	35	119	18	199	53	318
Real estate investment	3	28	—	1	3	29
Accumulated value in $US million at the end of March 1969	1,551	1,152	727	799	2,278	1,951

Source: Ministry of International Trade and Industry.

The motives for direct investment abroad are often classified in textbooks under three headings: market-oriented, resource-oriented and factor-oriented investment. We have seen from the above questionnaire study that in manufacturing industries, Japanese investment has been mostly market-oriented, but recently factor-oriented or human-resource-oriented investment has been rapidly increasing. In agriculture, fisheries and mining industry Japanese investment is mostly natural-resource-oriented. It is interesting to note, in the case of agriculture, fisheries and mining, the advantages due to more stable supply are reported by the largest number of firms, and the advantage due to lower price is the next.

One question worth asking at this point is why Japanese firms invest abroad instead of just importing the materials produced or extracted by foreign firms? If the foreign firms have access to all the technology, know-how, marketing and organising skill, and information that Japanese firms have, and if the market is neither imperfect nor regulated by the government, then it will not matter much whether Japanese firms invest abroad or whether they trade. If Japanese firms can only emulate native firms, it does not matter much whether we invest in resource-oriented projects or whether we import the material produced by native industry.

In order for natural resource-oriented direct investment to be profitable, it is necessary that there be some element of market imperfection and/or difference in technological or managerial skill between Japanese firms and native firms. If the advantages specified in (3) of Table 7.7 are real advantages, there must be some difference in technological or managerial skill or some monopolistic element in the raw material market. This is evident for advantages due to lower prices. As for advantages due to stable supply, if the native industry had identical technology and no monopoly power, the gain by investing abroad would not be very great. When the supply is short and price is high, Japanese firms supplying parent firms at home are losing the opportunity of selling the commodity at a higher price somewhere else. Therefore, the monopolistic element is one of the conditions for investing abroad, whether it is on the side of Japan or the host countries.

Next, turn to the economic or profit performance of Japanese firms abroad. The same questionnaire study provides some basic data indicating the profitability of investment projects abroad (see Table 7.8). Among the firms in operation, 60 per cent earned profits during the most recent accounting period, 5 per cent broke even and 35 per cent made losses. With respect to accumulated profits, only 50 per cent are in surplus, whilst 48 per cent are in deficit. Moreover only 29 per cent have ever paid dividends. This suggests that Japanese firms invest with a long-run perspective.

By industrial classification, textiles, electrical machinery, and others (mainly sundries) are doing relatively well, while agriculture and forestry,

Table 7.6 Japanese manufacturing firms: motives for investment abroad, by industry and region (no. of projects)

(1) Classification by industry

Objectives	Food-stuffs	Textiles	Chemical	Ceramics	Iron and metal	Machin-ery	Electric machinery	Other	Total (%)
Export of machines and equipment (from Japan to firms abroad)	3		2	1	4	1	6	2	30 (7)
Export of materials or half-finished goods (from Japan to firms abroad)		22	7	4	28	5	12	8	86 (21)
Defending foreign markets		25	22	2	8	20	9	6	92 (23)
Developing foreign markets	14	14	18	6	7	15	18	16	108 (26)
Subtotal	17	72	49	13	47	41	45	32	316 (77)
Export of products to other countries	4	9	3		1	1	9	11	38 (9)
Export of products to Japan	22		2				1	3	28 (7)
Earning dividends	1	7	1	1				3	13 (3)
Other	2	1	2	1	3	3	2	1	15 (4)
Total	46	89	57	15	51	45	57	50	410 (100)

(2) Classification by region

Objectives	East Asia	South-East Asia	West Asia	Latin America	Africa	Sub-total	North America	Europe	Oceania	Sub-total	Total
Export of machines and equipment (from Japan to firms abroad)	14	10		2	4	30					30
Export of materials or half-finished goods (from Japan to firms abroad)	23	29	1	16	11	80	2	3	1	6	86
Defending foreign markets	32	41	1	8	5	87	1	3	1	5	92
Developing foreign markets	32	29		37	3	101		4	3	7	108
Subtotal	101	109	2	63	23	298	3	10	5	18	316
Export of products to other countries	30	2		2	1	35		3		3	38
Export of products to Japan	18	3		4		25	3			3	28
Earning dividends	4	6		3		13					13
Other	6	6		1	1	14	1			1	15
Total	159	126	2	73	25	385	7	13	5	25	410

Source: Export-Import Bank of Japan.

fisheries, foodstuffs and machinery are not. Among the relatively profitable are cotton textile firms which, founded many years ago, are now at a stage of reaping rewards, and electrical machinery firms which make use of low cost labour in East Asia. In agriculture and forestry, fisheries and mining, there are many firms with deficits in accumulated profit. They are, however, successful in the sense that, as the same study shows, the realised imports of commodities developed abroad exceeded the original expectations of 60 per cent of the firms which responded in this industrial division. In this case, profit abroad is not necessarily a good indicator of success. The consolidated accounts of the firm abroad and the parent firm at home would be more relevant. Of course, this applies more or less to every kind of direct investment.

Regionally, firms in East Asia (except Okinawa), South-East Asia and Africa are relatively profitable, and those in Latin America are relatively unprofitable. As compared with the same survey in 1965, the percentage of the firms with positive accumulated profit in the 1968 survey has increased from 46 per cent to 50 per cent.

Firms in Asia and Africa experienced improvement but those in Latin America have experienced deterioration (see Table 7.9). Firms in Asia show a relatively good performance because the economy in Asia is booming as a result of the Vietnam war and firms in Asia have projects with shorter gestation periods. Then why do a considerable number of firms run deficits? It appears that 65 per cent of the firms that have run deficits during the more recent period are in deficit on operating account, while 18 per cent are in deficit because of interest costs, despite a surplus on operating account. According to the questionnaire study of manufacturing industry, insufficient sales or falling product prices is the major reason for deficits on operating account. The shortness of time since initiation and the higher cost of raw materials are the reasons that rank next. Insufficient sales or falling prices are mostly attributed to competition with imports and competition with other firms in the host country. The answers of some firms indicate that potential demand abroad was miscalculated.

Among the difficulties which Japanese firms encounter in various regions, low productivity of labour, unstable economic environment, troublesome and slow governmental procedures and inefficient administration are the main concerns. Interest costs are not the major difficulty. The supply of short-term funds is not the major problem except in Latin America, where inflationary pressure makes it hard to obtain funds. Generally, long-term funds for fixed investment are mainly supplied by shareholders. Short-term funds or operating funds are mostly supplied by banks in the host country or branches of Japanese banks.

Finally, it is interesting to note that 82 per cent of firms are expecting improvement in their profit performance. Some 55 per cent of the 383

Table 7.7 Japanese agriculture, fisheries, and mining: motives for investment abroad, by industry and region

(1) Classification by industry

Objectives	Agriculture, forestry	Fisheries	Mining	Total	(%)
Import of products to Japan	12	13	45	70	(71)
Export of products to other countries	1	6		7	(7)
Sale of products in the host country	2	11	3	16	(16)
Other	1	2	3	6	(6)
Total	16	32	51	99	(100)

(2) Classification by region

Objectives	East Asia	South-East Asia	West Asia	Latin America	Africa	Sub-total	North America	Europe	Oceania	Sub-total	Total
Import of products to Japan	4	27	1	8	3	43	15	1	11	27	70
Export of products to other countries		2		4		6			1	1	7
Sale of products in the host country		5	1	4	1	11	2	1	2	5	16
Other		1		3		4	2			2	6
Total	4	35	2	19	4	64	19	2	14	35	99

(3) Products advantages

Objectives	Agriculture, forestry	Fisheries	Mining	Total	(%)
Lower price	7	5	12	24	(31)
Better quality	2	4	1	7	(9)
More stable supply	5	7	31	43	(55)
Other		2	2	4	(5)
Total	14	18	46	78	(100)

Source: The Export-Import Bank of Japan.

Table 7.8 Profitability and dividend payments of Japanese firms abroad (no. of projects)

(1) Classification by industry

	Profit during most recent period			Accumulated profit			Dividend payments		Total number of respondents
	Surplus	Break-even	Deficit	Surplus	Break-even	Deficit	With dividends	No dividends	
Agriculture, forestry	2		4	1		5		6	6
Fisheries	11	3	9	9		14	2	21	23
Mining	12		9	9		12	5	16	21
Foodstuffs	16		24	14		26	9	31	40
Textiles	51	3	16	44	1	25	29	41	70
Chemical	26		10	17	4	15	13	23	36
Ceramics	8	1	4	7		6	4	9	13
Iron and metal	24	2	14	19	2	19	14	26	40
Machinery	14	1	15	11	1	18	7	23	30
Electrical machinery	27	7	10	25		19	12	32	44
Other	23	1	12	23		13	8	28	36
Total	214	18	127	179	8	172	103	256	359
(per cent)	(60)	(5)	(35)	(50)	(2)	(48)	(29)	(71)	(100)

(2) Classification by region

	Profit during most recent period			Accumulated profits			Dividend payments		Total number of respondents
	Surplus	Break-even	Deficit	Surplus	Break-even	Deficit	With dividends	No dividends	
East Asia	71	5	43	59	3	57	35	84	119
(Okinawa)	(16)	(4)	(20)	(13)	(2)	(25)	(9)	(31)	(40)
(Other)	(55)	(1)	(23)	(46)	(1)	(32)	(26)	(53)	(79)
South-East Asia	70	4	44	60	2	56	35	83	118
West Asia	1			1			1		1
Latin America	34	7	25	27	3	36	15	51	66
Africa	14	2	3	14		5	11	8	19
Subtotal	190	18	115	161	8	154	97	226	323
North America Europe Oceania	24		12	18		18	6	30	36
Total	214	18	127	179	8	172	103	256	359

Source: The Export-Import Bank of Japan.

firms are planning to expand equipment investment and 36 per cent are planning to develop new products. Some 17 firms (4 per cent) are cutting back or quitting, two of these due to the exhaustion of mines, one due to the expiration of a contract (the Japanese share will be sold out to a native firm), and fourteen due to a slump in business. This exhaustive survey concludes by emphasising the following four serious problems for Japanese investors abroad: the need for the co-ordination between the parent firm and the firm abroad, the need for better labour management relations, the need for the financing plans, and the need for preliminary research before actual investment abroad.

Policies and Regulations Governing Direct Investment Abroad

Transactions and transfers for outward direct investment must be individually authorised by the government. The granting of all authorisation is the responsibility of the Ministry of Finance. Projects under $US0.2 million are authorised automatically, and those under $US0.3 million are authorised in practice by the Bank of Japan. Thus, Japan keeps careful control over outward direct investment, I/B in List A of the Capital Movements Code of the OECD.

The reasons for Japanese government restrictions on the outflow of direct investment are as follows. First, a large amount of capital outflow may cause deterioration in the balance of payments. Secondly, domestic monetary policy may lose effectiveness if a large amount of capital flows out of the country. Thirdly, direct investment abroad may have unfavourable effects on Japanese industries. For example, firms abroad may be-

Table 7.9 Japan: relationship between profit performance and year of initiation of investment (percentage of number of projects which are profitable)

Region	Permitted before 1964	Permitted 1965-7	Total 1968 survey	Results of 1965 survey
East Asia	49	50	50	46
South-East Asia	51	52	51	46
West Asia	100	—	100	—
Latin America	49	21	41	53
Africa	77	67	74	20
Subtotal	52	46	50	48
North America Europe Oceania	50	50	50	32
Total	51	47	50	46

Source: The Export-Import Bank of Japan.

come involved in what is called 'excessive' competition. Or the product made by Japanese firms abroad and imported to Japan or exported may affect unfavourably the business activities of other firms in Japan.

It is the first reason that Japanese government seems to have relied on most heavily in justifying the regulation of direct investment abroad in the past. Recently, however, Japan's balance of payments has improved considerably and she has become one of the major surplus countries in the world. Hence, the third reason seems to have become the main ground for regulating Japanese investment. Since the phenomenon commonly called 'excessive' competition is sometimes nothing but the process of natural selection normally observed in the working of price mechanism, the third reason cannot be maintained too strongly.

The effect of regulation on direct investment abroad should not be exaggerated because most of the large projects so far proposed by large firms seem to have been permitted. Authorisation has become more formal than substantial. And this contrasts with the restriction on direct investment by foreign countries in Japan. More effective is the restriction imposed by governmental financial institutions like the Export-Import Bank of Japan, when a large-scale private investment project needs financial assistance from governmental institutions.

The general attitude of Japanese people towards outward direct investment is commonly favourable. It seems that government, businessmen and most academics agree that Japan should liberalise outward direct investment. This is in great contrast to attitudes towards foreign investment in Japan where the formation of national consensus is very difficult. Theoretically, labour unions have grounds for resisting a large capital outflow, especially factor-oriented outflow, but Japanese unions seldom express a systematic argument on the matter. Some academic economists, however, urge against increasing direct investment too rapidly, because they consider that undesirable social or political repercussions of direct investment abroad are not completely offset by its economic benefit.

Economic Growth and Direct Investment Abroad

It is worth turning to an examination of the relative magnitude of Japanese investment abroad from the standpoint of macroeconomics or growth theory. Suppose the movements of capital across national borders are made perfectly free. Then, as far as movements of capital as a factor of production are concerned, there must be some equilibrium or normal value of capital movements. This value should depend on the differences in the growth rates of labour, in the types and rates of technical progress, in the savings ratios and possibly in the rates of monetary expansion among countries. For capital as a factor of production moves from the country with a higher rate of return to the country with a lower

Table 7.10 Direct foreign investment, accumulated assets, by major countries (book value in $US million)

	Investment by industrial sector						Share in the world		Percentage of investment in advanced countries	Ratio to GNP		Ratio to exports		Accumulated assets per capita	
	Petroleum	Mining and smelting	Manufacturing	Other	Total 1966	Total 1968	1966	1968	1966	1966	1968	1966	1968	1966	1968
U.S.	16,264	4,135	22,050	12,113	54,562	64,756	60.9	60.8	69.1	7.3	7.4	182.5	190.6	277	322
U.K.	4,200	759	6,028	5,015	16,002	17,774	17.9	16.7	61.4	15.2	17.3	109.1	115.8	292	321
France	—	—	—	—	4,000	4,697	4.5	4.4	47.5	3.9	4.2	36.7	37.0	81	94
Germany	200	100	1,800	400	2,500	3,921	2.8	3.7	66.2	2.1	2.6	12.4	15.8	42	65
Canada	—	250	2,988	—	3,238	3,479	3.6	3.3	83.5	6.0	5.6	33.9	27.7	162	168
Japan	—	—	—	—	1,000	1,972	1.1	1.9	39.5	1.0	1.1	10.2	15.2	10	20
World	25,942	5,923	36,246	21,472	87,583	106,438	100	100	66.5	6.2	6.3	67.2	67.1	133	155

Sources: Ministry of International Trade and Industry and *Foreign Trade of Japan*, 1970.

rate of return while the differences in the rates of return depend essentially on the relative scarcity of factors of production.[5]

However, if we consider direct investment, which is the movement of capital combined with technology and managerial ability, the story is not so simple. Given the growth rates of factors, the types and rates of technical progress, and the degrees of monopoly in various markets, there may be some equilibrium value of direct investment, or ratio of it to national income, to which the accumulated value of direct investment converges if it is made perfectly free.

Of course, there are, aside from legal barriers, several kinds of barriers which prevent direct investment from reaching this hypothetical equilibrium value. First, barriers due to the lack of information about the host country exist. As a consequence of this, investors may feel a very large degree of subjective risk attached to investment abroad. This risk, however, will be lessened by the improved transmission of information or by learning obtained from investment experience in a particular country.

Therefore, a spurt of direct investment, especially to a relatively unfamiliar part of the world, can be described as follows. The country starts off with little information about the situation abroad. People are not particularly eager to invest abroad at this stage. Then, little by little, people learn about the economic conditions of host countries. They revise their subjective probability from *a priori* to *a posteriori* and they increase investment quite rapidly. This may be reinforced by the effect of external economies. Thus, direct investment reaches some normal and equilibrium value (or ratio).

This is an interesting observation and, most probably, theoretically true. But, it would be difficult to figure out even approximate figures for equilibrium or normal levels of direct investment. Table 7.10 sets out data for accumulated direct investment by major capital exporters. The relative magnitudes of direct investment abroad to national income or to exports for these countries are given. But unfortunately there seems no systematic tendency in these values.

Attempts to relate the accumulated asset-income ratio in Table 7.10 to macroeconomic variables indicate a very slight negative correlation between the rate of growth and the asset-income ratio. A possible interpretation is that investment opportunities abroad are more attractive for a country with a lower rate of growth. However, it is highly probable that this is only a spurious correlation. There appears hardly any systematic way of relating the relative level of 'direct investment' with macroeconomic variables.

The Japanese data in Table 7.10 allow the following observations: the Japanese share in the total direct investment in the world is still small

[5] See Koichi Hamada, 'Economic Growth and Long-term Capital Movements', *Yale Economic Essays*, Spring 1966.

although it is growing very rapidly. The ratio of accumulated investment abroad to national income and of that to export is smaller than the same values for any other countries listed in Table 7.10.

Two features are remarkable. First, the share of Japanese investment in developing countries is larger than for any other country. Secondly, even though the current level of Japanese direct investment is small, its rate of growth is the highest. From 1966 to 1968, the annual growth rate of Japanese investment abroad was 40 per cent, whereas that for other countries was about 25 per cent for Germany, 9 per cent for United States, 8 per cent for France and United Kingdom and 3 per cent for Canada. This seems to indicate that Japanese direct investment is now just at the beginning of a rapid growth phase.

To what extent then, will Japan increase its foreign investment in the future? An exact answer to this question is impossible. To obtain a very rough idea of what is likely to happen, a comparative study of German and Japanese experience in investing abroad is useful. The case of Germany is interesting itself, but it is the more interesting to us because Germany and Japan have many economic aspects in common, for example, a high rate of growth and the surplus in the balance of payments.

Because the balance of payments of Japan has followed more or less the same pattern as that of Germany, it is probable that the outflow of direct investment of Japan will, in the future, follow a similar pattern to that of Germany. In Germany the asset-GNP ratio exceeded one per cent for the first time in 1960, while in Japan it exceeded one per cent in 1966. Thus, an extremely naïve rule of thumb suggests that this ratio may reach around 2.5 per cent six or seven years after 1968, that is, in 1974-5.

A few words of caution should be given here. Because the composition of German and Japanese direct investment is quite different, the analogy should not be carried too far. German direct investment is concentrated in advanced countries and in manufacturing industries. That is, market-oriented investment is dominant in the German case. On the other hand, about two-thirds of Japanese direct investment is in the developing areas of the world, and industry-wise it has a more balanced structure. While Japan seems to follow the path of Germany in the aggregate level of direct investment, the structural difference between the two countries may become more marked in the future.

Problems Ahead

Japan's GNP achieved $US200 billion in 1970. It is said that Japan's GNP may reach $US400 billion by 1975. With its scarce natural resources, Japan is forced to rely on external trade in order to sustain large-scale economic activity. The more dependent the Japanese economy becomes on foreign trade, the more likely is Japan to be engaged in foreign investment activities. If 5 per cent were the normal or equilibrium ratio of accumulated direct investment to GNP, $US20 billion would be the normal level of Japanese investment abroad corresponding to $US400 billion GNP. Of course, there is no assurance that Japan will reach the normal value by 1975 if such a value actually exists. Alternatively, suppose 2.5 per cent was the level in 1975 as calculated by the comparative study with Germany: still $US10 billion would be the forecast value for foreign investment. This large value is not at all improbable, however, if we take into consideration the fact that Japan has increased the level of its direct investment by about ten times in the last ten years. Moreover, if we consider the moral requirement by DAC that advanced countries should aid developing countries every year by at least one per cent of GNP, Japanese foreign investment, which is counted as a part of this assistance, may increase quite rapidly.

Thus, expansion of Japanese direct investment is in a sense inevitable. And the tendency that a larger part of Japanese investment is directed to developing rather than advanced countries will continue or will be probably reinforced. The only way Japan could reduce foreign dependence, is by reducing its rate of growth to a considerable degree.

So far we have considered quantitative trends in prospective direct investment. What will be the problems accompanying Japanese investment? What will be the obstacles to the expansion of Japanese direct investment and its efficient operation? The questionnaire study quoted above shows what kinds of complaints firms abroad have. Current problems will persist in the near future. Concentrating attention on investment in the developing area, the major difficulties may be summarised under two headings.

One is the attitude of governments in both host countries and Japan. The Japanese government does restrict the outflow of direct investment, and in most cases permission can be obtained only after a formal inspection. So long as the balance of payments remains favourable, regulation will be relaxed in the future. Some firms abroad complain at the slow pace of administrative procedures in the host country. Some of the governments in host countries, even though they welcome Japanese investment, insist on nationalisation schemes, such as 'Indianisation', 'Malaysionisation', 'Filipino first policy' and so on.[6] Some of them want to replace Japanese employees by local people, and restrict the extension of visas. The length of stay for Japanese employees is made shorter than necessary. Needless to say this kind of attitude reflects the nationalistic feelings of people in the host country.

The second is that there are cultural or social differences among various countries. Something very similar to what Japanese people feel about

[6] These policies are not necessarily typical.

American firms in Japan is felt by the people of host countries. Every nation has different characteristics or patterns of business and social behaviour. The behavioural pattern of foreign companies, or multi-national corporations, is more or less in conflict with the behavioural or cultural patterns of domestic people. By investing abroad, Japanese firms should always be ready to adjust themselves to the business environment of the host country. If Japanese firms are not successful in adjusting, nationalistic feeling may be combined with some sort of anti-Japanese feeling from the past for which we were responsible. In order to overcome this cultural or behavioural gap, Japanese firms should not behave just like rich men. They should make every effort to make contact with various groups of people, not exclusively people who speak Japanese or English, to propagate their skills and their knowledge. For, as we ourselves know as a host country, foreigners with technology and skill are much more welcomed than foreigners with money alone. The questionnaire study seems to indicate that we need the exchange of engineers on a larger scale, that Japanese should study the languages of host countries more intensively, and that some of the employees should stay in a particular country much longer.

This large outflow of Japanese venture capital to the world, and particularly to developing areas, will by itself promote the allocation of resources in a more efficient way if we adopt the Paretian efficiency criterion. Even though some monopolistic elements are involved in direct investment,[7] we can still argue that the movement of capital funds combined with technology or managerial resources will contribute to the improvement of productive efficiency of the world as a whole. Let us take the view that the process of direct investment is a two-person, non-zero sum game, as Kindleberger maintains.[8] As long as both participants have economic incentives to co-operate for a particular investment project, they must be better off than the initial position in the absence of direct investments. Therefore, as far as private direct investment is concerned, there will be a positive effect on economic wellbeing unless the external diseconomies offset these gains.[9]

If we measure the welfare of developing countries only by materialistic wellbeing, private direct investment is most likely to benefit developing countries. However, if we enlarge our welfare criterion by including social or political aspects, the evaluation of direct investments becomes much more involved.

In the real world, no participant is a single entity in this non-zero sum game. There are various groups of people within both countries, and each

---

[7] Stephen Hymer, 'Direct Foreign Investment and the National Economic Interests', in Peter Russell (ed.) *Nationalism in Canada*.

[8] Charles P. Kindleberger, *American Business Abroad*.

[9] In the immediate future, we should guard against the *de facto* export of pollution.

of these groups has different political views and has different economic interests. The formal calculation may justify the welfare effect of direct investments, if we rely on the marginalist principle. But for some groups of people, direct investments may mean the deterioration of their welfare. It is one thing to solve a two-person game. It is quite another to take account of various repercussions of many different groups of people having different views.

Consider two typical or extreme situations. In one situation, Japanese direct investment really helps create the economic climate for the development of national economies abroad, that is, by promoting the formation of organised nation-wide markets, by heightening the level of education and the level of technology in host countries. This type of direct investment will be welcomed by a consensus of various groups of people in developing countries.

The other extreme case might occur if Japanese investors combine with corrupt groups in host countries, governmental or private, which make use of funds without really embodying them in productive activities. In this kind of unfortunate situation, anti-Japanese feeling may be connected with a political movement aiming to oust the corrupt power groups.

These two cases are, of course, unusual. And in most cases, the nature of direct investment projects lies in between these extreme cases. Which elements are stronger in a particular project is a difficult question that can be answered properly only after one makes empirical investigations. In order that direct investment may promote productivity in host countries, efforts are required in various directions. First, multilateral and global investment relationships between countries should be developed. We should not try to monopolise some part of the world for Japanese firms.

Multilateral capital movements in both directions are to be welcomed more than movements in one direction alone. Nor should we rely too heavily on the formation of an exclusive region with special connections to Japan within an economic bloc. Therefore, Japan should try to invest in all parts of the world, and excessive concentration on one region like Asia is not to be recommended. Incidentally, for the same reason, the financing of development projects should be channelled through international organisations like the Asian Development Bank.

Secondly, the pattern of co-operation should be in such a form as to develop the skills and knowledge of people in host countries. As mentioned above, if we go abroad and invest simply as owners of funds or patents, without real thought for propagating sufficiently the knowledge and skill we possess, Japanese may be disliked as 'ugly Japanese'. But if the form of direct investment is such as to improve and develop skill in host countries, it will be welcomed.

Even though Japanese firms take every kind of precaution, there may still remain some element of hostility among the people of host countries, a hostility which is sometimes coexistent and intermingled with a feeling of familiarity. And there is an increasing probability that Japan will be involved in the social or political affairs of host countries.

Thus, the choice is two-fold: for the developing countries, the choice between (short-run) material wellbeing and political independence, and, for Japan, the choice between economic growth and non-involvement in affairs of other countries. The choice itself is beyond the realm of economics, but the frontier of the trade-off between economic prosperity and political independence can be improved by cultivating an environment which channels funds into more productive projects which can serve as a lever for the autonomous drive in self-sustaining economic development.

Comments and Discussion

DONALD BRASH opened the discussion: The future development of East Asia—and indeed the whole Pacific Basin—is so clearly intimately bound up with the pattern of Japanese development, that to be ignorant of the major characteristics of Japanese foreign investment is serious indeed. In my own view, there are three particularly interesting features of Hamada's paper. The first is the small size of Japanese investment abroad. Though such investment is now running at an annual rate well over twice that of foreign direct investment *into* Japan, the annual outflow is still only about 5 per cent of the level of United States foreign investment. The *accumulated* value of Japanese foreign investment at the end of 1969, at little more than $US2 billion, was still substantially less than the annual outflow from the United States, and well below the accumulated foreign investment of Canada, a much smaller and traditionally capital-importing country.

The second is the knowledge gained that so many of the Japanese companies operating abroad do so at a loss. Certainly, one must be careful to avoid attaching too much importance to the book profit of foreign investment, and this is especially true in the case of Japanese investment which is so heavily concentrated in parts of the world where political factors and restrictions on profit remittances probably give a special incentive to understate the true earnings of the subsidiary by 'fiddling' with intra-company prices. But still it seems a matter for surprise that only 60 per cent of the firms covered in a recent survey were operating profitably when surveyed. In fact, this is undoubtedly the result of the fairly recent establishment of many of the Japanese foreign investments but, as Hamada shows in Table 7.9 (which appears to refer, incidentally, to accumulated profit and loss rather than profitability as normally understood), there is remarkably little difference in the profit performance of the most recently established ventures and those established for more than five years.

Thirdly, it is particularly interesting to see the high proportion of Japanese investment in developing areas—about 60 per cent of the total, and a remarkable 60 per cent (Table 7.4) of foreign investment in manufacturing. These proportions are in striking contrast to the pattern of both United States and United Kingdom foreign investment. Perhaps the explanation for this is to be found in the pattern of Japanese exports, or the fact that Japanese techniques and technology have a relatively greater competitive advantage in developing countries than in developed. If the latter is a factor in the allocation of Japanese investment, one could expect a shift in favour of investment in developed countries with the relatively rapid rate of Japanese technological progress, but in fact the tendency has apparently been in the opposite direction, in favour of a relatively greater investment in developing countries.

Hamada also sheds considerable light on the future trend of Japanese investment abroad. He mentions the growing attraction of low wages in other parts of East Asia and, interestingly, the proposal to give the exports of developing countries preferential access to the markets of developed countries. He mentions Japan's obvious need to import raw materials, and the lack of any systematic opposition to investment abroad by Japan's trade unions. Presumably, this lack of opposition on the part of organised labour, especially as an increasing proportion of Japanese foreign investment is explicitly aimed at taking advantage of lower wages abroad, is a result of the unique personnel policies practised by Japanese companies, but I for one would be interested to hear whether Hamada expects organised opposition to foreign investment to increase as Japanese foreign investment itself becomes more significant.

It is indicative of the quite different climate in which private business operates in Japan that Hamada gives learning effects as one of the reasons for his expectation that Japanese foreign investment will rise rapidly in the future. He notes that initially 'people are not particularly eager to invest abroad . . . Then, little by little people learn about the economic conditions of host countries. They revise their subjective probability.' There is almost certainly some validity in this view for all foreign investment, but had Hymer been writing about this aspect of American investment abroad, he would have emphasised the reaction patterns of oligopolistic competitors rather than learning effects. Perhaps only in Japan, where the government acts to check 'excessive competition' between Japanese companies abroad, would it be possible to place emphasis on learning effects as normally understood.

Hamada notes the normal factors inhibiting foreign investment— notably economic environment, slow and troublesome governmental procedures, some restrictions on capital outflow exercised by the capital-exporting country, a hostile political environment in recipient countries. In this last respect, some of his suggestions appear a little strange. In the light of a quite widespread resentment against the tendency of Japanese companies to employ large numbers of Japanese in their overseas operations, for example, the suggestion that Japanese employees should remain for *longer* periods in the host countries seems odd. His belief that a company which promotes the formation of an organised nation-wide market and improves the level of education and technology in host countries 'will be welcomed by a kind of consensus' in developing countries also seems excessively optimistic.

Hamada suggests that there may be some normal or equilibrium ratio between accumulated foreign assets and GNP. It is not at all obvious why, or in what sense, this should be true. He himself appears to doubt the meaning of the ratio, and yet uses it to estimate the level of Japanese foreign investment in the mid-seventies. He notes that there is a slight negative correlation between a country's rate of growth and the foreign asset/GNP ratio, and speculates that countries tend to find foreign investment opportunities attractive when their own growth rates are low. It is at least possible, of course, and other writers have argued as much for the United Kingdom, that the causal relationship runs the other way, in other words that countries which invest very heavily abroad over a period of years for institutional or other reasons suffer a reduction in growth rate as a result.

Perhaps the most provocative section of Hamada's paper is the final paragraph which, in one sentence, suggests that developing countries, in considering whether to welcome Japanese foreign investment, face a choice between 'short-run material wellbeing and political independence'. Faced with this choice, few countries would welcome foreign investment, but perhaps that is not what Hamada intended to imply.

The main focus in the ensuing discussion was upon the characteristics of Japanese business overseas and the general nature of the multinational corporation.

An American participant observed that Japanese trading companies were perhaps the first great multinational corporations, operating traditionally in the field of commerce but newly entering direct investment and other entrepreneurial activities. It was usual to conceive of the multinational firm as being a production unit: the Japanese trading companies had begun at the marketing end and were now moving into the production end.

This observation prompted one participant to question what he considered a confusing use of terminology. As he understood it, Japanese trading companies were fully integrated national companies and their operation was difficult to encompass within that of the multinational corporation. However, an American participant explained that the term multinational corporation was first coined with reference to the phenomenon which occurred in the fifties and sixties when large corporations began to see their marketing strategies in terms of the whole world market. There was an endless rosary of names for this phenomenon—multinational, transnational, or multiterritorial corporation—but worldwide marketing strategies were the essential element. In this respect, Japanese firms, in their traditional operations abroad, were little different. Now the big new industrial firms—in automobile manufacture, for instance—were moving in the same direction. The particular form of operation, whether it be through a wholly-owned subsidiary or joint venture or branch—is not crucial in this view of the multinational corporation. Where Toyota, say, cannot penetrate a motor car market effectively by exporting because GM is protected to manufacture locally, it is likely to want to move into manufacture or enter a joint-venture arrangement.

Several issues specific to Hamada's paper were raised. One participant from a developing country asked whether the suggestion that Japan was concerned about the export of pollution was serious. He noted that most developing countries were anxious to develop processing and manufacture based on their raw materials and he saw fewer problems with pollution control than were evident in Japan if they were given the opportunity to do this.

Another participant was interested in the role of MITI in curbing excess competition among Japanese foreign investors and in other areas. This had happened in Thailand because of the reluctance of Japanese firms to withdraw from unprofitable ventures. A participant from a developing country suspected that Japanese companies often tried to play their home government off against the host government, for example, by suggesting to one side that approvals were forthcoming from the other and *vice versa*. He suggested that a system of regular consultations between host country and exporting country officials would eliminate confusion and prevent conflicts of interest from being aggravated.

Several participants questioned Hamada's conclusions, however qualified, about the profitability of Japanese firms abroad. The nature of the industries in which Japanese firms were primarily engaged, a Japanese propensity to have a national rather than company sense of profit, and intra-company pricing all cautioned against easy interpretation of the profitability data. A participant from a developing country remarked that, if this kind of data were the sole basis for judgment, one was forced to conclude that everyone is doing very poorly out of foreign investment except the natives.

The more extensive use of Japanese personnel in Japanese business abroad than Americans and Britishers in American and British business abroad was cause for additional comment. Japanese firms appeared to bring personnel right down to the foreman level. But it was argued by at least one participant that this might not be a disadvantage to host countries. The cost of the use of alternative local personnel was high, especially in the early phases of a project, and this may justify the more extensive use of foreigners. A Japanese participant felt that the explanation of Japanese practice lay more in unfamiliarity with local people and labour resources than in purposeful economic rationality. Conservative personnel procedures were attributed to Japan's cultural remoteness, even in South-East Asia. Hamada explained his remark that Japanese personnel should stay longer in host countries in similar terms. He said that Japanese overseas had a transit-passenger attitude which encouraged aloofness from the foreign environment.

8 Foreign Investment in Developing Countries: Indonesia[1]

MOHAMMAD SADLI

Foreign investment is an old as well as a new phenomenon in Indonesia. Before World War II, foreign investment, predominantly Dutch, flourished extensively. It contributed significantly to the opening up of new areas for modern economic activity and the development of natural resources. The development of the so-called modern sector of the economy was mainly due to infrastructure development by the Dutch colonial administration and to private foreign investment. Some important public utilities were also private companies. These investments, however, were much associated with the colonial regime and became the political target of the nationalist movement. The 'dual economy'—a highly productive sector run by westerners existing side by side with a stagnating subsistence economy, and a grey area in between dominated by alien Chinese who controlled the distributive trade—aroused political resentment and partly accounted for the influence of Marxist ideology in the independence movement.

During the brief Japanese occupation, the western managers were replaced by Japanese administrators and for the first time Indonesians had a chance to rise to middle-level management positions. The Japanese interlude in many respects stimulated social and political development and was an eye-opener for Indonesians. Wartime control of enterprises became the forerunner of a more ideologically motivated type of state control of the modern sector of the economy.

At the end of the war came the Revolution, followed by the struggle to defend the fledgling Republic against Dutch attempts to restore their colonial empire in Asia. At the end of 1949 the formal transfer of sovereignty took place and, as a result of a political compromise, the Dutch enterprises were returned to their foreign owners.

The following seven years were a spell of relative quiet in the economy during which foreign enterprises resumed their once dominant position.

[1] The author wishes to thank H. W. Arndt for his help in preparing this chapter.

201

In 1957, the continuing controversy with the Dutch culminated in the dispute over the future of West Irian. Again, the Dutch-owned enterprises became the victims of political conflict. In 1958 they were taken over and subsequently nationalised. They were administered as state enterprises and became the cornerstone of an experiment to set up a socialist mixed economy in which public enterprise controlled the 'commanding heights'. New foreign direct investment was not welcome in this period, although many new industrial projects were financed by foreign credits, mainly government-to-government credit but also some private suppliers' credit. Before long, control by the Indonesian government was extended to British and other western enterprises ostensibly to protect the factories against hostile labour organisations.

In 1966, in the twilight between the old (Sukarno) and the new (Suharto) regimes, a financial settlement was reached with Holland, under which compensation was provided for the nationalised industries. In 1967, when the new government returned foreign enterprises to their original owners and began courting new investment, the former Dutch enterprises were left out. It may be asked why the new government did not cancel the nationalisation of the Dutch enterprises and offer to return them. The answer to this question provides a clue to the indigenous political forces of economic nationalism, a potent force in countries like Indonesia caught up in the process of decolonisation.

One of the major aims of the new states created in this period was the building of a truly national state. This was taken to imply a national economy, that is an economy free from control or domination by foreigners. This sentiment has remained sufficiently strong in Indonesia for a policy of returning all enterprises in the modern sector to their former owners to be politically unacceptable, even to the present regime and political leadership.

Thus, if Indonesia appears to have covered a full cycle in its political orientation, this does not mean that it is, or could ever be, right back where it started. Nationalism remains a strong force. It may be tempered by experience and by the emergence of a new generation of leaders more pragmatic in their political and economic outlook. Nationalism, and specifically economic nationalism, in some—if not all—of the newly independent countries may be growing more flexible, less doctrinaire. The rhythm may be influenced by experience. But its basic aspirations, its long-run objectives, are still alive and powerful. A key element in the aspirations of these countries is to show that they can do the job of nation-building themselves.

Now and in the future, foreign enterprise operating in developing countries has to take these factors into account. Foreign investment is needed to accelerate economic development, but the foreign investors have to live with the forces of economic nationalism in the host country which can display various forms and intensity and will not remain static for very long. In the spirit of partnership for development, enlightened foreign enterprise should accept this as a challenge. Equally, the governments of the industrialised countries, the leadership of the international agencies, as much as the host governments in the developing countries, should be concerned to harness these energies into constructive channels. They should appreciate nationalism as a positive, constructive force, and as a potential ally. Given time to gain self-confidence, it may gradually reach beyond the boundaries of the national state towards co-operation on a regional or later even global level. Thus, if foreign enterprise can find the right accommodation—which is a two-way process—then the pay-off can be great and the experience rewarding.

A New Approach

The government led by General Suharto which took over power from President Sukarno after the abortive coup of October 1965 had on its hands an economy on the verge of collapse: unable to meet payments due on external debts of well over $US2 billion; with export earnings barely covering one-half the cost of imports of goods and services; inflation running at 20-30 per cent a month; far-reaching breakdown of budget control and tax collection; rundown infrastructure and much diminished productive capacity in the industrial and export sectors. During 1966, the new government developed a new approach to economic policy, including a two-year stabilisation program leading on to rehabilitation and resumption of development, decontrol of foreign trade and payments, restoration of orderly price relationships and greater reliance on market forces. Among the government's first pieces of legislation was a Foreign Investment Law, passed by Parliament early in 1967.

Conscious that foreign bilateral aid would for some years be fully mortgaged for balance of payments support and food aid, while such project aid as would be available from foreign governments and international agencies would be needed to rehabilitate the country's infrastructure of roads, ports, irrigation, and public utilities, the government's economic advisers believed that new capital, and technical and managerial know-how, for natural resource development and industrialisation would have to be secured largely through private foreign investment. The Foreign Investment Law was designed to attract such investment by providing fiscal incentives, transfer guarantees, legal security against nationalisation, procedures for settlement of disputes and assurance of management autonomy. It was realised from the start that tax concessions, transfer facilities and guarantees by themselves would not attract much capital. Plans were therefore made for more basic reforms of economic policy, and of the administrative and legal structure, aimed at improving the 'investment and business climate'.

As a demonstration of its sincerity in calling for new investors from abroad, the government promptly began to return to their foreign owners the enterprises that had been placed under government control (though not the Dutch enterprises that had been nationalised and for which compensation had been negotiated). The restoration of these enterprises, with the exception of some groups of estates that took longer to negotiate, was completed within two years.

The Foreign Investment Law.   Following the example of many other developing countries, the main emphasis among inducements to attract foreign investment was laid on tax concessions. These included: a tax holiday on taxation of company profits for a period up to six years for new projects; exemption from import duties on initial equipment and (for up to two years in 'pioneer' industries) on raw materials needed by the enterprise; exemption from stamp duty on capital raisings; carry-forward of losses during the tax holiday period against profits earned subsequently; and accelerated depreciation.

The right of foreign companies to transfer abroad at the current rate of exchange was guaranteed for all profits after tax and other obligations, part of the earnings of foreign employees in Indonesia, costs such as insurance premia, interest, patent fees, etc., and compensation in the event of nationalisation. Repatriation of capital would not be permitted during the tax holiday period.

The government guaranteed that it would not nationalise a foreign enterprise unless a law was passed stating that such a measure was necessary in the national interest. In such a case, the government would pay compensation under the rules of current international law and with provision for agreed procedures for arbitration.

The law guaranteed to foreign companies full power to appoint the management of the enterprise and also to employ foreign technicians in positions for which no qualified Indonesians were available. But a general obligation was imposed on foreign-owned enterprises to provide training facilities so that foreign technicians could be gradually replaced by Indonesians. Permits to operate under the Foreign Investment Law were to be limited to thirty years, but subject to the right of the foreign company to negotiate in the last two years of the period for extensions.

Foreign investors were given the option of straight investment or joint ventures with national firms, with a strong invitation to opt for the latter. In most cases, the foreign business would be required to be incorporated and legally domiciled in Indonesia; operation as a branch of the parent company was permitted but little use has been made of this option.

All fields of investment were declared open to foreign investors, with a few exceptions in which foreign investment would be permitted only in special cases, in co-operation with the Indonesian government or public enterprises. The exceptions included most public utilities (such as harbours, railways, electricity, water supply and telecommunications), mass media and atomic power stations. Priority would be accorded to investment in industries which would earn foreign exchange (such as mining, agricultural export industries, processing for export, or tourism); would save foreign exchange through import substitution; or would provide significant new employment opportunities or introduce new technology or productivity-increasing innovations. An additional year of tax holiday was offered for investment outside Java or for exceptionally risky or capital intensive projects in Java.

Special provision, outside the Foreign Investment Law, was made for the oil industry and banking. Until 1963, the Indonesian oil industry was dominated by three major international oil companies, Shell, Stanvac and Caltex, operating on the basis of 'concessions' which stemmed from contracts concluded with the Dutch colonial administration. In 1963, the Sukarno government had forced the oil companies to change these concessions into 'contracts of work', basically profit-sharing arrangements between them and the Indonesian government. Just before the change of regime, Shell sold out to the government oil enterprise, Pertamina, which also expanded in other ways in the following years and became responsible for negotiating (in conjunction with an inter-departmental committee) and administering all new foreign contracts in the oil industry.

The re-entry of foreign banks was provided for by banking legislation passed early in 1968. Foreign banks were required to pay substantially for the licence to operate in Indonesia ($US1 million in commercial bank-

Table 8.1 Indonesia: approved foreign investment projects (excluding oil and banking)

	Approved by Foreign Investment Board		Final approval by government	
	No. of projects	Intended investment ($US million)	No. of projects	Intended investment ($US million)
1967	29	189.3	23	174.8
1968	77[a]	223.6	69[a]	221.1
1969	118[b]	775.8	85[b]	705.1
1970 (as of 31 May)			58	96.3
Total (as of 31 May 1970)			235	1,197.3

[a] Withdrawn: 4 projects ($US6.9 million).
[b] Withdrawn: 1 project ($US1.25 million).

Source: Foreign Investment Board, Djakarta.

Table 8.2   Indonesia's foreign investment projects: final approvals, by investor's home country, 1967-9[a] (excluding oil and banking)

Country	1967	1968	1969	1967-9
United States	5	10	14	29
Japan	2	8	15	25
Hong Kong	1	10	10	21
Singapore	—	6	8	14
West Germany	1	4	7	12
Netherlands	2	7	2	11
Philippines	2	1	8	11
Australia	2	1	3	6
France	3	2	1	6
Malaysia	—	1	5	6
United Kingdom	2	3	1	6
Belgium	1	2	1	4
Thailand	—	—	4	4
Canada	—	3	—	3
Denmark	1	1	1	3
Norway	—	3	—	3
Switzerland	—	2	1	3
Panama	1	—	1	2
Korea	—	1	—	1
Liberia	—	—	1	1
Sweden	—	—	1	1

[a] Excluding projects withdrawn.

Source: Foreign Investment Board.

Table 8.3   Indonesia's foreign investment projects: final approvals, by industry, to 31 May 1970 (excluding oil and banking)

Industry	Number		Intended investment $ million
1. Mining		9	535.5
2. Manufacturing		131	196.1
a. Heavy industry	24		32.3
b. Light industry	73		72.3
c. Textile industry	9		51.9
d. Chemical industry	6		17.2
e. Pharmaceutical industry	19		22.4
3. Forestry		46	377.4
4. Fishery		7	9.2
5. Transport and communication		7	8.1
6. Trade (including crumb rubber)		10	7.8
7. Construction, housing, real estate		10	18.0
8. Infrastructure		4	4.1
9. Hotels		5	10.5
10. Estates, agriculture		6	30.7
Total		235	1,197.3

Source: Foreign Investment Board.

ing, $US2 million in development banking), the rupiah counterpart of the fee constituting in each case the initial capital of the branch.

Foreign Investment, 1967-70. The response of foreign investors to the new Indonesian policy has been gratifying. By the end of January 1970, some 170 investment projects (outside oil and banking) had received final government approval and another 50 had been approved by the Foreign Investment Board. Total 'intended' investment under these projects amounted to almost $US1.2 billion. Tables 8.1 to 8.4 give breakdowns of these projects by year of approval, size, sector, investor's home country, and location in Indonesia.

Only a small proportion of all this 'intended' investment, perhaps 10 per cent, had been disbursed at the end of 1970. As was recognised at the outset, investment in several sectors, notably natural resource exploration and development, has a long gestation period. Typically, signing of an agreement in mining is followed by one year of general survey and up to three years of exploration. If the results are encouraging, a year is allowed for feasibility and engineering studies. Only then is the investment decision made, probably requiring some additional time to secure finance and marketing. Finally, construction time for major mining projects is two to three years. Thus, it may take eight years from the signing of a contract before a mining project comes to fruition. During the first years of survey and exploration only a small fraction of the 'intended' investment (which may amount to $US75 million or more) is spent, but even this expenditure may run into some millions of dollars and the employment effect is

Table 8.4 Indonesia's foreign investment projects: final approvals, by location of project, 1967-9[a] (excluding oil and banking)

Location	1967	1968	1969	1967-9
Djakarta	12	32	38	82
West Java	2	2	5	9
Central Java	—	2	3	5
East Java	1	6	8	15
North Sumatra, Atjeh	—	5	1	6
Central Sumatra	4	4	3	11
South Sumatra	—	6	3	9
Kalimantan	1	5	13	19
Sulawesi	—	3	2	5
Nusatenggara	—	—	1	1
Maluku	2	—	4	6
West Irian	1	—	1	2
In several provinces	—	—	2	2
Total	23	65	84	172

[a] Excluding projects withdrawn.

Source: Foreign Investment Board.

not negligible. In 1967, for example, scores of Indonesian geologists were without work; now the market for geologists is very tight.

Even in manufacturing, where the rate of disbursement has been higher —after three and a half years, some 25 per cent of projects have been completed and another 25 per cent are due to be completed by the end of 1970—the lag has been longer than usual in advanced or even in some other developing countries. Several factors have contributed to delays. First, confidence that the government's stabilisation program would succeed did not become firm until the end of 1968. Quite a number of the early foreign applicants were probably interested in the first instance in securing approval and then preferred to wait until the economic situation in Indonesia inspired sufficient longer-term confidence. Secondly, given the woeful state of infrastructure and ancillary services in Indonesia, getting factories built and operating has proved a time-consuming process. It takes at least six months to find a suitable location and procure land, and another six months for design and other preparations before construction can start. A construction period of eighteen months is normal and of two years not unusual. Bureaucratic procedures in handling the multitude of permits and clearances required constitute another source of delay.

Administration. Since the Foreign Investment Law was couched in very general terms, policy on a great many important matters was gradually evolved, case by case, in the negotiations between individual foreign companies and the various agencies of the Indonesian government to whom the administration of the law was delegated.

Executive authority for determining policy and making regulations with respect to foreign investment as well as making final decisions on all applications was given to the Economic Stabilisation Council, consisting of seven Cabinet Ministers as well as the Chairman of the Planning Commission (Bappenas) and the Governor of the Central Bank, under the chairmanship of the President. The administration of the law was shared out between a Foreign Investment Board, the government departments responsible for the various sectors of the economy (industry, agriculture, mining, etc.), the Ministry of Finance and the Central Bank. The Foreign Investment Board, which is responsible to the President as chairman of the Foreign Investment Council, consists mainly of senior officials of other departments and had only a small staff of its own, was given the duty of assisting and preparing recommendations for the Economic Stabilisation Council. Formal applications for permits have had to be directed to the government department with jurisdiction over the proposed field of operation, and all policy decisions and contract details on particular projects have been the responsibility of the department concerned, with the Foreign Investment Board acting only in an advisory capacity.

The negotiating authority for all foreign contracts in the oil industry has been a special inter-departmental committee, responsible to the Minister of Mining, with Pertamina officials doing the secretarial and staff work; for permits to foreign banks it has been the Minister of Finance. In both cases, final approval has required the President's signature.

The New Investors. The first international firms to venture out after the welcome signal was given were natural resource development companies, oil groups, mining firms and logging operators. Their motives were probably mixed, the lure of handsome profits, the fear that if they did not move in their competitors would, and the chance to collect a commission (for example, a finder's fee) for taking the risk while the general political and economic climate was still uncertain. Natural resources development is connected with fluctuating world markets, hence risk premia and rates of return are generally higher than those prevailing in industries producing for domestic markets.

Indonesia's pre-war reputation as a profitable field for foreign investment in resource development, and the existence of a pool of experience and knowledge in the western world, mostly embodied in Dutch reports and technicians (some of them now in the employ of international companies) contributed to the early resumption of interest. The fact that new investors were not immediately committed to large investments but only to a million dollars or so over a couple of years for survey and exploration, and had at least four years to make up their minds or sell their interest, also provided a hedge against uncertainty.

The first group of industrial firms consisted of the enterprises returned to their original foreign owners and a few major international firms with an existing export share in the Indonesian market. The former did not wait long to claim back their assets and have them run again. At present, most of these enterprises (Goodyear, Unilever, Heinekens, British American Tobacco, etc.) are thriving concerns in the forefront of industrial rehabilitation and expansion. To make up for their losses and discomfort during the years they lost control, the government granted them three years' tax holiday on a promise of rehabilitation or expansion of their plants. Eleven manufacturing plants were returned to the original owners.

The return of agricultural estates took longer. Two American plantation owners (Goodyear and Uniroyal) came back early and their estates are now well managed and productive. The other nationalities came back rather more slowly. By now, practically all such plantations have been restored. The owners of a few small plantations did not elect to resume possession; financial compensation is now being negotiated. On the Indonesian side, there were at first some reservations with respect to foreign-owned or managed plantations because of sensitive problems of land tenure and community relations. There was fear that returned foreign plantations might incur labour hostility. So far such fears have proved unfounded, most likely because Indonesian labour organisations are no longer under communist influence.

The early entry of major international companies with established names and market shares in South-East Asia can probably be explained as follows. On a short view, the years 1967, 1968, and probably also 1969, were not a safe bet, especially if the amount of investment required was large. But these companies had a market share to protect, or a market share to conquer or reconquer. If developments in Indonesia continued in the right direction then, over a longer run, significant market shares were at stake. Hence the need to come in early and plant the flag. Two things might happen later: the Indonesian government might close further entry once a number of firms were established, or the government might erect tariff walls to protect domestic industries. Jumping a future tariff wall could be a good insurance in the company's long-term interest. Here, too, the initial risk was small since, to establish such a beach-head, an assembly or formulation plant costing some $US1 million or even less was enough, although some firms have spent $US1½-2 million inclusive of working capital. The pharmaceutical industry, the motor vehicle industry and some consumer goods industries with strong labels (dry battery, shoe polish, condensed milk, cosmetics, etc.) are good examples of this category.

Gradually, as economic and political conditions improved, others came, lured by the potentially large domestic consumer market. Investments from Hong Kong and Singapore now occupy third place after the United States and Japan. From these countries, as well as from Japan, a number of manufacturing ventures with no great capital requirements was launched. They have tended to be relatively labour intensive (employing one or more workers per $US5,000 of capital invested) and their products not so sensitive to brand names. In the low income Indonesian consumer market there is a place for low priced, unadvertised commodities (articles of daily use, household or kitchenware, processed food, textiles, etc.). Since mid-1968 when the government provided credible assurance to the Chinese in Indonesia, they and their Hong Kong and Singapore relations have come forward with a steady flow of such investments. There are by now some 100 new foreign-owned manufacturing plants actually in operation or under construction, with an average investment of a little over a million dollars.

Investments in manufacturing or other sectors for the domestic market larger than $US5 million are still very scarce. Of course, Unilever, Goodyear and British American Tobacco are in this category, but these plants existed before the war. I.T.T.'s ground station for satellite telephone communications, which began operating in September 1969 with a total investment close to $US10 million, is as yet a lonely landmark. But more projects are in the pipeline. In the textile industry, for instance, the minimum requirement for a new foreign investment is an integrated plant (spinning, weaving, printing and finishing) and there are five Japanese projects and one large American project already approved. The American project promises a plant of over $US20 million, with a phased build-up stretching over four years. Typically they will start at the end of the production line and work gradually backward. A $US26 million cement plant is to be constructed by an American firm, a $US10 million sheet glass plant will soon also be approved. These multi-million dollar plants producing intermediate goods or producer goods and mainly working for the domestic market apparently require much more careful prior scrutiny of the economic and political situation. Usually the investing party also awaits the encouragement of its home government because this may entail some guarantee or insurance (for example, against political risk) or availability of softer-term loan money.

Another category of foreign investment which is potentially important for Indonesia, but in which only one has so far come into operation, is the labour-intensive assembly or processing plant for export. The typical examples in countries like South Korea, Hong Kong and Taiwan are electronics, garments, toys, shoes, and so on. The one operating firm, working on a small scale as yet, runs an electronics assembly plant. But several inquiries have been made and some of these may eventually come to fruition. Wages in Indonesia for this type of industry are lower than in other countries of the region ($US0.60 to 1.00 a day, depending on circumstances), but other factors are also relevant to costs, such as speed of customs clearances, bonded warehouse or customs area facilities, domestic transport, and availability of industrial estates. At the moment Indonesia can offer only the low wage rate plus government willingness to extend customs area facilities on the site to any plant producing solely or mainly for export.

Credit-Financed Projects. The new policy of encouraging direct private investment represents in part a reaction to Indonesia's unhappy experience with most of the industrial projects financed under the old regime by foreign credits.[2] These had taken four main forms. In the early and mid-1950s, French, German, Italian and other West European industrial firms had offered supplier's credit, in some cases under insurance or guarantees provided by their own governments. Most of these were for public utilities, such as electric supply or harbour facilities, but they also included some industrial plants. Japanese firms, under Japan's $US800 million war reparations commitment to Indonesia, undertook to construct

---

[2] Cf. A. Shakō, *Foreign Economic Assistance in Indonesia, 1950-1961* (Tokyo: Foreign Office, June 1964); D. H. Pond, 'Foreign Economic Assistance to Indonesia, 1956-1963', *Malayan Economic Review*, April 1965; H. W. Arndt, 'Indonesia's Foreign Aid Experience to 1965' (unpublished), Canberra, 1968.

several multi-purpose dams, textile and paper mills, shipyards, hotels and a department store. The United States, as part of her economic aid program, built two large plants, the Gresik cement factory and the Pusri urea factory, on a 'turnkey' basis in the early 1960s. Finally, the Soviet Union and other countries of the Communist Bloc, from 1956 onwards provided government credits totalling some $US646 million which were spent partly on supplies of equipment, such as ships, tractors, diesel generators, buses and railway rolling stock, but were largely allocated for the construction of a large steel mill, a superphosphate plant, a hydro-electric project and aluminium smelter, as well as textile, paper and sugar mills, and cement, tyre, electric bulb and engineering factories.

Indonesia's experience with these projects varied greatly. Japanese reparations financed a large volume of imports of consumer goods and equipment and the construction of some useful buildings, but little use was made of them for industrial development. The two American 'turn-key' plants were built relatively quickly, though at rather high cost, and have been operating effectively since they were handed over as going concerns. Of the projects financed by Western European supplier credit, quite a number of smaller ones ran into difficulties which were at least in part the contractors' fault. Of the many industrial projects undertaken by the countries of the Communist Bloc, only two were completed before 1966, a Czechoslovak tyre factory and an East German sugar mill. Two or three others, including a cement plant and a cotton spinning mill, have been completed since 1966. Of all the large Soviet projects (apart from the Asian Games stadium) not one was completed. Most of them have proved so ill designed or located that, despite the large expenditures already incurred, it is doubtful whether any of them will justify the additional cost required to complete them.

The trouble with the credit-financed projects was not only that many, being largely politically motivated, were quite insufficiently prepared by surveys and feasibility studies. Nor was it only that the suppliers lacked experience and often found it difficult to cope with Indonesian conditions and that the prices at which equipment and services were supplied were often seriously inflated (no doubt partly reflecting the premium for political risk the suppliers were taking). But it lay in the fact that, even in the few cases where the projects were efficiently carried out and resulted in operating units, they had two unfortunate features in common. They saddled Indonesia with large foreign debt commitments which were quite independent of the economic return on the investments to Indonesia, and they did not in most cases transmit to Indonesia the technical know-how needed for their continued operation.

The unhappy experience of those years has been a major factor leading the present government and economic planners to abandon the policy of setting up industrial projects based solely on foreign government or suppliers' credits and to encourage instead private direct investment. It has come to be realised that a viable industrial project is more than just a plant, that the infusion of technical and managerial know-how on a continuing basis is no less important. When a tyre factory, for example, is financed by suppliers' credit, there is no guarantee that up-to-date tyre-making technology will continue to be available once the plant has been handed over. Arrangements for this might be made, but in the past this was overlooked, with the result that after ten years the plant was hopelessly obsolete.

Indonesia may well again resort to supplier credit financing, but care will be taken to profit from past mistakes. One or two approvals have been granted, mainly in the private sector, but they have been confined to cases where the viability of the project is easily established, for example, expansion projects of going concerns or projects with a secure market, and on condition that no Indonesian government or central bank guarantee is required.

'Production-Sharing' Agreements. From 1960 until 1965, Indonesia concluded a number of so-called 'production-sharing' agreements with foreign contractors. Put forward by the Sukarno government as 'the preferred form of foreign investment' since it involved no foreign equity or control in the Indonesian enterprises, these agreements were frequently interpreted abroad as profit-sharing arrangements. In fact, they were motivated mainly by the prevailing scarcity of, and restrictions on, foreign exchange. They involved supplier credit, with repayment scheduled on the basis of 'production-sharing', that is, the foreign supplier agreed to take an agreed proportion of the output in payment for principal and interest, with an Indonesian central bank guarantee covering risks. Most of these agreements were concluded with Japanese firms in resource development projects, such as petroleum, timber, nickel, and pearl and other fisheries. A few were concluded with Western and Eastern European countries but none of these had made much progress by 1966. Although plausible enough on paper, these contracts were found to have serious shortcomings for both parties, though the overriding reason for their failure was probably the unfavourable overall business climate of those years.[3]

In the Indonesian oil industry, the term 'production-sharing' has acquired another meaning. As was mentioned before, the Sukarno government in 1963 forced the international oil companies to change their former concession contracts into 'contracts of work', basically profit-sharing arrangements subject to a 25-year time limit. The rationale was

[3] See Joyce Gibson, 'Production-Sharing', *Bulletin of Indonesian Economic Studies*, Nos. 3 and 4, February and June 1966; G. Clark, 'Japanese Production-Sharing Projects, 1966-1968', *Bulletin of Indonesian Economic Studies*, No. 10, June 1968.

that the country's natural resources were the property of the state up to the point of export and that the foreign company was only a 'contractor' for exploration, exploitation and marketing. Under the agreements, the government had an option to market its share itself if it so elected, but the usual arrangement was for the foreign company to sell the whole output, subject to a profit-sharing formula.

Since 1966 the 'contract of work' has been replaced by a 'production-sharing' arrangement. The foreign party is still a contractor but in principle management is in Indonesian hands. At least, the Indonesian party to the agreements (that is, the state oil enterprise, Pertamina) has greater say in the scope of the work program. The Indonesian party cannot force the foreign contracting company to spend more than it is willing to spend but it has the right to tell the foreign contractor where to drill and where not, how much to produce, and the like. In practice there is a give and take, Pertamina recognising the expertise and the interests of the investing party. The fixed equipment brought in by the contractors becomes Indonesian property upon entry but the foreign contractors can write it off in their cost calculation. An innovation of the production-sharing contracts is agreement on a 'cost ceiling', that is to say, the surplus available for distribution between the two parties is defined as the excess of physical output over 'costs', where costs are actual costs or 40 per cent of sales proceeds, whichever is the smaller, translated into physical value terms at the disposal price of the foreign contractor or, if Pertamina can demonstrate its ability to obtain a higher price, at the latter price. The surplus after deduction of costs is divided in the ratio of 65 per cent to the government and 35 per cent to the company. The government (that is, Pertamina) can elect to receive its share in kind and do its own marketing. Pertamina is responsible for all domestic requirements (housing, transport, etc.) for which it is compensated (the compensation forming part of the costs) and for customs clearance and other relations with the government.

In 1966 and 1967 practically none of the major oil companies was willing to accept these conditions. The ice was broken by a few so-called independents, small companies or consortia, which ventured to sign the first contracts. By now, most of the major oil companies have overcome their reservations and have concluded exploration contracts, and others have bought into the independents who secured promising areas. There are now over thirty oil contracts with many well-known companies, including Japex, Kyushu (presently teaming up with Union Carbide), Sinclair, Union Oil, Mobil Oil, Gulf Oil, Stanvac, Caltex Pacific, Shell, BP, Continental, Texaco, and many others. Typically these contracts require them to spend on exploration for some six years agreed minimum amounts averaging $US1½ million per year. Between 1970 and 1975, therefore, these companies are expected to spend altogether at least

$US50 million. Another feature of the oil exploration agreements is the 'turn-back of area' obligation. Every three years the contractors are required to relinquish 25 per cent of their exploration areas so that they retain in the end only a small fraction of their original areas.

Because the oil companies under production-sharing contracts technically will not hold property (which is transferred to Pertamina), the contracts do not fall under the Foreign Investment Law. The procedures are also different. Tenders are invited and there is a special committee to receive these tenders. The contract is awarded to the highest bidder, in terms of attractiveness of commitments and offer of payment of a cash (or signature) bonus and production bonuses.

Some Policy Issues

Role of Foreign Investments. In the economic policies or 'philosophy' of the new government, foreign investment is accorded a 'supplementary' or 'complementary' role. In principle, or in the long run, foreign investment should not become a mainstay of the economy. The major pillars of the economy should be domestic firms and the indigenous business class. Foreign investments are conceived as filling gaps, deficiencies in the array of domestic factors of production which it is hoped will not be permanent. The ideal still is to build a 'national economy' well rooted in the domestic soil. Foreign investment should also be 'domesticated', in other words integrated into the national economy. Enclaves of foreign enterprise, insulated from the vagaries of the domestic economic and social environment, are anathema.

How far this conception is a practical proposition remains to be seen. But it should be recognised that this idea has the force of belief. It is therefore of political consequence, now and in the future. It is part of the ideology of economic nationalism. Today Indonesia is willing to make compromises to attract foreign investment. Provided the incoming foreign ventures subscribe broadly to these goals, Indonesia does not insist on immediate fulfilment of the implied requirements. But the expectation is there and some day it must be met. Otherwise the governments of the day and/or the investing companies may from time to time experience rough political weather.

Welcome to private foreign investment is also recognised as a *quid pro quo* in international aid diplomacy. The aid donor countries often count non-official capital flows like foreign investment and export credit as part of the total 'aid' to a developing country, for instance in relation to the one per cent aid target.

In general, Indonesian government policy does not favour the coupling of official aid to the requirements of a private investment from the particular donor country, for instance where a private company is willing to undertake the investment only if part of the aid commitment of its government is earmarked for related infrastructure investment. Wherever possible, the private investor is expected to take care of his own infrastructure needs. The reason is simply that all the foreign project aid that can be secured is needed for the priority requirements of the government's development plan. But it is recognised that for smaller private investment projects, such as small manufacturing plants which cannot be expected to carry the cost of necessary port or public utility development or the construction of industrial estates but which meet the government's general priority criteria, exceptions will be made.

Operation of the Foreign Investment Law. The Foreign Investment Law has a number of features which have given rise to difficulties and cause for second thoughts. One is its relative brevity. It is general rather than specific, leaving numerous important details to be handled by government regulations or decrees or by departmental policies. It conforms in this respect to a general legal tradition, probably a heritage from the Dutch period. Power lies more with the administration than with the legislature. For the tastes of foreign investors the summary laws provide too little protection. They are also disconcerted by the custom in Indonesian legislation of superimposing one new law on the body of existing laws regulating the same subject, so that the whole structure does not become transparent by reading one or two documents. Efforts have been made to assist foreign investors by collecting the main regulations in handbooks[4] and recently by setting up an Investment Information Centre in Djakarta. But these do not entirely meet the problem.[5]

A conceptual bias in the Foreign Investment Law, reflecting a general preoccupation and probably some blind spots in the thinking of policymakers at the time of its formulation, is that only equity capital qualifies for the protection and facilities of the law. Loan capital is excluded, although not explicitly, and the same is true for investment in the form of intangibles, such as goodwill, industrial know-how or patents, or management. This bias makes it difficult to handle investment in the form of credits or intangibles. But if loan capital is not too large relative to equity, debt servicing should constitute no problem. If a direct investment package includes royalties to be paid on patents this can also be done easily. On the other hand, capitalisation of know-how or goodwill is still frowned upon.

Another shortcoming of the law is that it does not state a formula for distinguishing foreign from domestic enterprises. This stems from the preoccupation with capital. In practice, one needs such a distinction, for

---

[4] See, e.g., *Economic Data for Investors in Indonesia* (Djakarta: Bank Indonesia, 1968).
[5] On this and other problems mentioned in the following paragraphs, see also M. Clapham, 'Difficulties of Foreign Investors in Indonesia', and M. Sadli, 'Difficulties of Foreign Investors: A Comment', *Bulletin of Indonesian Economic Studies*, March 1970.

instance, for international arbitration, or for certain rights and facilities enjoyed only by domestic or by foreign enterprises. If, for example, a foreign investor makes a 10 per cent equity investment, so that the Indonesian partner is in full majority, what will happen in case of a tax dispute? A foreign investor could, after exhaustion of local remedies, eventually seek international arbitration but a domestic enterprise cannot do so. The tax dispute will normally involve the whole enterprise, not merely the foreign partner. Again, a foreign enterprise may not engage in retail trade outside the big cities. What are the rights of an Indonesian firm which has entered into a joint venture with a foreign partner but retains a majority? Will it lose its distribution rights?

The Incentive System. The incentives for incoming new foreign investment consist mainly of the granting of tax holidays to new ventures in priority industries. The maximum tax holiday period is six years, with leeway for only one or two years to be decided by the government. The formula is probably not an effective system for influencing the direction of foreign investment. For instance, a foreign investor, having free choice, will not go outside Java just to pocket one extra year of tax holiday. The government reserves and has already exercised the right to close Java for foreign investment in a particular industry which is believed to be sufficiently catered for; in such a case, where the foreign investor has no choice, the extra year will serve at best as a consolation prize.

There is a school of thought that discounts the effectiveness of tax holidays as an incentive system. According to this argument the size of a tax holiday is very seldom an overriding factor in the decision of a firm to enter a country or not; it does not affect the crucial issues of short-run survival or the long-run prospects of profit. This may be true. But too many underdeveloped countries have adopted this system in their frantic competition for outside capital for any one country like Indonesia to contract out. A unilateral withdrawal of tax incentives might be construed as denoting a less welcoming attitude to foreign firms which tend to measure a country's welcome mat from faraway boardrooms aided by memos of corporation lawyers. Alternatively, if a tax holiday is granted for long enough to affect the long-run rate of return, as in Puerto Rico where a 10-year tax holiday is given, most companies are tax free for the whole of their payout period.

A second incentive is the exemption from import duties for first-round capital equipment, spares and some supplies. This is a normal feature of foreign investment legislation in developing countries. In the Indonesian experience it has not in itself created major difficulties (except in determining what constitutes capital equipment—a telephone set, an air conditioner, office equipment, and how many?—and what quantity of spares and supplies is appropriate). The main difficulty stems from the fact that subsequent rounds, and particularly replacement requirements, are not exempted. How is the line to be drawn between replacement and new plant? One can argue that fine distinctions do not really matter much since the revenue forgone at the margin is small. In practice the main cost is the nuisance of frequent hassles between investors and customs authorities about definitions and amounts.

Customs duty exemption on equipment, spares and supplies sometimes also runs counter to the requirements of domestic industry protection. Suppose textile and crumb rubber equipment can be produced at home but normally at a price, say 15 per cent, above that of a comparable import product. Should the government prohibit the duty free importation of such equipment? Whatever is decided there will be unfairness towards one party or the other, the domestic industrialist or the foreign investor.

Another fiscal incentive is the possibility of duty free imports of raw materials for two years, provided the industry is given pioneer status and the raw materials conform to customs definitions. This privilege has been a constant source of complaints, disputes and friction between new investors, customs officials, officials of the Department of Industries (about pioneer status) and old firms that readily complain about discrimination if they do not enjoy the same privileges as new firms. Even if pioneer status is reserved for entirely new industries, there remains a ticklish problem. A new industry may produce a close substitute competitive with an established industry. A synthetic fibre plant, for instance, requests pioneer status because it is new, but its products compete to some extent with cotton fabrics.

Definitions also matter to the customs authorities because they are reluctant to give import duty privileges to pure assembly operations. The degree of industrial processing needs to be sufficiently substantial to warrant the loss of revenue. After all, the object is to promote industrialisation. Mere screwdriver-type operations or simple mixing and blending of chemicals do not deserve the incentive concessions.

The incentive system normally consists of exemptions, reduction of rates, and other exceptional concessions. It is a constant source of headaches for the administration in the exercise of its discretion, a source of irritation to all concerned and a source of ambiguity in the rules of the game. In the long run it should be abolished, but meanwhile the developing countries are stuck with its problems.

Transfer and Other Guarantees. The transfer guarantees, at the most favourable official exchange rate, for investment income, foreign employees' earnings and certain costs incurred abroad, which are given by the Foreign Investment Law, are not of immediate importance since Indonesia's foreign exchange system is now extremely liberal and virtually free of multiple exchange rates. But they were undoubtedly important in 1967 when exchange controls and multiple exchange rates were still extensive, and they remain important for the future. Foreign investors are unlikely to share in full the confidence of the present Indonesian government that re-imposition of exchange controls can be indefinitely avoided; and while their trust in the assurances provided can be no greater than their confidence about the survival of a government determined to honour them, the inclusion of guarantees in formal legislation provides some additional safeguard.

The Foreign Investment Law also provides a guarantee of freedom of management and a guarantee against expropriation without adequate compensation. Much the same applies to these. Disputes between foreign investors and the government concerning interpretation of agreements or of the investment law can be submitted to international conciliation or arbitration. Several bilateral international agreements have been signed reaffirming this principle.

Obligations of Foreign Investors. The law stipulates that foreign investors should employ Indonesians as much as possible and should provide training to enable more Indonesians to qualify for employment at all levels. No quantitative norms are set in the law, nor is a time-table fixed. This again reflects the general nature of Indonesian laws. The stipulation could be elaborated by administrative decree but even this is not yet possible since its administrators still lack the experience to set quantitative norms over time. The government favours flexibility but this is often not appreciated by the foreign investors who see in such a situation only a measure of uncertainty.

The Foreign Investment Law also imposes an obligation on the investor to sell part of the stock of the Indonesian subsidiary to the Indonesian public. Again neither time nor amount is spelled out. Most foreign firms have no objections to this. Others have voiced concern about having to sell shares to an unknown public; they would prefer to sell to parties in whom they have confidence.

There is also an obligation, stemming from government policy rather than from the law, on incoming foreign firms to try to find a local partner and form a joint venture. This requirement can be waived for large investments (e.g. in mining) where there are practically no local partners who can sensibly share in the venture. The joint-venture obligation has both economic motives (Indonesians are given a chance to participate in gaining entrepreneurial and industrial experience) and political ones (joint ventures are believed to be more palatable to the community).

Restrictions. The law gives the government power to close certain industries to foreign investment for various reasons, including security and domestic enterprise protection. The period for which a foreign investment licence is given is also limited—thirty years, subject to extension. These restrictions reflect the spirit of economic nationalism which remains a strong undercurrent beneath the otherwise pragmatic attitude of the present regime. Most people recognise that for the foreseeable future foreign investment will be prominent in certain industries, such as oil, mining, timber and even quite a few manufacturing industries. But Parliament in passing a law thinks far ahead and often the law expresses a 'matter of principle' rather than practical rules for the day. At its best, an Indonesian law is a combination of the two, of *das Sein und das Sollen.*

The laws governing land ownership are also somewhat discriminatory. A foreigner may not own land. He can, however, have a long-term lease. For many foreign investors this also constitutes a source of insecurity, although the law dates back to the colonial days when the Dutch administration tried to protect the small indigenous farmers from land alienation to foreigners. Indonesian land law is still oriented towards agriculture rather than industry and other urban uses.

Protection of Domestic Industry. This is provided mainly by tariffs on imports of competing goods, but complete prohibition of imports has been resorted to in some cases as more easily enforceable than either tariffs or quota restrictions. This list of banned imports could conceivably grow as domestic industry becomes capable of meeting total domestic demand for particular products.

Occasionally protection is granted to established firms, both domestic and foreign, by periodic closing of an industry to further entry, and if necessary also to capacity expansion by existing plants. Government regulation to balance industrial capacity with demand is still accepted as legitimate, but practical difficulties of projecting demand and determining 'capacity' throw serious doubt on this policy as an instrument for protection. There is much to be said for using it sparingly and leaving the achievement of balance to the market.

National Planning and Priorities. A question often raised in Indonesia has been to what extent foreign private investment can be fitted into the national development plan, or at least be subjected to the national development priorities. The answer is not clear. There is a chapter on private investment in the national Five Year Plan which came into operation on 1 April 1969. But since the Plan is merely a set of policy guidelines, rather than an integrated quantitative investment plan, such a chapter had no regulatory implications. Some efforts were made to estimate the inflow of foreign as well as domestic private capital, but these were at best educated guesses.

Reference was made above to the priorities laid down in the regulations for implementation of the Foreign Investment Law. In effect, foreign investments are declared beneficial if they tend to improve the balance of payments or create a lot of employment or introduce an innovation. These are worthy priorities but so broad that not many investments are likely to be rejected on their basis. Some effort has been made to qualify the import replacement criterion since this may easily be abused.

Domestic assembling of, say, cosmetics is always foreign currency saving in the first instance, but price effects (the products of the domestic assembly are often cheaper than imports on account of very high import duties) and advertising effects (once an international company has a domestic plant it advertises more intensively) may raise total consumption and cause a net increase in the import bill.

A persuasive argument against any attempts to impose priorities on the inflow of foreign investment is that if particular industries are regarded as less desirable, then something should be done to regulate demand for the product and in this way the capacity of the industry as a whole, rather than single out the foreign investors. After all, domestic investment in the cosmetics industry would presumably have the same effects on the balance of payments. This is true, but not only are foreign firms liable to be more aggressive (for example, in their advertising) but such an approach may not be so easy. Once the foreign firm is part of the family of domestic industries its lobbying carries more weight, re-inforced by all sorts of arguments about employment, multiplier and scale effects, all legitimate in their own context.

Public sector planning is an exercise in the allocation of scarce resources which are substantially under public control. Private capital is not an allocable resource in quite the same sense, and this applies especially to foreign private capital. The opportunity costs of permitting or limiting investment in a given field are much less clear. If investment in one part of the public sector is limited, more capital will generally be available for expenditure in another field. In the case of private investment, and particularly foreign private investment, this is not necessarily so. If a foreign cosmetics firm is barred from entry it is most unlikely to come into the country to set up a rubber estate or engineering plant instead. Hence, the opportunity cost of refusing such investment may need to be measured by the absolute benefits forgone, in terms of employment creation, skill formation or industrial linkage effects, rather than in terms of the relative advantages of foreign investment in alternative fields.

As against this, it can be argued that if an industry is regarded as a low priority industry because it caters for a luxury demand but is highly profitable because purchasing power is unequally distributed, it should be left to indigenous enterprise. Cosmetics may not be a good example because it demands qualities of product development, advertising and distribution which a developing country may find it difficult to achieve on its own. But one can readily think of others. Clearly, cost-benefit analysis in this field is a tricky business.

There is also the practical problem of the policy instruments available to direct or regulate the inflow of direct investment if regulation is thought desirable. The approval requirement is one. The government can refuse entry or make it subject to certain conditions. Usually these conditions aim at maximising the industrial development effects. Incoming pharmaceutical firms wanting to assemble (or formulate) their products in Indonesia are asked to commit themselves to producing at least one basic raw material or ingredient in the country after so many years; incoming milk plants assembling imported powdered milk are asked to do something to upgrade the local dairy industry; forestry firms get large concessions if they promise to set up processing industries over time; and so forth. One problem that has been encountered here is the firmness of the contract. A foreign economic adviser has suggested that many of the contracts negotiated by Indonesia in the past three years have been too lenient, too full of loopholes through which the foreign investors would be able to delay the fulfilment of these conditions. The relevant clause normally contains the phrase 'if feasibility studies warrant the establishment of such projects'.

The Size of the Domestic Market. Large-scale manufacturing investment in developing countries is frequently inhibited by the limited size of the domestic market. Although Indonesia is a large country of 120 million population, the low level of per capita income (probably not more than $US100) and the present stage of industrial development keep the domestic market for many industrial products small in relation to optimal capacities of plants. The situation is aggravated by aggressive competition in some fields from the industrialised countries and by the exports of industrialising countries in the region, such as Mainland China and Hong Kong, Taiwan, Korea, India and Pakistan. Moreover, the geography of Indonesia, an archipelago close to free-port cities, renders a policy of tariff protection of the domestic market difficult to enforce against smuggling.

The limited size of the domestic market has led potential foreign investors to demand a variety of special concessions. Among them are the granting of temporary monopolies, that is barring further entry (especially of other foreign investors) for, say, five years; requests for protection duties of 25 per cent or more; and demands for adequate protection against 'dumping' (on their definition of dumping).

Demands for temporary exclusion of international competitors as a *quid pro quo* for coming in pose awkward problems for the host government. The Indonesian government is committed to the principle of a market economy, and monopolies, certainly foreign monopolies, are not popular. Often what is requested is not merely a monopoly but tariff protection as well, since the size of the market is insufficient for a plant of optimum size. In a developing country a new enterprise also suffers the handicap of lack of 'external economies'. For instance, even a good sized tyre plant in Indonesia will have to buy its chemicals from abroad, while the costs of electricity, power and transport are generally higher than in a country like Japan. Since a large multinational company is usually engaged in monopolistic competition with rival companies, a concession to one company often invites protest, sometimes even diplomatic moves, from the other parties. For a country like Indonesia, dependent at present upon the goodwill of a number of donor countries, this can pose a delicate problem. Hence, for practical purposes, even with a possible loss of efficiency, an open door policy is the only alternative. The result may be: a score of automobile assembly plants, fifteen pharmaceutical formulation plants, four condensed milk plants, two (if not more) electric cable plants, several galvanised iron sheet plants, and so on.

Often enough it becomes clear that the interest of a foreign company in putting up a factory in Indonesia is to protect or acquire a market share. Before the country opened its doors to foreign investment the international companies were content to supply Indonesia from abroad. Once the possibility of local production through foreign direct investment opens up, the international companies face a dilemma: whoever gets in first may eventually control the market behind a tariff wall and enjoy other, non-tariff, types of protection. Hence they offer small assembly plants, usually without great economies, and promise a progressive deletion program if the market expands. For the host government it may be wiser at times to forgo a local investment altogether and remain, for the time being, a buyer in the international market, where effective competition may keep prices down. But departmental officials are often tempted by the prospect of the benefits of industrialisation. Here again, if analysis of opportunity costs and benefits could be refined and quantified, governments would be helped to make better decisions. Even if politics will not allow an optimal solution, at least policy makers would have a better idea of how far they were deviating from the optimum.

Production for Export. One obvious escape from the limitations of the domestic market is production for export.

Indonesian experience so far has not encountered any reluctance on the part of subsidiaries of international corporations to embark on efforts to export some of their local production. Normally these companies state in their applications that they will consider exports to neighbouring countries, and some of the already operating companies such as Philips, Unilever, Bata, Goodyear have concrete plans in this direction. Several major international firms have stated that they would undertake large-scale investments in Indonesia if they could have adequate assurance that in the foreseeable future a wider regional market free of tariff barriers could be created for their products. An example is a major international automobile company which has proposed a significant investment in assembling and local production of parts provided it forms part of a regional scheme; they would produce one range of parts or components in Indonesia, another in Singapore, others again in Bangkok and Manila.

Between the plants in the different countries of the region there should then be the possibility of a 'barter' of components and parts. In some such way, these major multinational companies could play the same role in South-East Asia as they have done in other continents, helping to integrate national into regional economies.

Conclusion

The three or four years that have elapsed since the change of Indonesian policy towards foreign investment under the new regime are too short a period for broad generalisations.

Indonesia perhaps illustrates the Hirschman thesis that the economic development effects of foreign investment differ from country to country depending on its stage of growth. One reason why foreign investment in Indonesia is probably more beneficial than, for instance, in Latin America is that in Indonesia it does not yet replace indigenous resources already productively employed or stifle potential domestic investment.

There will be problems of potential clashes of interest. In natural resource development, such as the oil industry, the interests of the foreign companies and the Indonesian government may diverge on such matters as rates of exploitation, investment spending, marketing, prices, or the degree of local content and local procurement. At present, Indonesia relies for defence of her national interests *vis-à-vis* the large foreign corporation on competition between the foreign companies, between major companies and independents, and between companies of different countries.

In manufacturing and service industries, the most important impact of foreign investment on economic development is likely to come from its intangible rather than its physical aspects, on Indonesia's human rather than its physical capital. Through the presence in Indonesia of foreign companies and their managers, foreign investment may transmit to the Indonesian business community a new set of attitudes—aggressiveness, alertness to new business opportunities, self-confidence and self-reliance —as well as information and know-how. Foreign businessmen may also facilitate the development of more appropriate government policies towards business in general, because they are more vocal, because they present their proposals and problems more effectively, because they are able to deal with government as more nearly equal partners. The injection into the local society of a new strain of business culture should, if things go reasonably well, have a healthy and invigorating effect.

But in Indonesia, as elsewhere, foreign investment may have its negative aspects. Domestic enterprise and initiative may be pushed into the background. Foreign business may come to dominate the scene. Favourable spillover effects may benefit primarily the local Chinese whose business ability and head start may enable them to profit from the widening of

opportunities and horizons, but largely pass by the indigenous entrepreneurs. It will take all the imaginative initiative of the foreign investors,
in their own enlightened self-interest, to bridge the cultural gap that
separates them from the indigenous business community.

Research on the impact of foreign investment on the economic development of the host country needs to be done not by economists alone but
on a multi-disciplinary basis.

Comments and Discussion

ED SAFARIAN opened the discussion: Because of their general interest and
importance, two issues, which Sadli notes, are worth underlining—namely
incentives and fragmentation. These lead to a broader question about the
range of choices open to a country developing with the aid of foreign
techniques.

To an outsider, the size of the incentives which Indonesia finds it necessary to offer foreign direct investors seems quite large. These cover not
only various tax holidays and concessions but special protection of various
kinds. Admittedly, the size of these incentives reflects the need to regain
the confidence of foreign investors, and also the high risk involved in
primary industry. But one wonders how much the size of the incentives
reflects also the competition from other countries seeking to attract
foreign investors, and perhaps also competition within Indonesia.

The theory of the effects of foreign direct investment suggests that
much of the gain comes from increased tax revenue unless passed back in
subsidies. If the incentives differ between countries, and if they are
effective in attracting industry, they can lead to international misallocation of capital. If they are offsetting, there is an unnecessary subsidy to
investment and a reduced general tax yield. Moreover, as Sadli notes, the
administration of the incentives is a constant source of difficulty for all
involved.

Might not some harmonisation of the incentives be possible by co-
operation between the countries involved, in order to increase their net
gain from foreign investment? Someone noted earlier that the interests
of the countries diverge, and that not even relatively rich federal countries
such as Canada have succeeded in harmonising such investment incentives internally. One wonders, however, why economic and political
wisdom must begin in high-income countries.

A second issue is the fragmentation of industry (what has been called
the 'miniature replica' effect) which was attributed earlier in the conference to protection and the lack of effective competition. Given the strong
desire for development and employment, it may seem necessary to attract
firms even at the cost of some (hopefully) initial inefficiency. The long-run
problems for industrial structure can be severe, however, as Canadian and
Australian experience suggests. In any case, much of the fragmentation

effect may reflect a lack of integrated industrial policy as such, or competition between regional governments or government departments. It seems to me that countries such as Indonesia are in a position to minimise directly some of these wastes of short production runs and excessive product differentiation, given the control over new foreign investment. It does not seem convincing to say that an open door policy for firms from every country is necessary, with the fragmentation which results. Elsewhere Sadli makes it clear that moratoria on entry to an industry can be declared. If this approach leads to continuing monopoly situations, it can be corrected by reducing or eliminating protection against imports.

Finally, Sadli's chapter suggests a broader question. The rate of development depends on many variables, and not just those associated with foreign direct investment. Depending on a country's stage of development, its resources and history, and how well it has exercised policies, it has a range of options available to it in terms of any desired access to foreign technology. Japan's growth rate, for example, gives it a wide range of options in this respect. Given the domestic situation, however, the question remains whether there is any leeway in the choice of a technique for importing foreign technology. (I appreciate that these are not entirely independent questions.) To what extent can the package brought by foreign direct investment—capital, techniques, markets—be broken up? What are the costs and benefits theoretically and empirically of foreign direct investment (with and without the minority share issue in the subsidiary), joint ventures, licensing, management contracts, state purchases of techniques, and other forms of access to foreign techniques? How do the net benefits differ by types of industry? What further points can be made if political variables are introduced? It would be of great value if more models and empirical studies could be made of the effects of alternative forms of access to foreign techniques, as well as comparisons with the net benefits of domestic emulation as such via infant industry protection or otherwise.

Further discussion is reported at the end of Chapter 10.

9 Foreign Investment in Developing Countries: Thailand

AMNUAY VIRAVAN

Before World War II, foreign investment in Thailand was largely limited to the field of trade and mining. Industrial activities at that time accounted for a very small proportion of national income and centred almost exclusively on agricultural processing.

The war and its aftermath brought the need for industrialisation and a greater degree of self-sufficiency into sharp focus and the government decided to take the necessary steps to start a number of industrial enterprises ranging over paper, gunny bags, plywood, sugar, and glass containers. A policy was established then that the government should pave the way for the private sector in industrial development.

It was not until towards the end of the 1950s that monetary and fiscal reform in Thailand began to have a favourable impact on economic growth and stability. With a more favourable investment climate, the government decided to shift its industrial policy in favour of private initiatives and to promote foreign investment, the latter as a means of facilitating the flow of capital and advanced technology from external sources.

For the same reasons as in other South-East Asian countries, in Thailand it was felt that the pace of industrialisation could be greatly accelerated through an investment incentive program. Such a program could also serve to overcome many existing investment impediments like an unfavourable tax structure or excessive market risks which might take a considerably long time to overcome under normal circumstances.

Thailand's first effort to stimulate industrial investment through incentive measures was the Industrial Investment Act of 1954. For various reasons including the general economic and political conditions, the Act proved ineffective and had to be repealed in 1958.

The Incentive Program

A new industrial investment act was promulgated in 1960 and subsequently revised in 1962. It is interesting to note the differences in the promotional privileges offered under the two Acts.

Industrial Investment Act of 1960	*Industrial Investment Act of 1962*
1. Approved industry exempt from import duties on machinery, component parts and accessories, reduction or exemption on materials, tools and instruments and prefabricated frames and equipment for factory construction at the discretion of the Board of Investment.	Approved industry exempt from import duties on all these items.
2. No exemption from business taxes (equivalent to sales taxes, but collected at time of importation) on imported capital goods.	Approved industry exempt from business taxes on machinery, component parts and accessories used on industrial activities, and other equipment and prefabricated framework for factory construction.
3. No exemption from business taxes on exported products.	Approved industry partly or wholly exempt from business taxes on exported products for a specified period at the discretion of the Board of Investment.
4. New and approved industry exempt from income tax on profits for two years only, within first five years from date of issuance of promotion certificate.	New and approved industry exempt from income tax on profits for five years, beginning the first accounting year business sells products or earns revenue.
5. Approved industry may remit abroad in foreign currency only if it is repatriated investment capital or profit derived therefrom.	Broadened to include loans from foreign countries, interest, profits derived from such loans abroad, and currency which it is committed to pay for the use of patent rights, incentives agreements, or other services of a third party.

6. Approved industry exempt from import duty on raw materials, degree and length of time at the discretion of the Board of Investment, no exemption from business tax on import of raw materials.

Five-year exemption or part exemption of import duty and business taxes on imported raw materials. Since February 1967, only a one-third exemption of such duty and tax may be given to any industry at the discretion of the Board. But after September 1969, this privilege is no longer granted.

However, there were similarities:

1. Approved industry shall receive a guarantee that the state will not initiate any similar industrial activity and will not transfer any private industry to its ownership.

2. If approved industry is a duly registered company or partnership, it shall be permitted to own land for carrying on industrial activity to the extent the Board of Investment deems appropriate. This applies only to foreign owned companies, since Thai companies can own land anyway.

3. Approved industry may bring alien skilled workers or experts into the country, together with their families, regardless of immigration law quota provisions.

4. Exports of the approved industry's products shall be permitted, unless contrary to the national interest.

5. When the Board of Investment deems it appropriate, certain special rights and privileges may be given to an approved industry: prohibition or restriction of import of competitive product, increase of custom duty on competitive product, and, in case of export, exemption from or reduction of export duty (if any) and business tax on products of an approved industry.

The Investment Promotion Act of 1962 has provided a basic framework for investment promotion activities in Thailand up to the present time. Although the Act itself provides a more liberal incentive program than the 1960 version, there have been strong indications that after a certain stage of industrial development, a reduction in incentives may be appropriate.

Industrial Promotion and National Economic Development Plans

Thailand launched its first 6-year National Economic Development Plan in 1961. The plan spelled out national development targets and economic policies to achieve the desired objectives including the policy to encourage private industrial investment through incentives. The First and the Second Plans (the latter for 1967-71) were somewhat similar in scope and addressed themselves mainly to the public development projects. They did not make a serious attempt to establish industrial targets in terms of productive capacities nor recommend specific programs or measures to accelerate industrialisation beyond those already available under the existing institutional arrangements.

The thinking at the time was that the industrial sector should be left to private initiative with minimum government interference. The government might guide the flow of private investment under its incentive system but should not get involved in other aspects of industrial planning and development. Such an approach is now being reappraised, and there seems to be a strong movement in favour of specific industrial targets and development programs in the national plan.

The economic planners of Thailand have, from the very beginning, attached great importance to the creation of a favourable investment climate. Political and economic stability have been singled out as the key factors for economic development in the private sector. Incentive measures under the Investment Promotion Act may be effective to a certain extent but they do not and cannot compensate for other shortcomings. The long-run policy is, therefore, to find ways and means to improve the existing structure and system in a manner that would lessen reliance on special incentives in the future.

A case in point is a current program to bring about improvement in our fiscal and monetary system in order to mobilise savings for investment in desired areas. Expansion and co-ordination of government and private activities which would assist industrialists in obtaining the necessary capital, technology, and managerial know-how is also aimed in the same direction.

Past Pattern of Industrial Development

Industrial development in Thailand since 1960 has followed a defined pattern. New industries were first attracted into the area of import substitution to take advantage of the existing local market which is adequate to support domestic production of many types of consumer goods. Agricultural and mineral processing also attracted substantial new investments, thus increasing the export earnings of Thailand from the primary sector.

New consumer goods industries, of course, tend to start a backward linkage effect and provide new investment opportunities in the raw material based industries such as synthetic yarn, tin plate, chemicals, and packaging materials.

In the raw material based industries, economies of scale become a critical factor. Consequently, the opportunities for investment in this area are more limited. There is also a limit to growth of pure import-substitution industries in view of the relatively small domestic market in terms of purchasing power.

New Emphasis on Export-Oriented Industries

It is because of this limitation that Thailand has shifted its emphasis in investment promotion to industries which depend mainly on indigenous raw materials or those with high labour content. It is believed that such industrial activities will be more oriented towards exports because of their competitive advantages.

The past pattern of industrial development in Thailand has come about more by accident than design. It is fair to ask the question, 'Why is Thailand not more outward-looking like some of her neighbours, namely, Singapore, Korea, and Taiwan?'

A number of factors may be attributed to Thailand's past approach to industrialisation. Among them are the following: first, lack of pressure to produce industrial output for export because of the favourable foreign exchange position and high export earnings from the agricultural sector; second, inadequate incentive to export and lack of institutional arrangements to promote industrial exports effectively; and third, excessive taxes on production which make manufacturing costs too high to be internationally competitive.

As Thailand enters the new development decade, its foreign exchange position is less favourable. A decline in international reserves which started in 1969 is expected to continue at least for the next few years, due partly to its stagnant exports and partly to a decline in foreign spending in Thailand. The need to diversify and increase exports from the industrial sector has become increasingly apparent. It is equally obvious that some structural and policy changes will be needed to make the industrial export drive more effective.

Another pressing problem is the need to distribute industrialisation to provincial areas. To be sure, many industries, like agricultural processing and mining, find it desirable to locate their factories close to the raw material sources. But most manufacturing industries tend to concentrate around the capital and port city and there is an apparent need to bring industry out into rural areas.

In the case of Thailand, Bangkok is the growth centre. There is no comparison between Bangkok and other Thai cities in terms of infrastructural facilities. Naturally, industry will not move to a remote area if it is not economically desirable to do so. New growth centres must be developed in other parts of the country to stimulate the geographic distribution of selected industries.

The Role of Foreign Investment

Manufacturing activities, especially those with foreign co-operation, have been a most dynamic force in the Thai economy, registering an average annual growth rate of over 10 per cent in real terms during the past decade. Industrial growth compares favourably with other sectors, including agriculture and trade, and the manufacturing sector has increased its contribution to national income from about 12 per cent in 1960 to nearly 15 per cent in 1969.

One of the major reasons behind industrial growth in Thailand is the active response of the local and foreign investors to the Investment Incentive Program first launched by the government in 1959. Under this program, approximately $US1 billion have been approved and approximately three-fourths has already been invested in enterprises dealing with agricultural processing, manufacturing, mining, transport and tourism. The remainder is in the process of implementation (see Table 9.1).

Although capital participation from external sources has accounted for only one-third of total equity investment in this promotion program, its relative contribution is much greater in terms of industrial technology, labour skill improvement and managerial know-how. This is quite evident

Table 9.1   Thailand: industrial investment promotion, 1966-9

Item	1966		1967		1968		1969
(A) Promotion certificates issued (no.)	33		89		96		83
(B) Promotion certificates issued (number, by nationality of ownership)							
Thai establishments	14		41		43		34
Foreign establishments	2		2		8		1
Joint venture establishments	17		46		45		48
(C) Promotion certificates issued (number, by new or expanded activities)							
New investments	28		77		79		52
Expansion	5		12		17		31
(D) Total registered capital (million baht)		506		985		639		1,338
Thai	315		723		360		861	
Foreign	191		262		279		477	
(E) Total investment (million baht)	1,713		4,531		2,648		4,423
(F) Machinery (million baht)	1,036		2,555		1,361		2,674
(G) Direct local employment (persons)	4,419		10,940		11,210		18,780

Source: Board of Investment, Thailand.

in many leading manufacturing activities: from such highly labour-intensive industries as garment and accessories and watch dials to capital-intensive activities like oil refinery and steel rolling, from import-substitution industries like textiles and sheet glass to export-oriented industries like food-canning and wood products.

The industrial sector of Thailand has also relied substantially on external credit to finance its capital requirements. Much of this comes in the form of suppliers' credit on machinery and equipment with the terms of repayment varying from 5 to 8 years and interest rates at 5-6 per cent.

Because of the difficulty in raising equity capital for industrial investment, this sector is being developed with a relatively high financial leverage. On the average, industrial projects under the Board of Investment's promotion program have a debt-equity ratio of about 3.3 to 1.

More than twenty different countries take part in the industrial development of Thailand as foreign investors (see Table 9.2). The leading investing nations are Japan, the United States and the Republic of China, in that order.

Table 9.2 Thailand: promoted investment, by country

		Total registered capital[a]		
Rank	Nationality of ownership	million baht	percentage by country	Cumulative percentage
1	Thailand	4,199	66.5	66.5
2	Japan	670	10.6	77.1
3	United States	363	5.7	82.8
4	Republic of China	303	4.8	87.6
5	United Kingdom	116	1.8	89.4
6	Malaysia	85	1.4	90.8
7	Netherlands	50	0.8	91.6
8	West Germany	47	0.7	92.3
9	Hong Kong	31	0.5	92.8
10	Denmark	28	0.4	93.2
11	Singapore	26	0.4	93.6
12	Switzerland	22	0.4	94.0
13	India	19	0.3	94.3
14	Australia	14	0.2	94.5
15	Sweden	14	0.2	94.7
16	Italy	12	0.2	94.9
17	Portugal	11	0.2	95.1
18	Philippines	11	0.2	95.3
19	Other	296	4.7	100.0
	Total	6,317	100.0	100.0

[a] Based on promotion certificates issued until the end of March 1970.

Source: Board of Investment, Thailand.

Most, or nearly all, foreign investment in promoted industry has taken place in the form of joint ventures. Out of nearly 500 new enterprises under promotion, only 26 are 100 per cent foreign owned investment. The present policy is to encourage more joint ventures on a more equal basis as the local industrial sector becomes stronger. Politically and socially, industrial co-operation on a joint venture basis is likely to prove more stable and more lasting.

Foreign investment has also contributed substantially to the balance of payments of Thailand. The Bank of Thailand reported that the annual inflow of foreign capital during the late 1960s exceeded the outflow by about $US50 million. The equity capital from foreign sources registered with the Bank of Thailand also showed an upward trend with a peak inflow of about $US30 million in 1968 (see Table 9.3).

Japan, which is the leading foreign investor in Thailand, attracts special attention. The presence of Japanese in Thailand is conspicuous not only in industry but in export-import, in wholesale trade, and in banking and services as well. The situation has raised fears among many observers about possible Japanese economic domination. To be sure, Japanese business policy is highly aggressive and market-oriented, a great deal more so than its western counterpart. The Japanese way of doing business, which is effective, sometimes causes resentment from local competitors. It is not surprising, therefore, that some business interests would occasionally attempt to promote nationalism as a shield against Japanese competition.

The broader base of manufacturing industry has also produced a strong movement for protectionism. This feeling has become apparent in a few industries and could be extended to others if such a movement proves effective.

Nationalism and protectionism may have their place in the process of industrialisation as long as one can look at the problems objectively and

Table 9.3   Thailand: foreign investment 1961–9 (million baht)

Year	Yearly inflow of foreign equity capital	Total yearly inflow of investment	Total yearly outflow (profits, etc.)	Net yearly investment
1961	32.4	120.9	204.9	−84.0
1962	43.7	156.7	204.7	−48.0
1963	152.1	348.2	194.5	153.7
1964	153.8	373.3	201.6	172.7
1965	112.4	603.7	205.0	398.7
1966	198.5	587.7	345.6	242.1
1967	400.4	869.5	377.4	492.1
1968	598.2	1,312.5	339.0	972.5
1969	230.2	1,090.0	420.3	669.7

Source: Bank of Thailand.

make the decisions accordingly. Our effort to industrialise the economy could, however, be hampered if we were carried away by emotional and irrational considerations. Fortunately, the authorities in Thailand seem to be well aware of the extent of economic nationalism that Thailand should realistically follow.

Basic Policy Questions

The interaction of many forces, both rational and irrational, have led to a number of dichotomies in investment promotion. These dichotomies will be identified and discussed. The investment process is so dynamic that continuous examination of policy and promotional strategy is desirable in order to cope with the changing requirements.

Foreign Investment versus Nationalism

The first dichotomy is the need for foreign investment in Thailand and the fear of foreign economic domination. On the one hand, we welcome foreign capital, technology and managerial know-how to accelerate and modernise our industrial sector as well as to make Thailand and especially Bangkok the business centre of South-East Asia. On the other hand, some of us fear economic domination from external sources and resent the economic freedom of the foreign business community. It is a simple case of nationalism versus internationalism and firm decisions must be made by the political leaders. This issue is further complicated when we bring our aspirations for regionalism into consideration.

Argument has been advanced in favour of nationalism on a selective basis. Economic activities in the form of natural resource exploitation, in commodity trade, banking, agricultural processing and domestically already well-established industries, should under this policy be reserved to Thai nationals. Others would like to see a more protectionist policy by requiring all new business and industrial ventures to have Thai investors in a majority ownership. Yet, a counter argument is also made to the effect that if we want foreign investment, which we do, we must adopt a completely open-door policy. Foreign investment promotion would never work effectively on a half-hearted basis.

Some neighbouring countries have insisted on local majority ownership in all investment projects in order to avoid problems and difficulties. Whether this is the best approach is subject to discussion. Thailand's position is that we should be more flexible and open-minded. Majority ownership does not necessarily mean control of management, nor does it give a better assurance for success. A multitude of factors must be considered in order to evaluate the long-term contribution of an investment project. In some cases, like an electronic assembling industry for export which is highly labour intensive, 100 per cent foreign ownership may be allowable. This may be the only way of ensuring such new industrial development. In other cases, foreign investors may consider a majority holding initially, but should allow the local investors to take a greater share of the enterprise after a certain period of time.

The current policy in Thailand is therefore to strike a balance in foreign investment by encouraging greater participation from foreign countries and by discouraging the complete control of a particular industry by a single foreign nation.

Diversification of foreign investment has, however, not been very effective under present political conditions in the region. Many western investors may have begun to adopt a wait-and-see attitude and may be holding back their investment plans until the political situation becomes clearer. If political stability does not return to the region, foreign investment in Thailand and in Asia may come from Japan to an even larger extent because of the Japanese investors' greater willingness to take risks.

Outward-Looking versus Inward-Looking Policies

The second dichotomy concerns the relation between import-substitution and export-oriented industries, or inward-looking versus outward-looking policies. Previous industrial investment in Thailand was largely oriented towards import substitution. Such a pattern of industrial development could be accepted and encouraged in the initial stages of industrialisation. But it could not be pursued indefinitely. Internally-oriented industrial investment in developing countries is limited by the domestic market factor and, in most cases, will require tariff protection against competition and dumping from external sources. Such protection requirements will be even greater in an economy which depends largely on tariffs as the source of public revenue. But excessive protection in the industrial sector may run a danger of making the next stage of development more difficult due to higher costs of production permissible in over-protected industry.

Developing countries are therefore urged to be more outward-looking in their industrial policy. If necessary, we should overcome local market limitations by promoting industrial exports through various forms of fiscal incentive. Such a policy would offset the danger arising from over-protection and ensure better utilisation of economic resources, with benefits accruing from economies of scale.

Export incentives combined with tariff protection have been used effectively in many countries in their industrialisation programs, most notably in Japan, Korea and the Republic of China. Their effectiveness is, however, conditioned by a proper selection of industrial activities. Naturally, developing countries can be more competitive in industries with higher labour content or industries which depend mainly on competitively priced indigenous raw materials.

Export incentives do not necessarily involve subsidy payments to the exporters. What is needed is a system which will enable the industrial producers for export to avoid absorbing high taxes or duties in their production costs. The need is more apparent in a high-duty economy like Thailand.

One alternative is to extend market boundaries beyond the national borders by adopting regional industrial co-operation and harmonisation programs. This would call for specialisation in specific industrial activities by each member country in the region of arrangement and market-sharing through a preferential trading system. For example, the ASEAN countries could decide to undertake an industrial co-operation program by investing in five different industries, one in each country, on a scale large enough to supply the ASEAN region. The industries could be paper pulp, food processing, automotive parts, rubber products and iron and steel.

A co-operative program for regional or subregional industrialisation has been under study by the ECAFE. This effort is commendable but much more is needed to bring political leaders to the conference table to discuss the program seriously. Regional co-operation in South-East Asia is still in its early stage of development and the member countries seem to be content at the present time with the low-cost, low-risk projects such as joint training and research programs, joint promotion activities, and regional exploration surveys.

An Integrated Program for Industrial Development

The third problem deals with the role of the government in promoting industrial development. Our economic planners and those who are responsible for guiding the flow of private investment have long advocated labour-intensive and agriculture-based industries. Yet, private investors, both local and foreign, do not give this type of industry its deserved attention. Foreign investment, in particular, appears to be more concerned with producing for the domestic market and some even make investment conditional upon partners' not being allowed to market outside of Thailand. Such restrictions should be lifted but the question remains whether the private sector needs greater support and assistance from the government in order to fulfil these objectives.

Greater fiscal support and understanding from the government and its tax-collecting agencies are being requested by industrial enterprises. An argument is advanced that export-oriented industries, to be successful, must be able to obtain full tax rebate on their exports and obtain it in the shortest possible time. The Customs Department should also be more understanding of the needs and requirements of the industrial producers in working out a rebate formula. The revenue department can also be more sympathetic in its legal interpretation and in business tax collection. The 7.7 per cent business and municipal taxes on every level of output can put tremendous financial strain on industrialists, especially in such industries as textiles. High rates of business taxation tend, of course, to favour vertical integration. Perhaps business tax on value-added should be used to overcome the existing problem. The accounting difficulty with the value-added system could be a blessing in disguise, for it could provide useful information and make tax evasion rather more difficult.

Greater budgetary support for the government may also be necessary in the industrialisation program, especially in the development of industrial estates and bonded manufacturing areas to promote exports. One can easily understand the difficulties of the government in allocating limited financial resources to public development projects, but industrial estates are also an important infrastructure for industrial development.

Industrial parks and export-processing zones are in fact self-financing in the same way as public utilities. Perhaps the best way to realise this objective is to set up an independent organisation responsible for industrial estate development in the kingdom. Such an organisation can get initial funds from the government but can obtain long-term loans from external sources for its development program.

Local industries can also be developed more rapidly with successful diversification in the agricultural sector. Some of our industries experience difficulties in getting adequate supplies of agricultural raw materials because of a slow response from the primary sector. The problems can be attributed partly to market imperfections and partly to inadequate research and extension services. A strong effort to overcome these obstacles may contribute significantly to our industrial development.

Conclusions

Foreign investment has undoubtedly been a dynamic force in the development of Thai industries and its contribution is expected to continue to be important for a long time. The question is not whether foreign investment is needed but how foreign capital and technology should be put to work in the economy of Thailand.

On past performance, foreign investment has not been an unmixed blessing. While many industrial successes are due to foreign co-operation, some mistakes in private investment decisions have also been made. This is, perhaps, part of the free-enterprise system. The encouraging note is that we can always learn from our past mistakes and the knowledge can be used to avoid future failures.

Looking back over the past decade of industrial development, our investment promotion policy might profitably be reshaped in the following manner, in order to answer more effectively the needs of the nation.

First, foreign investment should be welcomed and promoted on a selective basis. Its contribution to the national economy in terms of income and employment must be substantial to justify governmental support. Assembly-type industries would be ruled out except in the case of labour-intensive items for export. Furthermore, foreign participation should serve to supplement and strengthen local effort, not to overwhelm it.

Second, new investments should be more outward-looking or oriented towards export. Such projects must, of course, have comparative advantage and economies of scale. In the case of Thailand, our strength is associated with labour, agricultural supplies and mineral resources. Ability to trade internationally is the ultimate test of industrial efficiency.

Third, industrial development should be promoted on a regional basis to overcome the market limitations. Major industrial powers should also be invited to co-operate in our regional endeavours. Although regional industrial co-operation in South-East Asia is still at an exploratory stage, there is much to be gained from joint efforts. The pace should be accelerated.

Fourth, while industrial development must become more important, the agricultural sector will remain economically, socially and politically dominant for many years in the economy of Thailand. This does not mean, however, that the government should not extend more efforts in promoting industrialisation. Much can still be done to provide better services and assistance to private enterprises. In this respect, developed countries can be more co-operative in providing economic and technical assistance to enhance our capacity to assist the private sector.

Fifth, most developing countries are looking for ways and means of mobilising private savings for productive investment. Attempts are being made to promote general public participation in business and industries through public sales of stock and securities. Such an approach requires public confidence in corporate management and foreign investors can play an important role in promoting local capital market. Established foreign companies always attract public confidence, and they should capitalise on it to induce public capital participation.

The policy considerations outlined above are not unreasonable. They take into full acount the fact that foreign investment is a business decision and must be made in view of business objectives. Foreign investment must have an adequate rate of return and security but, as a host nation, we can rightly expect to share equitably in the benefits from our joint efforts.

Comments and Discussion

ARTHUR PAUL opened the discussion: What seems to me to be of most interest in Amnuay's work is not his description of Thailand's present practices in respect to the inducement and regulation of foreign investment; rather it is the outline of the way in which it is to be reshaped. Thailand has had several decades of experience with policies that have promoted private foreign investment by offering various inducements, but the performance has not been one of unmixed blessings. Nevertheless, in

Amnuay's opinion, the question is still not whether foreign investment is needed, but how foreign capital and technology should be put to work in the economy.

As to the reshaping of Thailand's investment policies, Amnuay's first point is the need for greater selectivity. Priority is to be given to labour-intensive projects and export-oriented industries and also to projects related to the agricultural sector and to those that could be geographically located in the provincial areas.

It is hard to quarrel with this program other than to point out that private foreign capital is not an allocable resource and that the scope for applying selectivity is therefore limited. Sadli called attention to this fact in his chapter on foreign investment in Indonesia.

Nevertheless, Thailand is certainly in a position to alter the terms of its inducements to foreign capital and in doing so may, in fact, effect a considerable degree of selectivity.

There are emerging problems in the developing countries of Asia to which foreign investors seem as yet to have given little consideration. One of these is the manpower absorption problem. In many Asian countries the new additions to the labour force each year far exceed the number of people absorbed by the expansion of industry, and the underlying demographic factors generating this imbalance are so strong that the situation can only get worse in coming years. Even if the most optimistic assumptions are used in estimating the demand for labour created by industrial expansion, the tensions that will arise from rapidly rising levels of unemployment seem likely to become sufficiently alarming in some countries to affect adversely the climate of investment in those areas.

The extent to which this set of circumstances will emerge varies in each country. To lessen its impact will require changes in developmental plans that will influence selectivity in foreign investment policies, particularly in respect to preferences for labour intensive industries and projects more directly related to the agricultural sector. When these are export oriented, they raise trade policy as well as foreign investment issues.

The transfer of technology is so closely related to investment policy that I would like to add a few comments on that subject. Certainly more selectivity in this field is needed, but it requires great skill to apply it properly. New technology specifically designed for the needs of developing countries has not been offered by many prospective investors, most of whom want to find wider uses for their existing devices with as little modification as possible to meet the very different circumstances encountered in the various developing areas.

It is interesting to note that it was not the multinational corporations that developed the high yielding seeds that have advanced agricultural production so rapidly in recent years. But the large manufacturers of the equipment for making synthetic fertilisers and for irrigation projects benefited greatly from this technological achievement. The research that developed high-yielding seeds was carried out by private institutions, but it is quite possible that some of the more far-sighted multinational firms, looking several steps ahead, would be willing to divert their research resources to the special technological needs of developing countries. In that case developing countries themselves could well afford to offer greater inducements to those firms that tied such an approach to their investment proposals.

Amnuay's thoughts about regional industrial integration as a means of overcoming market limitations are interesting. The results of ECAFE's efforts to foster regionalism in the economic field, as well as those of sub-regional groups, have so far been disappointing. The suggestions in the Sadli chapter that some international firms are now proposing that their investments should be tied to regional arrangements regarding the supply of parts and raw materials and access to wider markets are also interesting. It is hard to see how these arrangements could, in fact, be carried out because they require the same kind of regional intergovernmental negotiations that have proved so difficult at ECAFE. However, it is possible that some multinational firms could be induced to adjust their proposals so that they became sufficiently attractive to overcome the existing resistance to regional integration. Both the investing firms and the countries involved, especially smaller countries, would have much to gain by creating new patterns of investment along these lines.

Further discussion is reported at the end of Chapter 10.

10 Foreign Investment in Developing Countries: Korea

YOONSAE YANG

Devastation of the land and industrial capacity, and the despair of people on the verge of starvation, were the remnants of the 3-year-old Korean war at the time of the Armistice in July 1953. Rehabilitation and reconstruction of the war-torn land were the immediate tasks confronting the government and people of the Republic of Korea. This took approximately four years, from 1954 to 1957. Economic activities during this period were marked by extensive relief and resettlement of the populace, aimed primarily at providing them with the basic necessities of life— food, clothing, and meagre shelter.

Restoration of industries in the consumer goods area, such as flour milling, sugar refining, and textiles took place rather rapidly due to the inflow of aid commodities in these fields. This is reflected by the figure of 18.1 per cent average annual growth in the manufacturing sector during this period and a 5.5 per cent annual average growth in GNP. The foreign aid inflow amounted to over $US1.2 billion worth of goods and services, mostly from the United States.

From 1958, the economic growth rate began to decline; GNP grew at only 4.1 per cent between 1958 and 1961. The manufacturing sector recorded an annual average growth of only 6.7 per cent during this period. Heavy emphasis by the government on stabilisation to check rising inflationary pressures could have been a factor affecting growth performance. But the over-expansion of the consumer industries in the earlier period was probably the most important cause of this later decline and stagnation in the economic activities. Decline in the amount of aid from the United States was also a factor dictating re-evaluation of past policies. And finally, Korea experienced two revolutions in 1960 and 1961. Some shift in emphasis in investment from consumer industries to capital goods began to take place in this period.

It was with the military regime in 1961 that the government began to adopt economic development as the primary objective of national endeavour. The first 5-year plan implemented in 1962 marked a new era in the nation's economic history by endeavouring to foster growth based on a comprehensive economic program. For the first time in the country's history, the Korean government adopted goals and guidelines for development. The plan, although somewhat hastily prepared, reflected the ambitions and aspirations of the government and people and represented a sincere effort to establish a self-sustaining economy. This effort continues, 1972 being the last year of the second 5-year plan, and the next plan being implemented from 1972 through to 1976.

The major economic achievements between 1959 and 1969 can be summarised as follows: GNP grew 2.3 times, 1.5 times for agriculture, 4.2 times for mining and manufacturing, and 2.4 times for social overhead and the service industries. Exports increased 33.4 times, whereas imports rose 6 times. Investment increased 7.7 times, while domestic savings reached W240.6 billion in 1969, up from minus W2.6 billion in 1959. Thus, domestic savings constituted 62 per cent of capital formation in 1969. This situation differs greatly from that in 1959 when Korea relied almost totally on foreign savings for investment. Population increased by 30 per cent during this period. A sustained high rate of growth, rapid industrialisation, a remarkable increase in exports and domestic savings, emphasis on social overhead capital (power, transportation, and communications), and an ever-increasing awareness of the importance of, and emphasis on, the attainment of stability were the salient features of the economy in the sixties. Koreans now view these developments with satisfaction and are encouraged in their will to further economic progress. The determination of a well-educated, readily trainable people, and the decisive leadership provided by President Park Chung Hee, who was identified closely with the aspirations of the people, were the instrumental factors in economic success during this decade. Korea was also fortunate in effective support from friendly countries. Substantial grants-in-aid in the fifties and economic co-operation in the form of loans, both concessional and commercial, in the sixties, have also contributed to Korea's development. Foreign investors emerged as an important factor in the economic activity of the nation during the latter half of that decade.

Attempts to Attract Foreign Capital

Foreign capital had been channelled into Korea in the form of grant aid in the 1950s. However, a large part of this aid was spent on the consumption needs of the people rather than on financing independent industrial projects. The introduction of foreign loans, both concessional and commercial, has led to a great increase in capital for investment in the sixties. The Foreign Investment Encouragement Law (FIEL) was promulgated in 1960 to induce direct equity investment by foreign businesses, either independently or jointly with Korean partners. The term 'investment' is confined for the purposes of this chapter to equity, not loans.

The Foreign Investment Encouragement Law contained all the essential incentives that currently prevail in similar laws of other developing countries. It provided for a 5-year tax holiday. Following the initial five years, tax was reduced by two-thirds for the first two years and by one-third for another year. Machinery and raw materials brought into Korea as capital were duty-free. Remittance of principal and profit was guaranteed under this law. On the principal, the investors could remit 20 per cent of their investment every year after two years of operation, while they could remit profit not exceeding 20 per cent of their investment beginning the first year. Protection of property against expropriation and prompt and fair compensation in case of such expropriation were also defined in the law. In order to draw benefits from this law, an investor had to hold shares of at least 25 per cent in the corporation. The law was, in general, liberal and well designed to induce foreign investment, although it was not without defects, since it was born out of the experience and example of other countries and had yet to be tested on the Korean scene.

Table 10.1   Korea: summary status of foreign equity investment as of May 1970 ($US '000)

1. Type of Ownership	Projects approved	Equity amounts
Sole ownership	43	32,223
Joint venture	172	126,163
Total	215	158,386

2. Equity investment by year		
Approved year	Projects approved	Equity amounts
1962	2	2,120
1963	3	5,442
1964	5	757
1965	11	22,281
1966	12	5,333
1967	24	25,812
1968	49	30,382
1969	49	44,682
1970	60	21,577
Cumulated total	215	158,386

Source: Economic Planning Board, Korea.

Investment up to 1965 under the law was insignificant. There were no applications in 1960 and 1961, and only ten between 1962 and 1964, with a total value of $US8.3 million. Poor performance during this period is attributable to the lack of confidence by the international business community in the Korean economy and a high rate of inflation.

The signs of a significant increase in interest by prospective investors began to appear in 1965. Eleven applications totalling $US22.2 million were approved during 1965 (see Table 10.1). Among them were two fertiliser plants, one involving $US10 million equity investment with a $US24.4 million aid loan, and the other $US10.5 million equity investment with a $US24.6 million aid loan. Thus, up to this point, investment was primarily made to form an acceptable equity base to induce aid loans or other kinds of credit backed by the repayment guarantees of the government. Investors did not commonly take the total risk on ventures by themselves.

Strong anti-inflationary measures taken from the latter part of 1963, including a reduction of budgetary expenditures as well as tighter control on monetary expansion, brought about considerable results by 1965. Wholesale price indexes rose only 10 per cent during this year, as against 20.5 per cent in 1963 and 34.7 per cent in 1964. Major reforms, such as the institution of a floating exchange rate system and the raising of domestic interest rates, also took place during this period. An increased inflow of potential investors was noticeable. The need for a single agency of the government to guide potential investors, to answer their questions, and to provide services was acute, as these visitors did not know where or how to approach the government and business. They were often subjected to a merry-go-round type of treatment by the different government ministries. Also, further improvements in the Foreign Investment Encouragement Law were called for to remedy some of its defects. Both needs were fulfilled in 1966 with the establishment of the Office of Investment Promotion and the passage of the Foreign Capital Inducement Law (FCIL).

The Foreign Capital Inducement Law, promulgated in August 1966, consolidated the Foreign Capital Encouragement Law, the law concerning the importation of capital goods on deferred payment, and the law concerning repayment guarantees by the government. This was done with the hope that a single law governing all of the importation of foreign capital, of a non-aid type, would be more convenient for all concerned. It has seven chapters and fifty-four articles, of which Chapter 1, General Provisions, and Chapter 2, Investment by Foreign Nationals, are the parts most relevant to direct investors.

In essence, the Korean government further liberalised the incentives in the Foreign Investment Encouragement Law. It still provides five years' tax holiday on corporate income tax, acquisition tax, and property tax, followed by three years' half-holiday. All equipment and raw materials approved as investment requirements can be imported duty-free. The percentage of shares that investors had to hold to qualify for the benefits under the FIEL was deleted. There is no limitation as to the percentage of shares that foreign investors must hold to get the benefits of the FCIL. Free remittance of profit, in the form of dividends, was made possible, while the FIEL placed a ceiling at 20 per cent of the investment. FCIL maintained the same provision for repatriation of principal as was contained in the old law. A clause to oblige investors to employ at least 90 per cent Korean personnel under the old law was removed.

Other Laws and Regulations. Liberalisation of the laws and regulations was not limited to the Foreign Capital Inducement Law. It extended to trade laws, various tax and custom laws, labour laws, the law concerning acquisition of land by aliens, and a whole set of implementation laws and working rules under these laws. In fact, liberalisation to meet the convenience of investors has been a continuing process and will be for quite some time. As long as the desire of the government to encourage foreign investment exists, these laws will have to accommodate to changing conditions over time, and to the different needs of investors. Innumerable changes have taken place in the laws, decrees, and working rules to reduce the red tape, to simplify daily business, and to reduce the time necessary to process investment applications. Changes in the rules and regulations are only good when the people who handle the actual cases act in accordance with the spirit of these changes. Nevertheless, I would like to point out some of the important changes that have been made to add incentives for the investors as well as to reduce bureaucratic red tape.

The personal income tax law now has a provision to exempt from income tax foreign nationals working in foreign companies. All raw materials brought into Korea to be processed for export are duty-free and also exempt from commodity tax. The use of inter-company accounts is permitted for companies operating as subsidiaries of parent companies in their home countries. Industries manufacturing exclusively for export can be bonded, entitling them to free-port operations for their imports and exports. Financing of raw material imports of products to be processed for export is available at concessional rates.

A special labour law governing the foreign company is, in effect, one which eliminates the possibility of strikes or demonstrations by unions in their negotiations with management.

The Office of Investment Promotion (OIP). Concurrently with the enactment of the Foreign Capital Inducement Law, the Office of Investment Promotion was established in the Economic Planning Board, the senior ministry of the Korean government, headed by a minister who is *ex officio* Deputy Prime Minister. The director of the Office of Investment Promotion is charged with the responsibility of promoting foreign investment by providing the services investors require and by processing their applications in a speedy manner, as well as by providing pre-investment and post-investment consultations. The Office was also given responsibility for cutting through the red tape existing among the various other government agencies that investors have to deal with. The results have been satisfying. The Office is able to process several applications, well-documented, within a week. Most are processed and approved in a month. Twelve applications at a total value of $US5.3 million were approved in 1966, 24 applications at $US25.8 million in 1967, 49 applications at $US30.4 million in 1968, 49 applications at $US44.7 million in 1969, and 60 applications at $US21.6 million to May of 1970. As the number of applications increased, the variety of businesses increased sharply. Post-investment consultations have become an increasingly important part of the daily business of the OIP. Bureaucratic mentalities operating within existing rules and regulations were unable to cope with the sophistication and subtleties of doing business with a highly complicated foreign society. This was brought to the attention of the President, who immediately ordered an enlargement in the scope of operations of the OIP by bringing in men from the various ministries concerned in order to serve the needs of the foreign investors in one spot.

The One-Stop Service Office was established in April of 1970 by a Presidential decree. Two middle-grade officers from the Ministry of Commerce and Industry, one from the Ministry of Justice, and one from the Internal Tax Office have been assigned to this office with one assistant each. The decree defined the areas in which these officers must get the approval of their ministers for action. Other than this, they were given the authority to act on behalf of their ministers on all matters relating to their ministries and were given the official seals of their ministers. The One-Stop Service Office in the OIP is therefore engaged in a wide range of business, such as securing and renewing of visas for the investors and their families, licensing imports and exports, and reviewing the technical feasibility of applications. The difficulties for investors in their routine operations have decreased substantially.

The One-Stop Service Office is far from being complete, as it does not have representation of all the government agencies, both national and local, affecting in one way or the other the daily functions of the investors. However, the OIP acts with other agencies on behalf of the investors as soon as any difficulty is brought to its attention.

The Response of Foreign Investors

At the end of May 1970, the total number of applications approved and on the active list reached 215, amounting to $US158 million. Forty-three cases at a total value of $US32 million were solely owned by the foreign investors and 172 cases, amounting to $US126 million, had local partners, these varying greatly in the split of shares between the parties.

American investment was largest, with 89 cases valued at $US93 million, while Japanese cases brought in $US26 million. Korean residents abroad had forty-four applications approved to the amount of $US22 million. Four Netherlands cases were approved for $US6.3 million, seven Panamanian cases for $US5.5 million, four West German cases for $US864,000, two Hong Kong residents for $US1.5 million, and five others for $US2.8 million.

This country breakdown shows that United States firms accounted for 41 per cent of the projects in number and 60 per cent in value, thereby ranking first in both respects. Japan ranked second with 28 per cent of the projects and about 16 per cent of the value. Thus, Japanese capital was primarily in the form of smaller units than was American (see Table 10.2).

The industries in which these investors have engaged vary widely. Electronics and electrical appliances are the most common with 40 projects involving $US36 million. Textiles and garments had 29 projects with $US18.5 million, chemical products had 22 projects with $US17 million, oil had five projects with $US13 million, tools and parts, 26 projects with $US5.6 million, and there were 21 general merchandise projects with $US3.4 million. Other areas include pharmaceuticals, animal husbandry, food processing, transportation, hotels, metal and steel, and ceramics. Eighty-seven out of 215 projects were for export only and the rest were either for a combination of exports and domestic use or were solely for domestic sale. There were thirty-one projects approved for an increase in the original investment, either through using retained profits or by bringing in additional capital to enlarge the operation. Twenty-seven cases had separate technical assistance agreements with provisions for payments of royalties. Almost all of the rest of the applications had some kind of technical assistance clause in the joint venture agreement.

Table 10.2   Korea: foreign investment, by country

Country	Projects approved	Equity $US '000
United States	89	92,938
Japan	60	26,212
Overseas Resident	44	22,204
Panama	7	5,510
West Germany	4	864
Netherlands	4	6,293
Hong Kong	2	1,530
Others	5	2,835
Total	215	158,386

Source: Economic Planning Board, Korea.

Processing of investment applications may take over a month. For example, projects are sometimes a combination of equity and substantial loans, and consequently the completion of agreements with the partners, financial organisations and governments concerned are complex and time-consuming. Sometimes applications submitted may not be complete or final, since an investor may file an application in order to register his intent with the government and take time to crystallise his project plan. Third, some applications may encounter opposition from local concerns, as these mean competition with superior financial and technical ability. While in some instances local concerns are justified in their fears, most frequently their protests merely represent resistance to innovation and improvement of an inefficient industry. It takes time to mediate in such circumstances.

All applications must be screened by the Foreign Investment Deliberation Committee organised under the provisions of the Foreign Capital Inducement Law. The members of this committee include ministers of the relevant government ministries, governors of banks, business representatives and others appointed by the Minister of the Economic Planning Board. The committee meets on an *ad hoc* basis when there are enough cases to be screened, and though the Economic Planning Board tries, in any event, to plan these meetings at least once a month, sometimes this cannot be arranged.

It takes time for investors to proceed with investment after approval is

Table 10.3   Korea: foreign investment, by type of industrial project

	Projects approved	Equity $US '000
Textiles and garments	29	18,504
Electronics and electrical components	40	36,016
Chemicals	22	16,909
Fertilisers	3	21,200
Petroleum	5	13,166
Pharmaceuticals	6	2,419
Poultry, livestock	6	619
Food processing	11	2,091
Machinery and parts	26	5,571
Iron and metal	11	9,148
Automobiles and transportation	11	4,848
Shipbuilding	3	3,347
Power generation	1	5,000
Ceramics	6	4,337
Tourist service	4	7,850
General merchandise	21	3,364
Others	10	3,997
Total	215	158,386

Source: Economic Planning Board, Korea.

obtained. Out of the total of 215 projects on the active list, 97 projects, or 45 per cent of the total number, amounting to $US95 million or 60 per cent of the total value, had completed the approved investment. One hundred and eighteen cases, representing 55 per cent in number and 40 per cent in value, are in various stages of preparation. Out of 97 cases which have completed the investment and are now in operation, 65 cases completed their investment within one year after they had obtained government approval, while 15 cases took one to one and a half years, and 17 cases more than 18 months.

Thirteen cases have so far been dropped from the active list by cancelling approval. Utmost prudence on the part of the government is employed in cancelling any projects.

Critical analysis as to the effects of these investments on the Korean economy is premature, as our experience is limited. However, those 97 cases which have completed their investments are now providing jobs for over 25,000 people. They also have made contributions to expanding Korea's exports in the past few years—$US27.8 million between 1962 and 1968, and $US82 million in 1969. I am confident that the rate of increase in exports from these industries will grow rapidly in the years to come. A positive impact has been made in the fields of construction, local technology, and expansion of local industries to supply needed materials to the new industries, and in other areas intangible benefits have been achieved through the introduction of modern technology and methods of doing business. However, it is very difficult to assess and quantify accurately these improvements.

Lessons Learned

I have no reservation in stating that private equity invested in the form of either joint ventures or enterprises owned solely by the foreign investor is the best form of economic co-operation. It is based on the principles of free economy and the pursuit of profit. It is the fairest and most honourable way of mobilising needed capital and know-how as well as creating jobs for the developing countries.

Free pursuit of profit by our private citizens can maximise the benefits of the division of labour and economies in production, improve utilisation of available resources, and accelerate the equalisation process between the developed and developing nations in lasting ways. This is not a give-and-receive 'relationship' but a give-and-take 'game' furthering the mutual advantage of the parties involved.

The developed countries can help the developing countries, while at the same time their enterprises can benefit by producing and marketing their products most economically. Nevertheless, the developing countries sometimes argue that they are losing their business to foreigners or that their economy is being dominated by foreigners. The developed countries argue with equal force that their jobs are being taken away by foreigners or that their balance of payments positions are being threatened by foreigners. Nationalistic and provincial sentiments do exist today in countries at all levels of development. Yet we must all recognise that in reality the world is, in fact, more interdependent than many of us are willing to recognise. Governments in the developed countries state that they encourage overseas investment by their citizens in the developing countries. The governments of the developing countries respond enthusiastically that they encourage and welcome foreign investors. There is certainly a big gap between what they say and what they do. This gap is often called, loosely, a poor investment climate, red tape, or provincialism and nationalism. I shall here deal with these as negative factors for foreign investment promotion.

One cannot pretend to treat all the factors inhibiting international capital flows among nations. The topic is too deep and wide. Any one factor might itself form the subject of a comprehensive paper. I shall therefore try to point out only some of the most important factors that exist both in the developed and the developing countries.

There are many ways in which nationalism in developed countries is important in inhibiting foreign investment. All the measures restricting the outflow of foreign exchange, gold or dollars, complex protective tariff systems, and immigration and travel restrictions on aliens are still very effective in deterring the incentive to invest abroad.

More often than is justified, developing countries are accused of monopolising bureaucratic red tape. Probably no less red tape is prevalent in the developed countries both on the part of their governments and of corporations, under the name of prudence, economics, technology, and financial feasibility. Justifications to the various committees or boards of directors are the most familiar excuses for simple bureaucratic delays. This often disheartens eager and enthusiastic partners in the developing countries.

The investment climate is also an inhibiting factor in developed countries. The political and economic conditions of the developed countries are no less important than those of developing countries. Poor political and economic conditions in the developed countries restrict overseas investment by firms and private citizens.

Cultural differences and linguistic barriers are probably the most important factors. A significant part of the way of doing business and handling of business affairs by a government is a reflection of a country's cultural background. More often than not, the government officials and businessmen from the developed countries have a hard time understanding the ways employed in developing countries in terms of the logic and ways that are familiar to them. Language barriers, on top of this, can magnify the extent of the problems arising from this situation. All of these are similarly denounced as 'red tape' or 'a bad investment climate' by the developed countries. In reality, however, they are often simply different ways of handling similar affairs by different people, rather than evidence of special red tape for foreign investors.

Exactly the same kinds of factors in developing countries can frighten off the potential investor, but in quite a different way.

Nationalism is illustrated by explicit or hidden limitations on the shares that can be held, areas of investment, and the amount of invested principal and profit which can be remitted. There are frequently fears that foreigners will take over entire business interests and will exploit weaknesses that exist in developing countries, whether this sort of fear is justified or not.

Backwardness in administrative skill, more stringent controls, and authoritarian attitudes on the part of the government and its officials in the developing countries as compared with the developed countries often place unaccustomed outsiders in a very frustrating position. Problems are further intensified as one goes down the ladder to the level of petty officials. They simply refuse to look at anything but the mechanical trans-lations of the letter of the rules and regulations given to them. Problems can further be aggravated by the lack of communication in foreign language and even in their own language. Too many papers from too many organisations and people are demanded which are beyond anyone's capability for digestion in the conduct of quite routine and normal business.

Political and economic stability are the most important prerequisites for foreign investors to become interested in any developing country. It is clear from Korea's experience that only from the latter half of the sixties has there been a meaningful inflow of foreign investment responding to the political stability and economic boom during this period.

Infrastructural facilities, such as electricity, water, transportation and communications are generally less adequate than those to which investors are used. Whole sets of tax and customs rates and systems vary widely from the international practice among developed countries. Expert ser-vices of public accountants, lawyers and bankers are lacking. Living conditions for the investors and their employees are less than adequate in terms of housing, schooling, food and community services. Finding local assistance armed with such facilities as language and expertise, both administrative and technical, is not always simple.

It is not always easy for the people in the developing countries to under-stand the behaviour of the investors. Sometimes, for the indigenous people, foreign businessmen are too demanding, too arrogant, and too eloquent. 'How can a businessman who is out to make his own buck talk like that?' This is a familiar comment of indigenous people who do not want to see that in the majority of cases, foreign businessmen are the same salarymen as they are. They are not after their own buck, but simply are trying to perform their responsibilities to their company. Inability to communicate because of the language barrier often produces a negative conclusion about the investors.

But things are not as bad as they sometimes appear. Positive factors to encourage co-operation in improving the economy of the free world through private initiative greatly outweigh these negative factors.

All the leaders of free countries, developed and developing alike, publicly emphasise and encourage on behalf of their governments private investment to and from abroad. In Korea's case, President Park Chung Hee is the most enthusiastic promoter of foreign investment. Presidents Johnson and Nixon of the United States have also publicly encouraged American investors to invest in developing countries.

Most of the developed countries have some kind of guarantee system to protect their overseas investors from political as well as business risks. Multilateral or bilateral arrangements have been made to provide protection and incentives in such areas as arbitration, avoidance of double taxation, and protection of industrial rights, to name only a few. International organisations such as the World Bank and the Asian Development Bank have been increasingly interested in this field and support various activities to foster foreign private investment.

Developing countries are aware of the negative factors and are constantly improving conditions in order to accommodate foreign investments. Korea has changed its laws and regulations, established an Office of Investment Promotion, and later expanded the authority and responsibilities of the Office. Korea is also establishing an export processing zone in addition to developing industrial parks on a nationwide scale, and shows a willingness to do more to improve the conditions in which investors can develop an international business community that can benefit all concerned.

Conclusions

Foreign investment in Korea will play an increasingly important role in the years ahead. With the disappearance of grants-in-aid from the United States, the scarcity of concessional loans from friendly countries leaves two major sources of capital inflow which Korea will continue to need for some time to come: export credit and private investment. Export credits, or supplier's credits to finance sales of capital goods, are reasonably abundant and readily available for the speedy conclusion of commercial dealings. Yet, excessive utilisation of this type of credit creates debt service problems which are too familiar to all of us. Foreign private investment is the ideal way of filling the investment gap, provided it is directed toward the right industries.

Korea has been applying four essential criteria in evaluating investment applications: export contribution, import substitution, creation of jobs, and technological innovation. Application of these criteria in our examination of proposals in the future will continue. The Korean government has done a great deal to improve the conditions under which investors conduct their business. It will not hesitate to correct or improve the conditions that can be handled by changing existing rules and regulations or even organisations. It is keenly aware that there are problems that cannot be licked overnight. Problems that come out of cultural and human factors take time to be resolved. A continuous educational process may bring answers to these problems. But there are areas in which the governments and the investors of developed countries can take action to encourage investment and assure its success.

The governments can take another hard look at their procedures for approving investment abroad. Liberalisation of these procedures by delegating more authority to a single organisation can be very helpful.

In many instances, we have found that the investors are not familiar at all with their own governments' rules and regulations governing their investment abroad. An effort to familiarise the business communities of developed countries with procedures and facilities to assist them could be helpful in these situations.

The gap between stated policies and existing rules must be re-evaluated. In some countries, tax is imposed on the profit repatriated. Some of the developed countries levy duties on commodities processed with their own raw materials abroad and re-imported. At most, duties should be levied on the value added, as is the practice in some other countries. Also, there should be a way that the benefits provided to investors by the developing countries could be protected in their own countries. Impressive amounts of technical assistance funds have been spent to support various exchange programs, surveys and studies by both developed and developing countries. Some allocation of funds for concrete project identification to be considered by private investors may be in order at this stage.

Investors should exercise greater care in selecting their personnel, especially the heads of establishments. Often, the head is selected on the basis of his technical competence and some experience in managing a plant. Once he is appointed, he becomes president of a corporation in Korea, which means something quite different from being the manager of another plant within his own country. A company president in Korea has to be far more paternalistic than a plant manager toward his employees, since Korea lacks such facilities as social security, medical care, and so on. The man must have an aptitude for enjoying and understanding different ways of life. He also needs to know how to handle international trade, as his business will require continuous imports of commodities even if his entire enterprise manufactures solely for domestic sale. A plant manager in a developed country might never have this experience in his own country and consider all the steps to be taken to acquire needed material as unnecessary red tape. In a single word, the man must be much more mature than the ones who often are selected.

Finally, nothing is more important than close co-operation among all concerned in this field. Generation of frank and straightforward discussion to find better ways of handling investments by foreign private business could greatly contribute to the betterment of all.

Comments and Discussion

TED ENGLISH opened the discussion: Yang's discussion of the Foreign Investment Inducement Law and of the Office of Investment Promotion is most interesting. Particularly appealing is the One-Stop-Service Office which sounds like a splendid way of reducing transaction costs. There is little evidence that Korea has had qualms about the impact of foreign control on the political or economic identity.

The difficulties I have in assessing the role of present investment in Korea could undoubtedly be largely eliminated if there had been room in this chapter for a fuller analysis of the development record in which the relationship between investment and other forms of capital flow (aid) and between investment and trade policies and practices had been spelled out. In particular, did trade opportunities provide the kind of guidance and selection among alternative investment activities that helped to guarantee against the wasteful diffusion of investment activity and inefficient kinds of import substitution? If this was the case perhaps it is trade rather than the investment that played the most strategic role.

Some of the policies mentioned in the paper raise questions about the pattern of investment, for example, duty free import of machinery and materials might by itself lead to an inefficient pattern of final product outputs given the increased effective protection it ensures. Again, the criteria employed by the Economic Planning Board in assessing investment applications do not appear in themselves to assume a desirable allocation of resources (export contribution, import substitution, creation of jobs, technological innovation). It would be interesting to have some further comment on the way the criteria have been applied, and the extent to which the Board was constrained by international market conditions, perhaps, and the fact that market information rather than a more positive screening process might well have produced the same result.

In the light of the earlier discussion of competition with incentives I would be interested in Yang's assessment of the extent to which Korea's tax and other inducements may, on the one hand, have diverted investment to Korea from other locations in the Western Pacific area, or on the other hand, to what extent they constitute matching inducements to those offered by other countries.

Finally, there are a few more specific questions arising out of my ignorance of the details of foreign investment relationships. First, under what circumstances would interest not be taxed? Second, which developed countries levy duties only on values added and on what major product categories? And third, what sort of protection for the benefits of developed country investment does Yang have in mind?

The papers presented by Sadli, Amnuay, and Yang were then discussed jointly. Four broad issues were given considerable attention: the role of nationalism in economic policy; the importance or otherwise of market fragmentation; the effect of incentive schemes; and the administration of investment programs.

The relationship between economic and political analysis was taken up in the specific context suggested by Sadli's paper. Countries consistently adopt policies, for reasons of nationalism, which reduce their income and rate of economic growth. Two main reasons were responsible for this, it was felt. First, there was often faulty advice from economists and economic practitioners confused by their own nationalism. Second, political rationality superimposed itself on economic rationality. Economists were prone to assume fallaciously that governments existed to serve the social, even economic, interest. Governments clearly had interests of their own, and political rationality did not necessarily coincide with economic rationality. At least one participant declared his preference for riding the one horse at the one time. Sadli thought of nationalism in the same light as the choice between future goods and present goods or investment and consumption: nationalism should be seen as an indulgence in present consumption. Taking up this issue from a different standpoint, an American participant asked whether participants from Asia would welcome the prospect of a quintupling of Japanese investment within their countries over the next decade. The consensus seemed to be that it would be accepted, possibly welcomed, but that few would be happy about it.

The issue of market fragmentation was raised again in the context of comments in the papers of Sadli and Amnuay. A Japanese participant asked what the host country had to lose from 'excessive competition' among foreign firms. In Thailand there seemed to be a policy to restrain entry to one Japanese firm in each industry, presumably to protect local business interests. The question prompted an extensive debate from which three main points emerged. First, Amnuay replied that there was no policy in Thailand of limiting Japanese entry to protect local business interests, but that there was a growing feeling that foreign competition in local markets should be more broadly based—largely for non-economic reasons. It was hoped to encourage European, American, and Australian firms as well as Japanese firms. Secondly, it was argued that there would be no disadvantage from allowing vigorous competition, even in small markets, so long as national resources were not being used to subsidise inefficiency. Where tariffs, subsidies and other forms of protection were taken advantage of, there was cause for concern over fragmentation. Thirdly, one participant suggested that, in some circumstances, there may be a case for auctioning off monopoly privileges rather like monopoly mining rights were auctioned off in Indonesia.

The rationale of incentives was also explained in some detail. Points made by English and Yang were pursued further. It was noted that when tax concessions granted in a host country were not validated by the capital exporting country, there was no gain or incentive to the private investor, merely a transfer of resources from the host government to the capital exporting country's government. The United States has few tax sparing agreements which alleviate this problem, because it feels that tax sparing will merely lead to competitive erosion of the tax base. In fact, the lack of tax sparing means that incentive schemes cannot function as they are intended. It was noted that Japan frequently has tax sparing agreements and that Singapore has negotiated such an agreement with the United States. It was also noted that the United States has a tax credit system, applied on a discretionary basis. Of course, the home-country tax burden to private companies falls only at the point when profits are repatriated.

On the question of whether there were too many incentives, some participants had different perspectives. Sadli thought that the view on incentives in the Asian region would change gradually as foreign investors established a confidence in the market. He reminded participants of the novelty of large-scale industrial investment in South-East and East Asia. What governments in the region had managed to do with their various incentives was establish a bargaining position. Amnuay denied that there was overt competition among host countries in incentive-giving. Indeed, the conference had exposed a large degree of ignorance among participants from Asia of schemes other than those in their home country. This called for consultations among them and others not present, and he was confident that they would soon eventuate.

Finally, the scarcity of administrative resources in developing countries was discussed. Yang's paper, and comments on the role of the Singapore Economic Development Board, prompted one participant to urge a concentration of administrative talent in the field of investment management, both foreign and domestic, for it was there that many of the most complex and important development problems would have to be handled and solved.

11 Foreign Investment in Developing Countries: The Philippines

CESAR VIRATA

The Philippines has had long experience with foreign investment. This started with state monopolies established by the Spanish government in the seventeenth century and was followed by an influx of trading investments by Chinese and English traders during the earlier part of the nineteenth century when the Spaniards opened the Philippines up to foreign trade. Then there was a major shift to American investment after the Philippines was conquered by the United States at the start of the twentieth century. American investment grew in the fields of public utilities and trade in agricultural products, as a result of the preferential trading relationship between the Philippines and the United States from 1909 to 1946. A trade and investment law was passed by United States Congress just before the Philippines gained independence in 1946 and this was converted later into a treaty retaining national treatment for American investments in the Philippines and preferential treatment in trade. This treaty will expire in 1974. The Philippines had the experience also of dealing with trading firms under the auspices of the Japanese military government during the war years. The foreign investments in the Philippines are not, of course, confined to these countries. Almost all free world countries have investments in the Philippines—the United Kingdom, Switzerland, the Netherlands, Australia, Belgium, Sweden, Italy, France, Austria, Canada and Germany.

After Philippine independence in 1946, the influx of investments was influenced by other policy considerations which I shall outline briefly. Initially, foreign investment flowed back to the Philippines for reconstruction, such as the rebuilding of sugar and coconut mills, rehabilitation of gold mining, and public utilities, like electricity, communications, and transportation. During this reconstruction period, the Philippines adopted import and exchange controls to conserve its reserves, but maintained the pre-war parity rate of the peso to the dollar (₱2 : 1) up to 1962. In consequence, many import-substitution industries were attracted, especially

258

those products that had found market acceptance and were being imported as finished goods from the United States. Textiles, drugs, cigarettes, household appliances, petroleum refineries, car assembly, rubber tyres, containers, food products, flour mills, milk canneries, confectioneries, biscuits and soft drinks moved in at a relatively rapid rate to preserve their share of the market to the exclusion of some traders who did not invest in facilities. Such investments were facilitated by liberal tax incentives and protective tariffs. This was a period when many wholly owned subsidiaries were established to assemble, package, fabricate or undertake light manufacturing in the Philippines. The contribution of the manufacturing sector to national income doubled within a decade.

These industries were basically operated for sales to the domestic market and very few exported at all. Within a decade, almost all the possibilities of import-substitution were exhausted. Further backward linkages were difficult because of the many product types allowed assembly. In fact, overcapacity developed since many industries tried to overstate their capacity during the exchange control period in order to get a higher dollar allocation from the Central Bank. This is a phenomenon which occurred not only in the Philippines but also in other places. One wonders why there is a propensity to develop overcapacity when capital is so scarce. This approach is a businessman's approach—a transfer from import business to light manufacturing. As foreign exchange reserves were being depleted rapidly by an industrialisation pattern which was heavily import-oriented and at the same time freezing in effect the basic colonial export structure, the Philippines had to devalue in 1962 to check the balance of payments problem. This move brought about encouragement to extractive industries like logging, iron and copper mining, additional pineapple cultivation, and more sugar, desiccated coconut, and coconut oil mills were set up.

After devaluation, the Philippines switched from exchange controls to an open economy. It was from one extreme to the other, and as a result of this sudden swing some of the Filipino joint ventures with foreigners were either taken over completely by, or majority control thereof was transferred to the foreign partner. Under an open economy, credit terms, advertising and the ability to put in capital quickly counted a great deal. Business and industry operated under these terms until the first half of 1969. While there were no exchange controls *per se*, the Central Bank adopted indirect controls and subsequently resorted to foreign exchange budgeting. An investment incentives law was passed in 1967 which delineated policies for orderly growth of the industrial sector. The economy expanded under an easy money policy which induced more import demand while the export sector stagnated partly due to bad weather conditions and to world trade conditions. Severe cuts in foreign exchange allocation were effected but later on the policymakers opted for a comprehensive exchange reform which took place in February 1970. The exchange rate was allowed to float and seek its own level. In summary, after all these developments, I would like to add that about 70 of the 100 largest corporations in the Philippines are foreign-owned. Their role in the development can be seen and felt. With this brief background it is possible to explain the basic policy direction of foreign investment in the Philippines.

Investment Policies

Along with the private sector development of agro-industries, mining and public transportation, the government pioneered several industries like textiles, cement, shipbuilding, shipping, airlines, railroads, power generation, and steel bars during the middle thirties up to about 1950. However, there are now very clear indications that the Philippine government is leaving the development of industry and business to the private sector. In fact, the government has sold some of its enterprises in such industries as textiles, cement, hotels, shipping, and steel bar making to private corporations and will in the future sell others. In only those vital industrial areas where the private sector is relatively timid in spite of incentives and financial assistance would the government discharge a pioneering function. This has been the most recent policy statement from the Philippine Congress.

Another fundamental element in Philippine foreign investment policy is that Filipino control of the basic industries is essential. The Constitution of the Philippines provides that the exploitation of Philippine natural resources such as forestry, mining, and the development of public land should be undertaken by corporations 60 per cent of the capital stock of which are owned by Filipino citizens. Likewise, public utilities shall be controlled by Filipinos to the same extent. Extending this principle, it is now stated in the Investment Incentives Act of the Philippines that any non-pioneering industry must be controlled by Filipinos to the extent of 60 per cent of its voting stock while there is no limitation as to foreign ownership of non-voting shares. On the other hand, pioneering industries can be established by foreigners even up to 100 per cent equity ownership. The investment act provides that the role of foreign investment should be in pioneering industries which require heavy capital investment and modern technology. Most of those industries which are considered pioneer were established in industrialised countries probably forty years ago. Note that the basic reason for this division is to harmonise the respective roles of domestic and foreign investments. I suppose it is difficult for a local businessman to be displaced by the sheer financial power of a foreign capitalist. Foreign investments can still assist established businesses in non-pioneer areas by providing supplemental capital. A joint venture could be a mutually beneficial arrangement.

The other concept which was introduced in the investment act is the programmed phasing out of foreign control in pioneering industries over a period of twenty years from the time of registration of the enterprise with the Board of Investments, although the period is extendable for another twenty years. Thus, the maximum period is 40 years of possible foreign control. It states that the corporation must tender shares to the public by the eleventh year, so that by the end of the twentieth year, 60 per cent of the *voting* shares would be owned by Philippine nationals. One of the first to register under this provision is an English company that will manufacture explosives for the mining industry. It should be emphasised that this requirement does not apply to non-voting shares nor does the law prohibit management contract with foreigners. The Congress seems to emphasise, in this provision, the pioneering role of foreign investments.

These rules are seemingly restrictive but it is the avowed policy of the Philippines to announce her plans in advance. We would not like to have liberal entry requirements and then suddenly to nationalise enterprises. When the retail sector was 'Filipinised', that is, 100 per cent Filipino ownership was required, foreigners were allowed to retain their businesses for as long as they lived and, in the case of corporations, they were given ten years to adjust to the requirements of law.

Pioneering industries, as defined in the Investments Act, are those industries which have not been operated on a commercial scale in the Philippines or those industries which represent major process improvements over existing ones. Generally speaking, these industries are in the intermediate fields, such as the smelting of ores, refining of metal, and rolling and extrusion of metal. Pioneer areas cover the wide open field of chemical industries—petroleum and salt-based chemicals. In the wood and fibre industries, pulping and integrated pulp and paper mills are considered pioneer industries. There are many mechanical and electrical components manufacturing that will qualify under the pioneering category. Briefly, light manufacturing and assembly operations have largely been filled by numerous enterprises and there is already a developed extractive industry; hence, areas that are open to foreign investments are mostly in the intermediate industries.

The major industrial effort, therefore, is to link the finishing industries with the extractive industries through the transformation of ores, agricultural products, and wood products into finished consumer and industrial products.

Overcrowded industries—where there is overcapacity—are relatively expensive for any developing economy, hence the concept of measured capacity has been introduced in the Investments Act. The Board of Investments indicates the capacity that will meet domestic and foreseeable export demands in the investment plan. The Board of Investments specifies the capacity of respective industries, which particular areas are open to investment and which areas are not. The areas open are declared through an indicative plan and it is up to private enterprise to claim specific areas, and where an enterprise qualifies a number of fiscal incentives are provided. Not only tax exemptions but also post-operative tariff protection, as well as anti-dumping protection, are assured.

A predominant factor in increasing foreign investment is the aim to keep an established, or enlarged, share of the market. Without capacity regulation, especially if an economy is open to all comers, excess capacity, especially in light industries, would most likely result since foreign investments are usually justified initially on the basis of marginal contributions to the company effort.

Another feature of the foreign investment law is that participation of foreigners with up to 30 per cent interest in any business enterprise is not regulated by government. It is only for participation which exceeds this amount that the Board of Investments enters into the picture. The basic purpose of this is to avoid wastage of resources through additional investment in overcrowded industries. This regulation is usually interpreted negatively, but, on the other hand, the Philippines only desires to utilise every bit of local and foreign resources to the maximum extent by not allowing excess capacity.

Once the business is established, the companies, whether foreign or owned by Filipinos, operate on an equal footing; the business tax and income tax rates are uniform. However, retailing and trading in rice and corn are reserved for Filipinos. The remaining preferential treatment applied to imports of United States origin is a tariff preference of 10 per cent on the applicable duty. Of course, United States preference has long been important since that country's goods entered duty free up to 1954. This treatment will continue up to 1974 unless the United States renounces the reverse preference earlier.

The current regulations on capital repatriation allow full remittance of profits and capital to non-resident shareholders if the company is involved in export-oriented activities, domestic companies whose shares are traded in stock exchanges, companies registered with the Board of Investments, and all companies which have not borrowed from domestic commercial banks. Repatriation by companies which borrowed from domestic sources are limited to 25 per cent of their profits. The main reason for such regulation was that many companies did borrow in order to remit profits and dividends in advance. The record is that the Philippines has always allowed repatriation of capital and profits even when exchange control was relatively strict. Remittances of profits increased a great deal when the United States required companies to remit 100 per cent of their profits to their parent companies. This resulted in a threefold increase in remittances, a situation which the Philippines could ill afford. This is one of the problems that might have to be faced when investments have matured, when the main effort of the managers is to maintain the market. The cash inflow to the company is heavy, hence the constant pressure to remit home the profits.

More and more the direction of investments is being geared towards exports. The Philippines has learned, through experience, the heavy demands for foreign exchange of import-substitution industries. Where import-substitution industries are highly protected by tariffs, and sales promotion is conducted intensively in the domestic market, then the foreign exchange outlay for industry becomes higher than projected. It also becomes more difficult to control the importation of raw materials from an administrative and political viewpoint than cutting importation of finished products. In order to offset the heavy foreign exchange requirements of the economy, export-oriented industries are absolutely necessary.

What was neglected initially during the time that import-substitution industries were being set up was a thorough analysis of the licensing agreements. We have found, to our dismay, that many of these licences contain provisions for export restrictions, such as complete export prohibition or limited exports to certain countries or the imposition of penalty royalties if there are exports. What therefore seemed to be a good initial export base became excess capacity of some of these import-substitution industries, and the international marketing experience of these companies could not be utilised. Now the Board of Investments carefully scrutinises these agreements so that such restrictive clauses can be removed. Another aspect of restrictive business practice is the tied purchase clauses for raw materials, especially in the chemical and drug industries. On the whole, probably the reaction to Philippine foreign investment incentives is that they are not as liberal as the incentives offered by neighbouring countries in South-East Asia. This is probably true because the Philippines has assigned a definite role to foreign investments. However, in an overall evaluation, other factors enter, such as the stability of the government, literacy, manpower, communications, and living conditions. Our policy-makers realise that the bulk of investment comes from domestic savings and no matter how liberal the fiscal incentives may be, only a small number of foreign investors do come. In fact, there is cause for the evaluation of fiscal incentives given by developing countries. Many of us are overly generous so that what may be exempted from imports by the host country may be taxed by the investing country. Hence, from an enterprise viewpoint the tax incentives may not be material to the investment decision. Loss of the much needed revenue to the government of a developing country should be a major concern.

In regional or sub-regional co-operation, the Philippines looks forward to the implementation of the ASEAN plans for marketing arrangements and the joint undertaking of projects where an individual country's efforts could not sustain a viable operation. It is also hoping that the developed countries, like Japan, will allow developing countries to process more of their raw materials rather than provide financial incentives for exporting them unprocessed. In this way, there could be some natural division of investment between developed and developing countries. The developing countries could start with industries that are based on their indigenous raw materials, whereas the advanced countries could maintain their role as machinery suppliers and play a pioneering role in establishing forward or backward linkage industries.

Patterns of Foreign Investment

Two points should be noted about foreign investment in the Philippines. First, the total amount has been relatively small. Second, for practical purposes, foreign investment is predominantly American. The largest foreign investors are actually the Chinese, who since the war have been investing about three times as much as all other foreign nationals put together. But these Chinese investors are almost all residents of the Philippines, who derive their funds from local sources and in general keep their profits in the country. Of the remaining foreign investment, about half is American.

The Philippine economy has been growing at a relatively fast rate since the end of the war, but relatively little of this growth seems to have been financed by foreign sources. Some indicators are given in Table 11.1. For convenience, the postwar years have been broken into five periods, the reasons for their beginning dates being that: in 1949 the Central Bank was established and import and exchange controls instituted; in 1946 came the Philippine Trade Act which was subsequently modified in 1956, and is now commonly known as the Laurel-Langley Agreement,

Table 11.1   Philippines: gross domestic investment and net inflow of foreign capital, 1946-69 (million pesos at current prices)

Period	Gross domestic investment		Net inflow of foreign capital		Foreign capital as per cent of GDI	Annual GNP growth rate in current prices (per cent)
	Total	Annual average	Total	Annual average		
1946-48	2,710	903	97	32	3.6	12.0
1949-55	6,685	948	545	78	8.2	6.7
1956-61	10,488	1,748	757	126	7.2	8.1
1962-66	20,964	4,193	506	101	2.4	10.8
1967-69	18,588	6,196	986	329	5.3	11.8
Total 1946-69	59,435	2,479	2,391	100	4.0	8.6

Source: Philippines Department of Commerce and Industry.

Table 11.2 Philippines: annual average capital investment by newly registered business organisations, by nationality and kind of business, 1967–9 (thousand pesos)

	Filipinos	Chinese	Americans	Others	Total	Total foreign	Per cent distribution of total	Per cent distribution of total foreign
1. Agriculture	12,601	94	88	6	12,789	188	2.95	0.57
2. Forestry, fishing and live- stock	16,087	141	88	147	16,463	376	3.80	1.14
3. Metal mining	108	7	10	—	125	17	0.03	0.05
4. Non-metallic mining and quarrying	14,107	107	380	52	14,646	539	3.39	1.63
5. Manufacturing	62,037	7,594	633	1,791	72,055	10,018	16.64	30.28
6. Construction	18,793	392	346	106	19,637	844	4.54	2.55
7. Electricity, gas and water services	780	3	13	—	796	16	0.18	0.05
8. Wholesale and retail trade	124,222	13,110	730	2,493	140,555	16,333	32.46	49.37
9. Banks and other finan- cial institutions	24,338	159	38	—	24,535	197	5.67	0.58
10. Insurance	1,350	21	3	5	1,379	29	0.32	0.09
11. Real estate	49,722	299	1,633	95	51,749	2,027	11.95	6.13
12. Transportation, storage and communication	29,776	70	63	65	29,974	198	6.92	0.60
13. Community and business services	33,621	658	335	258	34,872	1,251	8.05	3.78
14. Recreation and personal services	12,387	977	56	19	13,439	1,052	3.10	3.18
Total	399,929	23,632	4,416	5,037	433,014	33,085	100.00	100.00

Source: Philippines Board of Investment.

with its special privileges for American investors; in 1962 exchange controls were removed and the exchange rate of the peso *vis-à-vis* the dollar almost doubled; and in 1967 an investment incentives act was enacted into law. In 1970, another exchange reform was implemented.

Over the entire period, the economy grew at the rate of 8.6 per cent annually at current prices, and this required gross domestic investments at an annual average of ₱2.5 billion. Almost all of this, however, was financed from domestic sources. The annual net inflow of foreign capital over the same period averaged only 4 per cent of gross domestic investment.

The breakdown of foreign investment by nationality and industry is shown in Table 11.2. These figures are, of course, not directly comparable with Table 11.1 since they include types of investment which would not enter into the national accounts. The table shows that most foreign investment is Chinese, and that, of the remainder, about half is American. By industry, investment is concentrated in the manufacturing and trade sectors, these two accounting for about three-quarters of total foreign investments.

Direct United States investment, which according to the estimates of the United States Department of Commerce amounted to $US415 million in 1963, was concentrated in manufacturing, trade, extractive industries (mining) and the operation of public utilities. Some changes have taken place since 1963: the American interest in public utilities, such as power and telephone, was sold to Filipinos. Investments in manufacturing comprised 32 per cent of the total direct United States investment (17.2 per cent of this was attributed to investment in petroleum refineries). Trade made up 36.1 per cent of total investment, public utilities 6 per cent, mining 10.4 per cent, while the rest was distributed in forestry and other types of natural resources investment.

American investment in the Philippines, while concentrated in key sectors, has been small—less than 2 per cent of total investment. More important, it seems to have been generated less by the national treatment provisions of the Laurel-Langley Agreement than by restrictions on the repatriation of earnings during the period of controls—restrictions which were completely removed in 1962. New American direct investment has fluctuated around an annual average of less than $US1 million in the period of the Agreement. Most investments under Philippine statistics appear as imports of equipment rather than inward foreign exchange remittances. This represents about one-fourth of one per cent of the annual investment required to support the current economic program. The Chinese, who do not enjoy the same advantages, have contributed about six times as much investment as the Americans. With reference to American investments, discussions have been held for an orderly transition of affected rights by the termination of the treaty in 1974.

In conclusion, foreign investment has a definite role in the development program of the Philippines. Its contribution to advancing the industrial frontier through investment in pioneering industries is welcomed. Joint ventures with Filipinos in non-pioneering industries are also welcomed. Foreign investment, in terms of the transfer of technology, employment and training of personnel, promotion of export products and indigenisation of import-substitution are valuable contributions to the economy. It is true that the rules are being refined and there is a great deal of selectivity, but this is essential if domestic and foreign resources are going to be harmonised in an optimal way. As mentioned earlier, co-operation within the region or sub-region is also welcome. It may soon be possible to promote multinational and joint marketing arrangements on a regional basis.

Comments and Discussion

HISAO KANAMORI opened the discussion: Firstly, I must make the comment that the different treatment between pioneering and non-pioneering industry would seem wise. Virata says that in the Investment Incentive Act of the Philippines, any new non-pioneering industry must be controlled by Filipinos, while pioneering industries can be established by foreigners even up to 100 per cent equity participation. But is the distinction between pioneering industry and non-pioneering industry suitable as a criterion for foreign investment? Do pioneering industries not include infant industries which should be protected from foreign capital and non-pioneering industries include the oligopolistic or stagnant industries into which inflow of foreign capital may act as a good stimulus?

Secondly, the Investment Act apparently states that corporations in pioneering industries must tender shares to the public by the eleventh year, so that by the end of the twentieth year, 60 per cent of the voting shares would be owned by Filipino nationals. Does this not discourage foreign investment in the Philippines seriously?

Thirdly, it is indicated that the Board of Investment specifies the capacity of respective industries, which particular areas are open to investment and which areas are not. But is there not any danger that such a procedure encourages the production of oligopolistic industries? Moreover, does bureaucratic interference not have bad effects on the economy?

Fourthly, the exchange rate was allowed to float and seek its level in February 1970. What will be the effect of the floating rate on capital inflow?

Finally, the natural division of investment between developed and developing countries is proposed. This is an interesting proposal, but it is not clear what kind of factors decide the structure of the natural division of investment? In case of foreign trade, international division of labour occurs according to the principle of comparative advantage. Is there any such principle in case of international investment? It is understandable that in some key industries, a country would want to avoid domination by foreign capital. But why is it natural that the developing countries invest in industry which is based on the indigenous raw materials, where-as the advanced countries retain their role as machinery suppliers?

Further discussion is reported at the end of Chapter 12.

12 Foreign Investment in Developing Countries: Mexico

MIGUEL WIONCZEK

Past conflicts, present attitudes and policies towards foreign private capital, and potential future frictions between Mexican society and foreign direct investment can hardly be understood without a brief overview of Mexico's political and economic history. Its highlights were as follows.

In the beginning of modern development there was exploitation of the very extensive sub-soil wealth of Mexico for the benefit of the Spanish metropole over three centuries of the colonial period. There followed the achievement of political independence from Spain in 1821 that, like the recent decolonisation of Africa and Asia, did not affect in any substantial degree the country's social and economic colonial structure. Then there was a brief encounter with British private capital that went into Mexican mining in the 1820s to fill the void left by the disappearance of Spain as the exclusive market for Mexican precious metal exports. That encounter, accompanied by British loans to the newly independent country, ended in a disaster both for the investors and the host country due mainly to the British attempts to inject advanced European technology into a primitive post-colonial economy. Almost a half century of political chaos and economic stagnation (1830-70) ensued, accompanied by the loss of a major part of Mexican territory to the United States and by an endless chain of foreign punitive expeditions and outright interventions on behalf of Mexico's creditors aimed at making out of Mexico an appendage to rapidly growing European industrial economies.

Then came thirty years of political peace and economic development under the dictatorship of Porfirio Díaz (1880-1910) that opened the country to foreign private capital and technology, both European and American. The populist revolution of 1910 broke the back of the Porfirian society, whose main pillars were, first, landed aristocracy, mercilessly exploiting the masses of Indian and mestizo population, and,

269

second, foreign economic interests that had achieved, by the beginning of this century, the goal of making out of Mexico an important source of raw materials (mining and tropical agricultural products) for the industrial countries of North America and Western Europe. There followed a period of political and economic reconstruction (1925-40) including agrarian reform, following one and a half decades of savage civil war, and characterised by continuous overt and hidden conflicts between Mexico's post-revolutionary society and foreign private investors in mining, public utilities, transport and communications, conflicts that culminated in the expropriation of United States, British and Dutch oil companies in 1938.

The last quarter of a century is characterised by inward-directed heavily protected industrialisation (1945-70), broadly supported by the newly emerging domestic entrepreneurial groups and broadly based nationalistic public opinion, and accompanied by the progressive elimination of the foreign private investment still present in the traditional sectors (extractive industries other than the nationalised petroleum, public utilities, and transport and communications) through so-called 'mexicanisation' procedures—that is, the total acquisition of foreign assets by the state or partial acquisition by domestic private capital.

The 'mexicanisation' of traditional sectors was practically completed by the mid-sixties through two major decisions. In 1960, the Mexican state purchased two large foreign-owned electric power companies that had become, in the late thirties, the centre of a serious conflict, due in part to the foreign companies' refusal to invest in generating facilities and their growing dependence, as electricity distributors in major urban areas, upon electric power produced by the state-owned Federal Electricity Commission.[1] Moreover, in the mid-sixties, under the new mining legislation, all foreign mining enterprises were forced to sell 51 per cent of their properties to Mexican domestic interests, with the state reserving to itself the right to extend new mining concessions to enterprises with 66 per cent of domestic capital. The new legislation affected, among others, the only dynamic sector of the Mexican extractive industries (with the exception of the oil industry, owned by the state since 1938), especially sulphur mining, that made Mexico during the fifties the second largest world sulphur producer.[2]

Ex post, these two important policy measures are easy to explain. In

[1] For details of the relations between Mexican state- and foreign-owned electric public utilities between 1900 and 1960, see Miguel S. Wionczek, 'Electric Power—The Uneasy Partnership', in Raymond Vernon (ed.), *Public Policy and Private Enterprise in Mexico* (Cambridge: Harvard University Press, 1964).
[2] See my study of sulphur mining 'mexicanisation' in Raymond F. Mikesell (ed.), *Foreign Investment in Petroleum and Mineral Industries* (Baltimore: Johns Hopkins University Press, 1970).

the case of the electricity industry, the failure of the state-run system of public utilities' regulation, on the one hand, and the inflationary excesses of the forties and the early fifties, on the other, have aggravated the conflict latent since the inter-war period and are related to the fact that both the state and large sectors of public opinion considered the adequate provision of electric power as a pre-condition for an industrialisation drive. The breakdown of regulatory processes and the inflation of the forties made politically impossible an equitable increase in electric energy prices that would have satisfied the financial objectives of private electric energy producers and would have solved acute electric energy shortages faced by the Mexican economy after 1940. The growing technical skills of the state-owned Federal Electricity Commission, established on the eve of World War II, the increasing hostility of large sectors of the society to foreign electric power companies, coupled with the frustrations of their owners who considered themselves victims of public policies, made the nationalisation of the electric power industry in 1960 the only alternative.

The mexicanisation of the mining industry has a different rationale. It must be remembered that Mexico was the single largest producer of silver and gold in colonial times and an important source of metals and minerals for industrial countries between 1880 and the onset of the Great Depression. In both periods that sector was fully controlled by foreign interests. The appearance in the country after the Revolution of resource conservation policies, aimed at securing a hold over mineral wealth for future industrialisation, coincided with the shift of major United States and British mining companies to new sources of supply in South America and Africa. The contribution of mining to the Mexican national product and the share of Mexico in the world metal and mineral markets have continued to decline since 1929, with the exception of silver throughout the past three decades and of sulphur in the fifties. It was in the late fifties, however, that the inward directed industrialisation drive brought about, on the one hand, the appearance of the rapid expansion of domestic demand for industrial raw materials, and, on the other, the state's dissatisfaction with traditional policies of foreign mining companies exporting unprocessed or semi-processed metals and minerals for further elaboration abroad. These two factors together with the growing import bill for intermediate metal goods represent the background to the mining legislation of the early sixties and the subsequent mexicanisation of extractive industries. Except in the case of highly profitable sulphur mining, the state decision met with no obstacles from mexicanised foreign companies. Following the example of the electric power companies, they used most of the proceeds from sales of their properties for investment in highly profitable manufacturing and ancillary activities in Mexico.

In the field of banking no need for mexicanisation has ever arisen.

The pre-revolutionary banking system, particularly that controlled by European interests, had effectively been destroyed by the Revolution. The new banking system established in the inter-war period belonged, from the beginning, largely to nationals. Only one foreign commercial bank— a branch of the present First National City Bank—was set up in Mexico on the eve of the Great Depression. It still operates in the country but it accounts for less than one per cent of sight deposits of the whole banking system. The subsequent banking legislation barred the entry of foreign financial intermediaries in Mexico without—one must add—creating undue hardship to foreign enterprises operating in the remaining sectors. In the late sixties domestic financing of foreign enterprises exceeded 50 per cent of their total financial needs.

The Position of Foreign Capital in Mexico

As shown in Table 12.1, foreign private investment had practically disappeared from the traditional sectors by the late sixties.

The magnitude of the shifts in the sectoral distribution of foreign private investment in Mexico between 1910 and the late sixties has no parallel in any other Latin American country. At the end of the Porfirio Díaz era, out of the estimated total of $US1,200 million of foreign direct investment in Mexico, almost 80 per cent was in extractive industries, including petroleum, railroads and public utilities. Sixty years later, only 6 per cent of the total estimated in 1968 at over $US2,300 million was still in mining. Foreign investment has completely disappeared from petroleum, transport and public utilities. It is concentrated exclusively now in manufacturing (75 per cent) and services other than banking (over

Table 12.1   Mexico: sectoral distribution of foreign private investment, 1911-68 (per cent)

Sectors	1911	1940	1950	1960	1968
Agriculture	7.0	1.9	0.7	1.8	0.7
Mining	28.0	23.9	19.8	15.6	6.0
Petroleum	4.0	0.3	2.1	2.0	1.8
Industry	4.0	7.0	26.0	55.8	74.2
Electric power	8.0	31.5	24.2	1.4	—
Trade	10.0	3.5	12.4	18.1	74.8
Transport and communications	39.0	31.6	13.3	2.8	—
Other services	—	0.3	1.5	2.5	2.5

Sources: For 1911: Cleona Lewis, *America's Stake in International Investment* (Washington, D.C.: The Brookings Institution, 1938); for 1940-60: Banco de Mexico, S.A.; for 1968: estimates by the author. It should be noted that by 1911 foreign oil interests had just finished the first stage of their activities in Mexico; their participation in the total foreign investment increased considerably during the Revolution and reached its peak around 1925.

15 per cent). The shift that took place in the past twenty years reflected, first, the progressive and peaceful takeover, mostly by the state, of traditional foreign investment in the name of economic independence, and second, the working of direct and indirect incentives available—under certain rules—to foreign manufacturing and service investment, incentives originally established in the forties to protect domestic entrepreneurial groups.

The fact that these incentives (including the rapidly growing market, political and monetary stability, very high protection levels and a very liberal tax system) worked can be deduced from Table 12.2. While for the lack of other data the table covers only United States private direct investment in Mexico, which accounted for some 80 per cent of total foreign direct investment in the country at the end of the sixties, it reflects the sectoral distribution of all foreign direct investment flows in Mexico in the past two decades.

One might surmise that the elimination of foreign private capital from the sectors in which it used to be historically a source of conflicts and the entry of foreign capital in dynamic growth-inducing activities would guarantee the absence of future frictions between foreign investors and the political and economic interest groups in modern Mexico as long as dominating local economic interest groups were assured some participation in the growing market via special state privileges and joint ventures. Strangely enough, although the past situations of conflict had apparently been eliminated, the convenience or inconvenience of new foreign investment—in terms of political implications, the resources gap relief,

Table 12.2   Mexico: book value of United States direct investment, by major sectors, 1950-70 ($US million)

	1955	1960	1965	1968
Mining and smelting	154	130	140	125
Petroleum	15	32	48	38
Manufactures	274	391	756	1,370
Public utilities	91	119	27	—
Trade	50	85	138	260
Other, including tourism	30	38	73	67
Total	614	795	1,182	1,860

Sources: For 1955: *U.S. Investments in the Latin American Economy* (U.S. Dept. of Commerce, Washington, D.C. 1957) and *Survey of Current Business*, U.S. Dept. of Commerce, August 1956; for 1960: *Survey of Current Business*, August 1961; for 1965: Walter Lederer and Frederick Cutler, 'International Investment of the United States in 1966', U.S. Dept. of Commerce, *Overseas Business Reports*, OBR 67-72, November 1967; for 1968: estimates of the author based upon unpublished partial United States and Mexican data.

the balance-of-payments burden, the technological contribution—continues to be debated in Mexico today with an intensity similar to that which characterised discussion of traditional private foreign investment during the past half century. Outside of official agencies which, in the most recent years, decided not to publish any data on foreign investment except those pertaining to net financial flows which appear in the balance-of-payments statistics, the subject is discussed continuously and with highly emotional overtones. It is quite probable that more rational approaches to this issue are hampered, first, by the extreme scarcity of reliable information, second, by the absence of scholarly studies of the sectoral composition of foreign investment, its profitability and real impact upon the balance of payments, and, finally, by doubts about the contribution of foreign capital to the technological progress of a society whose backwardness, in this respect, is directly due to its inadequately designed educational system. Given the particular characteristics of the Mexican political system, the absence of serious and publicly available research strongly suggests that the issue of foreign direct investment is considered by the government as a politically highly sensitive subject. This political sensitivity seems to be related in part to the outcome of official industrialisation policies that have resulted in a large-scale entry of foreign private capital into Mexican industry and services.

Official pronouncements on the subject of policies toward foreign direct investment offer the following broad policy guidelines.

Basic sectors of the national economy, such as the oil industry, heavy petrochemicals, electric power, railways and communications are reserved to the state. Investment in agriculture and financial intermediaries is reserved to Mexican nationals; in other sectors (mining and manufacturing) the rule of domestic capital majority participation is applied to fields either closely linked with basic economic activities or considered of special importance for future industrial development. While no all-inclusive list of such activities has ever been elaborated, some six important industries, such as steel, cement, glass and aluminium, among others, were declared as falling under the 51 per cent domestic ownership rule in July 1970; in all remaining fields, no limitations upon foreign private capital are imposed, except that it must accept all legal obligations applied to domestically-owned enterprises. Unless it accepts domestic capital participation, it must renounce access to fiscal and other privileges provided by the Law for New and Necessary Industries, and Mexico is particularly interested in foreign investment projects that bring into the country new technology, create considerable sources of employment, and give preference to the use of domestic physical inputs.

While these general directives, elaborated over the past two decades, might look forbidding to prospective investors by restricting considerably the participation of foreign private capital in Mexico's economic development, the inflow of new investment into the country is larger than anywhere else in Latin America. Rapid industrial development, continuous diversification of domestic demand, and, finally, the extremely high level of profits in the private sector, more than offset the apparently restrictive features of present policy toward foreign private capital.

According to very preliminary estimates, the total book value of foreign private investment increased in Mexico from $US1,080 million in 1960 to some $US2,300 million by 1968; that is, it more than doubled in less than ten years. During the present decade, practically all new investment, reinvested profits and financial resources released by dis-investment in traditional sectors (especially in public utilities and mining) went into manufacturing and non-financial services, mainly commerce and tourist facilities. Between 1960 and 1968 the total book value of foreign direct investment in manufacturing grew from less than $US600 million to about $US1,700 million and in the service sector (excluding financial intermediaries from which foreign investment is barred), from $US225 million to about $US400 million.

The Role of American Investment

Because of the allegedly decisive contribution of foreign manufacturing investment to the solution of the balance-of-payments difficulties and its presumably highly positive technological and welfare impact upon the developing economies, the recent massive flow of foreign private capital into Mexican manufacturing and ancillary services is worth looking into closely. These alleged contributions are considered almost axiomatic by most of the literature forthcoming from the advanced countries, and particularly by studies sponsored directly and indirectly by the United States Department of Commerce.[3] Serious scholars have considerable difficulty in accepting these simplistic apologies.[4]

In the case of Mexico, one has to work exclusively with the data on the Mexican activities of United States owned transnational manufacturing companies.[5] A wealth of information on that subject has been collected by Harvard Graduate School of Business Administration as a part of a monumental study of United States transnational corporations,

[3] For the most recent example of such treatment see Herbert K. May, *The Effects of United States and Other Foreign Investment in Latin America* (New York: The Council for Latin America, January 1970), based upon partially released data of a long-overdue world-wide survey of United States foreign direct investment in 1966, made by the United States Department of Commerce the following year.

[4] See Johnson in Chapter 1, p. 4. See also Paul Streeten, 'The Contribution of Private Overseas Investment to Development', Pearson Conference, Columbia University, February 1970 (mimeo.) and Carlos F. Díaz Alejandro, 'Direct Foreign Investment in Latin America', University of Minnesota, 1970 (mimeo.).

[5] Throughout this chapter the commonly used term *multinational corporation* is replaced by *transnational corporation*. This term lends itself to less confusion by making clear that these corporate giants are characterised by the centralised control in the country of the parent and world-wide operations through manufacturing and other subsidiaries.

directed by Raymond Vernon.[6] According to these data, Mexico occupied in 1967 third place in the world after Canada and Great Britain as a haven for American investment. There are 187 United States-based transnational corporate parent systems, accounting for over 70 per cent of United States direct manufacturing investment overseas and over 80 per cent of United States foreign direct manufacturing investment outside Canada. Out of those 187 corporations, 179 have entered Mexico through subsidiaries during the present century. The comparable figures for Canada and Great Britain are 183 and 180 respectively. In respect to the number of affiliates of these parent systems, established over the same period, Mexico with 625 subsidiaries occupies the first place in Latin America and the fifth in the world after Canada (1,697), Great Britain (1,189), France (670), and Germany (632).

Because of mergers, sales to nationals or withdrawals, 162 out of 187 United States transnational manufacturing corporations were present in Mexico at the end of 1967 with a total of 412 subsidiaries. There were 255 subsidiaries in manufacturing (including assembling) activities, 31 in commerce, 14 in extractive industries, and 112 either in other sectors or unspecified by the Harvard researchers. Out of the original 625 entries into Mexico before the end of 1967, 268 were newly established subsidiaries, 225 involved acquisitions of existing firms,[7] and the remaining 132 either appeared as separate new branches of existing subsidiaries or their form of entry into Mexico was unknown. Out of 412 subsidiaries present in Mexico at the end of 1967, 143 were new entries, 112 acquisitions, and 109 were branches of subsidiaries established earlier. The mode of entry of the remaining 48 subsidiaries is not known. Some 56 per cent of the total was wholly owned by the parent system; 19 per cent had United States majority capital control and only 15 per cent had United States minority control. While the degree of foreign control of the remaining 10 per cent of subsidiaries could not be established, it is a fair assumption that half of them had majority control by the parent system. This would bring the percentage of Mexican subsidiaries of the 162 major United States transnational manufacturing corporations, fully-owned or with majority capital control, to some 80 per cent of the total.

The trend toward entry of United States-based transnational manu-

[6] All data used in the following section come from James W. Vaupel and Joan A. Curhan, *The Making of Multinational Enterprise—A Sourcebook of Tables Based on a Study of 187 Major U.S. Manufacturing Corporations* (Boston: Division of Research, Graduate School of Business Administration, Harvard University, 1969).

[7] Although no global data about both foreign and domestic acquisitions of Mexican firms are available for any period, the findings of a recent Canadian study strongly suggest that the entry of foreign firms into Canada through acquisition of domestic firms was of less importance between 1945 and 1961 in that country than in Mexico in 1958-67. For Canadian data see Grant L. Reuber and Frank Roseman, *The Takeover of Canadian Firms, 1945-1961, An Empirical Analysis* (Ottawa: Special Study No. 10, Economic Council of Canada, March 1969).

facturers into Mexico through acquisitions and the tendency toward full or majority control, measured in terms of flows, increased substantially in the period 1958-67. Compared with the first post-war decade (1946-57) the total number of entries jumped from 156 to 335, while the number of newly-established subsidiaries increased from 80 to 119 and that of acquisitions from 49 to 149. Looked upon in terms of stocks, a considerable number of mergers (presumably representing horizontal and vertical integration within the captive market) and an extension of activities into new fields can be detected in the behaviour of United States manufacturing companies' subsidiaries over the last ten years of the rapid industrialisation of Mexico (1958-67). Out of 178 subsidiaries established in Mexico after 1957, and existing ten years later as separate structures incorporated under local legislation, 34 were newly established firms, 62 resulted from acquisitions, 73 were branches of other Mexican subsidiaries and the origin of the remaining 9 is unknown.

This brief overview would not be complete without a mention of manufacturing industries in Mexico for which United States transnational manufacturing firms have shown strong preference in the postwar years and particularly in the 1958-67 period. Out of a total 315 United States entries into manufacturing in Mexico between 1946 and 1967, recorded in the Harvard directory, 99 subsidiaries, or close to one-third, were established in the chemical, pharmaceutical or cosmetics industries. The second place belongs to processed foods and beverages, with 65 entries; the third to the automotive industry including rubber products, with 34, and the fourth to domestic electric and electronic appliances including light electric machinery, with 26. These four industries represent over 70 per cent of all postwar entries of United States transnational manufacturing companies. All of them fall into the category of durable and non-durable goods, produced almost exclusively for the domestic market.

Under these circumstances one cannot be surprised if, out of the total sales in 1956 of United States manufacturing subsidiaries operating in Mexico, valued at $US643 million, 98.5 per cent ($US633 million) represented local sales and, ten years later in 1966, still 87 per cent of the total sales, valued at $US1,480 million, represented sales in the domestic Mexican market.[8] Except in the field of transportation equipment, where in 1966 sales of Mexican subsidiaries of two large United States automobile companies to their affiliates elsewhere amounted to $US149 million, total exports of all other United States manufacturing subsidiaries amounted to a mere $US38 million or 3 per cent of their total sales. They were composed as follows: sales to other affiliates of the same parent

[8] Figures for 1960 appear in *U.S. Business Investments in Foreign Countries* (U.S. Dept of Commerce, Washington, D.C., 1960), p. 110, Table 22. The U.S. Department of Commerce 1956 census covered all United States manufacturing firms in Mexico with control of more than 25 per cent of its voting stock by the parent system. Figures for 1966 are taken from May, op. cit.

systems $US15 million; exports to other clients in the United States of $US8 million, to Latin America $US7 million and to other destinations of $US4 million.[9] While at the close of the sixties, exports of the United States manufacturing newcomers to Mexican border zone, adjacent to United States territory, expanded considerably, their effect upon the balance of payments is minimal due to the fact that their activity is limited to assembling for re-export parts imported in bond, largely from the United States.

Costs and Benefits

All this information strongly suggests that the postwar wave of foreign, mostly United States, manufacturing investment in Mexico represented a clear case of the kind mentioned in Johnson's chapter, which takes advantage of high tariff barriers and gets, in addition, access to a wide array of state industrialisation promoting measures, ranging from tax exemptions to open and hidden subsidies offered to the industrial sector as a whole. These take the form of generous provision of infrastructure financed from public funds and through sales below cost to private industrial enterprises of state-produced goods and services, such as energy and transport. The tariff protection element seemed to play a particularly important role in investment decisions of foreign private capital.

Whilst in comparison with other Latin American countries, Mexico has been considered a relatively lowly protected market with its foreign exchange rate reasonably close to equilibrium, the most recent studies of the level of Mexican tariff protection undermine previous intuitive judgments based upon the concept of nominal tariff. Thus, it has recently been found that the average Mexican level of *effective* protection for manufactured goods is close to 50 per cent, varying from about 5 per cent in the case of processed foodstuffs to over 100 per cent in consumer durables.[10] Within this last group the automobile industry enjoys an effective protection of 255 per cent. According to the same study, manufacturing industries, able in recent times to export some part of their output (from 5 to 10 per cent), receive effective protection of 26 per cent; for those competing with imports the effective tariff is 73 per cent on the average and those that do not appear either on the export or import lists, 33 per cent. An effective level of protection for import substitution

[9] May, op. cit., p. 32, Table 4. Even these figures may overestimate the exports of United States manufacturing subsidiaries from Mexico in 1966. The author of that study (based, as previously mentioned, upon preliminary data supplied by U.S. Department of Commerce) made some adjustments to official United States figures, because the coverage of the 1966 world-wide census was limited to United States parent companies with majority of capital control and employing 100 or more people each. Figures quoted from May's study appear in his table under a heading 'presumptive exports'.

[10] Gerardo Bueno, 'The Level of Effective Protection in Mexico', in Bela Balassa (ed.), *Effective Protection in Developing Countries* (Baltimore: Johns Hopkins University Press, 1971).

industries close to 75 per cent can hardly be considered low. Its absolute level, which has probably increased in the past decade, explains to a considerable extent not only the rush of foreign manufacturing enterprises into Mexico in the past twenty years, but the coexistence of high profitability in manufacturing (within the range of 25 per cent a year on investment in fixed assets) with the use of about 60 per cent capacity on the average by the manufacturing sector. Inflexible protectionist policies coupled with the faulty design of the fiscal system and the absence of anti-monopoly legislation has created in Mexico a framework conducive to the inefficiency of the domestically-owned industrial sector and a foreign direct investment situation, aptly described by Johnson in the following way:

> where the foreign direct investment has been attracted by protection or fiscal incentives, the profits earned may not be matched by a genuine contribution to increased output, and the servicing drain on the balance of payments constitutes a real burden on the economy (see p. 13, this volume).

While it is impossible to disagree with Johnson's observation that such a situation should be ascribed to governmental error in providing socially undesirable incentives to foreign direct investment rather than blamed on the foreign corporation *per se*, a further inquiry into the behaviour of the subsidiaries of transnational manufacturing companies in Mexico and the implications of this behaviour for the host economy and the Mexican political system is in order. Such inquiry would help to define potential sources of conflict between a highly nationalistic Mexican society and foreign private investment, concentrated now in dynamic industrial sectors.

This inquiry has to start with rejecting three major propositions still fashionable in traditional economic theory. The first one considers international capital flows as the transfer of a single factor of production which is missing in the recipient country and which complements the existing factors. Once one substitutes this proposition with another stressing that private capital transfers represent only a part of a package of capital, technology and managerial skills, the measuring of potential benefits or losses from foreign direct capital flows, accruing to the host country, while becoming more complicated, offers more fruitful answers.[11]

The second proposition that must be discarded is that the flow of technology to the developing countries (technology treated traditionally as an aggregate entity which, introduced as an index in the production

---

[11] Examples of this 'conventional' approach can be found not only in official and private sector literature originating in the capital exporting countries, but in periodical reviews of flows of financial resources to the developing countries, published under the auspices of international agencies such as the OECD.

function, 'augments' the availability of some or all other inputs in terms of efficiency units) takes place on a microeconomic level between *two* firms—the seller and the buyer—under competitive conditions.[12] This proposition is as distant from the reality as the first one, because of the emergence in the postwar world of a growing number of transnational manufacturing giants that, in the case of Mexico among others, represent an important vehicle of the transfer of packages of capital, technology and managerial skills.

Finally, the third major traditional proposition, of little if any use, is that the reported profitability of a subsidiary of a transnational corporation, located in a developing host country, characterised by excessive protection and an oligopolistic market structure, is a correct accounting tool for measuring the foreign exchange costs and balance-of-payments effects of the operations of that productive unit. Paradoxically, the reported profitability of foreign subsidiaries and transfer of these profits abroad as compared with the inflow of new capital into a developing host country are used both against foreign private investment by its under-educated opponents in the developing world and, with some superficial degree of sophistication that takes into account the 'import substitution' and 'export creation' effect, by traditional apologists for foreign private investment. Instead of taking part in this spurious conflict between primitive accountants from 'the left' in the developing countries and from 'the right' in the capital exporting countries, one is forced to accept another novel proposition. Cost-benefit analysis of foreign direct investment must accept the reality of the package transfer, the monopolistic control of a large part of the modern technology (both patented and unpatented) by transnational manufacturing corporations, and the effect upon the host countries of global profit maximisation strategies of these large corporate bodies that according to some projections will account by the year 2000 for more than one-half of the world industrial production. Only then does one begin to deal with the real world.[13]

Looking at Mexican experience in the last twenty years, one sees that

[12] For an excellent study of the unreality of this assumption, supported by a case study of the experiences of an underdeveloped Latin American country, Colombia, see Constantine V. Vaitsos, *Transfer of Resources and Preservation of Monopoly Rents*, paper submitted for the Dubrovnik Conference of Harvard University Development Advisory Service, May 1970 (mimeo.).

[13] According to a thoughtful student of the foreign investment decisions affecting the capital importing countries: 'economic theory does not pretend to mirror reality. It only claims, by a process of simplification, to isolate some significant strands in economic causal sequences, and to describe how these strands operate. Economic theory, therefore, is rarely right or wrong, it is only more or less useful, depending upon whether the necessary simplification constitutes a very large or very small deviation from reality. My conclusion, nevertheless, reached over a long period of time, was that the simplifying assumptions of classical economic theory represented so gross a departure from reality that the theory was an extremely inefficient frame of reference from which to observe, project and prescribe on the subject of capital investment', Yair Aharoni, *The Foreign Investment Decision Process* (Boston: Graduate School of Business Administration, Harvard University, 1966), p. ix.

out of four major durable consumer goods industries, controlled almost completely by foreign private capital, three—chemicals and pharmaceuticals (including cosmetics of all sorts), automobiles, and domestic electric and electronic appliances have certain common characteristics. They did not involve heavy initial investment outlays, they used relatively constant technology and, at the time of their entry into Mexico, depended heavily on imported inputs. In all cases the technology is tied to the provision of imported inputs through intra-parent system standardisation of components (automotive and electric appliance industry) and by patents (the electric appliance industry and chemicals and pharmaceuticals). Under these circumstances, low capital investment needs, particularly at the assembly stage, considered along with the high income elasticity of demand in a society of rising middle classes (endowed with consumer preference patterns shaped by the proximity of the United States), the monopolistic control of tied technology by foreign manufacturing entrants, and tied sources of imported inputs, must have offered the parent systems, investing in a heavily protected market, extremely high profits that in no way could have been reflected in the balance sheets and profit and loss statements of the foreign subsidiaries in Mexico. They appear only in the profit and loss statements of the parent systems and this is why, among others, the parent companies' financial statements are generally published in consolidated form.

In fact, parent companies of transnational corporations do not show any enthusiasm for disclosing the detailed results of overseas operations to their own shareholders at home either, as was pointed out in a survey made by the United States National Industrial Conference Board in early 1965. According to this study:

> more than 80 per cent of manufacturers surveyed earn money through exports, foreign licencing agreements or overseas manufacturing. About half have increased earnings from such sources in recent years. Yet few share the good news with their stockholders.
> Any reader of annual reports will find that vital information on foreign sales and earnings generally is lacking, buried in small print in footnotes or discussed in terms a layman cannot understand.[14]

Reported subsidiaries' profits after local taxes, averaging in Mexico for the whole United States-owned manufacturing sector around 10 per cent a year, thus represent only the visible part of the profit iceberg, accruing to the parent companies through payments of royalties and 'technical assistance' and through intra-company pricing of imported inputs that obviously are priced in relation to the local protection level and not sold by the parent company at their incremental cost. World-wide practices in

[14] *New York Times*, 11 April 1965: 'Foreign Data Held Lacking in Reports'.

this respect by chemical and pharmaceutical transnational corporations are too well known to be discussed here.[15] The key to the measurement of profitability of a foreign investment venture for the parent company remains the inter-company pricing permitted by high protective walls and control over tied-in technology.[16]

These propositions explain, on the one hand, the extreme hostility of foreign manufacturing companies (and for that matter domestically-owned firms as well) to disclose to anyone but fiscal authorities any kind of financial information, and, particularly, any details of the cost structure in highly protected economies such as Mexico, and, on the other hand, the silent agreement between the state and the private sector to keep all this information secret. Under conditions of real or alleged scarcity of capital and technology and with a declared policy of economic nationalism, any breakdown of such 'gentlemen's agreements' on the secrecy of the internal financial operations of foreign-controlled enterprises might have many immediate and politically undesirable effects. First, it would destroy the 'good investment climate' for which Mexico is famous; second, it would permit outside parties to quantify monopolistic rents accruing to foreign manufacturing investors through overpricing of technology and intra-company pricing of imported parts and accessories; third, it would throw serious doubts upon the whole development strategy, based upon heavy protection and additional industrialisation incentives, that permits these rents to foreign firms and offers a premium for inefficiency to many domestic producers, in the name of economic nationalism. Finally, it might raise a political storm in a nationalistic society and provide strong ammunition to the political left.

In the absence of any alternative development strategy, the Mexican government has decided to face the challenge of the transnational manufacturing corporations in three indirect ways: by extending mexicanisation pressures to new segments of the manufacturing sector; by forcing foreign-controlled industries to increase the use of domestically produced inputs; and finally, very recently, by linking the issuance of permits for imported inputs with the export performance of industrial enterprises. The actual results of the first two measures, in terms of balance-of-payments relief and consumer's welfare, seem to be rather meagre. As one Mexican economist has put it, when questioning both the way import substitution is fostered at the present stage of Mexico's industrial development and the real effect of the mexicanisation policies encouraging joint industrial ventures:

[15] For details see volumes of Sen. Kefauver's hearings on administered prices of drugs, held in the U.S. Congress in 1953-4, and Lord Sainsbury's report on the British pharmaceutical industry, released by HMSO in London in September 1967.
[16] A neat theoretical analysis of this point can be found in Constantine V. Viatsos, *Transfer of Industrial Technology to Developing Countries Through Private Enterprises*, Bogota, Colombia, February 1970 (mimeo.), Appendix 1.

(given the dominant technological position of transnational industrial corporations) the actual effect of import substitution policies is extremely paradoxical. While one of the objectives of such policies was to diminish the dependence of the Mexican economy upon world economic fluctuations, it has obviously stimulated strongly the growth of foreign investment in Mexico . . . As a result of protectionist policies foreign corporations substituted trade by investment . . . Following the example of other underdeveloped countries, our authorities have attempted to solve the paradox through a mexicanization policy; however, even under the best circumstances, this policy does not help to improve the competitive capacity of Mexican enterprises. It only results in that some already privileged Mexicans may participate in oligopolistic profits, associated with technological innovations whose availability and control had led foreign enterprises to invest in Mexico.[17]

Forcing backward linkages upon such assembly activities as the automobile industry through a policy of increased integration into assembled units of domestic parts produced by new joint ventures has brought rather disappointing results. While no study of the new auto parts and accessories industries is available as yet, the official policy, according to the automotive enterprises, the majority of which are fully foreign-owned, resulted in an increase in costs and the decline in quality standards. A preliminary survey suggests, on the other hand, that most of the auto parts industry uses second-hand equipment brought mainly from the United States by foreign partners, and pays very considerable fees on account of patents, trademarks and technical assistance. Similar experiences are reported from other industries subject to 'domestic integration' programs, industries that, because of local inability to adapt imported technologies to Mexican conditions and intra-company standardisation of parts and accessories, depend heavily on technologies acquired—again at a cost defined by the increased protection level and the strong bargaining power of the sellers—from large transnational manufacturing systems.

It is only the linkage of import permits to export performance of manufacturing firms that starts showing positive results by curtailing heavily the possibility of monopolistic rents from the control of technology and overpricing imports of intermediate goods by the parent system. How large a benefit this policy will bring is hard to guess. It will largely depend upon Mexico's willingness to tackle, through fiscal measures and new industrial property and patent legislation (the present law is 25 years old and completely outdated), the problem of the restrictive practices of Mexican subsidiaries of foreign firms. Little if anything is known, for

[17] Carlos Bazdrech, 'Nuevas ideas sobre la inversión extranjera', *Reunión Nacional para el Estudio del Desarrollo Industrial de México*, Vol. 3, June 1970, p. 1791.

example, about restrictive export practices (market division clauses) of these subsidiaries. The only piece of evidence that such practices are extensive can be found in an unpublished report on United States foreign investment in Mexico, commissioned in 1969 by the National Chamber Foundation of Washington, D.C. The report, based upon 122 answers to questionnaires sent to some 650 United States owned or controlled manufacturing enterprises, contains information to the effect that one-half of the respondents (60) were enjoined from exporting from Mexico by their parent companies.

Since both foreign and domestic industrial producers are interested, for different reasons, in the highest level of protection possible, the Mexican state that a quarter of a century ago gave political and economic priority to industrialisation practically at any cost to the consumer, seems thus to be somehow stuck with 'infant industry' policies. Although it is easy to recognise that inward-oriented industrialisation, heavily dependent on foreign capital and second-class foreign technology, is expensive in terms of the foreign exchange burden and social welfare, any mentioning of the need to lower protection levels is drowned by protests from powerful coalitions of vested interests both foreign and domestic.

As long as Mexican industrial output was expanding at close to 10 per cent a year and balance-of-payments problems could be taken care of by growing tourist revenue, new foreign private investment and generous foreign public and private lending extended to the public sector, no imperative necessity could be seen in Mexico for a readjustment of crude industrialisation policies designed in the early postwar period. But in the past few years the situation has begun to change, though almost imperceptibly to the non-expert eye. The current balance of payments account is getting out of gear, the proportion of new foreign investment to reinvested profits has begun to decline, the inability of Mexican society to absorb and adapt foreign technology not tied to foreign direct investment is becoming clear, while attempts to expand industrial exports face serious problems because of the low efficiency of the industrial structure and the scarcity of the international marketing know-how among domestic firms, restrictive export practices of foreign manufacturing subsidiaries.

Only now some questions are being raised about the performance of the industrialisation model in force in Mexico since the end of the war and its social costs. A new generation of nationalist foreign-educated intellectuals questions also the generous treatment offered to foreign investment in the key sectors, in spite of an apparently impressive web of restrictions and regulations aimed at the mexicanisation of the manufacturing activities. What is more, sophisticated questions are being asked about the technological and managerial contribution of foreign private investment and about the real meaning of the mexicanisation policies. While the managerial contribution of foreign direct investment seems impressive, the costs of tied-in technology look staggering when compared with those of non-tied technology that might be easily acquired in international competitive markets by domestic entrepreneurs if only they would care to search for it.[18] As far as the results of the private mexicanisation of manufacturing and ancillary activities are concerned, there is a growing consensus that 'it is a tool used by the new middle class to accede to wealth and power'.[19]

Conclusions

It would, however, represent a gross underestimation of the strength of Mexican political and economic nationalism to consider it as a mere outcome of the social stratification process that has occurred in Mexico in the most recent decades and has brought about the emergence of middle classes and the concentration of wealth recalling the industrial economies of the end of the nineteenth century. If one keeps in mind the highlights of Mexican political and economic history, presented at the beginning of this chapter, one is forced to accept that Mexican nationalism has very deep roots related to rather unhappy encounters with the advanced outside world over the past two centuries. Given the declared commitment of the political system to use industrialisation as a major tool for increasing the country's independence from that outside world, and accepting at its face value the social content of the official post-Revolutionary ideology, it is difficult to envisage the long-term continuation of a situation in which the control of the dynamic new industrial sectors passes into foreign hands, or, at best, is shared by them with those members of the local middle classes that succeed in monopolising wealth and power. Neither of these situations helps to resolve the problem of the low efficiency in the industrialisation process.

What kind of new long-run strategy would Mexico need not only to ensure continuation of her impressive economic growth performance over the past decades, but also to translate this quantitative growth into increasing social welfare in a country with one of the worst income dis-

[18] While no data about the foreign exchange costs of technology imports to Mexico are available, the Mexican Treasury has lately found out that some $US80 million were transferred abroad for 'technical assistance' in 1968 alone, only in large part to such industrialised countries as Panama, Bahamas, Curaçao and Liechtenstein. For details see 'Asistencia técnica del extranjero', *Investigación Fiscal*, Secretaría de Hacienda y Crédito Público (Mexico), No. 45, October 1969. This writer's report, written for the United Nations in 1968, discovered that between 1961 and 1965, the only period for which such data were available, remittances abroad of net profits by foreign companies, established in Mexico, increased by 20 per cent only, while overt payments on account of interest, royalties and technical assistance grew by 40 per cent. For details see Miguel S. Wionczek, *Arrangements for the Transfer of Operative Technology to Developing Countries —Case Study of Mexico*, U.N. Economic and Social Council, E/4452/Add/3, March 1968 (mimeo.).

[19] Albert Breton, 'The Economics of Nationalism', *Journal of Political Economy*, August 1964, p. 381.

tribution patterns in Latin America and with one of the highest population growth rates? Such a strategy in respect of the contribution of foreign capital and technology to development would call for the following, among other things. First, it would require a sizeable but selective decrease in the level of effective protection in order to bring some degree of competition into the present monopolistic structures and increase Mexico's manufacturing export potential. It would also require the revamping of fiscal policies aimed at the abandonment of the whole array of superfluous incentives for 'infant industries' which long ago should have become, if not adults, at least adolescents. The knot that results in the package transfers of foreign capital, technology and managerial skills, lending themselves, as this chapter shows, to overt and covert abuses by foreign manufacturing enterprises, would have to be unravelled. Finally, it would require a general and far-reaching reform of the educational system, the performance of which has led to the appearance of acute bottlenecks on the middle technical skills level and has curtailed severely the country's ability to select and to adapt to the economy's needs untied technology available outside of transnational corporate systems.

While all these proposals run against the interests of powerful vested interested groups, both domestic and foreign, the delay in their implementation might create within the not too distant future severe conflicts between foreign private capital and Mexican society and add to domestic political and social stresses originating in the past strategy of industrialisation at any cost.

Comments and Discussion

STEPHEN HYMER opened the discussion: Wionczek describes the role of foreign investment in the transformation of the Mexican economy from a traditional export economy to a developing economy committed to a strategy of import substituting industrialisation. Mexico began with a system, early this century, in which there was a landed aristocracy exploiting the native population and foreign investors dominating the export sector. This is a very typical kind of structure in Latin America and in other parts of the world. Mexico is usually held up as an example for having dealt with that structure first of all through its thorough-going Revolution in which the landlord aristocracy was overthrown and a completely new society was established. Secondly, a series of measures, which lasted until recently, removed foreign control of the traditional export sector. This involved a long, hard battle, in the case of oil, in the late thirties and forties, and, more recently, has been effected forcefully through the 'mexicanisation' of electricity and mining described above. Thirdly, a major industrialisation drive has been successful, if success is defined in terms of a rapid rate of growth in the establishment of a large industrial sector. Mexico now stands, among the developing world, as one of the largest industrial countries. This is a major success. Also, during this time, it maintained very rigid control of foreign investment, or at least a mechanism for controlling foreign investment and supervising it. This is combined with an intensely nationalistic spirit, the cohesiveness of which is frequently compared with that in Japan.

Wionczek is not satisfied with this performance and he firstly observes that the industrialisation program has been heavily subsidised through tariff protection and other forms of incentives given by the government. The middle class in Mexico City have obviously benefited from this, and it must have been at considerable cost to a large number of people that they did. Foreign investors also shared in the incentives and the redistribution of wealth, as they took advantage of the programs offered. Of course, that is not the fault of the foreign investors, as the chapter points out. But it is suggested that the costs of foreign investment may, under these circumstances, never have exceeded the benefits. This is important, since a redistribution of the kind involved to non-nationals may have less chance of being 'paid back'. Naturally Mexicans resent the fact that subsidies which were supposed to help 'infants' grow up have gone to foreign firms which could not exactly be described as 'infants'.

Wionczek believes that the amount passed over to foreigners has been very large—much larger than indicated by profit statistics. As his chapter shows, the reason for this is that the foreign firms are in a strong bargaining position. There was a high income elasticity of demand for their products and their monopoly over one kind of technical knowledge or the other is strong. Government attempts to control or regulate foreign investment were not successful and the cost of these controls was effectively passed on to the Mexican consumer. If the foreign companies were required to buy more locally, for instance, there was either an increase in the price of their products or a deterioration in their quality; in other words, the cost of buying some locally did not come out of the profits of the firm but were passed on to the consumer. Another aspect was that certain Mexicans were allowed 'a share in the loot' as it were, through the policy of mexicanisation. In fact the amount of leverage from restrictions and controls was limited.

A big problem in thinking about the future seems to be the alliance that is forming between the local middle class and foreign interests, or, maybe, the local middle classes using the advantages that foreigners have brought. The problem is exemplified in an income distribution which is claimed to be the worst in Latin America.

To this point, I am in complete agreement with the argument. When it comes to the conclusions there appears to be a shrinkage from facts. The situation is described in very stark terms, and yet when we arrive at the solutions, they appear very mild. It is recommended that tariffs should be removed and controls tightened. But this is unlikely to change the returns to the foreigner. It will allow foreign investment to operate more efficiently, but will not change the return it is paid on its advantages. Moreover, will the local middle class be prepared to have these measures implemented? Rising middle class markets demand more of what foreign firms can produce, so that what foreign firms produce has to be paid for. The real solution would seem more fundamental. As long as the direction of development is towards the middle-class market, it will remain small, and generate little employment and welfare. Dependence on foreign investment is bound up with the problem of income inequality. I suspect that if the demand structure was changed, and goods were being produced to alleviate poverty in the bottom nine-tenths of society, that these would be goods in which multinational firms did not have particular advantages and could be handled by local technology and local entrepreneurship. This would seem to be one approach to solving the problems that seem to beset Mexico.

Thereafter, discussion of Virata's and Wionczek's chapters revolved around three themes: the relationship between income distribution and growth, the role of the joint venture form of foreign investment, and the effects of protection on industrial efficiency.

In answering Kanamori's specific questions, Virata agreed, firstly, that the problem of excess capacity in assembly industries was serious, but saw no easy solution to the problem through administrative discrimination. Secondly, he explained that the distinction between pioneering and non-pioneering industries was largely a compromise designed to prevent political reaction against foreign investment monopolising all segments of production. But it also had economic rationale in its attempt to encourage investors into areas such as copper smelting and fabrication, which could be competitive given the import of technology and capable management. Thirdly, he agreed that the phase-out conditions imposed on foreign investors were a deterrent but added that the period of grace was extendable up to another twenty years. Fourthly, he suggested that the floating exchange rate was likely to encourage capital into the extraction of natural resources and export activities. In reply to a further question about the existence of forward cover facilities, he said that these were too expensive but that investors were able to deduct up to 50 per cent of export earnings to pledge against imports of capital equipment and debt repayment, and these procedures offered some forward cover. Fifthly, he said that he saw the natural division of investment as being closely related to comparative advantage. Japan, for example, should consider investment in processing capacity and fabrication overseas to utilise more efficiently host countries' resources, cheaper labour, or environment.

An American participant found it difficult to understand Hymer's argument that lowering tariffs would not affect income distribution. Reducing tariffs lowers the rents to intra-marginal producers and affects the incomes within other sectors. He also observed that income distribution probably had little to do with foreign investment but had important implications for growth. On the historical evidence, it seemed probable that skewed income distribution encouraged high savings and high rates of capital formation. Hymer accepted the point on tariffs and income redistribution but suggested that the relationship between income distribution and growth was not so obvious as had been implied. High income-earners may well be high consumers rather than high savers. He produced an arithmetical example to illustrate the effects of income redistribution in Mexico, the arithmetic of which was subsequently challenged.

Another participant was uncomfortable at the connection which Hymer saw between the income distribution problem and the foreign investment problem. He thought that if there was justification for a thorough-going social revolution aimed, say, at redistributing the 40 per cent of national income acquired by the top decile in the population, it would have to be based on grounds other than its effect on any marginal improvement in efficiency in the location of overseas capital within the Mexican economy. Hymer replied that what he wanted to say was simply that, if any income distribution of the kind prevalent in Mexico persists, foreign firms will continue to dominate that economy and preserve their advantage.

Wionczek added that an important point made by Hymer was that the nature of Mexican income distribution (and perhaps this applied to the Philippines also) could lead to such increased social tensions that political scientists and economists ought to have an interest in it.

Consideration of the position of foreign investment in domestic political structures opened up discussion of the function of the joint-venture investment and its dominance in East and South-East Asia. Was the prevalence of joint-venture investments there a consequence of the cultural differences between the host and capital exporting country, and a requirement, under these circumstances, of local support? It was noted that joint ventures create a local interest which represents the foreign investor in various ways. In the Latin countries within Europe it appeared common for local participation to serve to establish the basis of taxation.

Further discussion was related to the political issues raised in Wionczek's chapter and Hymer's commentary. In many East and South-East Asian countries, joint ventures were encouraged by the host country government. Joint ventures were seen first as a business convenience, based on local monopoly of distribution outlets, resources, or familiarity with administrative procedures and business practice. In other cases, they might represent attempts to seek political patronage. Participants from Asian countries warned against the view that the latter cases were common and pointed out that reliance on patronage had its own risks. A

Japanese participant saw advantages in joint arrangements and observed that competition among potential partners before the venture, and mutuality of interests within the venture after, minimised the chances of exploitation of domestic interests.

There was also detailed discussion of the role of protection in fostering the inefficient use of foreign investment. Most participants had difficulty interpreting Hymer's view that the removal of protective devices would necessarily lead to withdrawal of foreign investment. He explained that his assumption had been a constant supply price and he agreed that this assumption might be qualified. Others pointed out that profits may fall, rise, or remain the same when tariffs are removed, depending on the degree to which foreign firms improve their level of efficiency. Thus, the effect of changes in tariffs or taxation policy and so on may, on balance, induce a substantial improvement in the efficiency of operation rather than an emigration of foreign capital.

In related discussion, at least some participants saw contradictions in Wionczek's argument which seemed at once to attribute the costs of foreign investment in Mexico largely to domestic policy and, at the same time, to infer from certain criticisms of the conventional approach to foreign investment that the costs were attributable to the nature of the investment itself. The fact that foreign direct investment involved the transfer of management and technology, as well as capital, had been seen as an advantage throughout the discussion, but Wionczek argued that the package was too expensive and should be unravelled. The real question was whether all or any of its component parts could be obtained more cheaply if this were done. It was advanced that foreign investment was expensive to Mexico because of protectionist policies, which reduced competition among investors, and perhaps because of the dominance of United States investors in that country. Mexico also appeared to have misdirected investment into inappropriate channels, and to have been unwilling to use its bargaining levers against the foreign investor. Wionczek replied that Mexico was getting second-rate technology very expensively through foreign investment and he doubted that local management, given the opportunity, could do worse.

Wionczek's argument for tying access to imports to export performance, for example, in the automotive industry, was also questioned on the grounds that it would lead to inefficient specialisation of the same kind embodied in the United States-Canadian Automotive Agreement. Wionczek saw his advocacy of trade balancing as a second-best policy where first-best policy options were not attainable.

13 Balance of Payments Effects of Direct Foreign Investment in the Pacific Area

J. O. N. PERKINS

This chapter considers in very general terms some of the likely effects of international investment flows among the Pacific countries. The principal effects discussed are those upon trade, rather than the more obvious effects on the balance of payments consisting of a given capital flow and of the subsequent remittances of dividends and interest that may result from it. The emphasis upon the less obvious trade effects is not to be taken as underestimating the importance of the more direct effects of capital flows. But the effects of international flows of investment upon trade are less widely discussed and are especially hard to foresee, largely because they cannot be assessed by reference to actual trade figures alone. Some reasonable assumptions have first to be selected about what the situation would have been in the absence of the investment in question, so that an estimate can be made of the way in which the actual trade flows differ from what they would have been if the investment had not occurred.

Two fairly recent studies suggest possible lines of approach to this subject. One of these is the Reddaway project at Cambridge, which estimated the effects of British direct overseas investment, mainly on the basis of material assembled through close co-operation between the research workers engaged on the project and most of the British companies involved.[1] The other is a survey of effects of overseas investment by United States manufacturing firms, undertaken by Hufbauer and Adler, on the basis of published statistical data (of types apparently not available in comparable detail for any other country).[2] The ensuing analysis draws on the methods and results of these investigations, in order to

[1] W. B. Reddaway in collaboration with J. O. N. Perkins, S. J. Potter and C. T. Taylor, *Effects of U.K. Direct Investment Overseas: An Interim Report*, 1967, and W. B. Reddaway in collaboration with S. J. Potter and C. T. Taylor, *Final Report* (Cambridge, 1968).
[2] G. C. Hufbauer and F. M. Adler, *Overseas Manufacturing Investment and the Balance of Payments* (U.S. Treasury Department, 1968).

suggest some of the factors that are likely to determine the effects upon trade of investment flows among the principal countries round the Pacific. The conclusions are no more than tentative, the aim being to promote discussion of the likely importance of various possible effects and to suggest hypotheses that might be capable of testing, either by econometric methods if the data are available, or by close consultation with firms involved in the relevant decisions.

In assessing the effects upon trade of a given flow of investment one has to consider two main groups of possible effects. There is, first of all, the effect of the foreign exchange accruing to the host country, and of the subsequent accruals of foreign exchange to the capital-exporting country as dividends and earnings are later remitted. The general effects of these payments are, however, analogous to those of any other payment of foreign exchange, in the sense that they enable the recipient to finance a higher level of imports (and of other out-payments) than he would otherwise find possible. On the other hand, it is true that such payments differ from payments for trade in goods and services in that the recipient does not have to provide in return for them any *quid pro quo* involving the use of his own real resources.

But some of the more interesting effects on trade arise from certain decisions that are often associated with the particular form taken by an international investment. In particular, important repercussions upon trade often result from the fact that most international flows of investment nowadays are in the form of direct investment, which carries with it effective control for the firm in the investing country over the operations of the branch or subsidiary in the host country. Indeed, this aspect is sometimes separable from the fact of an actual capital flow. A given direct investment by an American firm in Australia, for example, might be financed by fixed-interest borrowing within Australia. In this case, the consequent rise in the accumulated total of direct American equity investment in Australia may well affect the pattern of Australia's trade, even though there would be no accrual of foreign exchange to Australia by way of extra capital inflow. It is useful, therefore, in assessing the effects of direct investment, to consider initially the effects of an increase in the level of operations of firms controlled in other countries, whether or not this increase is accompanied by an actual flow of capital to the host country. It is true that there are usually only narrow limits within which direct investments can be financed within a host country; so that it is reasonable to assume that the effects of such increases in the operations of firms controlled outside the host country will normally be accompanied by a flow of capital to it (of a more or less comparable order of magnitude). But we may usefully separate the two matters conceptually, partly in order to facilitate analysis, and partly because the two aspects of international investment may often be (to some greater or lesser extent) separated in practice. The separability (within limits) of these two aspects of international direct investment has been evidenced in various ways in recent years. For example, American firms operating in Europe (especially when they have been limited by United States policy in their freedom to export capital) have borrowed large sums in Europe to finance these operations. Again, 'voluntary' control imposed by Britain over direct investment in Australia has clearly been intended to apply pressure to the Australian branches and subsidiaries of British firms to borrow more within Australia; whilst the operation of the Australian government's guidelines on local borrowing by such firms has been intended to have an effect in the opposite direction. In the analysis that follows, therefore, the effects of foreign control will be given attention separately from those of an actual flow of capital between the countries concerned.

The method of analysis is first to outline the approach of the Reddaway survey, and to apply some of its conclusions about effects on trade to the consideration of likely consequences of direct investments among the Pacific group of countries. In this analysis the Reddaway conclusions are supplemented by some of those of the Hufbauer-Adler survey. Something will also be said of the general effects on trade that might be expected to result from capital flows among the Pacific group of countries. One special effect on which the Reddaway survey throws some light—'technological feedback' from the host country to the parent firm—is considered briefly, even though this will probably not generally be, strictly speaking, a balance of payments effect. Incidental mention is inevitably made of some of the costs and benefits arising from capital flows, and many of these are related to balance of payments effects, but this analysis is not concerned with costs and benefits as such, and should not at any point be interpreted as making judgments on the net cost or benefit of particular flows to particular countries. For particular effects on trade do not, of course, by themselves normally throw much light on such assessments: many other matters have to be considered before one can use any assessment of effects on trade as any sort of indication of net costs and benefits.

The Liberalisation of Capital Flows in the Pacific Area

A number of situations can be envisaged in which the governments of Pacific countries might wish to consider the sort of effects on trade that are discussed in this chapter. For example, there might be some form of regional integration or regional payments system that facilitated international flows of investment among this group of countries. It is also possible that as living standards rise and as trade expands, countries will feel it to be more feasible and more desirable to permit freer flows of capital generally. Even when some form of voluntary or mandatory controls over capital flows is applied by a capital-exporting country, these are often varied to some extent according to the country in which the investment is being made; and likely effects on trade may reasonably be supposed to be one of the considerations taken into account by a government in determining the details of such policies.

Countries receiving flows of capital, especially of direct investment, are also likely to be keenly interested in the possible effects of such flows upon their trade.

It should be stressed that policies towards investment flows should be formulated in the light of many other considerations besides their effects on trade. Indeed, an analysis of the effects of a given investment flow upon the trade of the countries concerned may not be primarily of relevance for their policy towards capital flows, but for their general balance of payments policy. In other words, if a capital-exporting country finds that a given international investment will adversely affect its trade in some sense (at least over some particular period) this would not be an argument for preventing an investment that was in general felt to be in the interests of the capital-exporting country, but it would be a consideration to be taken into account in assessing the country's general balance of payments prospects, and would therefore be relevant for determining the country's general economic policies.

Effect of Direct Investments on Exports from the Capital-Exporting Country

The effects of a direct investment on exports from the capital-exporting country are likely to vary considerably according to the economic characteristics of both countries concerned.

Let us consider first direct investment originating in a highly industrialised country, as such direct investments account for the overwhelming majority of the total.

It will first be assumed that if the country in question had not made the direct investment a similar project would have been undertaken in the host country under the control of either a local firm there or a firm in some other capital-exporting country. We shall subsequently consider what difference is made to the analysis by varying this assumption, and then ask what assumption on this point is likely to be most relevant for the various Pacific countries.

The first effect to be considered is the once-for-all, 'initial' favourable effect upon the exports of the capital-exporting country that may result when the investment takes place. This is likely to consist mainly of capital goods, and of other items required in the construction of the investment project that is being undertaken. The Reddaway investigation of the effects of a large number of British direct investments over the period 1954-64 found that the initial effect of British direct investments was considerable when the host country had little by way of manufacturing industries, and was very small for investments in such industrialised countries as the United States and France; whilst it was of an intermediate order for smaller developed countries such as Australia, Canada, and Denmark.[3] The average initial effect for all countries was about 9 per cent of the value of the investment flow.

The other effects on trade are those that continue during the life of the investment. These continuing effects on the exports of the investing country may be on balance favourable or unfavourable. (The Reddaway survey for British direct investment found that on balance they were favourable, but small—of the order of $1\frac{1}{2}$ per cent per annum of the stock of the investments examined, on the average for all countries.) The favourable effects arise almost entirely from the likelihood that a branch or subsidiary will purchase more of its input items (materials, components and so on) from the country of its parent firm than would a comparable business controlled elsewhere. There may also be small favourable effects on the exports of the parent firm if the production by its subsidiary in the host country serves to advertise other lines of the parent company in such a way as to increase its exports of these lines to the host country.

But a more important continuing effect on exports of finished products from the capital-exporting country is likely to be the adverse effect on its exports that normally results when its firms set up branches or subsidiaries to produce within the host country items that were previously exported to it.

The Reddaway survey found that the continuing upward effects on British exports were relatively greatest for investments in the least industrially developed countries—and that they were least for investments in highly industrialised countries; whilst they were of an intermediate order in smaller developed countries or semi-industrialised countries, such as Australia, Argentina and India.[4] Again, the explanation—as for capital-goods exports—seems to be that where the host country does not have a diversified and competitive range of manufacturing industry, there is a relatively large volume of imports of input items whose source stands to be influenced by the fact that the parent company is located in a particular investing country.

Another influence on trade that seems to be important is the geographical and other ties that may cause a high proportion of the host country's imports to be purchased from the investing country even for projects not associated with direct investments by that country. The Hufbauer-Adler survey of United States direct investments in manufacturing found that

[3] Reddaway *et al.*, *Final Report*, pp. 216-17. It must be added, however, that a few of the countries considered did not fit exactly into this neat ranking. But in general the ranking of the relative effect was remarkably close to the ranking (in inverse order) of the countries by the extent and diversity of their manufacturing industries.

[4] Reddaway *et al.*, *Final Report*, pp. 63-8, 109-10, and 372.

United States direct investments in Canada and Latin America had a negligible continuing effect in raising United States exports. The Reddaway survey found that the favourable continuing effects upon United Kingdom exports of Britain's direct investments in Canada were small, and that they were actually unfavourable for Brazil, though about average for Argentina (the other Latin American country considered in that survey). It is reasonable to expect that United States investments in these countries would have relatively small upward effects on United States exports, as even locally controlled investments in those countries, or ones controlled by firms in other capital-exporting countries, would be more likely than those of similar firms outside the western hemisphere to purchase a high proportion of their input requirements from the United States. Moreover, the importance of the United States as an exporter of finished products to these countries increases the likelihood that the setting up of production in them by United States subsidiaries would adversely affect United States exports of these products to the host countries.

One may conclude that the effects of a direct investment upon the exports of the investing country are most likely to be favourable when the host country has to import a large proportion of its requirements of capital goods and input items, but where the capital-exporting country is not such a dominant source of these imports for all projects in the host country that these items are likely to be purchased from the capital-exporting country irrespective of where the importing firm is controlled. Obviously, a further requirement is that the capital-exporting country should be able to supply the capital goods and input items on reasonably competitive terms. For finished manufactures competing with those produced by the direct investment, the risk of an adverse effect on the exports of the capital-exporting country is least when the country would not in the absence of the investment be a major exporter of the relevant products to the host country.

Let us now compare the principal countries of the Pacific group with these considerations in mind, viewing them first as capital-exporters and then as host countries for direct investment (and for the moment still retaining the assumption that in the absence of the direct investment that we are considering some other firm, controlled elsewhere, would have undertaken a similar project).

As a capital-exporting country, Japan is in a comparable position to Britain; for both countries are considerable exporters of a wide range of input items and capital goods; yet neither is such a dominant supplier of such items to countries where they may undertake direct investment as to leave only small amounts of imports from other sources that their exports could replace as a result of the investment. On the other hand, both also export finished products, the sales of which may be reduced when their subsidiaries begin production in a host country. The United States shares some of these characteristics, especially that of being a major exporter of input items, capital goods and finished products. But the special feature of the United States position is that imports from the United States are, in some countries, notably Canada, so strongly entrenched as to leave relatively little scope for direct United States investment to raise Canadian imports of capital goods and input items, whilst a great deal of direct United States investment there is very likely to reduce United States exports of competing finished products, of which the United States is such a dominant source. On the other hand, for most other countries in the Pacific area the United States is comparable to Britain or Japan as a source of imports, so that similar considerations would apply to all three countries viewed as capital exporters.

By contrast, the smaller countries of the Pacific group, Canada, Australia, New Zealand (and, so far as the question may have any relevance, the less developed countries of the area), could normally assume that a direct investment by one of their firms in another country of the area would not have substantial effects on their exports of capital goods or input items, since they are not considerable exporters of these items—with the possible exception of Canada. But in cases where they are able to supply any of these items on competitive terms, the fact that they are such small suppliers of them gives them great scope to achieve large increases in such exports; and even an absolutely small expansion of their exports in relation to the total imports of the host country may well be of significance for a country whose manufactured exports are not large. At the same time, these countries are not likely to be major suppliers of imported finished products competing with the items produced by the subsidiary: the risk of a direct investment reducing their exports would thus normally be very small. It is possible, however, that direct investments by their firms might be most likely to occur in particular products in which those countries already had a strong competitive position; in that case adverse effects on their exports might well result.

Comparing the countries of the Pacific group as host countries for direct investment, one would expect that the least industrialised among them would be those where a given direct investment was most likely to increase imports of capital goods and input items. At one extreme, less developed countries in the area are most likely to import a large part of their requirements of these; but, on the other hand, in so far as finished goods of exactly comparable types would have been available at all in such countries, in the absence of the investment, these would probably have been mainly imported, so that the direct investment would to that extent be likely to reduce their imports of such products. But, as many less developed countries severely restrict their imports of many finished goods, imports of finished products would in such cases be less likely to replace goods that would otherwise have been imported.

For an intermediate group of small industrialised countries, certainly New Zealand, and perhaps Australia (at least in some periods of the fairly recent past), a smaller, but still a fairly wide range of required capital goods and input items are likely to be imported. Their imports of finished products are least likely to be reduced by the investment where the relevant imports are already severely limited by import controls (as generally in New Zealand, and as in Australia in the 1950s) or by tariffs. But the rapid growth and the diversity of Australia's imports of finished products in the 1960s implies a greater chance that the production of new items by direct investment will in future have more effect in reducing some imports of products of types so distinctive that it would be unrealistic to assume that in the alternative position an exact equivalent would have been produced.

For direct investments made in the United States or Japan, one would expect a high proportion of the capital goods and input items required to be obtained locally, so that any upward effect on exports of such items from the investing country would be much smaller than for the countries so far considered. Canada is probably in an intermediate position in this respect, with a high proportion of her imported requirements likely to come in any event from the United States. On the other hand, the wider distribution of sources of imported inputs into the countries of the Western Pacific makes it much more likely that the origin of a direct investment would have an appreciable effect on imports from the investing country.

As to the effects on imports of finished products, it is likely that where there is a broad range of suppliers from many different countries, an investing country will face a smaller risk of loss on this score, especially if it is not itself the dominant supplier.

At one extreme, the high proportion of Canadian imports of finished products that come from the United States must make it very likely that United States investment in that country will reduce Canadian imports from the United States, and very unlikely that direct investment in Canada from elsewhere in the Pacific group of countries will reduce Canadian imports of finished goods from investing countries.

For direct investment in Australia and New Zealand, on the other hand, there is much less likelihood of direct American investment reducing United States exports of finished products to those countries, as Britain is both a source of direct investment and a source of imports to them comparable in importance to the United States. Indeed, Britain, as the established and dominant supplier of a wide range of imported products to these countries, is far more likely to lose export markets in them as a result of direct investment there, whereas the United States and Japan (and, indeed, probably also Canada) are likely to gain by way of extra exports of capital goods and input items (net of any loss of exports of finished products) to a far greater extent than is Britain by way of direct investment in Australia and New Zealand. It is true, however, that the recent rapid rise in the share of the United States and Japan in the imports of finished products into Australia and New Zealand may be changing this picture to some extent; in future there would thus be more scope for the United States or Japan to lose export markets for finished products in these countries as a result of direct investments in them.

Varying the Basic Assumption

It has so far been assumed that in the absence of the direct investment whose effects we are considering there would have been a broadly comparable project controlled either in the host country or in another capital-exporting country. The present section discusses the direction in which the conclusions will be affected if this assumption is relaxed and which assumption on this point is likely to be the more reasonable for the various Pacific countries.

If a similar project had occurred in the alternative position, it might well have necessitated the import of some capital goods and input items from the capital-exporting country (though normally not as much as when the investment is controlled there). If, therefore, there would have been no similar project in the alternative position the upward effect on imports of these items resulting from a direct investment would be the greater. As we saw above, for countries where even firms controlled outside the capital-exporting country are likely to buy a large part of their capital goods and input items from there, there is relatively little scope for a direct investment by that country to increase its exports if we assume there would have been a comparable project in the alternative position. But, by the same token, if there would have been no similar project in the alternative position, this means that a greater rise in its exports would be likely to result in such cases from the direct investment.

In contrast to what has just been said about exports of capital goods and input items, exports of finished goods from the capital-exporting country would be much more likely to be adversely affected by a direct investment controlled there if it is no longer assumed that there would have been a comparable project in the alternative position. For under our earlier assumption of a comparable alternative, by setting up a subsidiary in the host country the parent firm would lose only those exports of its finished products that were so closely identified with its brand name that exact substitutes for them could not be produced by any other firm. But if there would otherwise have been no alternative undertaking to produce even partial substitutes for these items, the parent firm's exports would clearly have been much larger in the absence of the direct investment: that is to say, the adverse effects on its exports of undertaking this direct investment would have been much greater. The Reddaway survey estimated that even if one assumes that only 90 per cent instead of 100 per cent of the direct British investments it examined would otherwise have been replaced by production controlled elsewhere, the result would be the disappearance of virtually the whole of the small favourable continuing effect on British exports that was found to be likely on the basic assumption. This estimate resulted largely from the fact that Britain is normally a major exporter of the relevant finished products to countries where the direct investments occurred. The Hufbauer-Adler survey discovered a very large unfavourable effect on United States exports to be likely once one assumed that no comparative alternative project would have otherwise occurred in the host country.[5]

This analysis needs qualifying, however, if the direct investments are in minerals or other items produced for export, rather than for sale in the host country. In these cases there is no question of the product replacing items that would otherwise have been imported into the host country from the capital-exporting country. The effect on the exports of the latter can therefore not be unfavourable; and if no similar development would have occurred in the alternative position, the possibility of the investment increasing such exports is naturally greater, for even the alternative producer might have imported some capital goods and input items from the capital-exporting country. But if the latter does not export the relevant types of mining equipment or other specialised items needed for the project it would obviously not stand to obtain any rise in its exports in such cases.

Of the various Pacific countries, one extreme is the United States, which could often not assume that the alternative to a direct investment by one of its firms would be a similar one controlled elsewhere. For in many cases the know-how and resources of an American firm will not be closely paralleled by similar capacities in firms from other countries. For similar reasons, any of the Pacific countries could reasonably assume that if one of their firms neglects (or is prevented from exploiting) a promising opportunity there is very likely to be an American firm able and ready to undertake a similar project. Furthermore, despite the limitations on American overseas investment in recent years, it is still broadly true that government controls over external investments are more prevalent in the rest of the world; so that such controls may often prevent non-American firms from making good any neglected or thwarted investment by an American firm; whereas the opposite is much less likely to be true.

[5] Reddaway *et al.*, *Final Report*, pp. 299-300.

If the United States has to assume that a comparable project controlled elsewhere would not have arisen in the alternative position, this means that increases in her exports of capital goods and input items are more likely to result from direct overseas investment by her firms than our earlier analysis would suggest. Furthermore, one factor analysed above that tended to limit the favourable effects on these United States exports on our previous basic assumption would not be relevant if we assume the alternative would have been no comparable project. This is the consideration that favourable effects are less likely where the United States is the dominant supplier of these items to the host country, so that *any* project there may often buy these items from the United States. Clearly, if there would have been no comparable alternative in the absence of the United States investment, the United States would not have made even these sales of capital goods and input items.

For United States investments in Australia and New Zealand (and certain other countries where British investment is of the same order as that from North America), however, it would be hardly less realistic for the United States than it normally is for Britain to assume that the alternative to a direct investment by one of its firms would have been a similar project controlled elsewhere. Furthermore, the assumption of a comparable alternative controlled *within* the host country is likely to be the most realistic one for any country, including the United States, contemplating an investment in Japan. The generalisation that the United States can less readily assume that a comparable project would have been undertaken in the alternative position is, therefore, not necessarily applicable in every country; and it happens that these three countries of the Pacific group are ones where, for various reasons, it can be made less confidently than in the general case. But for any other capital-exporting country in the Pacific group, the most reasonable assumption is presumably that of a broadly comparable project being likely to occur in the alternative position.

General Effects of Capital Flows on Trade

We have so far been considering certain effects of direct investment in one country controlled by a firm in another country, irrespective of whether it is financed by a flow of capital into the host country. But, in fact, it is realistic to assume that generally a direct investment is accompanied by some addition to the foreign exchange receipts of the host country (and by an outflow of dividends in some subsequent period).

The original inflow of foreign exchange may be less than the increase in the capital of the branch or subsidiary in the host country, for part of the required finance may be raised within the host country, either because it is cheaper to do so, or because of legal or less formal pressures on the firm to sell part of its equity to local shareholders, or because controls imposed by the capital-exporting country put pressure on it to raise a large part of the finance in the host country.

But even if the whole of a given rise in the capital of the subsidiary is financed by an inflow of foreign exchange to the host country, before one can say that this raises its receipts of foreign exchange one must make some assumption about what would have happened otherwise. For in the absence of the investment in question, some other capital-exporting country might have found a similar project worthwhile, and might have financed it by a similar flow of foreign exchange. Even if the alternative were a local firm controlling a similar investment, it is possible (though much less likely) that a substantial part of this investment would have been financed by overseas borrowing by the local firm.

The investment we are considering is, then, likely to increase the flow of foreign exchange available to the host country (and the flow of interest and dividends away from it in subsequent years) if the alternative would have been a project controlled by a local firm, or one relying less on overseas finance; or, of course, if there would in the alternative position have been no comparable investment at all.[6]

At the one extreme an investment by residents of the United States is especially likely to increase the flow of foreign exchange to the host country, as the alternative of a similar investment by another capital-exporting country will be relatively unlikely. Again, dominance of American know-how and capital in so many industries makes it likely that in many cases there would be no comparable alternative. But in Australia and New Zealand, where British investment is comparable in size with that from the United States, this is less likely to be true than in other countries of the group. On the other hand, for almost any other capital exporting country, a much more reasonable assumption would be that the alternative would have been a project controlled and financed by another capital-exporting country (very often the United States).

Whatever the country from which the investment originates, however, if the alternative were a local firm, raising all or most of its finance locally, one could almost always assume that the project controlled outside the host country would be likely to increase the foreign exchange receipts of that country. (It is just possible, however, that in the absence of this capital inflow the government of the host country would sometimes have been more likely to borrow an equivalent amount overseas itself.)

For an investment in the United States or Japan one would expect that the alternative of a locally controlled firm, and of local financing, would often be a realistic assumption. This consideration maximises the

[6] A portfolio investment is in this respect akin to a direct investment financed entirely from outside the host country. But portfolio investments do not usually involve decisions about the source of imports (such as we have discussed in earlier sections in relation to direct investments).

chance of a given direct investment in Japan—provided that it is financed from overseas—increasing its foreign exchange receipts. For investments in other countries of the Pacific group one might consider the alternative of a project controlled in another capital-exporting country as more likely, so that there would then be less chance of the investment we are considering leading to a rise in the host country's foreign exchange receipts.

Assuming that the investment brings about some rise in the foreign exchange receipts available to the host country, the general level of its imports (in the near future) is likely to be higher than if the investment had not occurred.[7] It remains to ask whether this consideration—tending to raise imports from the capital-exporting country (among others)—is likely to be significant enough for the latter to take into account in deciding its policies.

The answer depends upon how important a source of imports the capital-exporting country is for the host country. Among the Pacific group of countries probably only the United States is a sufficiently large source of imports for each of the countries in the group to take some account of the favourable repercussions upon her exports that are likely to result from a flow of American capital to them. But Japan may be in the course of becoming a large enough supplier to many of them for this consideration to be of some relevance in determining its future attitude towards capital outflows.

In summary, then, this general effect upon the imports of the host country is most likely to be significant if the capital-exporting country is the United States; partly because it will not so generally be reasonable for that country to assume that the alternative would have been a project financed by another capital-exporting country, and partly because of the large share of each country's imports that now comes from the United States. But for the other Pacific countries (with the possible exception of Japan) one could not really argue that it would be realistic to take account of this possible general effect on exports from the capital-exporting country.

Effects on Exports of the Host Country

Direct investments of certain types may be especially likely to increase the exports of the host country, particularly those to the capital-exporting country.

Minerals. A direct investment in minerals may well be one of these, especially if the project is one that could not have been undertaken with-

---

[7] With a direct investment this may sometimes take the form (at least in part) of a higher level of imported capital equipment and input items for the direct investment project, so that this effect is not necessarily *in addition to* the effect on imports considered in earlier sections.

out the package of capital and know-how brought by direct investment. Recent investments by American, British and Japanese firms in Australian mineral production are examples of this type of investment, a major aim of which is clearly to increase the supplies of the minerals to the capital-exporting countries.

But this does not necessarily mean that they will increase the value of mineral imports into the capital-exporting countries. They may merely represent a change in their sources of supply—less iron ore from Brazil or India and rather more from Australia. Or they might just possibly reduce the prices paid for the mineral so much that even though the volume of their imports from Australia rises, the value of them might not do so.

In general, however, this type of investment is likely to stimulate the growth of trade (in value and volume) between the countries concerned.

But before we can confidently say that the direct investment was responsible for this effect, we need to ask whether the same result might not have been achieved by other means, such as long-term contracts. It may be of general significance that the Reddaway survey found no convincing evidence that the direct investments of the sort that it examined tended to reduce the prices paid by Britain for the commodities produced by overseas investments in this form, or to assure supplies of them, in a manner that might not equally well have been achieved by long-term contracts. One might, however, reasonably argue that when— as with the Australian minerals—a considerable element of know-how (of types that are normally obtainable only through direct investment) is required to produce the mineral exports in question, and where long-term contracts may be necessary to make the direct investment an attractive proposition, *both* direct investments *and* long-term contracts may be necessary. This leaves open the question of whether they should both be with the same country. Very often, as with the United States-Japan-Australia group, it may be more economic for one side of the triangle to be concerned mainly with the investment, whilst the long-term contracts are along another side of the triangle. This amounts to saying that if, in this context, one thinks of Japan and the United States (taken together) as a mineral-importing, capital-and-know-how-exporting entity, the imports of minerals by this entity, or at least those from Australia, are likely to be increased by a direct investment undertaken by this entity in Australian mineral production. It seems likely that other mineral developments in Australia, as well as Canada, and also on a smaller scale in New Zealand and some of the smaller Pacific islands, may lend themselves to similar arrangements.

It should be pointed out that some of the international investment in such ventures may well not be direct investment as normally defined. For Australian iron ore developments large sums came from American banks, and these flows are classified under the heading 'institutional' investment rather than 'direct' investment in the Australian statistics; for, unlike direct investment, this form of investment does not give the lenders control of the borrowing enterprise. But as these flows of institutional investment presumably made possible the direct investment (which brought with it the necessary know-how and concomitant overseas control), and as the institutional loans would presumably not have been forthcoming without the direct investments, such arrangements must clearly be thought of as being in many of the relevant respects akin to direct investment rather than to portfolio investment.

Manufactures. Exports of manufactures from the host country, including those to the capital-exporting country, may be stimulated by certain forms of direct overseas investment. Such investments by American firms seem to have been significant—according to the Hufbauer-Adler survey —many firms having been able to combine their know-how and capital with lower-cost labour and other factors of production in other countries, to produce items that can then be exported, even to the United States, in competition with goods that would otherwise have been produced within the United States (sometimes by the parent firm itself).

The Reddaway survey did not find cases of manufactured exports to Britain being stimulated by British overseas investment. This suggests that the combination of circumstances favourable to such investments is most likely to occur when North American firms undertake direct investments to countries with lower-cost labour (and where certain other costs may also be lower), especially in countries where the available know-how and capital resources in the relevant industries compare unfavourably with those of the American firms. One would suppose, however, that similar types of investment might well be also undertaken by Canadian, Australian and New Zealand firms investing in less developed countries, in industries where lower wage costs in the host country are an important consideration, and especially where the capital-exporting country has the appropriate know-how and capital in the relevant industry. In many cases this might be because the Canadian, Australian or New Zealand firm itself had access to know-how from an American or British parent; but it might also be the result of special forms of know-how developed in the capital-exporting country (for example, certain types of agricultural machinery, or milk-processing methods originating in Australia).

One might also expect to find cases where United States (and perhaps Canadian) investment in Australia, and perhaps New Zealand, could raise these countries' exports of manufactures, even those to the United States. For, at current exchange rates and in the light of recent relative rates of inflation, costs in some industries in these countries may well appear attractive to American firms considering the desirability of producing overseas for export to the United States and elsewhere. This would be especially likely in industries for which proximity to the sources of certain primary products originating or being processed in Australia and New Zealand (as with the current and prospective mining and processing of bauxite) was an important element in the manufactured item under consideration. Recent innovations reducing ocean transport costs may favour such developments.

The scope for investment in export-creating industries must presumably be very great for American investment in Japan, so far as Japanese policy may permit it. Indeed, one might expect that a very sharp rise in the export of manufactured goods from Japan to the United States would result from a freer flow of direct American investment in Japan, if that should occur in future.

Japan, too, may well find that lower labour costs than her own in some less developed countries will make investments in developing exports from these countries an increasingly attractive proposition.

Moreover, direct investment that originally concentrates on producing items formerly imported into the host country may develop to a point where it can facilitate the growth of exports of the relevant products. Whereas overseas investment in Australian industry during the 1950s was almost exclusively of products that were previously imported, the high level of direct investment in these manufacturing industries in the past has presumably played its part in facilitating the remarkable growth in Australia's exports of manufactures (of the order of 10-25 per cent per annum) in the last few years.

Knowledge-sharing and Technological Feedback

The process of direct investment often generates benefits to the investing country by way of economies in the use of the products of its own research and by way of the fruits of research done in the overseas subsidiary. The resulting interchanges of know-how may or may not be charged for, and may or may not be reflected in the profits of the subsidiary; and, where the parent company does charge the subsidiary, the net benefit to it of this direct investment can be estimated only after allowing for the loss of any licensing revenue that the parent company would have derived from overseas firms that might have used its processes in the absence of the direct investment under consideration. But for investments in a number of industries, and especially in certain countries, there remain certain benefits to the capital-exporting country resulting from the flow back to it of various types of informal know-how. These are often not charged for, but should certainly be taken into account where they are important, if one is assessing costs and benefits to the investing country, and even if one is concerned primarily with balance of payments effects, or balance of payments policy. In the absence of the relevant investments the parent company would have had to make some form of expenditure in the host country, if it were to acquire a similar feedback of know-how.[8]

The Reddaway survey showed that for the British firms investigated the net return to Britain from knowledge-sharing between the parent companies and their subsidiaries was considerable for subsidiaries in West Germany, France and the United States. Somewhat more surprisingly, however, it was by no means negligible for Canada, Australia and India. For the first three countries the extra return due to this factor was of the order of 2-3 per cent per annum of the accumulated value of those United Kingdom direct investments in the countries that were examined. For investments in Canada and Australia the corresponding figure was about 2 per cent: from investments in these two developed, net capital-importing countries of the Pacific area, therefore, this evidence suggests that a capital-exporting country might reasonably expect an appreciable return in this form, of which due account should be taken in formulating its policy towards capital flows. The Reddaway survey suggested, however, that the return from this source from those British investments examined in less developed countries generally was negligible—with the important exception of India, where it was just under 1 per cent of the value of the relevant United Kingdom investment. This form of return was closely related to the industry in which the investment occurred, being much higher for chemicals than for any other industries, and appreciably more significant for non-electrical engineering than for the remaining ones.

It is of some interest and importance to observe that (on the evidence in the Reddaway report) the gain to the capital-exporting country from this source tends to be greatest for investments in those countries where direct investments are least likely to have a substantial effect in raising the exports of the capital-exporting country. For, as we saw above, the effect in increasing exports from the capital-exporting country (Britain) was greater from investments in less developed countries, and least in the highly developed economies of Europe and North America, whilst the effects on exports of investing in smaller industrialised countries such as Australia was intermediate between these extremes.

Conclusion

This chapter has concentrated on certain aspects of the balance of payments effects of international investment that do not generally receive as much attention as do the actual flows of capital and the interest and dividends to which these give rise. In viewing trade effects in the context of the balance of payments as a whole it is important to bear in mind that effects on trade involve the use of real resources, so that a rise in exports from one country resulting from an overseas investment by that

[8] The problems of estimating the gains resulting from the various forms of knowledge-sharing are discussed in Reddaway *et al.*, *Final Report*, Chapter XXV.

country should not be considered in the same category as, say, a receipt of dividends or of capital by that country. As any additional exports require the use of real resources that could otherwise have been available for other purposes, an important question for the policymaker should always be whether these resources could have been used in more economic ways (whether or not there are other ways of 'improving the balance of payments'). Furthermore, any assessment that may be feasible of the likely effects on exports that may result from a given capital outflow is principally to be taken into account in determining overall balance of payments policy (or the likely exchange-rate fluctuations, where exchange rates are free to vary), rather than for determining whether particular investments should be permitted (for which purpose much wider considerations need to be applied). In any event, such generalisations as can be made on the basis of the sort of analysis given in this paper can properly be applied, not to individual investments, but only on the average of cases for a large number of investments between two countries with the broad economic characteristics on which the analysis is based.

On the basis of the foregoing analysis two desirable future lines of research suggest themselves. First the theoretical analysis of the various factors that determine the directions and the order of magnitude of the effects of investment flows on trade might well be developed. Secondly, more light could well be shed on the likely effects of international investments between various types of economies, by econometric investigations of the Hufbauer-Adler type (in the rare cases where sufficient data are available) or by extensive research projects in which research workers co-operate actively with those responsible for the investment decisions (as in the Reddaway project). Perhaps this is an area of research in which the principal Pacific countries, with their diverse characteristics and their various complementary interests in the effects of international investment, could usefully co-operate.

Comments and Discussion

FRITZ MACHLUP opened the discussion: The current fashion for behavioural studies has invaded international economics. Neo-classical economic analysis attempts to explain changes in economic quantities as the result of changes in relative prices and relative incomes, and econometric analysis tries to test the findings by substituting statistical data for the variables used in the theoretical models. Behavioural analysis has other interests. Perhaps I may characterise it by saying that it explains why an immigrant from Hungary continues to eat goulash and red paprika, and why a manager of an American subsidiary in Australia orders a computer from I.B.M. while a Britisher may give preference to another make, and the manager of a Japanese subsidiary will rather have Japanese appliances. Since many economists find it difficult to disentangle factual, theoretical, and moral judgments, the devotee of behavioural economics often becomes an expositor of 'misbehavioural' economics.

If I had the assignment to analyse the effects which capital flows have upon the major categories in the balance of payments of a group of countries, my first impulse would be to study how the major monetary variables, especially the money stocks, the bank reserves, the domestic assets and foreign assets held, acquired, or disposed of by central banks and commercial banks have been reacting to the inflows or outflows of long-term capital. The behavioural economist, however, is more interested in the national and ethnic background of the senior executive managers of the firms receiving the capital, the channels of control, and the influences which the owners of the capital and the potential overlords of the foreign investors exert upon the decisions of particular companies. I know that I shall not be able to impose my methodological preferences on other analysts. But I may say that I incline to regard behavioural analysis in international trade as not very significant in explaining large changes in the current accounts of the nations, though I concede that some of the findings of the behavioural researchers are quite interesting.

How do these methodological comments bear on Perkins's chapter? I believe that he was overly impressed by the behavioural research recently published in England and in the United States and that he devoted a disproportionately large portion of his chapter to an attempt at applying these findings to the Asian-Pacific area. He did this in partial contradiction to his own intentions announced in the title and initial paragraphs. It is quite obvious that he regarded his task as being the consideration of the effects of international capital flows; yet two-thirds of the chapter deal with other matters. When he comes to 'General Effects of Capital Flows on Trade', he admits that: 'We have so far been considering certain effects of direct investment in one country controlled by a firm in another country, irrespective of whether it is financed by a flow of capital into the host country'. In other words, the first two-thirds of the paper deal with foreign control or influence, not with the effects of capital movements. I submit that, whatever may be the role of foreign influence upon subsidiary firms, this role is not in determining the overall shape of the balance of international payments, except perhaps in the repatriation of profits by some very large companies.

Perkins was to discuss the effects of capital flows, and not just of foreign *direct* investments. But even if we were to confine ourselves to direct investment, we could not discuss its effects unless we asked the question 'compared with what?' Thus, the effects of direct foreign investments are the differences in outcome compared with: foreign investment being made in other forms, say, as portfolio investment or several other ways of providing finance; foreign investment financed by capital funds raised in other foreign countries; foreign investment financed by capital funds raised in the local markets of the host country; investments by companies locally owned and controlled, but financed by capital funds raised abroad; investment by local firms financed with local funds; and no investment at all. These six alternatives are offered only as a sample, but enough, or more than enough, for purposes of analysis. To go through all these paces is a rather tedious exercise. Sometimes it is preferable just to point out that the question about the effects of foreign direct investment makes sense only if it is clearly stated which alternative is to be used for the comparison.

I would consider it helpful if the analysis of the effects of capital flows upon the balance of payments had been divided into three parts: first, the initial flow of capital to finance the new investment and its effects upon the major items in the balance of international transactions; second, the subsequent changes, after the new productive facilities are in operation, in exports and imports due to the demand for current inputs and the supply of current outputs; and third, the eventual remittance of profits, interest, dividends, royalties, management fees, and perhaps also principal. These three parts of the problem differ in theoretical make-up and may also be separate in time, as they are apt to become relevant in different periods.

The first problem is theoretically and empirically more interesting because the effected changes in the major items of the balance of payments are likely to be larger than those associated with the other two problems. This does not mean, of course, that the effects of the initial flows of capital only, and not the subsequent changes, should be studied. But it happens that certain tools of analysis and certain sets of assumptions are of particular significance in the analysis of the effects of large flows of capital. It is in this connection that one has to inquire into the monetary institutions and policies of the countries concerned. A flow of capital of a given size may generate different processes depending on the adjustment mechanisms or adjustment policies employed. Some countries will allow aggregate-demand adjustment to proceed, and thus will allow the outflow or inflow of capital to have their classical effects upon aggregate spending and incomes and thereby upon the current balance. Other countries will allow foreign exchange rate adjustment to operate, and thus will allow the capital flow to be quickly translated into a transfer of goods and services. Finally, some countries will resist both routes to adjustment, will stick to rigid exchange rates and will offset through domestic credit policies most of the changes in money supply and aggregate spending that are generated by the flow of capital. In this case, capital flows will not be matched by changes in the current balance, except to the extent that restrictions and controls lead to partial and lopsided alterations in the balance of trade at a volume reduced below the level that would be obtained otherwise.

Compared with these problems, which are problems also of the international monetary system, the effects of foreign influence on management decisions about current purchases and sales by industrial firms are, in my opinion, insignificant. To be sure, relative prices are not the only variables that determine the network of international trade. Quality, delivery terms, credit terms and several other things are also significant—and *among* these other things may be the divided or undivided allegiances of the managers of international, multinational, plurinational, and transnational firms.

Subsequent discussion focused on two subjects: an appropriate theoretical framework for analysing the balance of payments issues and the significance of export franchise arrangements.

Some participants wondered whether more careful specification of a macroeconomic framework for analysis of the balance of payments effects of direct investment would not be desirable. It was recognised that the chapter had been produced partly because of the extreme weakness of the treatment of the balance of payments effects elsewhere, for example in the Canadian Watkins Report, but the real questions were seen not to be about the balance of payments at all. However, governments do worry about the balance of payments effects and introduce policies based on their assumed importance. If the international monetary system were stronger and more efficient, policies based on balance of payments considerations could be roundly denounced, but there is a regime of fixed exchange rates, and balance of payments effects are of concern. One participant thought it would be useful to explore these issues before trying out the exercises attempted in the chapter. Nonetheless, some felt that it was an error to think that if governments imagine there is a problem, there is a problem. On the methodological issues raised by Machlup, Kindleberger defended the work of the behaviourists and econometricians (between whom Machlup insisted on some distinction) and attacked reliance on simple *a priori* models in analysis.

Perkins replied that, although he did not deny the importance of the broader balance of payments aspects of capital flows, he was unrepentant for having concentrated on the effects of direct investment on trade and payments. He hoped that the kind of analysis undertaken would help to minimise the damage done by policies directed at presumed balance of payments impacts of foreign investment. As for the partial equilibrium nature of his analysis, he considered it useful to specify the direct and immediately traceable effects of foreign investment on particular flows of trade since they were of such concern to the policymaker and they offered a reasonably good guide to the final outcome. He illustrated this point with reference to the impact of Australian mining investments.

A major part of discussion was concerned with the effects of export franchises. An American participant drew attention to recurring references to the importance of export franchises and wondered how widespread these arrangements were and what effect they had on trade flows. He saw the possibility of a real divergence of interest between the host country and international firms in terms of the effects of export franchises on trade flows. It was argued by others, however, that it was not at all clear that the presence of export franchises affected host country interests adversely. Very often the basis of foreign investment is the application of some knowledge possessed by the international firm. It may well be willing to make that knowledge available at very little or no charge to the host market in order to enable its subsidiary to set up, but, since it has created the knowledge by research expenditure or other effort, it naturally wants a pay-off from that somewhere. Hence, the subsidiary is confined to its own market or certain markets and not allowed into others which pay for knowledge creation. That is the firm's way of protecting its investment in knowledge, and it is not always to the disadvantage of the host country which may obtain the knowledge at zero or nominal charge. Another participant classified this behaviour as similar to that of the price discriminator who is able to separate markets, and guessed that countries other than the United States paid less than their 'fair' share for the knowledge they are able to use. An Australian participant was doubtful whether export franchises resulted in a reduction of exports that would otherwise have taken place and reported work which demonstrated that the export performance of foreign firms was better than that of Australian firms of the same size in Australia.

14 Assessment of Policies Towards Direct Foreign Investment in the Asian-Pacific Area

HELEN HUGHES

The eastern and western shores of the Pacific are a study in contrasts rather than in similarities in the flow of direct foreign investment.[1] Considering the quite separate cultural, political and economic development of the Americans, on the one hand, and Asia and Australasia on the other, as well as the paucity of communications across the Pacific, this is of course not surprising. However, despite the diversity of investment policies and flows outlined in the first part of this chapter, some similar patterns in the benefits and costs of direct foreign investment emerge, and these are analysed in the second section. A consideration of measures to improve policies so that the benefits may exceed the costs for those countries deeming direct foreign investment worthwhile concludes the chapter.

The Direct Investment Flow

United States corporations were the principal direct foreign investors in Canada and in the countries of Central and South America in the nineteenth century when direct investment formed a small proportion of total foreign investment. United States direct foreign investment, moreover, grew in importance as indirect investment, which in Latin America had been predominantly European, declined. Mines and plantations were originally the principal direct investment venues, but trade and banking, and then manufacturing, grew in importance. As its manufacturing industries grew, Canada obtained, and retained, the principal share of United States direct foreign investment abroad, but the growing national and political aspirations of the Latin American countries were accompanied by a rejection of United States economic dominance. With this movement, which is to varying degrees still in progress, came some voluntary and involuntary disinvestment. After World War II, however, the desire for

---

[1] I am indebted to Ediana Harahap for assistance with the preparation of this chapter.

economic development, which mainly took the shape of highly protectionist industrialisation strategies, led to a new need for direct investment because of its 'package deal' of technology, management and foreign exchange. Protectionist industrialisation strategies, of course, at the same time, endangered United States exporters' markets, and provided new opportunities for profitable direct investment abroad at a time when direct foreign investment was becoming an increasingly important competitive diversification policy for large manufacturing corporations. Opportunities in mining, trade and banking have also continued to attract United States direct foreign investment although the climate has remained questioning and frequently turned hostile. Direct United States investment in Latin American countries grew from $US4,445 million in 1950 to $US10,265 million in 1967, and investment in manufacturing grew from $US780 million to $US3,305 million, increasing from 18 per cent to 32 per cent of total investment.[2]

In Asia, Australasia and the Pacific islands the experience of foreign investment has been markedly different. This was an area where Japan alone escaped direct or indirect colonisation, and where independence for the most part only came after World War II, and in some cases is yet to be attained.

In the nineteenth century, foreign investment and colonial power moved closely together, although some British investment moved across colonial boundaries, and there was some investment from non-colonising European countries. Plantations were the principal investment venue, there was investment in timber and mining and a substantial investment in trade and banking which were largely in the hands of the foreign investors. There were some pockets of direct manufacturing investment in mainland China, Korea and Taiwan, northern Vietnam and Indonesia, and, on a more significant scale in Australia and New Zealand, where protectionist industrialisation policies were adopted in the 1920s.

World War II was bitterly fought in South-East and East Asia, and it brought a sharp break in the economic as well as the political development of the area. When the ebb and flow of fighting had for the most part receded in the early 1950s, the independent countries of this area, like those of Latin America, began to look to manufacturing as the leading sector of development, and during the 1950s and 1960s most moved to stimulate the inflow of direct foreign investment into their manufacturing sectors. The achievement of independence had so improved their relations with the former colonial powers that they appeared to be much readier to accept direct foreign investment from them than most Latin American countries were, at least formally, to have United States investment. Japanese direct foreign investment, with a superficial resemblance to the 'co-

[2] United States Department of Commerce, *Balance of Payments: Statistical Supplement*, revised edition, 1963, and *Survey of Current Business*, October 1969.

prosperity sphere' of the 1930s and 1940s, was at first an exception, and initially it flowed mainly outside Asia. A peace treaty between the Republic of the Philippines and Japan is yet to be signed. However, by the 1960s Japanese firms were among the leading investors in the western Pacific. Only the socialist countries of Asia now reject direct foreign investment,[3] although some have placed limits on its extent. In the Philippines, the only western Pacific country with a history similar to Latin American countries, policies have been restrictive towards foreign investment with specially favourable conditions for United States investors under the Laurel-Langley treaty, but in general there has been a marked difference between the climate which foreign investors have encountered on the western and the eastern shores of the Pacific.

The countries of South-East and East Asia did not recover from war, independence struggles, and insurgency until the early 1950s, and Vietnam, Cambodia and Laos are of course at war today. For most of the area, economic activity began to exceed the 1930s levels from the early 1950s, and firms from the former colonial countries which already had experience of doing business in this area led the new investment inflow. In the first instance, this meant the restoration of plantation, forestry and mining, although as countries gained independence, there was some disinvestment, and in Indonesia, expropriation. There was little additional new investment in agriculture, and such investment as has taken place has been closely tied with food processing, that is, it has been largely in support of investment in manufacturing.

The main emphasis of new foreign investment as in Latin America has been in inward oriented manufacturing, following protectionist industrialisation strategies for economic development. Australia, New Zealand and Japan attracted investment in manufacturing from the late 1940s, the Philippines followed in the early 1950s, and by the early 1960s this was the general trend. The 1960s also saw a renewed interest in mineral exploitation. The freeing of iron ore exports from Australia was the immediate impetus to direct foreign investment in Australian mineral development, while the reopening of Indonesian mineral exploitation to foreign investors in 1966 marked a second stage of a mining investment boom in the south-western Pacific. Foreign investors have also maintained and extended their strong interest in trade and banking which were, of course, growing rapidly with increasing economic activities.

Two further areas of investment came into prominence in the 1960s. Rising incomes in developed countries and the ease of air travel opened the cultural heritage and scenic pleasures of the East to United States, Japanese and European tourists, and the demand for tourist facilities was reinforced by the presence of United States military forces in the area.

[3] Indonesia passed a Foreign Investment Law (Act No. 1), January 1967.

Investment in hotels, travel and associated facilities grew markedly, and is only likely to reach a peak (or nadir) with 'jumbo' jet travel. Secondly, the immobility of labour across national boundaries in the post World War II world led to a new form of direct foreign investment in export-oriented manufacturing industries. Unlike the nineteenth and early twentieth centuries which saw great movements of labour to the source of capital in manufacturing, labour is now immobile in the Pacific area, and capital moves to sources of labour supply. The beginnings could be seen in United States investment in Hong Kong and, across the Pacific in Panama, in the 1950s, but the main impact came only in the 1960s, with the growth of export-oriented industries based on low labour costs in Taiwan, Korea and Singapore, where this influx of capital has transformed the character of the industrialisation process. There has also been a little investment of this type in the Philippines, and across the Pacific, in Mexico, El Salvador and Costa Rica.

The national composition of the investment flow also differs markedly between the western and eastern Pacific. Some European firms have invested in manufacturing in Latin America in the last twenty years, but such investment has been more marked on the east than on the west coast, and direct foreign investment is predominantly from the United States. The western Pacific in contrast has the most complex pattern of direct foreign investment flows outside Europe, and is the only area of such complexity among developing countries. The former colonial investors—British, French, Dutch, American and Japanese—have retained either pre-eminence or an important role in the territories they formerly ruled.

New investment trends, however, have overlaid the pre-World War II pattern. As United States firms began to run out of relatively easy investment opportunities in the Americas and Europe, they began to turn their attention across the Pacific, firstly to Australia, New Zealand and Japan, then to other Asian countries, and recently to the Pacific islands. Japan's rapid economic growth, with its emphasis on the development of resources and foreign markets, focused attention on its neighbours. Japanese firms were vigorously competitive and firmly backed by their government, and, as a result, Japan's foreign investments have come to equal, and in some cases, surpass those of the traditional investors and the United States.[4] In recent years European investors began to build on pre-war contacts and to reach out to new opportunities as the pace of industrialisation quickened.

Other foreign investors have come from within the area itself. The

---

[4] This is true of 'promoted' industries in Thailand (see Amnuay Virivan, above, Table 9.3), and of 'pioneer' industries in Singapore (H. Hughes and You Poh Seng (eds.), *Foreign Investment and Industrialisation in Singapore* (Canberra, 1969), pp. 212-13).

'overseas' Chinese, who have been settled throughout the western Pacific for at least 2,000 years, long before the coming of the Arabs and Europeans, have been the most important group. Although some Chinese immigrants have been able to become citizens of the countries of the area over the centuries, assimilation has been difficult even for citizens. Many countries discriminate severely against ethnic Chinese whether they are citizens or not. This has driven the Chinese business communities into close-knit co-operation, and, with a strong trading bias, they have in any case always been more strongly outward-oriented than other entrepreneurs, local and foreign, in the area. While Hong Kong, Singapore and Taiwan have absorbed much of this investment, they are in turn leading investing countries, so that 'overseas' Chinese investment has been an important influence throughout the area.

Another group of foreign investors consists of firms which were originally foreign owned but which have become domiciled in the area. Some of these may still have significant ownership in the United Kingdom or other investing countries, but board and management decisions are made locally. Such firms include plantation and mining enterprises, trading companies, and some of the largest banks in the area.

By the 1960s, there was also a considerable flow, in the number of projects, though not yet in volume, among investors other than 'overseas' Chinese from the smaller countries of the western Pacific. Australian and New Zealand companies, with government prompting and support, were among the first, but companies in the Philippines, Thailand, Malaysia, and further afield from India and Pakistan began investment in the area. The imposition of import quotas by developed countries greatly accelerated the trend towards inter-areal investment, as Hong Kong and Taiwan manufacturers, whose markets were limited by import quotas, sought to expand their markets by geographic expansion; they have now been joined by Singapore manufacturers seeking investment opportunities in exporting industries. Intra-areal investment is in contrast barely discernible on the eastern shore of the Pacific.

The volume and characteristics of the investment flow have differed on the two sides of the Pacific because both 'push' factors on the side of supply and 'pull' factors on the side of demand have been different. While the oligopolistic search for raw materials and markets has been the principal thrust behind the supply of direct foreign investment throughout the area, the interests of small countries in maintaining and expanding their manufacturing and trading activities, and paradoxically, the barriers imposed by the United States and Europe against imports from developing countries, were instruments in diversifying the capital supply in the western Pacific. On the demand side, key factors in attracting direct foreign investment have clearly been natural endowments, and the levels, types and rates of economic development, but the investing climate in the host countries in relation to each investing country has also played an important role within these constraints. Here differences between the western and eastern Pacific appear to have been even more important than those on the supply side.

With the exception of Japan, the more developed countries of the Asian-Pacific area have been content to allow market factors to determine the investment flow. They have not gone beyond general policy statements welcoming direct foreign investment to accelerate the flow, but in spite of periodic waves of doubt about the balance of benefits and costs and political implications, they have done little to impede or restrict it.[5] Japan, on the other hand, took a restrictive view of direct foreign investment, in fact if not in law, and this is reflected in relatively low direct foreign investment in Japan.[6]

For most of the market economy developing countries of the western Pacific, however, particularly in the late 1940s and early 1950s, market forces seemed inadequate or inappropriate determinants of the investment inflow. The total direct foreign investment flow into the area was still small, and the more developed countries throughout the world, including Australia and New Zealand, clearly offered better investment opportunities and usually a better investment climate as well. Expropriation of direct foreign investment by some developing countries had aroused investors' fears about the rest, and political stability was far from self-evident for many developing countries. Although doubts about the possible costs of direct foreign investment were not entirely eliminated, most of these countries therefore took policy measures to accelerate the foreign investment flow.

Such measures generally consisted of assuring investors that their investments would be safe from nationalisation, or that if eventually nationalised they would be fairly compensated. Assurances, particularly important in countries with strictly controlled foreign exchanges, that capital and profits could be freely repatriated, followed. Having established a welcoming framework for foreign investment, specific incentives sought to offset the disadvantages of underdevelopment. These have generally been of two kinds. Firstly, import tariff reductions have been available on capital goods, and, sometimes, on raw materials, to offset the high costs of these inputs where import tariffs have been high. Secondly, income tax exemptions and accelerated depreciation allowances of varying degrees and of varying duration of from three to five, but sometimes up to fifteen years have been granted. These incentives were intended to offset the disadvantages the developing countries had in the

[5] The implicit and explicit exclusion of direct foreign investment from banking and mass media is the most general exception to a generally favourable attitude. See Brash, above, pp. 99-100.

[6] See OECD, *Liberalisation of International Capital Movements, Japan* (Paris, 1968), p. 15 and Komiya, above, pp. 138-43.

lack of infrastructure and external economies of scale. They have generally only been available to 'pioneer' or 'essential' firms beginning a new process or industry, or otherwise essential to a country's development. The evaluation of essentiality has been based on criteria such as contribution to growth in the value of output and employment, exchange saving and the use of local raw materials, and necessitated the creation of evaluation teams to determine whether investors qualified for incentives. Few investors failed to obtain them. However, because some fears of foreign economic domination remained, policies in many instances also included restrictions on the extent of foreign ownership in each firm, on the employment of foreign staff, either directly or indirectly through migration laws, and restrictions on the outright ownership of land. Complex laws, for example with regard to mining, could, moreover, be utilised to limit or prevent foreign investment.[7]

By the time that specific investment incentives for new investment were introduced, the countries adopting them had already created an elaborate policy framework for industrialisation with protection at its core. Investment incentives were as much a part of this industrialisation policy package as they were incentives to foreign investment, and for the most part local investors qualified for them.[8] Since some of the developing countries on the western side of the Pacific had also given some assurances to foreign investors and evolved similar packages of industrialisation policies and incentives, incentives to foreign investors were not in fact greatly different on the two Pacific shores. Thus, while the specific enumeration of incentives in the context of foreign investment affected the investment climate in the western Pacific so that the flow of direct foreign investment appeared to follow the enunciation of guarantees and incentives for foreign investment, investment also grew in the eastern Pacific. It seems that it was the entire protectionist policy mix rather than special incentive legislation which led to the increasing capital inflow, and determined the ensuing balance of benefits and costs.

Characteristics and Principal Effects of Direct Foreign Investment Flow

It is extremely difficult to discuss the characteristics of the flow of direct foreign investment in the Asian-Pacific region because of the paucity of statistical data. Limited data are available for the inflow of capital from the principal investing countries, and, despite the very great difficulties of valuation, these at least give some indication of the extent of direct foreign investment both by selected host countries and for Japan, United

[7] This is, for example, true of Thai mining and allied legislation and administrative procedures. See Department of Mineral Resources, *The Mining Industry of Thailand* (Bangkok, 1969).
[8] Indonesia was an exception. The Domestic Investment Law, Act No. 6, 3 July 1968 was passed a year and a half after the Foreign Investment Law.

Table 14.1 Republic of Germany: Stock of direct foreign investment abroad, by area, 1955 and 1966 ($US million)

	1955		1966	
Europe		37.6		1,427.4
Common Market countries	17.1		717.6	
EFTA countries	13.4		562.3	
Other countries	7.1		147.5	
Africa		6.7		149.4
America		55.7		793.0
North America	27.7		359.0	
South America	25.7		356.2	
Other countries	2.3		77.8	
Asia		3.7		87.9
Australia		1.6		41.2
Total		105.3		2,498.9

Sources: 1955: *Mitteilungen Rhein,* Westfalisches Institut für Wirtschaftsforschung, 1965, Heft 10, S.256.
1966: *Bundesanzeiger Jahrgang* 10, Nr. 136 vom 25.7 1967, S.2.

Kingdom and the United States, by types of industry.[9] Unfortunately such figures can rarely be matched against inflows into host countries.[10] With few exceptions collection of statistics by the developing countries has been extremely poor and data are not comparable from country to country.[11]

The developing countries of the Asian-Pacific area for which data are available have shown a slightly increasing share of total direct investment abroad by the United States, United Kingdom, and Japan. It also appears that among developing countries those that are most developed and growing fastest have received the highest relative share of direct foreign investment. This includes such countries as Hong Kong, the Republic of China (Taiwan) (see Table 14.4) and Singapore (see Table 14.6)[12] while at the other extreme, investment in countries such as Laos has been very small.

The ownership form of direct foreign investment has undergone considerable change in the last twenty years. At the beginning of this period branches or wholly-owned subsidiaries were typical and local participation was negligible. This situation has changed considerably, so that, in many countries, the bulk of direct foreign investment both by the number of projects and volume has at least some local participation, even if it forms only 10 to 20 per cent of the total.

[9] See Tables 14.1 to 14.3 and also Hamada, above, Tables 7.1 to 7.4.
[10] This is of course true of most international capital flow statistics between individual countries.
[11] See Sadli, above, Tables 8.1 to 8.3, Yoonsae Yang, above, Table 10.2, and Virata, above, Tables 11.1 and 11.2, also Tables 14.3 to 14.6.
[12] Note Singapore data only include investment in 'pioneer' companies and this only covers investment in recently established enterprises.

Table 14.2   Stock of United States direct foreign investment in the countries of the Asian-Pacific area in 1968 ($US million)

	Mining and smelting		Petroleum		Manufacturing		Public utilities		Trade		Other		Total	
	1955	1968	1955	1968	1955	1968	1955	1968	1955	1968	1955	1968	1955	1968
Canada	904	2,636	1,381	4,088	3,093	8,546	329	599	411	1,115	643	2,505	6,761	19,488
Chile	421	586	a	a	37	68	a	a	11	39	174	270	643	964
Colombia	a	a	178	324	58	193	33	29	42	58	25	25	336	629
Mexico	143	112	15	44	262	998	87	27	54	181	16	27	577	1,389
Peru	154	421	a	39	23	96	a	22	36	51	79	62	292	692
India	c	a	a	a	29	131	a	1	10	41	55	107	94	281
Philippines	a	a	a	a	31	237	62	39	40	88	97	303	231	668
Oceania[b]	26	367	255	646	258	1,503	1	3	35	163	16	138	590	2,821
Australia	25	365	a	a	240	1,418	c	3	26	126	201	734	492	2,645
Japan	—	—	a	a	28	521	a	3	5	98	96	426	129	1,048

[a] Included in other industries.
[b] Includes New Zealand.
[c] Less than $500,000.
— No investment.

Sources: United States Department of Commerce, Office of Business Economics, *Balance of Payments: Statistical Supplement*, rev. ed., and *Survey of Current Business*, October 1969.

Table 14.3 Stock of United Kingdom direct foreign investment in the countries of the Asian-Pacific area in 1965 (£Stg million except where noted)

	Agriculture	Mining	Electrical and mechanical engineering	Vehicles, ship-building and marine engineering	Other manufacturing	Construction	Distribution	Transport and communications	Shipping	Other activities	Total	Total $US million
Canada	54.1	←	66.1	n.a.	224.5	4.3	114.2	6.1	n.a.	57.6	531.4	1,487.9
United States	37.5	←	4.9	n.a.	243.0	1.6	42.6	5.4	n.a.	44.5	387.6	1,085.2
Chile	—	—	—	—	2.2	—	1.5	n.a.	—	n.a.	4.2	11.8
Mexico	36.7	—	1.9	—	37.5	—	1.4	—	—	0.2	41.0	114.8
Ceylon	n.a.	—	←	6.0	7.8	n.a.	2.2	n.a.	n.a.	0.8	49.8	139.4
Hong Kong	n.a.	6.9	↑	↑	↑	n.a.	13.9	n.a.	n.a.	6.1	29.7	83.1
India	79.4	10.4	25.8	9.4	116.0	n.a.	23.7	4.0	n.a.	36.6	304.0	851.2
Malaysia	95.6	—	n.a.	—	19.8	n.a.	15.0	n.a.	n.a.	1.9	144.0	403.2
Pakistan	11.9	—	1.0	n.a.	16.9	0.3	5.3	n.a.	n.a.	0.8	39.5	110.6
Singapore	n.a.	—	←	2.1	↑	—	1.4	—	—	1.5	5.4	15.1
Other Far East	1.1	2.5	0.1	—	4.9	—	4.5	0.2	—	0.5	13.8	38.6
Australia	43.7	58.4	97.1	36.4	272.3	8.4	47.5	5.3	13.8	130.0	712.9	1,996.1
New Zealand	n.a.	n.a.	4.9	2.9	50.5	0.5	14.8	n.a.	22.1	40.0	137.1	3,838.8

Note: — means nil or negligible (less than half the final digit shown).

Source: Board of Trade Journal, Volume 194, 26 January 1968, pp. ix-x.

Table 14.4   Republic of China (Taiwan): Flow of direct foreign investment, 1953-69

Year	United States		Japan		Overseas Chinese		Others		Total	
	No.	$'000	No.	$'000	No.	$'000	No.	$'000	No.	$'000
1953	1	1,881	1	160	12	1,654	—	—	14	3,695
1954	3	2,028	1	14	3	128	1	50	8	2,220
1955	2	4,423	—	—	3	176	—	—	5	4,599
1956	2	1,009	—	—	13	2,484	—	—	15	3,493
1957	1	11	3	37	10	1,574	—	—	14	1,622
1958	—	—	3	1,116	6	1,402	—	—	9	2,518
1959	1	100	1	45	—	820	—	—	2	965
1960	6	14,055	3	309	8	1,393	—	—	17	15,757
1961	1	4,288	3	1,301	21	8,340	1	375	26	14,304
1962	8	738	16	2,664	10	1,660	3	639	37	5,701
1963	9	8,734	6	1,397	22	7,703	1	216	38	18,050
1964	8	10,223	2	728	28	8,007	4	916	42	19,874
1965	17	31,104	14	2,081	32	6,537	5	1,955	68	41,677
1966	15	17,711	35	2,447	53	8,496	2	746	105	29,400
1967	20	19,026	78	15,974	125	21,312	13	7,005	236	63,317
1968	20	34,555	98	25,292	213	39,408	7	4,539	338	103,794
1969	31	27,881	79	17,641	91	27,551	6	36,697	207	109,772
Total	145	177,767	343	71,206	650	138,645	43	53,138	1,181	440,756

Source: Council for International Economic Co-operation and Development, January 1970.

New attitudes in developing countries, sometimes backed by regulations which have established statutory minima for foreign investment,
have been important, but so have the new investors. Japanese, 'overseas'
Chinese, and investors from other small countries in the western Pacific
have tended to embark on joint ventures in which local investors own
land which they lease to the enterprise, provide distribution channels
for a product, take care of contact with government officials, and, in
manufacturing, look after labour problems. For Japanese firms this has
typically been a partnership of a parent Japanese company, a Japanese
trading company, and a local company. Joint ventures of this type have

Table 14.5   Malaysia: stock of direct foreign investment in pioneer
enterprises at December 1963 and December 1968

	Number of enterprises	Foreign capital ($ '000)	Total capital ($ '000)	Foreign as a percentage of total
1963	101	41.5	66.3	62.6
1968	140	85.3	145.4	58.6

Sources: Department of Statistics, Kuala Lumpur; Federal Industrial Development
Authority.

Table 14.6   Singapore: stock of direct foreign investment[a] in pioneer
enterprises, by industry sector,[b] at 31 December 1967

	Number of establishments	Foreign investment ($ '000)	Total investment ($ '000)	Foreign as percentage of total investment
Food and beverages	29	4,213	12,329	34.2
Textiles and garments	32	2,635	6,935	38.0
Wood and paper products	11	1,001	4,079	24.5
Rubber and leather products	6	3,513	4,108	85.5
Chemicals and chemical products	38	2,872	5,528	51.9
Petroleum and petroleum products	8	10,272	12,069	85.1
Non-metallic mineral products	10	1,173	2,866	40.9
Basic metals and engineering	48	7,571	17,012	44.5
Electrical products	18	1,741	4,070	42.8
Plastic products	11	282	1,045	27.0
Miscellaneous[c]	23	1,263	3,024	41.8
Total	234	36,536	73,065	50.0

[a] Paid-up capital.

[b] Includes enterprises in production and course of construction.

[c] Includes tourist enterprises.

Source: Economic Development Board, *Annual Report 1967*, p. 82.

partly been a response to the wishes of the host countries, but also reflect the fact that for small firms this is a more efficient form of investment than outright ownership. Investors from countries such as Australia which have themselves been subject to foreign investment by firms which have not allowed local participation are aware of the hostility that such investment engenders, and are therefore inclined to avoid it in their own investments abroad. Some of the older investing firms in the more developed developing countries (as well as in developed countries) have issued shares to local investors in the host countries to combine local participation with a retention of effective controls. Even some of the European and United States firms which have been opposed to local ownership participation have sometimes not been able to avoid at least a token ownership share, although others have chosen to license local entrepreneurs instead, thus minimising the extent of their involvement. Perhaps paradoxically the pressure for local participation seems to have been greater and more effective in the western Pacific, and together with the more diverse nature of the investment flow, it appears to have led to more local participation in direct foreign investment.

The behaviour of the firms with direct foreign participation, however, suggests that there is no close correlation between the nature of ownership and the degree of local control. The extent to which a firm conforms to local business and social mores depends largely on its management, and there is no direct relationship between the speed with which foreign managers are replaced and the form of ownership. The training of local managers depends on the complexity of the firm's investment, the parent firm's attitudes and the local partners' or trainees' aptitudes, and these vary a great deal. Similarly, factors other than the form of ownership tend to determine internal pricing between the local and parent firm, the degree of reinvestment and profit payout and investment in backward and forward linkages. In general, the effectiveness of economic policy in encouraging efficient production and offering opportunities for further investment appears to be more than the firm's ownership structure in determining such factors.

In a number of developing countries, direct foreign investment plays a very important role in the economy as a whole and particularly in some of its sectors. In the traditional areas, in mining and petroleum development, foreign investment predominates in most developing countries, and this is also true of some plantation agriculture. In forestry, foreign investment may be important in the export trade but it is rarely of importance in timber industry as a whole. In agricultural development other than plantations, foreign investment has only played a small role and this is also true of livestock and fishing. In the latter, however, there is an important area of relatively large-scale fishing, particularly for freezing and canning for export, which is sometimes dominated by foreign firms.

Direct foreign investment in primary industries has a number of characteristics which distinguish it from investment in secondary and tertiary industries, and link it to the foreign 'enclave' investment which was typical of the nineteenth and early twentieth centuries. Some of this investment has developed resources, particularly in the least developed countries, which otherwise would not have been developed at all. Only the foreign firms had the capital resources, access to technology, management, and markets, and above all, all these in combination. The impact of such investment has principally been felt in contribution to national product, to foreign exchange earnings and to revenue, for the contribution to employment and creation of skills has to some extent still been limited by the isolated nature of the investment. Such investments have usually also improved the infrastructure of the project's countryside, and even if such infrastructure is generally related to the needs of the investment projects, and would otherwise perhaps not have had a high priority, its existence generally benefits the surrounding countryside. It is also true that the enclave nature of this type of investment has been modified in comparison with the past. There is now a much greater tendency to local processing, particularly of minerals, but also of plantation products, such as copra, and this trend is still expanding although it is severely limited by the tariff structure of developed countries which discriminates against the processing of primary products in developing countries. Better transport has also tended to break down the isolation of such investment projects, modified their social structure and made them more acceptable to developing countries.

Particular problems, however, remain. Firstly, there is a danger that once foreign investors are assured of a potential source of supply of raw materials, they will delay their exploitation according to their own global preference for raw material development, and this may not coincide with that of the host countries which wish to develop their resources as rapidly as possible, particularly if the rest of the economy is not well developed and if exchange earning is urgent. Secondly, many difficulties arise from the ambiguous nature of rents, profits, and revenues due to the owners of the resources, the investors in its development, and the government. While such differences may be distinguished theoretically, in practice all three tend to merge, and infrastructure costs impinge on revenue questions. Prices frequently cannot be clearly distinguished because of the nature of international markets.[13] Since all these factors, moreover, change over time, it is extremely difficult to establish general rules or terms for large-scale natural resource exploitation. These problems as well as the fears of permanent alienation of national assets have led to the accumulation of mining and other relevant regulations, frequently to the

[13] These problems are discussed in Helen Hughes, 'The Political Economy of Nauru', *Economic Record*, December 1964, pp. 523-4.

point where their complexity makes them unworkable in practice, and they have to be circumvented by individual negotiations. In such bargaining, moreover, developing countries have tended to be at a disadvantage against more experienced investing corporations. Excessively generous conditions for the foreign investors have inevitably led to great bitterness, and sometimes to expropriation if appropriate re-negotiation of conditions was not undertaken in time.

In many countries the bulk of direct foreign investment since World War II has gone into manufacturing and in this sector the share of direct foreign investment in total manufacturing output may be quite high, ranging from about a sixth in Mexico[14] to 20-30 per cent in most of the countries of South-East Asia. Foreign investment has, however, been much more important in new, usually technologically complex industries, than these estimates would indicate. Such industries include a variety of non-durable consumer goods (such as soaps, toothpastes and cosmetics, flour milling, reconstituted milk manufacture and textiles), most durable consumer goods (where foreign investors generally dominate in electronic and electrical products and motor vehicles), some intermediate products (such as petro-chemicals and sheet glass) and most of the few capital goods which are produced in the developing countries of the Asian-Pacific area. In these industries direct foreign investment generally accounts for up to 50-60 per cent of total output, and in some cases reaches 100 per cent.[15]

On both sides of the Pacific, therefore, the greatest impact of direct foreign investment in the last twenty years has been in manufacturing. Briefly, the direct foreign investment package of technology, management and capital has often been critical to the industrialisation process; without direct foreign investment it would have cost more to introduce new industries or processes, or it may not have been possible to introduce them at all. In countries industrialising with foreign exchange constraints, and this includes most of the developing countries on both the Pacific shores, the foreign exchange component of direct foreign investment has also been important to the industrialisation process in a broader balance of payments context. For outward-oriented industrialisation, foreign investors' markets have frequently been equally important. The impact of industrialisation on the rest of the economy spreads the effects of direct foreign investment more broadly than investment in primary production.

Direct foreign investment in manufacturing has also had costs, but many of the costs frequently associated with it have not been due so

[14] R. Vernon, 'Private Long Term Foreign Investment in Latin America'; Inter-American Economic and Social Council, *The Role of Foreign Private Investment in the Development of Latin America* (Washington, D.C., 1969), p. 40.
[15] Direct foreign investment in pioneer industries in Malaysia and Singapore is an indication of the share of direct foreign investment in the new manufacturing industries in those countries. See Tables 14.4 and 14.5.

much to the nature of foreign investment itself, but rather to the choice of development policies by the host countries. The principal costs arise out of the lack of internal and external competitiveness of manufacturing industry and the associated balance of payments effects. In most developing countries on both sides of the Pacific a conjunction of heavily protectionist policies with controlled entry,[16] which has sought to avoid monopoly but recognised that in limited markets only a small number of investors were viable, has resulted in the fragmentation of production, the absence of economies of scale, low productivity and correspondingly high costs. While this situation is also typical of many industries in which local investors predominate, and local oligopolistic groups may be less competitive than foreign ones, the oligopolistic character of the principal foreign firms seeking entry into such markets has increased the pressure on governments to permit an excessive number of entrants into an industry and to protect it accordingly. Once such an oligopolistic group is established there is frequently little internal competition and the efficiency of management is low, particularly for the marginal firm whose costs, however, tend to determine the tariff level. The marginal firms are sometimes local firms, while the intra-marginal firms are usually the more efficient of the international firms, and they earn substantial monopoly profits.

The first steps in import-substituting industrialisation are generally relatively simple, and at this stage the costs of the fragmentation of production are not as high as they become as the local component of production is increased, or processes such as petroleum refining move towards the production of petrochemicals. Oligopolistic international firms generally press backward and forward integration further than local investors who are less reluctant to rely on common suppliers or marketing channels. The tendency to fragment markets then persists at a growing cost. Developing countries sometimes consider that foreign firms do not pursue backward or forward integration because they wish to continue making profits on component supply, and this may occasionally be true, but more often the reasons lie in the high costs of backward or forward integration by a group of firms intent on vertical integration in limited markets.

High production costs limit domestic markets, reducing economies of scale from levels which would be possible with lower production costs, and deferring the time when tariffs could be reduced. Foreign intra-marginal firms often fear that too much competitive success would expose

---

[16] Most developing countries exercise direct controls over entry into industry through the incentive system by controlling the entry of foreign firms and by the licensing of new firms. Protection systems, particularly where barriers to trade are quantitative, exchange controls, export subsidies, and credit subsidies and controls frequently also become controls over entry.

them in a monopoly position, and prefer to make high unit profits on a limited turnover. The types of products introduced by internationally competing manufacturing firms, particularly in consumer goods, but also in some intermediate and capital goods which are inputs for other sectors, notably agriculture, are often not suitable for developing countries, but the investment push of such companies makes it easy to introduce them, and the policy structure of developing countries maintains their profitability. In general, protectionist policies favour high income durable consumer goods rather than mass consumption goods.

The adverse balance of payments effects of this pattern of industrialisation are well known. Where production fragmentation stops further backward linked development, imports of raw materials and components tend to be high, and because of the high local value added costs, high cost production and limited employment are achieved at small foreign exchange saving.[17] Traditional exports are hampered by high production costs in the manufacturing sector, and the exports of manufactured products are made very difficult for the high producers themselves and for those dependent on them as inputs. For the efficient intra-marginal firm the profits of the secure internal market are more attractive than the intensive competition of exports.

Such factors have been more important, and more intransigent, in the foreign firms' failure to export manufactured goods than export restrictions imposed by parent companies. It is true that export restrictions are sometimes used to enable the parent firm to gain maximum scale benefits at home or in a low tax country, but the extent of such barriers cannot be known until costs of production are sufficiently competitive to make exports possible. Although statistical evidence is not available, experience of manufactured exports from developing countries suggests that foreign firms tend to perform better than local firms, particularly in the export of manufactures other than primary processing. In some instances, parent companies allocate shares of their world markets to the associated company in a developing country to enable it to reach economic levels of operation. In some cases the parent company finds it profitable to have relatively labour-intensive components made up by the associated firm in the developing country. While comparative advantage is undoubtedly a factor in the ability to export, in countries which have a bias against exports, it is only the very efficient firms which export in spite of the bias. A large proportion of these are frequently foreign firms enjoying the benefits of advanced technology and management, and a favourable financial situation, as well as the parent company's foreign market knowledge.

---

[17] With subsidised imports or exports, high foreign exchange capital costs, or high profits for foreign investors, import substitution may even involve a higher foreign exchange cost than importing.

Sometimes, following the pattern of exports from developed countries, it is their monopoly advantage in the domestic market which makes exports possible.

The nature of many export markets favours the foreign firm in those countries which either have little or no bias against exporting such as Singapore and Hong Kong, and those like Korea and Taiwan which have offset a protectionist bias by subsidies of various types. Relatively labour-intensive industries with a low substitutability of capital for labour, such as garment manufacture, paper flower making, and electronic component assembly, exploit the developing countries' comparative advantage in low labour cost. But these industries are relatively few in number, and the total markets, though growing, are limited and often restricted by tariffs and quantitative restrictions. Several of these industries, such as component assembly, are dependent on captive markets and hence to a considerable degree on foreign investment.

A more promising area of competitive advantage for developing countries, because it is potentially larger, consists of industries in which the rate of substitution of capital for labour is quite high, but where developing countries can combine low labour costs with sophisticated technology and management. These are industries such as textiles, machine tools and engineering components, shipbuilding, and such items as highly labour-intensive components of individually specified heavy electrical equipment. The countries for which a combination of relatively low wages, high labour, technical and management skills, and supporting services, provides a comparative advantage are semi-industrialised ones like Hong Kong, Singapore, Taiwan and Korea, and direct foreign investment is playing an important role in their export-oriented industries. They require a continuation of such investment for further steps in this direction, and the less developed countries generally require direct foreign investment to catch up with them.

Developed countries threatened by such exports constantly have to improve their technical and managerial skills, and invest in more advanced processes to maintain their competitive position, particularly against the semi-industrial countries. Without such improvement they either have to move out of the industries in which they are failing to compete, or else protect them to an increasing degree. With the exception of Japan which is making a considerable effort to upgrade its industry mix, developed countries are tending to protection instead, and this is particularly so in textiles in which there is little direct foreign investment from developed countries other than Japan.[18] Direct foreign investment in

[18] This has benefited some developing countries in the western Pacific by pushing successful exporters abroad (p. 318) but at the expense of higher costs due to the fragmentation of production, for even labour-intensive industries such as garment manufacturing have significant economies of scale. See Paul Luey, 'Hong Kong Investment', in Hughes and You Poh Seng, op. cit., pp. 133-4.

exporting industries by developed countries tends to reduce the political pressure for protection in the home countries, and this may improve the prospects for exports from developing countries. Without such improvement, if supply moves ahead of demand, the industries which rely purely on labour cost advantage are likely to become overcrowded, terms of trade will move against them, and a situation analagous to primary commodity gluts is likely to arise.[19]

It has frequently been alleged that foreign firms tend to choose more capital intensive techniques than local entrepreneurs, but there is little evidence that this is so. Local entrepreneurs are usually just as constrained in their choice of technology as foreign entrepreneurs, and sometimes more so. Their ability to adapt equipment is usually more limited, and they may wish to demonstrate their modernity by investing in modern processes. But in any case there is very little choice of technique in modern manufacturing. The greater productivity of capital-intensive techniques generally exceeds the savings of relatively low labour costs in labour-intensive processes, and raw material utilisation tends to be much more economic with modern processes. Where products have competition from imports, or are wholly or partly exported, quality requirements frequently impose modern techniques. Labour-intensive techniques generally make much heavier demands on skilled and supervisory labour than capital-intensive techniques, and such labour is usually in acutely short supply. Government policies may encourage capital-intensive techniques by artificially lowering the cost of equipment through special credit arrangements[20] or tariff concessions, and taxation concessions related to fixed investment or depreciation allowances. In some countries labour costs have been allowed to get out of line with productivity through excessive fringe benefits,[21] thus raising relative labour costs, and poor labour relations encourage capital-intensive techniques. The effects of such measures are, however, generally exaggerated. In most modern industries there is little room for substitution of labour for capital except in preparation and finishing, and here the substitution of labour for capital is common. The choice between capital and labour is not in production processes, but in products and industries, and the relatively low employment generated by foreign investment is due to its concentration in capital-intensive industries encouraged by high protection.

---

[19] For the developed countries this is, of course, not simply an issue of commercial policies. To be politically viable a turn towards free trade would also require support for re-orienting industries and a new social welfare and education orientation for many developed countries. Such supporting action only appears to be forthcoming in Japan.

[20] General credit subsidies do not, of course, necessarily affect the choice of technique, since cheap credit can be used for labour-intensive as well as for capital-intensive techniques.

[21] This is particularly true of special conditions for women workers which, in some countries, far from favouring women, make it too costly to employ them.

The contribution of foreign investment to the revenues of developing countries depends on the structure of the tax system, the host country's taxation agreements wtih lending countries, and the revenue expenditures on infrastructure. If taxes are higher than those in developed countries, that is, generally above 45 per cent or so, they appear to deter investors; on the other hand, if taxes in the host country are lower than they are in the investing country and if there are double tax arrangements, there will be a transfer of revenue from the host country to the investing country's revenue. This may also occur with income tax exemptions. Unless host countries have clear agreements with investing countries that the taxes exempted in the developing country will also be exempt from taxation in the lending country, tax exemptions will not benefit the investor, but his country's revenue. Japan is the only country which, as a matter of course, includes 'tax sparing' arrangements in double tax agreements with developing countries. In other cases, the inclusion of 'tax sparing' clauses depends on a developing country's negotiating ability, and if it is not included in double taxation agreements, it will depend on case by case decisions by the lending country.[22] Although foreign investors have sometimes in the past been accused of tax evasion, in recent times a foreign firm's exposed position generally means that it is a better taxpayer than local firms unused to modern business mores. Foreign investment, moreover, tends to spread the attitude that taxes are a reasonable call on a firm's gross profits, particularly through local partnerships.

In the long run, the foreign investors' contribution to revenue will usually exceed the government's expenditures on infrastructure and social services, specifically for foreign firms, even if at first such expenditures are high. However, if a substantial construction program for facilities such as industrial estates and factory buildings which are not charged at market prices is accompanied by considerable exemptions from tax revenues, then revenue gains will be small for some time.

The profitability of direct foreign investment does not vary so much by countries and by industries as by firms. To some extent this reflects the range of efficiency among firms, but it is mainly the result of the market structure. High profits are usually due to monopolistic situations created by protectionist policies, and the remedy does not lie in moral exhortations but in policy change. Foreign firms, of course, also enjoy some quasi-rent profit elements arising out of their superior technical, managerial, and sometimes financial resources, and this tends to lead to higher profitability and a more rapid rate of growth than local firms, lacking these advantages, can achieve. This is usually the reason why in an oligopolistic grouping the local firms are the marginal firms, while the

22 The United States government has used a variety of arguments, including the desire to discourage the loss of revenue by developing countries, for not allowing tax sparing. See also Hughes and You Poh Seng, op. cit., p. 186.

foreign firms are intra-marginal. It makes policy changes particularly difficult because an increase in competition would injure the local firm. The encouragement of reinvestment of profits by taxation incentives differentiating between reinvested and paid-out profits exacerbates the problem rather than relieves it. Most countries, far from wishing to discriminate against local firms, of course desire to encourage their growth, so that the local firms at least maintain, but preferably increase their share of manufacturing activities. The principal long-run problems associated with direct foreign investment in manufacturing are thus those which affect the competitiveness of local manufacturers.

Investment in service industries—trade, commercial services such as advertising, tourism and banking—has mainly affected the modern service sector associated with new developments in mining and manu-facturing. Traditional service sectors have been little affected, but in some services such as advertising and insurance, foreign investment plays a very important role. Investment in service industries tends to be more visible than in other industries and therefore provokes more political contro-versy, and in some areas, notably banking, it poses some additional problems.

Many countries, including developed countries, fear that the exercise of monetary controls over the banking system would be weakened by the presence of foreign financial institutions with large foreign resources. There is some evidence that this tends to be the case. Some of the large South-East Asian banks operate as international units, and it is only countries like Singapore and Hong Kong, able to eschew monetary instruments because of their unique situation as city states, which remain unconcerned by their presence. Developing and developed countries there-fore tend either to exclude foreign banks altogether, or restrict their activities in effect to international transactions.

Foreign investment can make a substantial contribution to savings by institutional savers and the growth of capital markets by making well known and backed shares available in local issues. Investors, particu-larly institutional ones, reluctant to invest in unknown shares, frequently welcome the opportunity to purchase the local issues of internationally reputable companies, and it is common, in Singapore and Malaysia for example, for such issues to be oversubscribed.

On the other hand, problems may arise if foreign investors seek to borrow the bulk of capital for a new venture in a developing country on fixed loan terms. Foreign firms tend to be favoured borrowers because they present less risk than smaller, local companies, but this limits loans to local borrowers. Developing countries therefore tend to discourage this type of lending. A great deal depends on the circumstances in which such loans are requested and made. Some foreign companies seek local funds, particularly from official sources, to ensure the government's involvement with their enterprise so that the firm's interest will be secured in times of economic or political upheaval, and such loans may be justified in a country struggling to attract foreign investors. In most cases, however, a country will be well advised to seek competing foreign investors, who may be willing to bring a similar package of technology and management and contribute substantial financial resources as well.

Conclusions

The flow of direct foreign investment to both the Pacific shores is now well established. Natural resource endowment and the existing levels of development play a very important role in the rate of flow to each country, but within these limits the flow to each country, as well as its effects, largely depends on the policies pursued.

Protectionist policies have been the most powerful policy incentives to direct foreign investment in the Asian-Pacific area, for they have been the most important incentive to manufacturing investment, but protectionist policies, particularly in conjunction with investment controls and the oligopolistic motivation of many foreign investing firms, have resulted in the principal costs of direct foreign investment. Many of the developing countries of the area are becoming increasingly aware of the costs of protection in terms of efficiency and external competitiveness, but reducing the levels of protection, or mitigating its effects by increasing internal competition is in practice very difficult. With a sharp reduction in protection marginal firms would go out of business, intra-marginal firms' profit margins would be cut, and workers now employed, albeit at a low level of productivity, would, at least for some period of time, be unemployed. In most countries manufacturers have found a *modus vivendi* with other producers, and in some cases governments protecting precarious balances of payments are reluctant to relinquish import controls.

Because of the difficulties of a substantial decrease in the level of protection, a change in orientation towards more outward-looking policies involves a process of decontrol and tariff reduction, and generally takes time to accomplish. For some countries in the area, in fact, some import substitution possibilities still offer a promise of immediate industrial expansion and employment growth, though at high cost. With foreign investors pressing for entry it is politically difficult not to open up such opportunities through higher tariffs, and in these countries the first step towards a more competitive economy may lie in holding the line against further tariff and direct import control increases rather than in a reduction of protective levels.

For other countries a review of the structure of tariffs and import control by industry group could progressively seek to rationalise the structure of protection, firstly eliminating particularly high tariffs 'tailormade' to the needs of marginal firms, and gradually reducing the overall incidence of effective protection. A planned reduction of protective levels can be used to give manufacturers notice of increasing competition, enabling them to improve their efficiency and expand their operations by looking toward foreign markets. Such action can be supported by other government policies. Credit and taxation measures may give assistance to mergers by local companies to increase economies of scale, although mergers are generally impossible to arrange between competing subsidiaries of internationally competitive foreign firms. In some cases limited and strategically designed price controls may be effective in pushing manufacturers to more efficient production and a more vigorous search for markets. In some countries action may have to be taken to offset the costs of protection for potential exporters before protection itself can be substantially reduced. Efficient drawback and temporary admission systems and credit and marketing support may suffice, but where costs of protection are high, subsidies may at first be necessary. Such policies are usually effective in shifting outward even those foreign firms which initially, implicitly or explicitly through restrictions on their ability to export, entered a market for purely domestic sales. The planned reduction of protection could also be used to foster regional trade as economies become more diversified and specialised, and as regional communications improve. This would lay a basis of regionally based international investment decisions which would in the long run overcome the high costs of excessive oligopolist entry into limited national markets.

Currently, however, the problem of control over entry into limited and protected markets remains. If a country's market is not large enough for competitive production it may be prepared to continue to import a product, but as the domestic market grows the question of domestic production arises for most products, and particularly for differentiated products for which there is usually no 'world market price' but rather a range of prices. A country with domestic production in mind may consider it worthwhile to do so at the point where its costs of production, and prices, equal the exporters' domestic prices rather than their export prices. Production generally entails a product mix, and while some products may be competitive, others may need further domestic market growth for an economic scale of production. Thus, for several reasons, a moderate level of protection, perhaps in the form of a temporary, progressively reducing tariff for the 'infant' industry may be deemed desirable. At this point it is likely that a number of internationally competitive foreign investors may become interested in local production.

A country faced with a limited market is ill-advised to fragment it along the lines so frequently followed in the past. There are, indeed, a number of alternatives. One of the competing producers may be eager enough to capture the market to begin production without a tariff, and external competition will in that case keep down prices. However, if a moderate and temporary tariff is necessary, the country may be wise to choose one monopoly firm, and exercise surveillance over it until international competition takes over. The suitability of the product to local conditions and the firm's performance in similar circumstances may be among the criteria for selection, but countries may wish to add other criteria which seem to them to be of importance. These may include local participation in the investment, a proven record of training and appointing local executive staff, a commitment to further backward and forward linked investment, or a further commitment to export. The benefits of monopoly are thus likely to be considerably greater, and the costs substantially less, than in the currently typical case of international oligopolistic competition. Once established, oligopolistic groups become the most intransigent cause of high costs, and in the industries in which they operate it is particularly difficult to reduce protection.

The structure of protection also affects the industry mix, and the possibilities of encouraging more labour-intensive industries oriented towards domestic mass consumption and agricultural outputs rather than high income markets should be borne in mind in the course of policy revisions, and supported by appropriate policies which would stimulate the growth of this section of the market. In such industries local entrepreneurs are likely to be more able to compete with foreign investors, thus making for a better balance of industrial entrepreneurship. New investment opportunities for foreign investors will generally arise in supplying such industries with intermediate and capital goods.

Commercial policies form only part of the 'rules of the game' which determine the extent to which the benefits exceed the costs of direct foreign investment. Indirect taxes frequently require adjustment, within the limits of revenue requirements, to avoid cumulative taxation which encourages vertical integration, and to ensure that the effective levels of protection are not distorted by their uneven incidence. Direct tax schedules may need revision so that they do not discourage foreign investors unduly, or that, alternatively, they do not result in a contribution of revenue to the governments of lending countries. This, of course, presupposes that double tax agreements with appropriate 'tax sparing' clauses are negotiated. Land and land sales taxes, and capital gains taxes, can frequently be used to divert investment from speculation in real estate, and the capital market can be encouraged by taxation measures where this is appropriate, without, of course, undue incursion into the redistributive effects of taxation. Labour legislation can usually only be adjusted in periods of rapid growth, but when such an opportunity arises, the reduction of fringe benefits and the tying of a worker's income closer to his productivity to increase real earnings is often advisable to avoid distortions in relative labour and capital costs.

A favourable investment climate which at the same time does not permit foreign investors to earn excessive profits and otherwise burden the economy not only requires sensible 'rules of the game', but also that the rules be not changed frequently. It also requires that policies be administered efficiently, and this may be where reforms are most urgently needed but hardest to achieve.

Investment incentives have been important in showing goodwill towards foreign investors if not in actually attracting investment,[23] but they have been the cause of some of the costs of direct foreign investment. Tariff exemptions on capital equipment imports and accelerated depreciation allowances may have encouraged capital intensiveness unduly, and similar exemptions on raw materials encouraged import dependence in some cases. Exemptions from income tax were intended to offset the lack of infrastructure and external economies, and internal excessive costs of infant industries, but these were also compensated by tariffs and other protective devices, credit incentives, and in some cases by low-priced infrastructure facilities. The sum of incentives has been excessive in many countries in relation both to the need and the possibility of attracting additional direct foreign investment. Foreign investors' behaviour suggests that specific incentives are particularly ineffectual in the least developed countries because in such countries investors rarely make decisions to invest at the margin where specific incentives may be most effective. For these countries the revenue forgone by incentives is relatively more important than for countries with a higher level of infrastructure, and expenditures of such revenue on infrastructure facilities are more likely to be effective in attracting further direct foreign investment.

While unilateral abolition of investment incentives may be difficult because of the possibility that this be interpreted as a withdrawal of a favourable attitude to foreign investment, regional rationalisation and reduction of incentives, at least to stop neighbouring countries from competing with each other in offering 'give-aways' is highly desirable.[24] This, moreover, is an area in which the developed countries might take a lead in eliminating investment incentives by international agreement.

---

[23] This is as true of incentives by investing countries as those by host countries. United Nations, *Foreign Investment in Developing Countries* (New York, 1968), p. 21, concluded on the basis of several studies that 'such empirical enquiries as have been made to elucidate the actual inducement effect and overall operation of various schemes confirm the expectation that, while prohibitive and discriminatory taxes may effectively impede otherwise worthwhile investments, temporary exemptions from normal tax burdens are unlikely by themselves to constitute a determining factor in many investment decisions'. This finding is supported by the study of foreign investment in Singapore in Hughes and You Poh Seng, op. cit., pp. 183-7.

[24] The Central American republics set a precedent in this respect in the Protocol of San José in 1962 by agreeing to grant uniform incentives, but unfortunately, instead of leading to an immediate reduction of incentives, this resulted in competition among the Central American Republics pending their introduction. Secretaria Permanente del Tratado General de Integración Economica, *Convenios Centroamericanos de Integración Economica* (Guatemala, 1963), pp. 13-18.

Even with a satisfactory policy and administrative structure, development agencies specifically oriented to the problems of investors, local as well as foreign, can play a major role in encouraging new investment and ensuring its economic operation. In areas involving natural resource exploitation or the alienation of urban land, negotiation is inevitable, and the developing countries' negotiators should be equal to the task. This generally means that a special agency, somewhat outside the public service, to ensure political independence and salaries commensurate with the task, undertake the review of existing investment, the search for new investors, and the investigation of difficulties of firms already in operation. An efficient agency of this type can do much to ensure local participation in direct foreign investment by finding suitable local entrepreneurs rather than Ali-Baba partners. It can seek foreign investment from a variety of sources to prevent undesirable overtones of political control which may arise if the capital inflow is predominantly from one foreign country, and it can assist local entrepreneurs to take up available opportunities so that local investment does not fall behind the direct foreign inflow.

Direct foreign investment follows economic opportunities: it is business, not aid, and it responds to policy stimuli and restrictions accordingly. Developing countries can influence its flow and its effects to a marked degree by appropriate policy decisions, particularly if these are made in co-operation rather than in competition.

Comments and Discussion

MOHAMMAD SADLI and CESAR VIRATA opened the discussion; SADLI made the following comments: Hughes says that: 'Many of the developing countries of the area are becoming increasingly aware of the costs of protection in terms of efficiency and external competitiveness, but reducing the levels of protection, or mitigating its effects by increasing internal competition is in practice very difficult.' And then she continues to suggest how it could be done. In practice, much will depend upon the political possibilities and impossibilities. If there is a strong government and political leadership (that is, *vis-à-vis* domestic political interest groups or parties) then it could be done, provided the leadership wants it. The obvious example is probably Korea.

Small countries and city states in East Asia and South-East Asia are more successful in engaging in outward-looking industrialisation and there are success stories enough in this area. These smaller countries simply have fewer alternatives. The bigger countries can always afford to start their industrialisation programs with an orientation towards the home market and a protectionist policy is usually their first resort. I have read that even for Japan, Korea and Taiwan the major market was, and probably still is, the domestic market, and these countries also have resorted to protection. We must, therefore, try to understand why Korea and Taiwan, and before, Japan, succeeded better in developing industrial exports as spillovers from domestic excess capacity probably, and why countries like the Philippines are not, or not yet, successful. Maybe their foreign exchange policy is the key. Protection plus an overvalued exchange rate is pre-empting exports of industrial goods, where protection plus a relatively undervalued exchange rate at least lowers the threshold. A purposeful and determined government policy designed to foster industrial exports is also necessary.

Since we are discussing the role of foreign investment, we must verify whether or not the existence of a good number of foreign firms will, by itself, be helpful, or detrimental, to the achievement of an export-oriented industry.

Hughes asserts that foreign firms typically are intra-marginal firms in terms of efficiency. Most of these firms know how to market abroad. She observes that, in the 1960s, United States investments in export-oriented industries based on low labour costs in Taiwan, Korea and Singapore transformed the character of the industrialisation process. It could be that United States firms in the Philippines are not so export-oriented, because the impediments are too many and the incentives too few. Hence, they may very well have excess capacity which could be profitably used as a jumping board for exports if other conditions were right. I am inclined to speculate that foreign firms and foreign investment *per se* are not a liability for constructing a progressive, competitive and outward-looking industrial structure. Potentially they are even an asset and there is no inherent laziness in them to engage in exports. But sometimes it is just not profitable, often because of overvalued exchange rates, sometimes also because of other, institutional, impediments of a cost-increasing nature; for instance, labour laws, and the high cost of domestic transportation.

On the other basic problem mentioned in the chapter, the cost of foreign investment in terms of tax revenues forgone because of too liberal incentive schemes: my colleagues from the region and I feel that improvements can be expected soon and apparently do not have to wait collective, or multilateral, action. The ideal end situation would be the absence of temporary concessions. Every government will find out, sooner rather than later, that the administration of these concessions and exceptions creates more problems and headaches than they solve, and the realisation has dawned upon us that foreign investments are much more attracted by market prospects than by temporary tax and duties exemptions. The dramatic proof is Japan. No matter how hard the admission requirements, foreign firms keep banging at the door.

This ideal situation will probably not be attained in one year or two, but it will probably also not take a decade. If a developing country is successful in her growth she does not need special incentives to attract foreign capital. If her economy is stagnating she may have to do other things to improve her investment climate.

The other tax leakage, so frequently discussed in the foregoing chapters, resulting from intra-company pricing, should be given proper attention by the governments of the developing countries. Tax administration should be improved and the quality, and salaries, of tax officials upgraded. This is easier said than done. Economic underdevelopment goes hand in hand with public administration deficiencies. Maybe the more developed, but still capital importing countries like Canada and Australia, could lend their experience to countries like Indonesia, the Philippines and Thailand, about how not to forgo tax money from the big multinational firms. Kindleberger is also optimistic; he believes that bargaining power may shift over time to the host country after a large foreign investment is installed, as with petroleum (Chapter 4). Perhaps international agencies, such as the International Monetary Fund, could, or would, do something to redress fiscal bargaining power balances, *ex ante* and *ex post* of an investment. So far we have heard little discussion of the fifth point in Johnson's paper: international policy issues. Or do we have reservations about such international institutions? A rich man's club can camouflage and perpetuate the unequal distribution of power, a poor man's club is at best a noisy, ineffectual congregation.

Finally, I must make a comment on Hughes's remark that 'problems may arise if foreign investors seek to borrow the bulk of capital for a new venture in a developing country on fixed loan terms'. The difficulty for national governments here is the administration of the principle of 'national treatment', 'most favoured firm treatment', or 'non-discriminatory treatment'. Adoption of these principles seems to be part of the musts of a favourable climate for foreign investment. National governments have no choice than to subscribe to them. But how should we interpret 'equal' or 'non-discriminatory' treatment between firms all incorporated under national law, be they foreign or domestic? One can assert that treating unequals as equal is discrimination, and the national government can claim that foreign firms and domestic firms are unequal. But can they get away with it?

VIRATA went on:

Generally speaking in the game played between investors and host countries, the host countries have three bargaining levers. They are internal market size, human resources, and natural resources. The investors have capital, technology, and the choice of location plus the fact that the investor could keep on selling its products from existing production centres, provided they recover direct costs. On the other hand, many business executives, according to various surveys, are primarily concerned about losing market shares or losing the market. Hence, host countries have used control over entry and protection as the main tools for attracting foreign investment. If the internal market size is relatively small, then, the emphasis on incentives is control over human organisation, such as low wages, longer working hours and fewer fringe benefits.

In a bargaining process, there are trade-offs, so the results could be overcapacity, inefficient production units or business conditions bordering on monopolistic conditions.

Hughes rightly focused attention on the adjustments to be made, the bargaining levers that have to be adjusted. She remarked, though, that the host country operators realise the importance of adjusting the levers. I agree with her suggestion for using international competition as a country's vetoing power over franchised manufacturers (or monopolists). Public utility concepts, in effect, are being used by developing countries in the field of manufacturing, through limitation of choice of the products available to consumers. In connection with the problems of taxation rates of return and balance of payments effects, there is real need for harmonising incentives among host countries.

As a participant from a developing country I would like to say that Hughes's observations are accurate and her suggestions practical. As evidenced by the discussions during the conference the participants from host countries are implementing suggestions that she has outlined in her paper on tariff levels, selectivity of projects, reduction of give-away incentives, improvement in the public administration of investment incentives.

The remainder of the discussion explored two major themes, namely, the rationale of incentive schemes for foreign investors and the case for industrial protection in developing countries.

The implication in Hughes's paper that positive lessons could be learned from Central American experience with attempts to harmonise fiscal incentives for foreign investors was questioned. It was suggested that, although the positive lessons were few, there were important negative lessons. Before the signing of the San José Protocol in 1962, there had, in fact, been a rush of incentive-giving by the signatories. Moreover, the agreement was not implemented for seven years, until 1969, during which time two signatories were given special conditions on the grounds of extreme underdevelopment. In consequence, the agreement represents the lowest common denominator by incorporating the most extensive and generous allowance schemes. The nature and history of the agreement are well documented by Fagan, of the Center for International Studies, at the University of California. The Andean Common Market is still working towards harmonisation of treatment for foreign investors and their problems in negotiation were also considered instructive to developing countries contemplating any similar action.

Several Asian participants cautioned against easy judgment of the generosity or otherwise of incentive schemes out of context. Taxation and commercial policy systems vary greatly from country to country and some systems of protection are so comprehensive that 'concessions' are necessary if investment is to be directed into useful channels. Take the treatment of foreign investors' imports of equipment and materials. Concessional tariff entry implies revenue forgone, but under what circumstances is such concession-giving inadvisable? The case of Korea was contrasted with that of Singapore. In Korea, where the tariff and tax structure mitigated against the efficient allocation of resources into export-oriented activities, concessions might be justified as compensatory devices. In Singapore, where tariffs on materials and equipment are low or zero, no such concession is required. It would be easy to advocate removal of the inefficient policy devices which have to be compensated for, but that fails to recognise the phases of development through which policy must pass in a newly emerging nation. It is frequently difficult to make first-best policy adjustments in sufficient time; meanwhile some substitutes have to be employed.

It was also argued that countries at different stages of development, of different size, and with different administrative backgrounds would have different requirements in the way of offering encouragement to foreign investors. There appeared no universally appropriate recommendations on incentives policies, and for this reason it may well be difficult to engineer any agreement among South-East Asian countries, for instance, to adopt common policies. The cases of the city states of Singapore and Hong Kong were contrasted with that of Indonesia where administrative difficulties were great, incomes lower, past performance and future prospects less certain.

Hughes agreed substantially with these comments and explained that what she had intended to advocate was regular consultation and exchange of information among interested parties, so that a better appreciation of the issues and appropriate shifts in policy emphasis would develop as required. She also reiterated her earlier advocacy of a concentration of administrative talent in agencies dealing with foreign investment and the domestic investment program.

Consideration of the question of incentives prompted discussion of the effectiveness of tariff protection in encouraging economic development and industrialisation. The differences between Latin America and Asia and the Western Pacific in respect of the extent and commitment to protectionism were first clarified. A participant from a developing country noted the role of protectionism in the development of presently industrialised countries and wondered at the strong undercurrent of anti-protectionism in the conference discussions. At least one participant asserted that the optimum tariff was always zero except where there existed a terms of trade case for protection. There was consensus on the need for holding tariffs in check and generally low tariffs. Some accepted the need for selected infant industry protection where externalities were strong; others admitted tariff protection in this case only as a second-best policy to other forms of subsidisation.

Further comment urged developed countries to play a more active role in assisting developing countries with the administration, taxation, and negotiation of foreign investment. Another inquiry sought exploration of the impact of developed country policies on the distribution and volume of investment flowing to developing countries.

15 Summary

HARRY G. JOHNSON

The subject of this volume, the role of foreign direct investment in Asian-Pacific economic development, is an extremely topical and relevant one. As has become clear from the Pearson Report and its reception, in future private foreign investment will have to take over from official development assistance the burden of transferring capital resources, and, more important, advanced technology, from the rich to the poor nations. In contemporary circumstances, this is both a highly controversial change, and one respecting which there is a dearth of relevant theoretical and empirical knowledge. As it happens, most, though not all of the relevant research—particularly with respect to policy issues—has been done in Canada or by Canadians elsewhere—though one must recognise the work of Brash in Australia and Dunning and Steuer in the United Kingdom, and the stimulus that Kindleberger has given to this field of study by his own work and by his academic entrepreneurship. One of the main achievements of the argument above, in my judgment, is to bring this Canadian work and thought to the attention of those from other countries, and to reveal to the Canadians present the extent to which Canadian concerns are special to the circumstances of their country rather than general concerns afflicting all host countries.

The book begins with my survey of the issues. Komiya's very useful commentary started the corrective process by stressing the difference between horizontal and vertical integration, and the fact that vertical integration is explained, not by product-differentiated oligopoly, but by dynamic considerations of reducing uncertainty. His analogy with owner-occupied housing, however, seemed to me to be pressed too far, and to overlook the key economic consideration, the imperfection of markets and of information. Komiya also made the important point that the profitability of direct foreign investment is not necessarily related to the factor endowment of the host country.

The general discussion thereafter ranged rather widely. Our attention was called to the importance of portfolio investment, and the possible adverse welfare implications of restrictions on it imposed by home and host countries; this is a subject that should be pursued further, although consideration of it was beyond the present scope. Others noted the fuzziness of the definition of direct foreign investment; portfolio investment in the form of loans with strings attached poses many of the same problems for host countries as equity investment. The general feeling, however, was that foreign direct investment is in the main clear-cut enough to be discussable. Much of that discussion was concerned with fairly familiar problems, or perhaps more accurately potential problems, notably the possibility of 'defensive investment' reproducing in lower-income countries the oligopolistic market structure characteristic of the home country, and the possibility that tariff or 'natural' protection (through transport costs) might lead to a long-term loss by encouraging market-sharing among a number of small companies where one large-scale company would be more efficient. The latter possibility emerges from both the Canadian and the Australian literature; but one should perhaps be more careful than some were in distinguishing between actual losses and potential losses by comparison with a hypothetical ideal; in remembering the time-dimension and the necessity of applying a discount rate to future losses; and in distinguishing between those losses attributable to the foreign-ness of the investments and those attributable to national policies of protection and/or of tolerating oligopolistic market organisation. English, who has worked longer and harder on these aspects of foreign direct investment than anyone else present, distinguished between the effects of tariffs, the effects of oligopoly, and the effects of foreign versus domestic ownership, and expressed the view that, once the effects of the first two were segregated, there was little left in the ownership issue.

Chapter 2 was Hymer's contribution on United States investment abroad. The participants at the conference, without exception, found his Old Testament prophetic style hard to take; more accurately, perhaps, no one was comfortable with the methodology, common to Marx and Myrdal, of viewing mankind as subject to inevitable economic determinism unless he does something about it. Wilkinson in his commentary pointed out that Hymer's paper presents two alternative sets of hypotheses about the future role of the giant corporation—either it wins, or governments win over it. He also took the occasion to float a trial balloon on his proposal that host governments in surplus should invest their accruing reserves in parent company stock, a balloon that Machlup punctured with an effortless back-hand shot! English disputed the factual basis of Hymer's view that industrial concentration has been increasing, and argued that agglomeration is limited by the exhaustion of scale economies, and that anyway government can play one corporation off against the others. A number of other speakers, who collectively constitute a conference view, argued that the political power of corporations, especially non-United States corporations, is weak; that they are quite deferential to political pressure; and that the political pressure of nationalism will hold them in check. Hymer's response to these criticisms, correctly but not too helpfully, was that his paper was an exercise in projection rather than prediction.

The third chapter is Safarian's on host country problems. Its author expressed dissatisfaction with the traditional analysis of the welfare effects of direct foreign investment, because that analysis ignores the reasons for such investment, which stem from the difficulties of enforcing contractual arrangements, in other words from transaction costs. He argued that the reduction of transaction costs through direct foreign investment, while privately beneficial, may not be socially beneficial, and discussed alternative methods of acquiring foreign industrial knowledge. The chief political problem of direct foreign investment was extra-territoriality. One comment distinguished among economic, political and social costs; the main concern was the possibility of displacement of domestic by foreign entrepreneurs, and of alliances of foreign and domestic capitalists leading to capitalist domination. These concerns are, of course, mutually exclusive—nothing would consolidate political control so much as a non-voting and suspect foreign entrepreneurial class. It was also suggested that extraterritoriality is a Canadian and not a general problem, a view which I think is correct as a general proposition.

The equations in Kindleberger's chapter were accorded respect but not regard, and the discussion concerned itself with general issues. Wionczek made three important points: the apparent conflicts between host country and corporation over extractive industries are really exchanges of economic losses for political gains by the host countries, and do not harm the corporations so long as they retain control of marketing; nationalisation may benefit the multinational corporation by releasing more capital and managerial resources for use elsewhere; the world picture regarding extractive industries has changed—natural resources are not scarce, what is scarce is the capital and the managerial talent required to develop them. This I think is the most important point to emerge from that session —that developing countries are wrong to think and act as if their natural resources were priceless pearls that should not lightly be cast before multinational corporate swine.

There followed discussion of Brash's chapter on United States investment in Australia, Canada and New Zealand—the benefits and costs. Brash's main points were that New Zealand had gained relatively little, due to faulty macroeconomic policies, and that he had concentrated on costs rather than benefits since costs had aroused much more popular confusion. Deane expressed some criticism of this choice of emphasis, called attention to the many inconsistencies of host country policies and

attitudes towards foreign direct investment, especially the lack of substance in most popular objections to such investment, and rightly questioned Brash's endorsement of the Australian guidelines policy for foreign
enterprises. The discussion carried the matter little further, and was
diverted into unfruitful channels by Hughes's question whether Australia might not have been further ahead if it had kept American firms out
of its manufacturing industries. Kindleberger produced an equally 'iffy'
question—whether it might not be a good idea to keep out foreign firms
to prevent rupture of the relations between local firms and the local
capital market.

The conference then turned to the consideration of the two very
informative chapters on direct foreign investment into and out of Japan
by Komiya and Hamada. In the Komiya session, which was initially concerned with the goals of Japanese policy—as Patrick defined them, to
obtain foreign technology without other involvements—I raised the question of how far Japan had been able to pursue this policy because the
political objectives of the United States in the Pacific made it willing to
tolerate policies on the part of Japan that it would not tolerate on general
principle elsewhere. The discussion on this point I thought rather disappointing, since a number of commentators interpreted the point as a
question of deliberate and official United States policy, whereas it really
was directed at a tacit policy of not raising issues that could legitimately
be raised. However, the majority opinion seemed to be that United States
firms were not until very recently interested in investing in Japan, and,
hence, had no interest in raising the question of Japanese policy with the
United States government. Subsequent discussion centred on why foreign
firms, which before World War II had had a substantial stake in Japan,
had elected to abandon it. The consensus was that for various reasons
they had lost interest, rather than that they had been forced out by
deliberate policy.

Hamada's chapter on Japanese investment abroad was perhaps the
most novel of the conference for the non-Japanese present, since the
data were unfamiliar. The chief question raised in the discussion reverted
to Hymer's contribution, and concerned how far Japanese foreign investment could be regarded as part of the trend toward the development of a
multinational corporate world economy. Some took their stand on
legalities, and argued that the Japanese companies were essentially
Japanese enterprises and not international enterprises. Hymer, on the
other hand, argued that the essential question was whether or not the corporation took the world market or the national market as its frame of
reference, and that on that basis the Japanese firms were multinational—
whatever their current practices, they would eventually have to do what
the American and European firms do, that is, invest in local production
facilities rather than export to the market from Japan. Kindleberger

challenged this with the question whether eventually Japanese firms will invest a lot of money in production facilities in the United States. Hamada judged that it will take a new generation of Japanese business-men before Japanese firms behave like American firms. The rest of the discussion was concerned with the special virtues of Japanese investment and the problems of controlling it. Amnuay argued that the Japanese can play one government against another, and recommended harmonisa-tion of government policies in relation to the foreign corporation and the encouragement of competition among foreign investors in relation to individual national governments. It was pointed out that Japanese cor-porations sent in Japanese down to the level of foremen, which was good given the local scarcities of skilled labour, and it was wondered how soon the Japanese would begin to develop export industries in developing countries, based on cheap labour.

This argument raises a consideration I have come across recently, and which seems to be a particularly Australian contribution to the debate. In Canada and elsewhere there has been considerable concern about the extent to which foreign companies employ local residents in managerial capacities, the assumption being that such employment is a desirable objective. But if management rather than capital is the primary contribu-tion of the foreign firm, it may be that policy should seek to maximise rather than minimise the employment of foreign-trained (not necessarily foreign-born) personnel.

Chapters 8-12 are concerned with less-developed host country prob-lems. The chapters on Indonesia, Thailand and Korea raised more detailed issues than I can deal with in the space available, so I will merely list some of them. First, there was disagreement over the desira-bility of selectiveness in policy favouring particular new industries over others, on the grounds of arbitrariness and political corruption. In this connection, some argued strongly for investment in the improvement of the government department concerned with administering the selective policy, on the grounds that administration rather than general incentives to foreign investment made the difference between success and failure. Safarian argued for the use of selectiveness to prevent market fragmenta-tion and for harmonisation of policies among countries to restrain com-petition in the offer of concessions to foreign enterprises. There was a general feeling that the countries involved had been over-generous in offering tax and other concessions to foreign enterprises. On the other hand, it was noted that there was now a trend towards reducing such incentives, and observed that as the developing country economies become stronger they could afford to reconsider such incentives. A side discussion was initiated with myself by Rosen on the treatment of nationalism as a factor in policy formation. Finally, initial alarm was aroused by asking how these countries would react to a quintupling of

Japanese investment in them in the next decade; but on sober reflection the country representatives concluded that, while they would be unhappy about it, they would accept it. (In some ways, this was a misleading question, since some forgot that their economies would also grow rapidly, so that the relative increase in Japanese investment and control would be far smaller than the quintupling suggested.)

The two remaining country case studies encouraged a repetition of a number of points already made. Virata's paper on the Philippines, in particular, revived the selectivity debate. Kanamori's comments on this paper made an important criticism of the Philippines distinction between pioneering and non-pioneering industries, with foreign investment confined to the former, that primary industries may be infant industry cases deserving protection of local enterprise, whereas non-pioneering industries may be monopolised and require foreign competition to discipline them. Some attention was devoted to the Philippine experience with a floating exchange rate. Most of the discussion of the chapters on the Philippines and Mexico, however, were directed to debate over Hymer's comments on Wionczek's paper on Mexico. These centred on the idea that Mexico would remain dependent on foreign technology and the foreign corporation until some sort of revolution changed the income distribution and the pattern of final demands away from types of luxury goods that only the foreigner could supply. The result was a confrontation between Kindleberger, on the one hand, and Hymer and Wionczek on the other, at a level of theory not really appropriate to a verbal debate.

The conference then turned to a discussion of Perkins's chapter on balance of payments issues. Unfortunately, Perkins succumbed to the fallacy of believing that if the policymakers think that there is a problem, then there must be one, and proceeded to develop a quantitative partial-equilibrium analysis of a general equilibrium problem. As I pointed out in the session, the fault was partly in the nature of the topic. Nevertheless, his contribution occasioned one of Machlup's famous, and always delightful, sermons on economic methodology, known in the trade as the death of a thousand (gracious) cuts. The discussion thereafter got into the question of arrangements to limit—formally or informally—exports by branch plants to various foreign markets. As Nevile pointed out, the evidence does not support the conclusion that branch plants are less export-oriented than domestic firms; but this evidence does not go to the heart of the issue. The discussion raised, but did not really come to grips with, the question of industrial knowledge as a public good, private investment in which has to be rewarded by profits, and the implications of this fact for the marketing policy imposed on subsidiaries by their parent companies, policies which have to be interpreted in the light of the theory of price discrimination.

Hughes's chapter assessed policies towards foreign investment in the

Asian-Pacific region. Both the author and the two people who opened the discussion agreed that the policy of giving concessions to foreign firms has gone too far, and that in Virata's words, 'the bargaining levers have to be adjusted'. The view seemed to emerge that, provided a country manages its affairs properly, it will not need to give special concessions to attract private foreign capital. Amnuay argued that one should be careful not to follow Hughes's arguments into a complete negation of protection, advocating both protection and export subsidisation; he argued also that perhaps incentives for foreign investment should be absorbed into the general tax system. The supposition that protection is a desirable policy for developing countries was questioned since it has no theoretical support. On the other hand, the problems of uncertainty facing investors in the less developed countries were also emphasised. Sir John Crawford raised a different question, how significant may be policy in the developed countries designed to push investment towards developing countries. In final comment, there was argument in favour of low protection as against high protection; some protection is justified by the infant industry and the employment arguments, but excessive protection eliminates the incentives to compete and to export. The give-away incentives, especially in taxes, should be the first to be tackled by international agreement. In conclusion, the plea that developing countries should concentrate administrative talent in the agencies dealing with foreign investors was reiterated.

In summary, the contributions ranged widely over the theoretical issues, and settled on the empirical conclusion that developing countries in the Pacific have competed too hard in attracting direct foreign investment, and should retreat from this position, and especially should try to harmonise their tax and other policies towards direct foreign investment so as to increase the benefits derived therefrom.

Comments and Discussion

CHARLES KINDLEBERGER opened the discussion: Johnson has been the alpha and omega and it remains for me only to try to add epsilon to his masterly summary. I shall not dwell on what was said but attempt to suggest those issues which were raised but on which discussion has been inconclusive or which somehow got lost in the shuffle.

As a first example let me cite the question of the package of capital, technology, and management constituting direct investment. Wionczek and others want to take the package apart and hire such technology and management as are needed in the developing countries, and borrow the capital, but eschew direct foreign investment, while some insist that the package is still needed in developing countries in South-East Asia for assistance in the development process. The difference may lie in the stage of growth the participants have in mind, Wionczek thinking of Mexico with its impressive achievements in growth, while others focus on much less developed countries in this region.

One should bear in mind, however, that whether the package is decomposable or not is a function not only of the desires of the host country but of the bargaining power of the owners of technology and management. Technology may be available on licence, or it may not. Management advice of the sort needed may be hirable from consultant firms, but if it is needed continuously, there may be no escape from ownership and control. Where special types of technology or management are sought, therefore, the developing country may be faced with a choice of direct investment or no technology, no management.

Secondly, it seems to me that we were far from resolving whether the problems of direct investment are different on the two sides of the Pacific, and if so why. Hughes, for example, maintained that these differences are deep and real, and that direct investment is less dangerous in the Western Pacific area than in, say, Canada. The conclusion was not universally agreed, however, nor the reasons made clear. Is it a function of the stage of development, or nearness to the United States, of competition in the area of Japanese and European business, or the example of Japan in resisting United States firms?

We have failed to explore the question of international machinery for the resolution of disputes in the field, posed in the first chapter by Johnson and raised again in discussion by Sadli. Is it enough to improve the policies of the host countries—lowering tariffs, reducing incentives, improving the fiscal system, and reforming education, for example? Or is further action necessary on the part of developed countries—along what lines?—and is there a need for international machinery? In my own view, international machinery is needed to cope with problems of extraterritoriality, anti-trust, conflicts of national balance-of-payments regulations and national tax systems, but that on the whole, while any organisation created for these purposes should be open to any developing country which wants to join, most will choose to stay out, with no real harm to the effort. Most developing countries would regard an organisation created by international agreement among the developed countries as directed against them and especially designed to limit their freedom of action in the face of real or imagined threats to their sovereignty posed by the multinational corporation. The code on nationalisation worked out by the International Bank for Reconstruction and Development, for example, has evoked little adherence, or even interest, on the part of developing nations. Canada, Japan, Australia and New Zealand may be interested in a General Agreement on the Multinational Corporation, but as in trade, where there are separate organisations, GATT and UNCTAD, for developed and developing nations, I would anticipate that the developing countries would stay out of a general agreement sponsored by the developed countries. I do not, however, think it likely that developing countries would organise by themselves on a worldwide basis. It is much more likely that agreements for the purpose, among others to limit incentives, will be worked out on regional lines, such as the Andes pact.

There was less than exhaustive attention to the criteria for accepting proposals for direct investment adopted in Thailand, Indonesia, the Philippines, and, I think, Korea, according to which special consideration is given to projects which are export-increasing or import-decreasing, bring new technology to the country, or employ large quantities of labour, as opposed to projects which respond to market opportunities to make a profit. In his paper on Australia, New Zealand, and Canada, Brash denounced this second-best solution where resources are adaptable and macroeconomic policies for stability in the balance of payments are practicable. Does this leave out the less developed countries of the area and by indirection justify the second-best criteria described? Nor has the question of superseding market opportunities by so-called 'selectivity' criteria which single out natural resources, 'pioneer', 'essential' and other broad categories of industry as permitted or excluded for foreign investment been penetrated deeply. Banking is prohibited to foreign investment in many countries, among them Australia, Canada, and New Zealand. Is this rational or designed to protect local monopoly? There was one hint at the need for investment in banking in the Pacific. Is there a difference here between the more and the less developed countries which runs oppositely to those in, say, balance-of-payments criteria?

Discussion of the political aspects of direct investment, within and between countries, arose on a number of occasions. It would be too much to expect consensus here, and it is not to be wondered at that there was no resolution of subjective opinions, strongly held.

The theory of direct investment was discussed at length. Johnson's emphasis on knowledge as the basis of the investor's advantage over local businessmen, and Komiya's insistence on superior management, seem to me less to contradict the more general theory of Hymer than to be special cases within it. As Hymer points out, the foreign investor is at a disadvantage in operating far from his decision centre; he must have some compensating advantage. It may be superior technology or knowledge, or superior management, but it may lie in other directions— the co-ordination of production at various stages in various countries, and access to markets—or it may be undertaken defensively, to maintain a market position even with limited profits, for the sake of preventing a competitor from stealing a march.

Index

Book designed by Arthur Stokes

Text set in 10 pt Linotype Times
and printed on 85 gsm Burnie English Finish
by Wilke and Company Limited
37-49 Browns Road, Clayton, Victoria